HEALTH AND ILLNESS

Michael Senior
with
Bruce Viveash

0004606
JD020340
£15.50
362.1 STANDARD LOAN
ROBY

© Michael Senior and Bruce Viveash 1998

All rights reserved. No reproduction, copy or transmission of this publication may be made without written permission.

No paragraph of this publication may be reproduced, copied or transmitted save with written permission or in accordance with the provisions of the Copyright, Designs and Patents Act 1988, or under the terms of any licence permitting limited copying issued by the Copyright Licensing Agency, 90 Tottenham Court Road, London W1P 9HE.

Any person who does any unauthorised act in relation to this publication may be liable to criminal prosecution and civil claims for damages.

The authors have asserted their rights to be identified as the authors of this work in accordance with the Copyright, Designs and Patents Act 1988.

First published 1997 by
MACMILLAN PRESS LTD
Houndmills, Basingstoke, Hampshire RG21 6XS
and London
Companies and representatives
throughout the world

ISBN 0–333–66249–0

A catalogue record for this book is available
from the British Library.

This book is printed on paper suitable for recycling and made from fully managed and sustained forest sources.

10   9   8   7   6   5   4   3
07   06   05   04   03   02   01   00   99

Printed in Malaysia

Contents

Chapter 5: The Relationship between Social Class and Health

Acknowledgements

The authors would like to thank the following for permission to use copyright material: Action for ME and Chronic Fatigue for extracts from *Interaction*, No. 16, 1994; Associated Examining Board for the use of past examination questions; R. Balarajan and V. Raleigh for four tables; The Big Issue for 'Mental Health on the Streets', *The Big Issue*, 6–12 February 1995; Blackwell Publishers for two figures from Thomas McKeown, *The Role of Medicine*; a table from M. Calnan and S. Williams, 'Images of Scientific Medicine', *Sociology of Health and Illness*, Vol. 14, No. 2, 1992; a table from G. Bendelow, 'Pain, Perceptions, Emotions and Gender', *Sociology of Health and Illness*, Vol. 15, No. 3, 1993; a table from M. Boulton et al., 'Social Class and the GP Consultation', *Sociology of Health and Illness*, Vol. 8, No. 4, 1986; a table from S. Macran et al., 'Women's Socio-Economic Status and Self-Assessed Health', *Sociology of Health and Illness*, Vol. 16, No. 2, 1994; BMJ Publishing Group for J. K. Morris, D. G. Cook and A. G. Shaper, 'Loss of Employment and Mortality', *British Medical Journal*, Vol. 308, 1994; P. Phillimore, A. Beattie and P. Townsend, 'Widening Inequality of Health in Northern England, 1981–1991', *British Medical Journal*, Vol. 308, 1994; Caledonian Newspapers Ltd for an extract from *The Herald*, June 1993; The Controller of Her Majesty's Stationery Office for figures, extracts and tables from *Social Trends 24*, 1994 and *Social Trends 25*, 1995; material from the 1987, 1990 and 1992 General Household Surveys; material from *the Black Report: Inequalities in Health* (1982); and material from M. Whitehead, *The Health Divide*, 1992; Elsevier Science for a table adapted from R. Punamaki and H. Aschan, 'Self-Care and Mastery Among Primary Health Care Patients', *Social Science and Medicine*, Vol. 39, No. 5, 1994; a table from A. Baker and S. Duncan, 'Prevalence of child Sexual Abuse in Great Britain', *Child Abuse and Neglect*, Vol. 9, 1996; Grant Naylor Productions Ltd for an extract from R. Grant and D. Naylor, *Red Dwarf* episode entitled 'Quarantine'; Guardian News Service for N. van der Gaag, 'Ageing with Attitude', *New Internationalist*, February 1995; HarperCollins Publishers Ltd for a table from P. Trowler, *Investigating Health, Welfare and Poverty*, 1989; Health Visitors' Association for H. Graham, 'Women's Smoking: Government Targets and Social Trends', *Health Visitor*, Vol. 66, No. 3, 1993; M. Chevannes, 'Access to Health Care for Black People', *Health Visitor*, Vol. 64,

No. 1, 1991; L. Sayce, 'Preventing Breakdown in Women's Mental Health', *Health Visitor*, Vol. 66, No. 2, 1993; A. Pollock, 'Privatisation by Stealth?', *Health Visitor*, Vol. 68, No. 3, 1995; C. A. Jebali, 'A Feminist Perspective on Postnatal Depression', *Health Visitor*, Vol. 66, No. 2, 1993' Independent Newspaper Publishing PLC for an extract from A. Ferriman, 'Looking Younger on Prescription', *Independent on Sunday*, 26/8/95; L. Hunt, 'GP Attacked for Removing a 60-a-Day Smoker from List', *Independent*, 26/2/96; Independence Publishers for material from *Mental Health*, 1995; Manchester City Council for material from *Health Inequalities and Manchester in the 1990s*; Mental Health Foundation for 'Mental Illness: The Fundamental Facts', 1994; Philip Allan Publishers for material from S. Taylor, 'Measuring Child Abuse', *Sociology Review*, Vol. 1, No. 3; *Social Studies Review*; a table from 'Update', *Social Studies Review*, Vol. 1, No. 3, January 1986; Ken Pyne for reproduction of his cartoon, 'Me a Danger to the Public? – It's the Other Way Round!'; Royal Association for Disability and Rehabilitation for an extract from RADAR, June 1994; Sage Publications for table 1.3 from P. Coleman, J. Bond and S. Peace, *Ageing in Society*, 1993. Every effort has been made to trace all copyright-holders, but if any have been inadvertently overlooked, the publishers will be pleased to make the necessary arrangements at the first opportunity.

The authors wish to thank a number of key individuals who have helped us produce this publication: Tim Heaton and Tony Lawson for their invaluable help throughout the editing of the book; Richard Layte at Nuffield College, Oxford, for his skills on the internet; David Neal at the University of Hertfordshire for his extremely useful advice and encouragement; Margaret Whitehead for her comments about the recent changes to the organisation of the NHS; Sheila Bond for her help with material on ethnicity and health; Jane Rose for allowing Mick Senior to talk endlessly about health and illness; and finally the A Level Sociology students at Kingsbury High School who allowed us to try out the material on them during their lessons: particular thanks to the students who allowed us to adapt their essays for the examination focus sections, including Richard Welch, Tanzila Iqbal, Kreepa Gohil, Saloni Karia, Lisa Smith and Nicola Lawrence.

1 Introduction

The philosophy behind the book

This book aims to help students take an active part in understanding and analysing the sociology of health and illness. Despite rapid changes in the areas of health and illness (for example the changes to the structure of the National Health Service) this text allows students to deal with a wide range of issues and enables coverage of A level sociology syllabi.

A major feature of the book, along with the use of up-to-date material and the inclusion of recent sociological thinking such as the New Right and postmodernism, is the provision of exercises to help students develop three examination skills: interpretation, application and evaluation. Interpretation deals with the ability to examine and communicate an understanding of different types of information, such as that provided in tables and newspaper articles. Application is the skill students exercise when they examine sociological and non-sociological material and use it in relevant ways to answer a question. Evaluation means being able to assess sociological debates and arguments, for example through a consideration of evidence.

By carrying out the exercises featured throughout each chapter students should be able to improve their performance of the three skills. In order to indicate which skills are being developed, each exercise is clearly labelled with i for interpretation, a for application, e for evaluation. There are also link exercises to help students understand the interconnection between information in different parts of this book. The link exercises develop the three skills, but they also aid a more sophisticated understanding of the sociology of health and illness by interrelating issues such as social class and gender. For example to study the chapter on social class separately from the chapter on gender means that these two social groups appear to be unrelated; however working-class women may have different life chances from middle-class women. Understanding how these aspects of identity and social position interrelate is crucial to a more sophisticated sociological approach. Each link exercise develops an understanding of essential interconnections.

To help students pass the essay-based A level examination the book includes an examination focus at the end of each chapter. Each examination focus provides an opportunity to apply the issues and practise the skills developed in the chapter. All the examination exercises prepare students to use the skills of interpretation, application and evaluation to the essay questions in their final examination.

Subject content

The book is divided into eleven chapters. Chapter 2 outlines the problems of defining the words 'health' and 'illness'. It then critically examines various perspectives of health and illness and outlines a relatively recent sociological issue: competing views of 'the body'.

Chapter 3 deals with the way in which people come to be defined as ill: the social process of becoming ill. The chapter analyses the morbidity (illness) figures by showing how they are socially constructed.

Chapter 4 examines responses to illness (for example by examining the effect some conditions may have on self-identity), an issue that is gaining increasing importance in A level sociology.

Chapters 5, 6 and 7 deal with key social patterns of illness, namely social class, gender and ethnicity. Chapter 8 too deals with patterns of illness but this time within different age groups. This chapter also tackles the subject of abuse and dependency in terms of child abuse and elder abuse. Dependency is examined when focusing on an increasingly more important sociological topic: disability.

Chapter 9 switches from the subject of physical health and illness to explore mental health and illness. Defining mental illness, labelling and community care are particularly focused upon.

Chapter 10 explores the subject of health care. Both the formal health care structure (for example the NHS and the private health care system) and the informal health care that takes place within the family are examined.

Finally, Chapter 11 deals with sociological perspectives of health care, including Marxism, functionalism, the New Right, feminism and postmodernism. The link exercises in the final chapter connect these perspectives to key issues outlined in the preceding chapters.

2 The social construction of health and illness

By the end of this chapter you should be able to:

- understand different definitions of health and illness;
- evaluate the medical model of illness;
- assess alternative models of illness;
- apply notions of the sociology of the body.

Introduction

This chapter considers the social construction of 'health' and 'illness'. The meaning of the words 'health' and 'illness' cannot be taken for granted as they mean different things to different people. A condition one person considers to be healthy, for example simply being able to walk around the house without very much pain from arthritis, may not be considered healthy by somebody who sets a higher standard of health, such as being mentally and physically fit. Similarly the definition of 'illness' is essentially contested, that is, there is no consensus about what is considered to be an illness.

Whether people interpret symptoms as an illness or not can determine the way they subsequently behave: this is known as 'illness behaviour'. Illness behaviour affects the extent to which people visit their doctor. Visits to a doctor can contribute to the morbidity rates (illness figures), but these do not reveal all illnesses in society, just those conditions that doctors and patients have defined as an illness.

The way an illness is defined by patients and particularly doctors is important, especially if a sufferer needs a sick note for work. There may be some conditions that doctors are reluctant to consider as an illness, for example repetitive strain injury (RSI). Experience shows that the medical profession exercises control over the symptoms considered to be an official illness: conflict may therefore arise between patients' views and doctors' views about what constitutes an illness.

The medical profession has a very distinctive view of illness, known as the medical model. The medical model treats the body rather like a machine that needs to be repaired when it is faulty. The main treatments offered are drugs and surgery. However some people are very critical of the medical model. Some theorists claim that improving living standards (for example cleaner water, more nutritious food, better sewage systems, better-quality housing) and imparting a better knowledge of hygiene have a far larger impact on health than drugs and surgery. Some even claim that medical treatments can cause harm (for example side effects from drugs). The harm caused through side effects is referred to as 'clinical iatrogenesis' by Illich (1976).

Finally, the chapter examines the way dominant views of the 'body' (for example as thin, tall) affect the way many people view their own and others' bodies and thus the way they define a healthy body. Thus notions of the body affect the definition of both health and illness.

What is meant by 'health'?

Are you healthy? Can you immediately answer 'Yes' or 'No'? Before answering would you have to clarify what is meant by 'being healthy'? To study health and illness we must start by establishing what 'health' means.

Exercise 2.1 Defining health

 Write down your own definition of health. Ask yourself what condition you need to be in to regard yourself as healthy. Compare your definition with that of a colleague. Is one of the definitions easier to accept than the other?

In the *Health and Lifestyles* survey Blaxter (1990a) examined how people define health. The study was carried out in 1984–5 with a sample of 9003 respondents drawn from addresses chosen randomly from electoral registers. Over 70 per cent of respondents agreed to participate in the research. Two home visits took place. One visit was made by a nurse who conducted a limited medical survey including height, weight, blood pressure and pulse rate. A postal questionnaire was left with the respondent to provide a self-assessed review of personality and psychiatric status. During the second home visit the respondents participated in a long, open-ended, structured interview about health-related behaviour, for example smoking, exercise, diet, and how they rated their own health (self-reported health). The study concluded that individuals have many different definitions of health. The different definitions of health were classified as negative or positive, as shown in Item A.

Negative definitions of health:

- Health is being free of symptoms of illness, for example I don't have a headache or a backache.
- Health is not having a disease/disability, for example I have no medically diagnosed condition such as a broken leg or arthritis.

Positive definitions of health:

- Health is being physically fit, for example I am physically fit enough to play sport.
- Health is psychological and social well-being, for example I feel emotionally stable and able to cope with life.

(Source: M. Blaxter, Health & Lifestyles, London, Tavistock, 1990.)

Blaxter (1990a) highlights the variety of definitions that people use to measure whether they and others are healthy. Any study that uses self-reported health as a key measure must therefore be examined very carefully because the researcher will be using many definitions of health. Any study of health and illness, including an essay or project on health, must make it clear that health is essentially contested. 'Essentially contested' means there is no single agreed definition.

'Generally it's being carefree, you look better, you get on better with other people' (single woman of 20, a secretary).

'Health is being able to walk around better, and doing more work in the house when my knees let me' (woman of 70).

'I clean the windows and rush round like a mad thing. When I'm not healthy is when I want to sit down in front of the box' (single mother, kitchen assistant).

'Health is having loads of whumph' (married woman, of 28, office worker).

'He never goes to the doctor and only suffers from occasional colds. Both parents are still alive at 90 so he belongs to healthy stock' (woman of 51, talking about her husband).

'Health is when you don't feel tired and short of breath' (man of 51).

'Health is when you don't have a cold' (man of 19).

'You don't have to think about pain – to be free of aches and pains' (woman of 78).

(Source: M. Blaxter, Health & Lifestyles, London, Tavistock, 1990.)

Exercise 2.2   The problem of defining health

1. Read Item B, which consists of quotes from the *Health and Lifestyles* survey (Blaxter, 1990a) defining health.

 2. Try to match the quotes in Item B with the four definitions of health identified in Item A. To do this exercise complete the chart below.

Negative definitions	Positive definitions
(a) Health is being free of illness symptoms	(c) Health is physical fitness
(b) Health is not having a disease/ disability	(d) Health is psychological and social well-being

Do notions of health vary between social groups?

In addition to Blaxter (1990a), sociologists such as Pill and Scott (1982) and Williams (1993) have shown that definitions of health not only vary between individuals but also between groups of people. Positive definitions of health – for example being able to do tasks – have been found to be used more often by middle-class groups (d'Houtard and Field, 1984). However Calnan (1987) found that working-class women had very narrow views of health, for example 'health is getting through the day', although Blaxter (1983) comments that the short time allowed for the interview process may limit the responses of 'less educated' people. Given a longer time (for example to relax) less educated people can express very complex and varied definitions of health. Definitions of health may vary between different ethnic groups.

Other variations between social groups could occur by age – younger people may hold different views of health from older people. Definitions may vary by gender and occupation, for example a glamorous model may view acne differently from somebody whose work is not dependent on their physical attractiveness.

Some who regard themselves as healthy may be regarded as unhealthy by others, for example 'I am very healthy, yet I have arthritis' (housebound woman of 61 in Blaxter, 1990a). One respondent, a twenty-year-old nursing assistant in a psychiatric hospital, stated a varied and complex view of health, showing how difficult it is to define health:

I feel alert and can always think of lots to do. No aches and pains – nothing wrong with me – and I can go out and jog. I suppose I have more energy, I can get up and do such a lot rather than staying in bed and cutting myself off from people (quoted in *Blaxter* 1990a).

Health does appear to be 'essentially contested': we are unlikely to define it in a way everybody agrees with.

Why are competing notions of health sociologically important?

Measuring health

Firstly, to study health we can ask people if they regard themselves as healthy. Such research is therefore going to use different definitions of health, and using different definitions of health means we should ask whether the study has provided a valid (accurate/truthful) measure of health. We could also use statistics from general practitioners (GPs), which show how much illness is reported to doctors. These figures can provide a measure of what symptoms are reported and the extent of illness (not all GP figures are used to determine the nation's morbidity rates – only a sample of GPs who volunteer to participate are used in a detailed morbidity survey). However if people define health and illness in different ways then the GP statistics are not actually measuring how much illness exists, but how much illness people actually report to their doctor. Take the 61-year-old housebound woman who stated, 'I am very healthy, yet I have arthritis'. Had the woman reported the arthritis to her doctor? Thus definitions of health are important considerations in the sociological study of health.

Health services

Secondly, definitions of health can shape the type of health services provided, particularly by the National Health Service. The NHS consists of regions (changed in April 1996 to outposts but could be renamed in the future) and smaller districts (changed in April 1996 to health authorities but also could change name again in the future). 'Outposts' (ex-regional health authorities, RHAs) are responsible for allocating resources to 'health areas' (ex-district health authorities: DHAs), which then take control of the delivery of health services. If outposts decide that fertility treatment is not a health matter, then such a service may no longer be offered free as part of the NHS; yet for some infertile people who wish to become parents, fertility may be an extremely important part of being emotionally and spiritually healthy.

A negative definition of health that focuses on the absence of disease may mean that services dealing with the improvement of spiritual and emotional well-being will not be offered. More positive definitions of health (well-being rather than absence of disease) require the provision of a wider range of services. Thus definitions of health play a crucial role in shaping health services.

What is meant by 'illness'?

Sociologists need to investigate what symptoms count as illness. In other words, how do people 'operationalise' illness. To operationalise means to define something so that it can be measured or investigated, or simply to make its meaning clearer to others.

Exercise 2.3   Defining illness

[a] 1. How might you operationalise or define 'illness'?

[a] 2. Compare your answers with those of a colleague.

[e] 3. What does your comparison tell you about the definition of illness?

Like health, illness is a subjective notion that depends on people's own interpretation of their mental and physical condition and what symptoms they count as an illness. Some people may not define a hangover caused by an excess of alcohol as an illness. Yet similar symptoms labelled as a migraine may well be regarded as a legitimate illness. A hangover and a migraine can both cause a severe headache, but one might more easily be defined as an illness. In other words, what counts as an illness is 'essentially contested': there is not complete agreement on what counts as an illness.

Sickness is defined as reported illness. In many Western societies those with official power to label illness are doctors. The extent to which doctors interpret reported illness as actual sickness differs, so the way doctors diagnose a sickness should not be taken for granted as an objective process but should be viewed critically.

Exercise 2.4   What counts as an illness?

[i] Rate the following cases according to the extent to which you consider each one to be an illness. You are not being asked to measure how severe each case appears to be, in a sense you are pretending to be a doctor who is passing judgment on whether each case is an illness. Please circle the appropriate value for each symptom:

Set of symptoms	Definitely not ill			Definitely ill	
Pregnancy	1	2	3	4	5
A severe hangover	1	2	3	4	5
A migraine	1	2	3	4	5
Breast cancer	1	2	3	4	5
Lack of appetite resulting in serious weight loss	1	2	3	4	5
A broken leg	1	2	3	4	5
Wrinkles	1	2	3	4	5
Severe memory loss	1	2	3	4	5
Acne	1	2	3	4	5
Shouting at oneself in the street	1	2	3	4	5
An 80-year-old woman whose eyesight is failing	1	2	3	4	5
A 14-year-old boy who finds it extremely hard to hear	1	2	3	4	5
An overweight man with high blood pressure and shortness of breath	1	2	3	4	5
A man who wants a sex change	1	2	3	4	5
A woman who started smoking knowing the habit could damage her health and who now has lung cancer	1	2	3	4	5
An alcoholic	1	2	3	4	5
A young man who claims he is Napoleon	1	2	3	4	5
A teacher who has been off work for six months claiming not to have the energy to get out of bed	1	2	3	4	5
A 25-year-old woman who has become bald	1	2	3	4	5

(*Source*: Adapted from an idea by David Neal, 'The Sociology of Health and Illness', unpublished.)

1. Which of the symptoms did you regard as (a) definitely ill, (b) definitely not ill?

2. Compare your results with those of a colleague and try to come to an agreement.

3. Explain why it is easier to regard some symptoms as *not* being ill. (Hint: does it revolve around notions of malingering? Is individual responsibility – for example over diet, smoking or exercise – a factor? The absence of a well known cause? Not being officially defined as an illness unlike, say, cancer? Is age or gender a factor?)

4. What was your judgment about 'wrinkles'? (Hint: you might like to reconsider your answer when you have read more about wrinkles later in this chapter)

5. What does the activity show about our ability to define illness?

Why are competing notions of illness sociologically important?

Measuring illness

What counts as illness will vary between individuals. Different people will regard their set of symptoms in different ways. Some will report a lack of energy to a doctor and others might not. It is those who report to a doctor who provide sociologists, health officials and policy makers with the official morbidity (illness) statistics because a selection of GPs are used to provide morbidity statistics based on patients who reported themselves to the GP.

Illness behaviour

As sociologists we need to examine what views of illness people hold and how this affects their behaviour; for example do they alter their lifestyle knowing that shortness of breath and being overweight could suggest vulnerability to heart disease? Do people visit the doctor when they experience an 'abnormal' symptom? Why? Or why not? What views of illness do doctors hold, and are these views at odds with patients' views?

The medical model

The dominant view of illness held by many official health practitioners such as doctors, consultants and surgeons has been labelled the 'biomedical approach' or the 'medical model'. This view of illness gained prominence in the late nineteenth century in Britain. The medical model largely assumes the following:

- That illness is *caused* by bacteria, a faulty gene, a virus or an accident such as falling down the stairs. Illness is the result of an identifiable cause. It is not the result of an evil spirit or curse.
- Illnesses can be *identified* and *classified* into different types, for example diseases of the nervous system, diseases of the circulatory system. The process of identifying and classifying is viewed as an objective one and it has created very little disagreement among doctors.
- Illnesses are identified by *medical officials,* for example doctors, not 'lay' people (that is, those outside the medical profession).
- *Diagnosis* of symptoms is relatively *objective.* The diagnostic process requires little negotiation between medical officers and patients. Illnesses are relatively self-evident. Little debate is needed to identify an illness.
- Illnesses can be *treated* and *cured*, for example antibiotics can be used to treat infections. Treatment often involves removing the cause, for example the virus or bacteria.

The main assumptions of the medical model are not held by all doctors, nurses and consultants, and some of the assumptions may be held to different degrees. However the medical model is claimed to dominate the health professions, for example in the NHS.

Kryten: Quite extraordinary, Lanstrom postulated there were two kinds of virus: positive and negative. The negative we already know about.

Lister: Yeah like flu, rabies, that kind of stuff?

Kryten: But she also believed that there were positive viral strains which actually made human beings feel better . . .

Cat: Such as?

Kryten: Well at a very basic level she predicted a kind of reverse flu, a strain of virus that promotes an unaccountable feeling of well-being and happiness.

Lister: That's happened to me. My life's been turned to complete and utter crud and I've woken up in the morning feeling good for no apparent reason.

Kryten: The chances are, sir, that you had unwittingly contracted some of Lanstrom's virus. According to her notes, twentieth century DJ's suffered from it all the time.

Cat: So what's in the [test] tubes?

Kryten: Lanstrom claims to have isolated several strains of positive virus: inspiration, charisma, sexual magnetism. . .

Cat: Sexual magnetism is a virus! Well get me to a hospital, I'm a terminal case!

Kryten: But this one is the most intriguing of all. According to her notes, the virus strain *'felicitus Populi'*. Commonly known as luck . . .

Lister: Luck is a virus?

Kryten: A positive virus which most humans contract at some points in their lives for very short periods. And here it is. Lady Luck. In liquid form. Want to try some?

Lister: Is it safe?

Kryten: Absolutely harmless. Even so this is a minute dosage and will only last for about three minutes. Now if you want to pick out all the aces from this pack of cards.

Lister: Shuffle 'em? . . .

Kryten: Yes. *[Lister quickly selects four cards from the pack. All four cards were aces.]* Sir, I want you to throw this dart over here into that bullseye behind you using your left hand, without looking. . .

Lister: No chance.

Kryten: Trust me sir. . .

[Lister throws the dart into the back of Kryten's head]

Kryten: Ah. I think that indicates the luck virus has worn off, sir.

(Source: © Rob Grant and Doug Naylor, Red Dwarf episode, 'Quarantine'.)

ITEM C   *Exercise 2.5   The search for a cause: the medical model*

Item C is a transcript of a scene from the popular series 'Red Dwarf'. The crew of the Red Dwarf have stumbled on an abandoned spacecraft, boarded the vessel and found a series of test tubes in which Lanstrom, a famous and strange scientist, stored peculiar viruses.

[i] 1. What types of virus did the Red Dwarf team find?

[a] 2. Why do these viruses seem strange?

[i] 3. The medical model searches for organic causes of bodily abnormalities such as viruses. How does the Red Dwarf sketch illustrate the medical model?

The strength of the medical model is that it attempts to research the cause of each illness rather than assume that there is no identifiable explanation for an illness. It is difficult to disbelieve that heart disease is to do with restricted arteries or that lung cancer is related to smoking cigarettes. Many people may consider that knowledge of causes is of help in avoiding illness. However, whether as sociologists we can trust all the claims made by the medical profession about the cause of illnesses must be examined. Postmodernists are critical of theories that try to explain all phenomena (for example all illnesses), calling them metatheories. Perhaps the medical profession is useful in explaining and treating some illnesses, but not all illnesses.

Critique of the medical model

Critique of the medical model: the social constructionists

Social constructionists claim that medical knowledge is just one way of examining health and illness: the medical model has just been very successful in attempting to make its knowledge appear superior and legitimate. Social constructionists are keen to show how the medical model developed. Such examination shows how a dominant group of people have come to shape people's views of health and illness.

How did the medical model gain dominance?

In the sixteenth century a variety of people were involved in health care. Women, in particular, were a primary source of health care in the home (Clark, 1968). Depending on availability and money there were also faith healers and medical physicians. The distinction between medical and folk medicine was less entrenched than today. Among physicians and surgeons there was no overall theory to explain illness. Some believed very much in Galen's idea that illness was caused by an imbalance of the four humours (bodily liquids).

A variety of 'healers', 'quacks', 'physicians' and 'barber–surgeons' continued to provide a health service into the eighteenth century. By this time concern for health had increased. Care of the sick started to become localised: hospitals were developed and expanded using old buildings such as prisons and asylums. Private funding and charitable donations were often behind the development of these early hospitals, where the medical elite could practice medicine and improve their social position (Webster, 1988). Clinical medicine started to take off: research into human anatomy could be conducted now that the church had less influence over society and health care. Physicians could safely cut up bodies and release information about human physiology without fear of the church claiming they had violated the sanctity of the human body. Foucault claims that at that time illness started to be seen in a new way: 'the new gaze'. This 'new gaze' became a dominant way of looking at and thinking about the body and disease. Diseases were identified and classified. Observable causes were tested. Spiritual explanations of diseases (for example curses) were seen to be the realm of 'quacks' (unqualified healers). Propaganda was released to place a dividing line between official physicians and unofficial quacks.

By the nineteenth century legislation had been passed to ensure that all official doctors had university medical training. Only men could receive this training: thus the medical world became a male world (Abbott and Wallace, 1990). Slowly the medical world came to call itself a profession, seeking status in society and claiming to possess superior knowledge of the human body: illnesses had physical causes and doctors claimed to be able to identify these objectively and cure them.

Marxists such as Navarro (1979) claim that the health care system that evolved throughout the years of industrialisation mainly benefited the ruling class because health care ensured that sick workers were made fit for work, and thus the bourgeoisie benefited from a more healthy work force.

Is the medical model really dominant?

One criticism of Foucault's treatise on the rise of the medical model (which was largely presented in the *Birth of the Clinic*, 1963) is that it mainly describes the development of the model in France rather than Britain. A further criticism of Foucault is that he concentrated on language or 'discourse' as the *main* way the medical establishment gained dominance. For Foucault, knowledge was power. For his critics, Foucault appeared too 'discourse deterministic' (Turner, 1984), meaning that not all power comes through being able to dominate language. Foucault claimed discourse led to power through the creation of new terms developed to describe the body and its conditions. The new language was alien to many lay people and it also sounded 'scientific', thus it tended to gain the status held by the 'natural sciences' (for example chemistry and biology). Gaining such status meant the medical industry appeared to possess superior, objective knowledge. Superior knowledge leads to power. 'Scientific' discourse, for Foucault, led to the medical industry being able to call itself a 'profession', which possessed the 'truth' about human health and illness.

Marxists would claim that far from knowledge creating power, the control over the means of production (the means by which society produces goods and services) creates a class of people (the bourgeoisie) who have to control the workers (the proletariat) to force them to work. Control over health means people can be made healthy in order to return to work more quickly, or health control can mean that fewer medical certificates are issued in order to prevent people taking time off work. Critics of the Marxist view point out that power is more widespread in a postmodern society than simply control by the bourgeoisie.

Medical knowledge can control the way people think about themselves. The way people behave (whether they exercise, buy particular 'healthy' products, take risks) is influenced by the way people think. Controlling knowledge means controlling behaviour. Rather as structuralist sociologists tended to ignore the role of individuals resisting institutions and powerful groups and ideas, Foucault failed to focus on the way patients can disbelieve medical accounts of their illness and refute the idea that medicine can 'cure' them. Foucault may have needed to allow some room for individual social action (that is, individual thought and behaviour) to challenge and resist the 'new gaze'.

Critique of the medical model: iatrogenesis

'Iatrogenesis' means doctor-caused illness. Illich (1976) claims that those in the medical profession (that is, doctors, surgeons, consultants, pharmaceutical companies and suppliers of medical equipment and technology) have a vested interest in ensuring there is plenty of disease. They do this by claiming health issues are medical problems (medicalising human behaviour). The medical industry generates illness, which it claims it can successfully treat. Life has become 'medicalised', according to Illich, 'Thus experiences once seen as a normal part of the human condition, such as childbirth, pregnancy, unhappiness, ageing and dying, have now been brought under medical scrutiny and control', (ibid.) The medicalisation of human conditions Illich calls 'social iatrogenesis'.

Once a set of symptoms is defined as an illness drugs can be supplied and technology sold to the health professionals. Health is big business so health companies 'sponsor illness' to create sales (Taylor, 1994). Health care has become focused on treatment (using expensive drugs, labour and technology) rather than prevention (better sanitation, housing, diet, lifestyle). Thus according to Foucault's 'new gaze' the medical profession tends to examine treatment that requires highly paid medical expertise, expensive drugs and technology.

The role of official western medicine (part of Foucault's 'new gaze') is important particularly because the design decisions of the NHS were largely given to doctors. They, not surprisingly, made it a technological and curative-based system rather than a localised preventative one requiring fewer technologically advanced surgeons and highly trained doctors. Illich (1976) claims the medical industry has robbed people of the ability to cope with pain and illness: now people need drugs to help them through periods of perceived illness. This process Illich called 'cultural iatrogenesis'.

Medical treatment can itself be damaging. The side effects of some drugs (for example tardiv diskonesia – involuntary movements such as sporadic shaking) and some negative consequences of surgery, Illich called 'clinical iatrogenesis'. The three types of iatrogenesis are interrelated, as follows:

Social iatrogenesis

↓

Cultural iatrogenesis

↓

Clinical iatrogenesis

ITEM D

Abraham (1994) used publicly available testimonies of scientists, transcripts of parliamentary debates, leaflets, letters and consultation papers to conduct a study into the scientific tests on Opren, a drug once used to treat rheumatoid arthritis. Drugs to treat rheumatism and arthritis are big business: in 1980 in England and Wales, they accounted for 15.8 million prescriptions (Bland *et al.*, 1985). In 1982 the USA banned the use of Opren. However, it was some time later that Britain banned the drug. Abraham argues that medical decisions such as those relating to the use of Opren are far from value free.

All drugs need to be broken down by the body after being consumed. Tests of the time taken to break down Opren were carried out by a specialist in geriatric medicine, sponsored by Eli Lilly, the manufacturer of Opren. The tests showed that elderly patients may have greater difficulty breaking down drugs such as Opren. Abraham's study argues that Eli Lilly did not take sufficient note of these tests. In fact the company claimed it found it 'difficult to believe that benoxaprofen pharmacokintic [a chemical found in Opren] levels in the elderly are significantly different from those in young people in the absence of renal impairment'. Abrahams claims that Eli Lilly then allegedly attempted to restrict the publication of the research.

Such a close involvement between the pharmaceutical industry and scientific medical research can leave people unaware of the true nature of medical knowledge. While Abraham's study goes on to show how scientists are able to resist intervention in their research and publication of data, it also illustrates the fact that not all medical knowledge is objective.

(Source: J. Abraham, 'Bias in Science and Medical Knowledge: The Opren Controversy', Sociology, vol. 28, no. 3, 1994.)

In summary, medicalising human conditions (for example worry becomes a medical condition called anxiety) creates a demand for medical treatment. Thus social iatrogenesis makes us define human conditions as an illness. Cultural iatrogenesis makes us seek medical treatment. Clinical iatrogenesis can be the result of receiving this treatment.

ITEM D ### Exercise 2.6 Applying iatrogenesis: the Opren controversy

[i] 1. What was Opren used to treat?

[i] 2. How does Abraham use the case of Opren to illustrate that the medical world is not as objective as it may appear to be?

[e] 3. Why is a study such as Abraham's research into Opren difficult to carry out?

[a] 4. How do Illich's notions of iatrogenesis apply to the case study of the Opren controversy?

Exercise 2.7 Evaluating the iatrogenesis critique of the medical model

[a][e] Copy the following table and sort the statements below into strengths and weaknesses of the iatrogenesis critique of the medical model.

Strengths	Weaknesses

- Some medical treatment can cause serious side effects.
- Due to the availability of medical remedies and the uses to which they are applied – for example antidepressants for people that are 'feeling sad' – some people may not empower themselves to cope with problems faced throughout life (for example grief) on their own or with social support.
- Medicalisation of human conditions such as being overweight (obesity) or feeling sad (depressed) may result in sufferers being defined as ill when the problem may be the way the medical profession defines illness.
- Not all medical treatments cause serious side effects; some treatments are extremely effective with no discernible problems.
- Medicalising behaviour as an illness may be a positive process. The iatrogenesis debate does not examine how some problems may benefit from being medicalised. If certain illnesses are defined as a legitimate medical problem, treatment is more likely to be researched, as with repetitive strain injury (RSI) or chronic fatigue syndrome (myalgic encephalomyelitis, ME).
- Iatrogenesis ignores the fact that defining some problems as a mental illness can be positive. People who have committed serious crimes such as murder sometimes appear to be suffering from psychological disorders. If a prison

sentence is passed the sufferer may be being punished for a crime committed when they were not in their usual state of mind – they may also experience abuse by other inmates. However if the behaviour is medicalised the accused may receive psychological treatment.

Critique of the medical model: feminists

Graham points out that only 13 per cent of hospital consultants are women, yet 90 per cent of nurses and 75 per cent of ancillary workers are female, and a large proportion of those in the lowest tier are black women. Although most paid care seems to be carried out by women, it is under the control of male doctors and consultants. Abbott and Wallace (1990) claim that male control over women's health has evolved through men deliberately exercising a monopoly over health care. In professionalising health care, men have assumed control over nearly all aspects of health, including gynaecology and childbirth. Oakley (1993) claims that 69 per cent of first-time mothers felt they had little control over the process. Oakley also concludes that doctors and mothers view childbirth very differently: the former as a medical problem and the latter as 'natural'. Women have also complained of lack of attention to their views throughout pregnancy and childbirth. This is further evidence that male ideology within the medical model of illness controls women's health care.

Men may also see themselves as the norm by which women are judged; indeed some feminists argue that male doctors still hold very inadequate notions of female health, which leads to female problems not being taken seriously. For example depression has sometimes been viewed as an example of female weakness in failing to cope with children and housework. Scully and Bart (1978) claim that some doctors blame female emotional problems on their reproductive tract rather than the problems they face in society and the home. In other words the medical model looks to weaknesses within the body rather than social causes such as stress.

The side effects suffered from contraceptive devices and drugs (clinical iatrogenesis), prescribed predominantly by male doctors, are another example of male initiatives influencing female health care. For example the coil, the pill and depo-provera can all have very harmful side effects. Would these contraceptives have been developed and continuously prescribed by a female-dominated medical profession?

'The newest development in male contraception was unveiled recently at the American Women's Centre. Dr Sophie Merkin of the Merkin Clinic announced the preliminary findings of a study conducted on 763 unsuspecting male undergraduates at a large Midwestern university. In her report, Dr Merkin stated that the new contraceptive – the IPD – was a breakthrough in male contraception. It will be marketed under the trade name Umbrelly.

The IPD (intrapenile device) resembles a tightly rolled umbrella which is inserted through the head of the penis and pushed into the scrotum with a plunger-like device. Occasionally there is a perforation of the scrotum, but this is disregarded as the male has few nerve-endings in this area of his body. The underside of the umbrella contains a spermicidal jelly, hence the name Umbrelly.

Dr Merkin declared the Umbrelly to be statistically safe for the human male. She reported that of the 763 undergraduates tested with the device only two died of scrotal infection, only twenty developed swelling of the testicles and only 13 became too depressed to have an erection. She stated that common complaints ranged from cramping and bleeding to acute abdominal pains. She emphasised that these symptoms were merely indications that the man's body had not yet adjusted to the device. Hopefully the symptoms would disappear within a year. One complication caused by the IPD briefly mentioned by Dr Merkin was the incidence of massive scrotal infection necessitating the surgical removal of the testicles. "But this is a rare case", said Dr Merkin, "too rare to be statistically important". She and other distinguished members of the Woman's College of Surgeons agreed that the benefits far outweighed the risk to any individual man.'

(Source: 'Outcome' magazine, the East Bay Men's Centre newsletter, and The Periodical Lunch published by Andrew Rock, Ann Arbor, Michigan, US, in P. Abbott and C. Wallace, 1990.)

ITEM E   *Exercise 2.8 Values and contraceptive advice*

a   1. How does the Umbrelly compare with other popular methods of contraception?

a   2. Do other methods of contraception have side effects? For whom?

a e   3. Would you expect the Umbrelly to become a popular method of contraception? Why/why not?

How have men shaped knowledge about health?

For centuries men used the law and notions of scientific medical knowledge to take over roles traditionally played by women (for example midwifery). Indeed it was not until 1899 that a law was passed to allow women to become doctors. Men claimed they had 'superior scientific medical knowledge' and attempted to gain control over childbirth. In the 1800s 25 per cent of all women giving birth in hospital died from puerperal fever, an infection transmitted by doctors from other sources, especially dead bodies, to women in childbirth. For those giving birth at home, their chance of catching the potentially fatal disease increased if they were attended by a doctor – a rather dramatic example of iatrogenesis!

In 1902 the Midwifery Registration Act was passed, which governed the registration and education of midwives and essentially placed all midwives under the control of medical men. (There was a tendency for doctors to attend the childbirth of those who could pay more, whilst midwives were more likely to deliver the children of poorer women.)

Although nursing has traditionally been the task of females, nurses had to struggle to be recognised as a profession. Florence Nightingale did little to help when she commented that nursing should be done by those 'who were too old, too weak, too drunken, too dirty, too sordid or too bad to do anything else' (quoted in Abel-Smith, 1960). Nightingale also suggested that the roles of doctors and nurses should be like those of Victorian husbands and wives: women should clean and care and males should be in control. There was a strict boundary between nurses and doctors, for example doctors prescribed drugs whilst nurses handed them out. Even recently, Oakley (1993) admitted in her study of childbirth that she was blind to the role of nurses.

In 1943 the Nurses Act was passed governing the training and registration of State Enrolled and State Registered Nurses. More recently nursing degrees have been devised and more men have begun to enter the nursing profession. Recent changes in the NHS have created a further administrative layer dominated by men, and men who have entered nursing may take up these management roles. Thus the decisions made by them may affect the future nature and quality of care received by women.

Link Exercise 2.1 Evaluating the feminist critique of the medical model

Turn to the section 'Men and control of the health service' in Chapter 6 (page 149).

 1. Assess the evidence that suggests males do not benefit from control over the health service despite the claim that it is dominated by men.

 2. Complete the following text by filling in the gaps with the key words provided below:

Feminists have usefully criticised the . . . . . . role of doctors. Male values and self-interest may have dominated the area of health care. . . . . . . claims that the area of childbirth is a very useful example that illustrates the way men have deliberately taken control away from female . . . . . . Oakley shows how some pregnant women view their birth differently from . . . . . .: seeing pregnancy as a natural process rather than a . . . . . . one. The area of contraception is another example of how a male-dominated medical profession has prescribed the contraceptive pill to women despite their risk of . . . . . .

Thus the feminist perspective claims that medical knowledge and intervention is not objective (value-free). However the feminists' use of pregnancy may be an . . . . . . example. The values of male doctors may not dominate in the same way within an ear, nose and throat ward. Thus the extent of . . . . . . needs to be examined. In addition, the feminist perspective lacks a wealth of empirical . . . . . . (perhaps due to male domination of researcher and academics – 'malestream' sociology) of the way in which male doctors 'dominate'. The way in which doctors and female patients . . . . . . would be a useful area of study because male doctors may treat male and female patients in different ways, thus illustrating the way the values held by male . . . . . . are at play within everyday interaction in the medical setting.

Key words: interact, Oakley, midwives, medical, doctors, side effects, 'domination', extreme, evidence, doctors, objective.

What alternatives are there to the medical model of illness?

Although the medical model of illness has gained prominence in many Western societies there are alternative explanations of ill health in other cultures, as well as competing explanations in Western countries.

A cross-cultural case study: Gilbert Lewis' study of the Gnau of New Guinea

Gilbert Lewis was a doctor who conducted an ethnographic study (an in-depth study of a way of life) of the Gnau tribe in New Guinea. The Gnau do not see illness in the same way as medical doctors. The word for illness is 'wola', which also means 'harmful', 'forbidden' and 'bad'. Illness is not viewed as a set of physical or psychological symptoms: illness is far more than that. In fact for the Gnau it is almost any negative happening in a person's life. Just like the medical model, the Gnau attempt to identify a cause for illness. However any Gnau adult can help a sick individual by helping to get rid of evil spirits that might have caused the illness. There are no specialist healers and it is the patients, not a health official, who define themselves as sick. It is also the patients who define themselves as 'cured' (Lewis, 1976).

[i] 1. What does the word *wola* mean for the Gnau?

[a] 2. How does the word *wola* differ from the Western notion of illness?

[a] 3. (a) Write down how the Gnau notions of illness are both similar to and different from the medical model.

[e]   (b) Which of the two do you find most convincing and why?

The patient-centred model of illness

Rather than starting with the idea that patients' complaints have an identifiable cause, such as a virus or bacteria, we could examine the patients' perspective of their own bodily and psychological condition. In a study of doctors' and patients' perspectives on the diagnosis of repetitive strain injury (RSI), Arksey (1994) examines how doctors and patients sometimes view their condition in very different ways. RSI is a general term for a number of neck, shoulder, hand, wrist, forearm and elbow disorders occurring in both manual and non-manual workers. There has been considerable opposition to the diagnosis of RSI as there seems to be no identifiable physical cause, for example Judge John Prosser QC said that 'RSI was meaningless and had no place in the medical books' (quoted in Arksey, 1994). The medical model of illness suggests that it is health professionals who possess and share valid and objective knowledge about the body. However Arksey shows how a patient-centred approach uncovers a perspective that can be very valid and even inform doctors about a condition. An RSI support group organiser said about the doctor–patient relationship:

> When we started the project, one of the GP's said, 'Well, I think that sounds like quite a good idea but I'm not really into this RSI thing. I think that's a load of nonsense; I'm not really into it.' Since then, however, he has said that he's learned a hell of a lot from the experience of talking to the patients and that he now recognises RSI as a problem, quite a major problem at that (*Arksey, 1994*).

The study by Arksey shows that medical knowledge cannot be taken for granted as objective truth. Patients can also resist the knowledge imparted by their doctors and challenge it. Negotiation does take place between social actors (for example doctors and patients) to develop, extend and change knowledge. Patients are able to evaluate the advice of their doctors, believing some, but not necessarily all, medical advice. We might therefore want to examine when and why patients choose to accept medical advice.

Exercise 2.10 Patients' evaluation of medical knowledge

Calnan and Williams (1992) carried out a survey using self-completed questionnaires with a random sample of the population aged 18 and over in the local health district. Sixty-two per cent (454 respondents in total) participated; very little demographic bias occurred in the sample as it reflected – in terms of gender and age – the make-up of the general population of adults in Canterbury and Thanet. The results were as follows:

Patients' evaluation of medical knowledge (percentage of sample)

Doctors' recommendation	Accept without question	Accept with explanation	Not readily/ not at all
Antibiotics	54	41	5
Hernia operation	30	63	7
Bowel cancer operation	29	60	12
Tranquillisers	8	29	63
Hip replacement	25	62	13
Hysterectomy	20	65	16
Faith in doctors %	Lot of faith	Quite a lot	Not very much
	31	56	13

(*Source*: M. Calnan and S. Williams, 'Images of scientific medicine', *Sociology of Health & Illness*, vol. 14, no. 2, 1992.)

[i] 1. For what complaint did respondents most readily accept the doctor's recommendation?

[i] 2. For what complaint were respondents least likely to accept the doctor's recommendation?

[a] 3. Why do you think the patients' response varied according to each condition?

[e] 4. What additional information might you require to develop a more sophisticated view of the impact of doctors' recommendations? (For example figures for men and women.)

Exercise 2.11 Evaluating the patient–centred critique of the medical model

[i] [e] In the appropriate box in the table below, list the following advantages and disadvantages of adopting the patient-centred model as an alternative to the medical model:

Evaluating the patient-centred model of illness

Advantages	Disadvantages

- Patients may even develop successful ways of dealing with symptoms.
- Patients may gain a very important understanding of their problem by applying their own knowledge and experience of the symptoms.
- Patients may not have an accurate understanding of their condition and could mislead the doctor.
- Doctors can learn from patients' experiences of illness and their understanding of possible causes of the symptoms.
- Patients may attempt falsely to define themselves as ill in order to obtain a sick note, therefore doctors should not always take at face value all that patients state about their condition but must judge for her/himself.
- Listening to patients is more time-consuming, therefore fewer patients might be treated.

The social model of illness

The medical model of illness tends to focus on finding the 'fault' of an illness within the individual. Once detected the assumption is that it can be treated and the individual will return to a 'normal' state. Because the medical profession played a key role in developing the National Health Service, our present health care system is curative (involves treating illness) rather than preventative (involves changing lifestyles/behaviour and the environment/social structure, for example poverty, to prevent illness). The social model of illness is an umbrella term that includes many different health strategies, for example community health and public health programmes. The social model was put into action early in the nineteenth century when improved sanitation was a main social policy.

McKeown (1976) argues that the main reason for a decline in infectious diseases in the late nineteenth and twentieth centuries was not the medical response to the problem (that is, inoculations) but the social response, particularly improved sewage disposal and the supply of cleaner water to homes. In short, the social model of illness focuses on living standards as the key to improving health. Living standards can improve through education (for example teaching about hygiene) as well as improving the material quality of life (for example reducing poverty to allow people better-quality housing, more nutritious diets and better sanitation). Critics of McKeown's research point out that not all illnesses will respond to an improvement in the social environment. Some forms of disease may be completely unrelated to the quality of sanitation or clean water.

McKeown identified the following pattern in the incidence of tuberculosis:

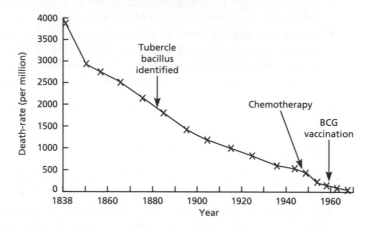

Respiratory tuberculosis: death rates per million, England and Wales

(Source: T. McKeown, The Role of Medicine: Dream, Mirage or Nemesis, London, Basil Blackwell, 1979.)

McKeown identified the following pattern in the incidence of measles:

Measles: death rates per million of children under 15, England and Wales

(Source: T. McKeown, The Role of Medicine: Dream, Mirage or Nemesis, London, Basil Blackwell, 1979.)

An article in the *Independent on Sunday* on 1 October referred to the 1994 campaign by the Department of Health in which over seven million children were vaccinated against measles and German measles in order to prevent a possible measles epidemic in 1995. The article pointed out that although the Department of Health did not think the campaign had harmed any children, a parents' support group called 'Jabs' believes that the health of a number of children has been seriously damaged by the vaccination.

McKeown identified the following influences on the decline of infections:

1. Improved standards of living, especially better food.
2. Behavioural changes, better personal hygiene, less overcrowding.
3. Improved public health, especially sanitation.
4. Clinical medical intervention.

It is important to note that in some cases, most notably diphtheria and polio, medical intervention was the decisive factor.

(Source: S. Taylor, Health and Illness, London, Longman, 1986.)

ITEMS F–I   **Exercise 2.12   What caused the reduction in tuberculosis and measles?**

[i] 1. According to Item F, what was the death rate from TB in 1850? In 1950?

[i] 2. When was the BCG vaccination introduced to combat TB?

[i] 3. What does Item F suggest about the influence of the medical response to TB?

[i] 4. (a) What does Item G suggest about the relationship between child deaths for measles and the availability of immunisation?

   (b) What does Item G suggest about the role of immunisation in reducing the incidence of measles?

[e] 5. Items F and G show the decline in TB and measles as identified by McKeown. McKeown based his research on death certificates. Do you believe these records accurately defined the cause of death? Why/why not? How might your answer affect the way McKeown's work is viewed?

[i][a] 6. With a colleague, rank the list of factors in Item I in what you think is their order of importance.

[a] 7. Can you suggest other illnesses that might be reduced by environmental improvements rather than medical intervention?

i *e*
8. What do Items H and I suggest about the impact of the medical profession on our health? Why might this lead us to underestimate the contribution made by medicine?

e
9. For which illnesses/medical conditions do you think the medical profession provides a very effective treatment? What conclusions might you draw from your answer about the effectiveness of the medical profession?

The body, health and illness

The notion of the 'body' as a sociological issue is relatively recent (the 1980s), and the issue appears to be absent from much sociology (Shilling, 1993). However recent debates on whether life should be taken (abortion and euthanasia) highlight the debate on the body. Increasingly, consumer culture is related to notions of the body: what should it look like (thin/fat)? What should people eat to keep the body healthy? How should people exercise to maintain a healthy body? The notion of the body as an entity or object that can be thought of in a variety of ways is one that is important to the study of health and illness. Dominant views of the 'desirable' body may affect people's ideas about whether they feel healthy or ill. In *The Body and Society* (1984) Turner states that 'In writing this study of the body, I have become increasingly less sure about what the body is'. Ideas about the body may be shaped by the perspective from which it is viewed.

The medical model and the body

The medical model views the body much as a machine that can break down and therefore needs repair. Lawrence and Bendixen (1992) studied anatomical textbooks published between 1890 and 1989 and found that the descriptions of the body and many diagrams treated the male body as the norm. Such texts may shape doctors' views of the body (that is, the male body as the norm).

Laqueur (1990) is critical of the way biology claims differences exist between bodies. He says the search for classification of types (for example people, plants, animals) started around the 1800s. The search for types was important because once 'types' emerged they could be treated unequally (think of the unequal treatment of racial types – white, coloured and black – under the former apartheid system in South Africa).

The social constructionist perspective and the body

Social constructionists have one belief in common: they all believe that the way people view themselves and others is not natural or truthful but shaped by the society in which they live. Foucault (1976) argues that the way people view the body is heavily shaped by the prevailing discourse (thought shaping language). Views of the body will therefore vary according to discourse: for example societies where thin people are viewed as attractive may give status to thin people; societies where fat is viewed as an attractive status will have different views on the body. Foucault would have people examine the language used to describe body size and would even try to make people question why language for body size even exists. For Foucault notions of health and illness are shaped by the discourse of the body.

Other social constructionists argue that notions of the body can shape the nature of the body (for example size, weight, strength). This point can be illustrated by the anthropological work of Douglas (1966), who points out that in societies where women are expected to lift heavy weights these expectations can shape the nature of the body. Therefore social expectations of the body can shape the physical body.

Feminism and the body

Feminists such as Martin (1989) claim gender expectations of bodies exist for both men and women. Bodily processes such as menstruation have received negative connotations, resulting in an unequal perception (or discourse) of male and female bodies. Martin claims the views held by women (and men) are shaped by medical notions as well as by social, economic and political factors. An example of Martin's point might be the way expectations of women changed during the Second World War when they performed more physically arduous work than had been previously expected (though women had worked in coal mines until the early Mining Acts legislated against this). For Martin women (and men) draw on medical notions of their bodies as well as constructing their own meanings about them (for example the significance of hormonal changes) and combine these with some social expectations of their bodies.

The phenomenological perspective and the body

The phenomenological perspective examines the way notions of self-identity are affected by notions of the 'normal' body. Kelly (1992) has examined the way people reshape their notions of the body after undergoing radical surgery (for example having a colostomy bag attached to the lower abdomen). Such a perspective might examine the way notions of being healthy and being ill are affected by our subjective/personal feelings about our own bodies. Thus to believe acne is ugly may force a person to visit a doctor. To believe being fat is undesirable may force people to change their self-identity, which in turn may lead them to seek medical assistance, and possibly even surgery. Whilst phenomenologists focus on individual self-identity, social constructionists and feminists would prefer to discuss the discourse that shapes such notions of the body.

Can the case of wrinkles be applied to the problem of defining health and illness?

Having read this far, you will be aware that when we talk about someone 'being ill' or 'being healthy' it is important to ask *how* we came to that decision; what do we *mean* by 'being healthy'? How do we judge whether someone is ill? You will realise that the medical model has been a major influence on ideas about health and illness in our society, particularly among the medical profession. However these ideas have been challenged: the iatrogenesis and feminist critiques suggest that the medical model can actually be seen as a threat to health. The patient-centred and the social models have provided us with alternative ways of looking at illness. Notions of the body are also important considerations that can be applied to the case of wrinkles.

<u>ITEM J</u>   *Exercise 2.13   Looking younger on prescription?*

 1. From Item J identify ways in which wrinkling can be seen as an illness. Does it fit the ideas of the medical model?

2. Who might benefit if wrinkles are classified as an illness?

3. In what ways could treating wrinkles as an illness be criticised? (Hint: could the ideas of the iatrogenesis or feminist critiques be applied to this example?)

4. How can the issue of wrinkles be applied to notions of the body. What would Foucault be concerned about? And feminists? And phenomenologists?

'Wrinkles aren't a natural consequence of ageing any more; they are a medical condition known as "photodamage". And according to large advertisements in the medical press, the condition can be cured. Retinova, says its makers, "effectively repairs years of photodamage to skin".

Retinova was originally developed as an anti-acne cream. It was developed by an American dermatologist, Albert Kligman, who said recently: "The wrinkle is a serious disease . . . everybody worries regularly about wrinkles". The cream, which costs £13.75 for a 20g tube is available on private prescription only.

But are wrinkles a medical condition? Should middle-aged or elderly women (for it is mainly women) occupy doctors' time seeking medical help for something many people would consider part of ordinary life?

Medical opinion covers a spectrum of views. Some doctors see wrinkling as almost exclusively the result of over-exposure to sunlight, and believe it worthy of medical intervention. Christopher Griffiths, professor of dermatology at Manchester University insists, "Wrinkles are not a normal part of the ageing process. Just because wrinkling is not life threatening does not mean we should not treat it. Few dermatological conditions are going to kill you, but we still treat them."

Ian Kennedy, professor of medical law and ethics at King's College, London is opposed to medical intervention. "The emergence of this cream raises yet again the difficult question as to what extent we should satisfy the ambitions of people who do not want to appear to grow old. This is part of the pursuit of Shangrila and is in the same category as bust lifts and bottom tucks."

But does Retinova actually work? Most doctors believe it makes patients' wrinkles look less obvious [and] causes mild dermatitis or swelling of the skin. Some doctors think that it is this swelling which causes the wrinkles to disappear. Others believe the cream actually restores collagen (the structural fibres in the dermis) and puts elasticity permanently back in the skin.

Whatever the cream's efficacy, its promotion can only amplify the message that ageing is a shameful process and must be disguised at all costs.'

(Source: A. Ferriman, 'Looking Younger on Prescription', Independent on Sunday, 26 August 1995.)

Were you surprised by the suggestion that wrinkles (a purely cosmetic issue?) could become a medical issue, or did you see little difference between treating wrinkles and other medical interventions designed to preserve the efficient functioning of our bodies (for example removing a cataract or replacing a hip joint)?

Structured exam questions

The following exercises should help you to apply the issues and practise skills you have learned in Chapter 2.

Question

1. 'Health and illness are socially defined concepts.' Examine the arguments for and against this view. (*25 marks*)

   (a) Read through the student essay answer below. The examination advice (in brackets) is intended to help you understand how to use your evaluation, knowledge and understanding, interpretation and application skills.

(b) Identify where the following key words should be placed in the text: medicalisation, obesity, positive, *lifestyles*, middle, gender, definitions, Illness, think, service, essentially contested, working.

Student answer

According to the World Health Organisation 'health is a state of complete physical, mental, and social well-being and not merely the absence of disease and infirmity'. The quote appears to suggest the the term health can be defined in a way that can allow consensus. However, the definitions of both 'health' and 'illness' can be viewed as. . . . . . . the terms mean different things to different people.

Comment *Knowledge and understanding: knowledge of the World Health Organisation's (WHO) definition is provided by way of a quote. Interpretation and application: the paragraph shows an interpretation skill because it directly addresses the word 'health' in the essay title by applying a definition provided by the WHO. Evaluation: the paragraph ends with a relevant evaluation point.*

Some people argue that health is a relative concept which means that the definition of health and how it is recognised varies from society to society. For example, in some societies being 'fat' is seen to be desirable whereas being 'fat' in many Western societies has been medicalised as a health problem and it is called ' . . . . . .'.

Comment *Interpretation and application: the health theme is addressed further by applying more information about cross-cultural notions of health.*

In the *Health and* . . . . . . survey, Blaxter (1990a) examined the way people defined health. The study had a sample of 9003 respondents with a response rate of over 70 per cent; this can be seen to be a large sample with a very high response rate. The study investigated the respondents' definitions of health and found that two main views of health could be identified . . . . . . definitions (e.g. being able to be fit enough to carry out tasks) and negative definitions (simply the absence of sickness). This study showed that people hold different . . . . . . of health.

Comment *Knowledge and understanding: knowledge of Blaxter's work on definitions of health is provided. Interpretation and application: the answer includes an accurate interpretation of the work undertaken by Blaxter, which is briefly summarised and applied to the question.*

Notions of health may vary between social groups. Researchers d'Houtard and Field in 1984 discovered that . . . . . . class groups hold more positive definitions of health whereas . . . . . . class people hold more negative views of health. However, Calnan (1987) did not find negative definitions of health held amongst working class women. Variations may also occur by age groups and even . . . . . . and ethnic groups.

Comment *Knowledge and understanding: knowledge of research into definitions of health among a variety of social groups has been provided. Interpretation and application: the answer now broadens to examine whether different social groups hold varying notions of health. Evaluation: some contrasting material has been included – that is, the work of Calnan – to show the skill of evaluation.*

Definitions of health are important considerations because they may influence the type of health . . . . . . offered to patients particularly by the NHS. If the issue of fertility is no longer regarded as a 'health' issue then the service may be withdrawn and many people wanting children but unable to conceive may have to seek private health care: not all people will be able to afford to purchase private health care.

Comment *Interpretation and application: the points show an implication of differing views of health that have been applied very cogently to the essay title. Evaluation: the final sentence shows yet more evaluation.*

. . . . . . is a notion which may depend on people's own interpretations of their mental and physical symptoms. Some people may define a 'hangover' as an illness but others may not.Yet a headache labelled as a migraine may be more likely to be viewed as an illness. The way in which people interpret illness symptoms may determine whether they visit the doctor: thus morbidity figures from GPs will depend on the way in which an illness is defined by people.

Comment *Interpretation and application: the essay now addresses the second part of the essay title: illness. Thus showing a clear interpretation of the essay question.*

Foucault (1976) claims that the way people think about health and illness is influenced by the dominant medical 'discourse'. Discourse refers to the way language is created that then affects the way people. . . . . . . Illich (1990) claims that Western societies make conditions of the body, eg. being fat, into medical problems: Illich calls this process . . . . . . Thus the medical profession may be attempting to influence the way we view symptoms so we see them as medical problems, visit the doctor and then buy drugs from private pharmaceutical companies who then make a profit. The way we think of 'health' and 'illness' may therefore be influenced by the medical model, which forms a powerful discourse in society. This medical discourse encourages people to define some problems as an illness: even being 'overweight' (medical term, obesity) and sad (medical term, depression).

Comment *Knowledge and understanding: knowledge of Foucault has been used to account for the work on discourse and the work on discourse shows a reasonable level of understanding. Interpretation and application: by drawing on the work of Foucault the essay is applying an interpretation of Foucault's work on discourse. A theoretical input was necessary as it had been absent for the most of the essay. Evaluation: the answer also applies the work of Illich to evaluate the medical model. The notion of 'discourse' is used to evaluate the way in which health and illness are viewed.*

Further work may have been added to show how varying notions of health and illness could affect the way doctors and patients define illness and the way the morbidity figures may depend on people's definition of illness and their subsequent illness behaviour (deciding whether to visit the doctor or not – see Chapter 3). The essay should also have dealt with the view that the medical model of illness assumes it is a relatively uncontested notion of which doctors, on the whole, share an understanding. Thus the essay only really dealt with the view that health and illness are socially defined.

Questions

2. Practice your essay skills by answering the following examination questions.

   (a) 'What counts as "health" and "illness" varies from place to place and time to time.' Examine this view, illustrating your answer with examples. (*25 marks*) (AEB AS Level, June 1991)

   (b) Critically discuss the view that the medical model is an objective way of understanding illness. (*25 marks*)
   Each of the following sentences introduces one key point that will help you with essay (**b**). Read through the introductory sentences, then expand each one into a paragraph using relevant information in Chapter 2 and other appropriate chapters, as well as any information you have gathered yourself. Each of your paragraphs should attempt to include some knowledge and some evaluation (strengths, weaknesses, criticisms), and where appropriate you should try to use evidence.

- The medical model is also known as the biomedical approach and is based on a number of key assumptions, including the view that diagnosing and classifying illness is objective.
- The issue of the medical model is an important one because it had a great deal of influence on the way in which the National Health Service was designed.
- The medical model assumes an illness is often the result of an organic cause that can be can be objectively identified. Cross-cultural notions of illness, identified by researchers such as Lewis (1976), have shown that illnesses do not have to viewed in the same way.
- The medical model assumes a doctor is the key person to diagnose an illness. The doctor's diagnosis is assumed to be an objective decision. This assumption excludes the views of the patient. The patient-centred model views illness as a negotiated process in which sufferers are able to contribute to an understanding of their bodily condition.
- The medical model promotes the use of biomedical treatment (that is, drugs and surgery).
- Illich, in his book *Medical Nemesis* (1976), is deeply critical of the treatments offered by the medical model.
- The medical model assumes that, like physical illness, mental illness has objectively identified causes that respond to medical treatment (that is, drugs and surgery).
- Social constructionists claim that the medical model is not an objective or value-free way of understanding illness. They believe that the medical model is just one way of understanding illness, but one that has gained dominance and legitimation.
- Some feminists, for example Graham (1984), support the view that the medical model is not objective, that doctors and consultants, predominantly men, impose their own values on women's health, and these values may not always benefit women. The issues of contraception and childbirth are two applications of the feminist perspective.
- Foucault (1976) claims that the medical model is not an objective way of understanding illness but merely a body of knowledge that has gained power in many Western societies. Foucault examines medical knowledge as just a type of discourse.
- Postmodernists reject theories that attempt to explain all aspects of behaviour (for example the medical model, which attempts to explain the cause of all illnesses). They refer to such grand theories as 'metatheories' (see Chapter 11).

Now try to think of some points to include in your conclusion. (Hint: the medical model is dominant in Western health care systems, so perhaps it is a way of understanding illness and treating certain health problems that has benefited many people. Should the medical model be totally accepted or completely rejected, or can it be useful in some cases but not others?)

Summary

This chapter has examined the way that 'health' and 'illness' cannot be taken for granted as they are concepts that mean different things to different people. Blaxter (1990a) explored the variety of definitions that people hold of health. Definitions of health may affect the type of facilities available, which is particularly important when examining the services offered free of charge by the NHS. Notions of illness also vary between people. Variation in definitions of illness is particularly important when examining the way doctors apply labels (or do not apply labels) to particular symptoms. One example explored in this chapter was repetitive strain injury (RSI), which some doctors have refused to regard as a legitimate illness. The issue here is of social control by the medical profession over patients' ability to have their symptoms taken seriously.

The medical model was explored and was seen to be the medical profession's main way of thinking about illness and the body. The medical model views the body as a machine that needs to be repaired, largely through drugs and surgery. Illich (1976) points out that some surgery and drugs can cause more harm than good: he calls this 'clinical iatrogenesis'.

Alternative ways of viewing health were discussed. A cross-cultural example of the way illness is understood by the Gnau tribe showed that some societies view illness and its potential causes in a very different way from the medical model. In addition, a contrast to the medical model was provided by the 'social model', which views improvements in health standards as due to better living conditions (for example better food, water, housing), as well as greater knowledge of hygiene and more effective sewage systems. The patient-centred model explored how patients differ from doctors in the way they view their bodily states and how a patient-centred approach might give a broader understanding of the causes of illness than the biologically informed medical model.

Finally, the way dominant notions of 'the body' affect how people view their own and others' bodies was explored. Notions of the 'body' may affect definitions of health and illness.

3 The social process of becoming ill

By the end of this chapter you should be able to:

- appreciate why the morbidity statistics may be socially constructed;
- understand the main stages involved in 'becoming ill';
- evaluate the validity of the morbidity figures.

Introduction

This chapter examines the way people come to be officially defined (or not defined) as ill. Six stages are outlined to illustrate this. The first stage begins with examples of some of the social processes (for example poverty, housing, poor diet) that along with genetic factors, cause people to become ill. The second stage examines the types of symptom that might develop, for example physical, mental and social symptoms. The third stage explores the factors (such as personal experience, family views, information spread by mass media) that influence whether symptoms are interpreted as an illness. Stage four explores the decisions people make when their symptoms are interpreted as an illness. What do people decide to do about the 'problem'? For example, will they choose to ignore the symptoms, to treat the symptoms themselves, to visit a GP or an alternative therapist? Stage five examines what takes place when a person decides to visit a doctor. Negotiation occurs between the doctor and the patient, after which the doctor will make an official diagnosis. It is during this stage that doctors label (or refuse to label) symptoms as an illness, thus exercising a form of social control over patients. Finally, stage six examines the way knowledge about illnesses is built up by the products of all the previous stages. Thus morbidity statistics (illness figures) cannot be taken for granted as they are 'socially created' – they are the outcome of the series of social processes outlined in the six stages.

How are the morbidity figures created?

The morbidity (sickness) figures cannot be taken at face value: they are not 'natural' figures that we can trust but are socially constructed, meaning they are developed by the sorts of decisions people make. Rather as crime figures often depend on people reporting an incident to the police, morbidity figures depend on decisions to visit a doctor. Once the symptoms are reported the doctor then has to decide whether to define them as an illness. Becoming a morbidity statistic is a complex process that we will now examine in more detail.

The process of illness can be identified by examining a series of stages, as follows.

Stage 1: social processes make people vulnerable to illnesses

A number of factors make people vulnerable to illness. Whitehead (1992) identifies a host of social causes, particularly poverty. Subsequent research has examined factors such as diet, poor housing, unsafe recreational play areas for children, pollution, stress and occupational hazards. Genetic factors may also cause people to become ill, particularly if combined with stressful environments that 'draw out' the symptoms. Both the social and genetic causes of illness need to be considered. Illness symptoms may not therefore strike randomly: some people may be more prone to illness than others for the reasons outlined above.

Exercise 3.1   Developing an illness

i   1. What factors identified in the text might cause people to feel ill?

a   2. What other factors might cause people to develop an illness?

Stage 2: symptoms develop

The symptoms that develop can be classified into three types: (1) physical symptoms such as a headache, runny nose or sore leg; (2) psychological symptoms such as feeling depressed, feeling that people are out to kill you, believing that you are constantly in contact with germs and need to clean yourself every few minutes, feeling overweight even though you are physically malnourished; and (3) social symptoms, such as feeling isolated or that your relationships are failing.

Exercise 3.2   The development of symptoms

 1. Using the appropriate boxes in the table below, separate the following conditions into the three types of symptom identified in the text:

Physical symptoms	Psychological symptoms	Social symptoms

(a) clinical depression, (b) food poisoning, (c) broken leg, (d) inability to relate to people, (e) AIDS, (f) schizophrenia, (g) migraine, (h) anorexia nervosa.

[a] 2. Write a list of symptoms that might not develop immediately after exposure to risk (e.g. polluted air) but occur after a long period of time.

[e] 3. Briefly outline one problem for health researchers caused by the delayed onset of symptoms.

Stage 3: symptoms are interpreted as an illness

The idea that once people develop symptoms of illness they automatically react by visiting their doctor is a common sense notion that is not supported by sociological research. Before people decide what to do about their symptoms they first have to interpret their physical, psychological and social state as a health problem.

The influence of personal experience

If you know that a large number of spots all over the body is a symptom of chicken pox then you may decide to interpret your condition as a problem. Experience of illness through other family members or friends, as well as your own previous illnesses, can affect how you interpret symptoms. Knowing that a relative was diagnosed with cancer after having reported a sore mole on his/her arm might affect how you react to a mole on your body that is irritating you. The British Heart Foundation is concerned that although heart disease kills one in four women, women tend to think of it as a male problem, and as a result women are more likely to ignore the early symptoms of heart disease (for example chest pains). Men are more likely to realise something is wrong and seek treatment at an earlier stage.

The influence of mass media

The mass media (newspapers, magazines, TV, radio, leaflets, posters and so on) communicate knowledge of illness. Having read a magazine article reporting that lumps on the breast could be a symptom of breast cancer, you might decide to take any lumps in this area very seriously. Through watching a television programme on health I found out that not only women but a small proportion of men suffer from breast cancer. This knowledge might affect the way I interpret a lump on my own (male) chest. In 1995 the British Heart Foundation launched a campaign to try to increase awareness among women about the dangers of heart disease, calling it 'Britain's No. 1 Ladykiller'.

Exercise 3.3   Mass media, health and illness

1. Try *either* activity (a) or activity (b):

   (a) Spend one week making a log of all the information about health and illness featured in the mass media. Read some newspapers and magazines and make a note of any information about health and illness. If this was your only source of knowledge, what would you understand about health and illness?

   (b) Choose just one medium, for instance TV, a newspaper that has a health section, for example the *Independent*; a magazine such as a women's magazine, for example *Cosmopolitan*. If this was your only source of knowledge what would you understand about health and illness?

2. Write a brief paragraph showing how the mass media influences what people know about 'being healthy' and 'illnesses'.

The influence of family

The reactions of others may also affect how we interpret a set of symptoms. If other family members view the symptoms seriously then perhaps we will change our own perception of these symptoms. In *The Man Who Thought His Wife Was A Hat*, Sacks (1985) provides the extreme example of a wife reporting her own husband to a psychiatrist (Sacks) in order to convince her husband he had a psychological problem. The husband was having difficulty perceiving the difference between objects such as a hat stand and people, for example his wife. It took his wife's frequent complaints to convince him that this behaviour was unusual. Family members, friends and colleagues can greatly affect the way we interpret a set of symptoms.

The influence of culture

Research suggests that the mere presence of symptoms is not enough to lead people to seek health care. Some research examines the way different groups perceive pain. Zborowski (1952) conducted research into cultural perceptions of pain and found marked differences between Italian Americans, Jewish Americans and 'old Americans' (Protestants). Zola (1966) also claims that there are cultural differences between Irish Americans and Italian Americans; for example when respondents were asked whether they became irritable due to deafness/hearing loss, an Irish response was 'No, not me', but an Italian claimed 'Yes . . . the least little thing aggravates me'. Zola claimed the Irish were more likely to be dismissive of physical symptoms, whereas Italians found physical pain less tolerable.

To become more sophisticated about perceptions of pain we might need to explore how different social groups respond to different types of pain, for example do women tolerate psychological pain better than men, and are men more tolerant of physical pain than women?

The influence of gender

Link Exercise 3.1 Gender and illness behaviour

 Turn to Chapter 6 on gender and health. Find the section that examines the validity of morbidity statistics (page 132). What does this section inform you about the extent to which men and women visit the doctor?

Bendelow (1993) examined whether there are gender differences in the notion of pain. One respondent said, 'it's quite hard to remember physical pain – I think probably mental pain is the worst – the physical is hard to remember, it goes but the mental stays there' (white male salesman, aged 26, Irish).

Men were found to hold a hierarchy of pain. Emotional pain was not considered 'real' pain. Some men considered that socialisation forced them to endure pain: several respondents thought that expressing pain would have branded them 'sissy' or homosexual. Pain could also be viewed as positive. Pain could 'strengthen' people by forcing them to cope with emotional problems.

Thus we can see that the way people interpret their symptoms (as painful or not) may vary between both individuals and social groups, such as men and women (Bendelow, 1994), and between cultural/ethnic groups such as Italian and Irish (Zola, 1966). These differences in pain perception may influence whether somebody decides to seek health care.

Exercise 3.4 Gender and pain perception

Bendelow (1993) conducted semistructured interviews with 11 men and women from a variety of ethnic groups drawn from a larger sample of 107 males and females who filled out questionnaires on their personal and medical history, their worst experiences of pain, and men's and women's ability to cope with pain. The results showed that the sample viewed women as being able to endure pain more than men:

(*Source*: G. Bendelow, 'Pain perceptions, emotions and gender', *Sociology of Health & Illness*, vol. 15, no. 3, 1993.)

Coping with pain (per cent)			
	Females	**Males**	**Total**
Women cope more	66	33	50
Men cope more	8	17	12
No difference	25	42	33
Don't know	1	8	5
Total	100	100	100

(*Source*: G. Bendelow, 'Pain perceptions, emotions and gender', *Sociology of Health & Illness*, vol. 15, no. 3, 1993.)

Interestingly, Bendelow reports that four men and four women changed their minds about what they each considered to be their most painful experience. For example in the questionnaire one respondent said that toothache was his most painful experience, yet in the interview he switched to recently occurring panic attacks as the most painful. The point suggests that the type of research carried out may affect the type of answers gained.

Bendelow's results are not consistent with other studies of gender and pain perception, some of which find that men and women have a similar tolerance of pain, others that women have a lower tolerance of pain.

1. Using the account of Bendelow's research, state one methodological problem that Bendelow might have had with her research.

2. Outline one main conclusion from Bendelow's research into pain perception.

3. Why are studies of pain perception important to the sociology of health and illness?

Stage 4: a decision is made to seek health care

The way we decide to react to a set of symptoms is called 'illness behaviour'. This behaviour is not straightforward because not everybody decides to visit a doctor.

Exercise 3.5   Health-seeking behaviour (1)

1. List the factors that influence your decision to visit, or not visit, your doctor.

2. Under what circumstances might you decide to visit an alternative practitioner, for example a herbalist?

Some people might not interpret their symptoms as serious enough to bother about; others might treat themselves, seek health care from their doctor, or seek other sources of help such as alternative therapists. The official morbidity figures depend on people reporting their symptoms to their GP, and because not everybody does this the morbidity figures may greatly underestimate the amount of illness in society.

There are other factors that may determine whether people decide to seek health care. People's previous experience of visiting a hospital or GP might encourage/discourage them from seeking medical advice. People who have never visited a hospital or GP might have preconceived ideas about what is likely to happen. Such beliefs and previous medical experience might affect illness behaviour.

Exercise 3.6 Health-seeking behaviour (2)

Health-seeking behaviour was examined in Finland by Punamaki and Aschan (1994). Respondents were approached in six Finnish primary health care centres located in different parts of the country. The respondents were selected using a systematic sample (that is, every 100th patient visiting the centre between December 1991 and January 1992). The sample was checked to represent the spread of illnesses reported to the centre, so no one illness was overrepresented. The respondents completed semistructured diaries over a two-week period and filled in their daily activities, intentions, thoughts and coping resources. Of the 258 participating in the initial interview, only 55 per cent returned their diaries. A check was made to see whether the 'successful returners' were significantly different from the non-returners in terms of age, sex and urban–rural residence.

Punamaki and Aschan point to other research showing that only about one third of people with medical symptoms seek medical advice. Their diary instructions for investigating decisions about health care were: 'every day, record what you do in order to care for your health and the health of those close to you'. The results showed that a wide variety of self-care responses occur when unpleasant symptoms are experienced:

Self-care responses recorded by respondents

Type of care	%	Example
Faith	18.0	I listen to religious music
Nature	8.6	I go out in the fresh air
Work and hobbies	42.5	I finished work/I went fishing
Leisure and relaxation	29.5	I went shopping by myself
Sports and exercise	63.3	I should do more walking
Food and diet	30.9	I should fast to purify my body
Sauna and hygiene	25.9	I go to the sauna to keep clean
Avoiding risks	10.1	I don't smoke
Lay care	49.6	I massaged my wife; I took an aspirin
Official health care	10.1	I booked a doctor's appointment

(*Source*: Adapted from R. Punamaki and H. Aschan 'Self-care and mastery among primary health care patients', *Social Science & Medicine*, vol. 39, no. 5, 1994.)

These results show that people are involved in many self-care activities apart from visiting their doctor.

i 1. In the table, what were the most popular forms of self-care?

a 2. What forms of self-care do you use (a) in daily life, (b) when you're feeling unwell?

a 3. What determines whether you rely on self-care or seek official health care (that is, visit your doctor)?

4. Why might it be easier for some people than others to visit their doctor?

5. Some people might be reluctant to visit their doctor even when they interpret their symptoms as illness. Does this matter?

Stage 5: labelling : doctor–patient interaction

Much as official criminal statistics depend on a police officer labelling an act of behaviour as a crime, morbidity statistics depend on a doctor labelling symptoms as an illness. The medical model of illness searches for identifiable causes (for example a virus or bacteria) and gives medical officers such as doctors the authority to label symptoms as a legitimate illness. A sick note can be granted, giving people the right to stay off work and claim sickness benefit.

A commonsense view of this stage may treat the labelling of illness as unproblematic: patients merely present their symptoms and the doctor applies his/her medical knowledge to diagnose these symptoms as 'proper' illnesses. However sociological studies show that patients and doctors enter a negotiating process in which a struggle sometimes takes place. This struggle may find patients accepting or rejecting the doctor's diagnosis. Sometimes patients even successfully persuade their doctor to accept their symptoms as legitimate when the doctor initially claims they are not; some patients may have more persuasive power than others. As sociologists we should treat the labelling of illness as problematic.

Doctors tend to be seen as those with the medical authority to classify illness. Patients are often expected to report their symptoms and listen to the official diagnosis. However this unequal relationship can be seen as a socially created one in which actors play parts: the doctor 'behaves like a doctor' and the patient 'behaves like a patient'. How are these roles created? Interactionist sociologists have examined the behaviour of doctors and patients to see how doctors create an environment in which patients may be encouraged to accept that the doctor is 'in charge'.

Have doctors the power to label illness?

Emerson (1972) said that doctors possess 'props' (much like those used by actors to convince audiences of the appropriate scene) such as white coats, medical equipment and medical notes. These create a 'medical scene' for the patient, and the medical scene adds to the doctor's power to label illness and have this label accepted as legitimate. In addition language is used in a way that is often exclusive to the medical setting. This does not just include medical jargon for various parts of the body, it also refers to a way of addressing the patient. 'Private' parts of the body may be referred to as 'waterworks' or 'down there'. Instead of using vulgar comments such as 'spread your legs so I can examine you', a doctor is more likely to say, 'part your knees'. Through language and props doctors may set a scene in which patients feel doctors are in charge. Being in charge or in control allows the doctor's definition of the patient to gain dominance.

Do doctors dominate the conversation with their patients?

Bloor (1976) examined patients' medical encounters with ear, nose and throat (ENT) consultants and showed how the consultants restricted the patients' participation in the conversation by demanding very specific answers to 'closed' questions (D = ENT specialist; M = mother of patient):

> *D*: How old is he?
> *M*: Nineteen months.
> *D*: He's had two bad attacks?
> *M*: Yes.
> *D*: He's fevered?
> *M*: Yes.
> *D*: And he came into hospital with one of them?
> *M*: Yes.
> *D*: In between times he's all right?
> *M*: Yes.
> *D*: He eats his food?
> *M*: Yes, fine.
> *D*: He hasn't had ear trouble?
> *M*: No.

This extract shows how doctors can shape the conversational flow and restrict their patients' ability to communicate on equal terms with them.

Exercise 3.7 Doctor–patient dialogue

 Rewrite Bloor's dialogue so that it becomes more open and negotiated between the doctor and patient.

Do patients resist being labelled?

Evidence suggests that patients are not passive during consultations with their doctors. Boulton *et al.* (1986) examined the interaction between doctors and their patients and showed how patients use a number of strategies to influence the dialogue between themselves and their doctor: for example they request further information, seek clarification, suggest their own 'lay' diagnosis, doubt or disagree with the doctor's diagnosis. Thus the doctor–patient relationship should be seen as one in which a struggle can take place between doctor and patient to dominate the conversation, as well as a struggle over competing explanations of the patient's symptoms.

Exercise 3.8 *A study of social class and doctor–patient interaction*

Boulton *et al.* (1986) examined doctor–patient dialogue. Consultations involving 328 patients from a number of social backgrounds with 16 doctors from a variety of GP practices were examined. Thirteen of the doctors were men and three were women. The doctor–patient negotiations were audiotaped with the permission of both parties. Follow-up interviews with patients were carried out in their own homes. Patients were divided into social classes on the basis of their occupation (using the Hope–Goldthorpe classification). The results were as follows:

Patients' strategies during consultation	Middle class (%) Service	Intermediate	Working class (%)
Gave a lay diagnosis of their own problem	42	50	26
Requested further explanation from doctor	46	29	27
Requested clarification of instructions	55	42	46
Expressed doubt or disagreement with doctor	55	55	58

(*Source*: M. Boulton *et al.*, 'Social Class and the GP Consultation', *Sociology of Health & Illness*, vol. 8, no. 4, 1986.)

[i] 1. What proportion of patients in each social class doubted/disagreed with their doctor?

[i] 2. What social class differences can you identify in the table?

[a] 3. Can you suggest what might cause these class differences?

[i][a] 4. What do the strategies listed in the table show us about the doctor–patient relationship?

Labelling: social class and doctor–patient interaction

Boulton *et al.* (1986) found that middle-class patients were more active in seeking further explanation, though both middle- and working-class patients were equally dismissive or disbelieving of their doctor's views and advice. The number of questions patients asked seemed to vary, with middle-class patients asking more questions. The explanation given by the doctors did not vary significantly with the social class of the patient. However Boulton *et al.* conclude that more evidence is needed of the extent to which different patients change their attitude and behaviour towards their health as result of consulting their doctor.

Can patients influence the doctor?

Doctors are often perceived as those possessing legitimate knowledge about health and illness. However Arksey (1994) shows how patients suffering from repetitive strain injury (RSI) can inform doctors about health issues. Medical knowledge can be seen as a two-way relationship rather than a one-way channel from doctor to patient. As stated earlier, RSI is a general term for a range of hand, wrist, forearm, elbow, neck and shoulder disorders. Arksey examined doctor–patient communication between GPs and RSI sufferers. One sufferer claimed that at first the GP believed RSI was a load of nonsense, but after the patient reversed the communication flow and informed the doctor about RSI, the GP claimed that he had 'learned a hell of a lot from the experience of talking to the patients and that he now recognises RSI as a problem, quite a major problem at that' (RSI sufferer, quoted in Arksey, 1994).

Medical interviews between doctor and patient are often perceived to be based on objective knowledge about health and illness, yet research is needed to examine whether there are a host of influences on the consultation. The mass media are one area of influence on the doctor–patient consultation.

Labelling and the media

Professional literature can also affect the doctor/patient consultation. Just because literature is published does not mean all doctors read it. Thus visiting doctors who regularly update their medical knowledge may be different from seeing those who do not take note of recently published medical research. In 1987 RSI was recorded in that year's edition of Hunter's *Diseases of Occupations*. Books, such as Huskisson's (1992) *Repetitive Strain Injury: the keyboard disease* have also been written about RSI. These official medical references may change doctors' views about whether to treat RSI as a legitimate illness. On the other hand, official references in medical publications have claimed that the large settlements paid to sufferers of RSI should alert doctors to treat potential RSI sufferers with suspicion.

ITEM A

'The recent settlement of £45 000 for "a disease caused by typing" has highlighted the rewards available to those who can convince the authorities that they have a disorder caused by their work. The public, unlike doctors, is well aware of these rewards, so understandably many people wish to have such a diagnosis made of their musculoskeletal aches. The history given by the patient is therefore likely to be biased.'

(Source: Barton, 'Repetitive Strain Disorder', British Medical Journal, no. 299, 1989, pp. 405–6.)

Exercise 3.9   Labelling and medical knowledge

1. Using Item A as one source of information, decide in what situations a patient might benefit from convincing their doctor that they are: (a) ill, (b) not ill.

2. Complete the table below to examine who else might be affected by doctors' willingness to classify people as sick and how they will be affected.

Who is affected?	How are they affected?
1. Government 2. 3.	Amount of sickness benefit

3. To what extent do you think that doctors have become aware of new diseases in recent years?

Stage 6:   morbidity statistics shape our knowledge of illness

As we have seen, not all illnesses are reported to the doctor and thus the morbidity figures only reflect a small proportion of illnesses. Wadsworth *et al.* (1971) conducted a study that provides an indication of how much illness is reported to the doctor. They surveyed 1000 randomly selected adults in London and information was collected on blood pressure, height and weight, as well as the results of urine sample and vision tests, chest x-rays and cervical smear tests for women. The respondents also reported their social and medical histories. The results showed that of 1000 patients over a two-week period:

- Only 49 respondents (that is, less than 5 per cent of the total) showed no symptoms at all.
- Of the remaining 951, who experienced at least one unpleasant symptom:
    - (a) the majority (562 or 59 per cent) were taking non-medical action to cope with them;
    - (b) 188 (20 per cent) were taking no action at all;
    - (c) only 201 (21 per cent) were actually involved in a medical consultation with their GP or as a hospital inpatient or outpatient.

The results of the study, although dated, suggest that morbidity figures reveal only the tip of the illness iceberg (see Figure 3.1). The majority of illnesses are not shown in the figures because a large number of people do not report every illness symptom to their doctors. The idea that only a proportion of illness (6 per cent, according to Last,

1963) is revealed by the morbidity figures is known as the 'clinical iceberg' (ibid.)

Figure 3.1   The clinical iceberg

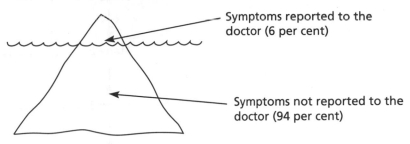

Symptoms reported to the doctor (6 per cent)

Symptoms not reported to the doctor (94 per cent)

(*Source*: Adapted from J. Last, 'The illness iceberg', *Lancet*, 6 July 1963.)

The morbidity figures show not only the amount of recorded illness (for example illness is increasing for men or decreasing for women) but also the types of illness reported, as labelled by the medical profession, particularly GPs. If doctors were to become more willing to label strains to people's hands, wrists, arms and shoulders as repetitive strain injury then the figures would make it appear as though RSI was on the increase, yet it would simply be the result of more doctors labelling patients as suffering from a legitimate illness. More recorded cases would cause greater medical attention to be paid to RSI. Thus it is doctors' behaviour (whether they classify an illness as legitimate or not) that shapes the morbidity figures. These figures in turn may influence the medical investigations that take place, which in turn feed back to doctors through medical journals, lectures throughout medical training, newspapers and word-of-mouth between doctors, or even from patients, which may then lead more doctors to view particular complaints as illnesses.

Exercise 3.10 Summarising the processes of becoming ill

The social process of becoming ill

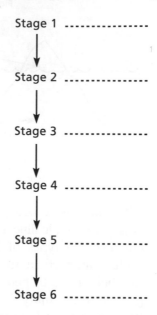

Stage 1 ....

Stage 2 ....

Stage 3 ....

Stage 4 ....

Stage 5 ....

Stage 6 ....

 1. Copy the above flow diagram and apply the following events to the correct stage:

- Labelled as ill and become a morbidity statistic.
- Symptoms are interpreted as an illness.
- Social processes make people vulnerable to illness.
- Symptoms develop, for example social, physical or psychological.
- Doctor–patient interaction.
- Decision is made to seek health care and visit GP.

 2. The following three examples show how people may be excluded from the morbidity statistics. Try to identify the three stages at which they could occur and place them at the left-hand side of your diagram at the appropriate stage:

- Decision is made not to see a doctor but to undergo self-care or seek alternative carer.
- Patient is not labelled as ill.
- No symptoms develop or they are ignored.

Structured exam questions

Question

1. Use the introductory sentences provided below to help you answer the following specimen essay question: Assess the view that 'becoming ill' is a social not a biological process. (*25 marks*)

The paragraphs are in order so all you need to do is draw on the issues you have encountered and the skills you have developed while studying Chapter 3. There are some suggested areas from other chapters to help you complete an essay that addresses the skills of knowledge and understanding, interpretation, application and evaluation. Suggestions have been provided in italics to help you address the three skills.

Student answer

People may 'feel ill' because they experience physical, social or psychological symptoms that may be due to a biological cause such as a virus, a biochemical problem or even a 'faulty' gene. The medical model suggests that illness, including many mental illnesses, have a biological basis. However the way in which someone is defined as ill depends on a number of social processes, such as interpreting the symptoms as an illness, deciding to visit a doctor, and negotiating the symptoms with the doctor. Symptoms may have a biological basis, for example measles or heart disease, but sociologists have argued that some people are more likely to become ill than others.

Comment *Knowledge and understanding: use evidence of social class and illness in Chapter 5, ethnicity and illness in Chapter 6, and gender and illness in Chapter 7 to show how some social groups may be more likely to suffer illness than others, and therefore biology may not be the only factor influencing the development of illness. Evaluation: by providing evidence that illness may have social rather than biological roots, marks may be scored for evaluation because a contrast is provided to the biological (for example genetic) explanation of illness.*

Once symptoms develop they need to be interpreted. Not all symptoms will be interpreted as an illness because people hold different views on what symptoms are considered to be an illness, that is, illness is an 'essentially contested' notion.

Comment *Interpretation and application: apply ideas of what factors may influence our understanding of illness, for example the mass media, family, culture, gender. Evaluation: by pointing out that illness is essentially contested – that is, there is no consensus on exactly what is considered an illness) – some marks may be scored for evaluation as the candidate realises that the term illness is problematic.*

Because people may define illness in different ways they may only report certain symptoms and not others, thus morbidity figures simply reflect those symptoms people report to their doctors. The process of being defined as ill involves being diagnosed by a doctor. The decision needs to be made to visit a doctor and present the symptoms. This decision is another example of how becoming (officially) ill is a social process and not necessarily a biological one.

Comment *Evaluation: marks for this skill may be awarded for questioning the validity of the morbidity figures. Note how the last sentence relates back to the essay title to show that you have interpreted the question accurately. Further marks for interpretation and application may be gained by applying an example of an illness that is contested, for example repetitive strain injury, RSI.*

If a person decides to present his or her symptoms to a doctor then a further social process needs to be examined: the interaction between doctor and patient. The medical model assumes that this interaction is a process whereby doctors objectively identify the biological problems of their patients. However illness can be considered as a label that doctors have the power to apply or withhold.

Comment *Interpretation and application: be selective in the way you apply issues and evidence about doctor-patient interaction, for example social class issues, domination by doctors in interaction with patients. Evaluation: you might consider patients resisting control by doctors – for example Boulton et al., 1986. You may use knowledge about the way patients inform the doctor, for example Arksey, 1994, on repetitive strain injury sufferers.*

Only when a person has been through the series of social processes involved in defining a set of symptoms as an illness does that person become officially ill. Therefore becoming ill is not just a biological process but a social one. The morbidity (illness) figures are the product of the social process of becoming ill, not simply the genuine amount of illness experienced by people in society.

Comment *Evaluation: you could draw the clinical iceberg diagram to show how recorded illness does not necessarily reveal all illness experienced by people.*

The medical model assumes that illness is simply a biological condition that is diagnosed by doctors. However Foucault believes that the way doctors view illness in biological terms is simply a powerful discourse.

Comment *Interpretation and application: select the relevant points from the information provided on Foucault in Chapter 2 and Chapter 11 to show how he challenges the biomedical discourse of the medical profession. In addition, apply the notion of discourse to the term* *'mental illness' in Chapter 9. In this way you will demonstrate knowledge and understanding.*

The issue of labelling can be applied to the area of mental illness. Psychiatrists apply their knowledge to label certain unusual behaviour as the result of a mental illness. Thus mental illness does not have to be thought of as a biological problem but one that is a social category or label.

Comment *Interpretation and application: selectively use information on the labelling of mental illness to show how mental illness may be a stigma applied to unusual behaviour rather than a simple description of a biological condition. Evaluation: use the information on schizophrenia to provide evidence that schizophrenia may have a biological basis – for example genetic, biochemical or neurological). If sufficient detail is provided about the biological basis of schizophrenia, then the information may score marks for knowledge and understanding.*

Marxists such as Navarro (1979) claim that illness is not simply a biological condition but one that is socially produced because of inequality in society.

Comment *Knowledge and understanding: by providing more detailed information on the work of Navarro as well as the Marxist perspective on the cause of ill health you will gain marks. Interpretation and application: use Chapter 5 on social class to provide evidence that poverty may cause people to be more prone to illness. By doing this you will also be demonstrating knowledge and understanding. Evaluation: you could also use more theory by extending the Marxist critique using the information in Chapter 11 on the Marxist perspective – remember to keep answering the essay question though!*

In conclusion, the medical model suggests that illness has a biological basis, however sociologists have shown how becoming ill can also be viewed as a social process. Sociologists would benefit from becoming more sophisticated about differences between people, for example do women become ill more readily than men? Additional sociological work may show how some people would benefit from being defined as ill rather than having their symptoms contested by doctors, for example RSI sufferers.

Comment *Interpretation and application: make sure that you are still dealing with the essay question when you add comments to* *the conclusion. Evaluation: you could add some further questions that would make a more sophisticated study of the way different people are defined as ill. You might add some points about the rise of alternative medicine in Britain: what would be the implication on the official morbidity figures if more people visited alternative therapists?*

Questions

2. Draw on the issues discussed in Chapter 3 and the skills you have learned to answer the following specimen exam questions. Try doing these essays in 45 minutes as timed essay practice.

   (a) Critically discuss the view that the decision to visit the doctor and the negotiation that takes place within the GP surgery are affected by social class and gender. (*25 marks*)

   (b) Evaluate the claim that illness is simply a label conferred by doctors on patients. (*25 marks*)

Summary

This chapter has looked at the stages involved in becoming 'officially ill'. It has been suggested that when we examine morbidity (sickness) figures we should appreciate that they have been socially created, and are not simply a set of objective figures. The processes involved in creating the morbidity figures include the social causes of illness (for example, poverty) as well as genetic or biological causes (for example, gene for cystic fibrosis, or a virus).

Once symptoms emerge (whether social, physical or psychological) they have to be interpreted by the individual. Interpretation depends on a number of factors, including past experience of illness and mass media information about illness. A decision needs to be made whether to seek health care. If a person decides not to seek medical attention, or wishes to be treated by an alternative healer or a family member/friend, then there will be no official record of the illness.

Once a person decides to visit the doctor then a negotiation takes place in which the doctor holds the power (as a 'gatekeeper' who decides which illnesses are legitimate) to label and define the patient as ill. This sequence of stages defines the extent and pattern of morbidity, a pattern that cannot be taken at face value because it is a social construction: the figures have been created by a series of decisions made by various social actors (for example, doctors, patients, family members).

4 Responses to illness

By the end of this chapter you should be able to:

- evaluate the issues involved in responding to illness;
- appreciate the impact of chronic illness on people's lives;
- apply the concept of self-identity, and assess its importance;
- evaluate studies on responses to RSI and other illnesses;
- appreciate that responses to illness vary.

Introduction

This chapter examines the way individuals respond to illness, particularly a chronic illness that may seriously affect a person's lifestyle. A series of in-depth qualitative studies of chronic illness sufferers are examined, including Ewan *et al.* (1991) on women diagnosed with repetitive strain injury (RSI), Kelly (1992) on people with ulcerative colitis, leading to radical surgery, and Williams (1989) on people with ankylosing spondylitis. These studies are used to examine individual responses to illness by focusing on the following issues:

- Making sense of a disorder.
- Being believed.
- Coping with changes in material circumstances.
- Dealing with life disruption.
- Dealing with self-identity.
- Role negotiation.
- Dealing with certainty and uncertainty.

How individuals cope with illness symptoms is also examined, using the work of Bury (1991). Whilst reading this account of the issues it is worth asking whether we would expect all people to react in the same way to the same condition, and whether different conditions are likely to lead to different responses. We will question whether the information in this chapter can be usefully applied to all illnesses, whether sociologists can produce an account that will suit all illnesses, and why it is important to avoid a fixed way of thinking about the way people respond to illness.

How individuals respond to illness

How might you respond to a set of symptoms that interrupt your everyday routine? Will your feeling of self-worth change? Will your symptoms disrupt your paid work, your other activities or your studies? What effect will your symptoms have on those around you: your friends, family or intimate partner? Some symptoms, such as a runny nose, sore throat or headache, are perceived as a fairly temporary departure from the way one usually feels. On the other hand chronic illness has, by definition, more long-term and sometimes permanent effects on patients. The time-scale involved means the sufferers' response is likely to be qualitatively different from their reaction to the flu or having their tonsils removed. An appreciation of how individuals respond to and cope with their symptoms often fails to be part of the problematic of sociology textbooks on health and illness, but in fact it is an important consideration in the sociological investigation of illness.

Exercise 4.1 Individual response to illness

  1. Write down your response to your last illness: what effect, if any, did the illness have on your self-esteem?

  2. What effects did any prolonged period of illness have on your lifestyle? For example did it affect your school/college work? Did it affect any paid work? What effect did it have on the people around you, for example your friends or family?

Making sense of a disorder

According to Bury (1991), once the onset and impact of a chronic condition have taken place individuals begin to think about the implications of their altered circumstances. Information may be gathered about their condition by contacting medical practitioners and reading relevant books and journals. In addition, people may join support groups in their search for further understanding of the condition and in order to legitimate their condition as a genuine complaint.

Seeking medical knowledge does not itself appear to be sufficient. Williams (1984) claims that official medical understandings of a condition are supplemented by 'narrative reconstructions' that attempt to explain more about what caused the illness to develop. These 'narrative reconstructions', or stories to explain the condition, combine a range of understandings about the symptoms (medical and lay notions) that help 'legitimate' the altered circumstances in which the sufferer finds him- or herself. These narrative reconstructions may also help preserve a sense of personal integrity and shore up self-esteem whilst serving to provide an explanation of the cause that makes sense to the sufferer.

Some sociological research has examined the way sufferers search for the answers to 'Why me? Why now?' Patients' answers focus on wider causes than simply biomedical ones such as the immediate infection or bodily disorder: for example fate, God, overwork, stress and diet.

A study of female RSI sufferers by Ewan *et al.* (1991) showed how the condition required an explanation beyond the limits of available medical knowledge. Some respondents found the cause of their condition in external factors: not taking enough tea breaks at work, working too hard, wanting to do a good job, health hazards at work or faulty equipment that forced them to hold difficult postures. Other examined causes focused on personal inadequacies or internal factors such as getting old or developing arthritis.

Sociological health research might find it useful to examine the ways in which sufferers' attempts to explain and rationalise their condition extend beyond the parameters of existing and available medical knowledge. Sociologically there are important considerations concerning the effects of sufferers' 'narrative reconstructions'. To what extent might these explanations aid a patient's recovery? To what extent do narrative reconstructions inform a patient's choice of health care? How might medical practitioners/alternative healers deal with these narrative reconstructions in a way that improves the quality of patients' lives?

Exercise 4.2 Making sense of heart attacks

Michael Crichton, best selling author of *Jurassic Park* and *Congo*, started a career as a doctor which he terminated before completing his medical training. In his semi-autobiography, *Travels* (1988), Crichton describes the way heart attack patients attempt to make sense of 'why me, why now?' Crichton interviewed a number of patients during his medical training and discovered they had a host of reasons for the causes of their heart attacks – the medical explanation was not often quoted. The extract below illustrates the range of explanations (Crichton, 1988):

Crichton: 'Why did you have a heart attack?'
Case 1: 'I got a promotion. The company wants me to move to Cincinnati. But my wife doesn't want to go. . . . That's why.'
Case 2: 'My wife is talking about leaving me.'
Case 3: 'My son won't go to Law school.'
Case 4: 'I didn't get the raise.'

[a] 1. Why do you think searching for the answer to 'why me, why now' is important? Important for whom?

[a] 2. Why might doctors ignore alternative explanations of heart attacks such as those illustrated in the extract?

[e] 3. Why is it important to consider patients' perspectives?

4. Find out what is meant by the patient-centred model of illness by turning to the appropriate section in either Chapter 2 or Chapter 11. How does Crichton's approach illustrate the patient-centred model?

Being believed

A set of symptoms needs to be labelled as an illness. This labelling process involves a number of social actors, including the sufferer, the sufferer's family, sometimes friends and work colleagues, and health officials such as doctors who provide the official label used for medical sick notes for extended periods of illness. Studies of patients show that the process of negotiation is an important response to their set of symptoms: the symptoms must be taken seriously if they are to be regarded as a legitimate illness.

Convincing others: doctors

Ewan, *et al.* (1991) interviewed fifty-two Australian women diagnosed as RSI sufferers – 28 in the telecommunication industry and 24 in a chicken processing plant – about their experience of the illness. The respondents claimed they had found it difficult to convince others, particularly doctors, that their pain was genuine. One respondent described how a doctor's hostility towards her symptoms was extremely upsetting:

> He [the orthopaedic surgeon] had me in tears.... He asked me what my problem was and I told him, and he started to yell at me. He said 'There is no such thing as RSI'. He said, 'I've just come back from the [United] States and they had computers for so many years and there is no such thing as RSI'. (Ewan *et al.*, 1991).

However other doctors can be more accommodating of a patient's condition. Bellaby (1990) shows how doctors sit between worker and employer in a position where they are neither an ally of capitalism (repairing workers to make them fit for work again) nor the workers' friend (able to provide sick notes so that they can escape work). Nonetheless, they sometimes do use coded expressions on sick notes that help employees claim sick leave more easily. One example of this is the term 'hyperemesis', which is medical jargon for morning sickness and is used to enable pregnant women to take limited sick leave. Doctors were also found to give employees a note for an 'anxiety state', a coded term used when people needed to time off to care for others in the family.

Convincing others: friends and family

Doctors are not the only social actors who need to be convinced that an illness is legitimate. Family, friends and intimate partners are also important. As an RSI sufferer pointed out:

> Nobody wanted to know you when you got it. During the six months that I was off [work], one person came to see me. They didn't want to know you or be around you. You were crying all the time and your hands were in the splints. I was going with a guy at the time and I lost him, because he got fed up with me crying all the time. He just shot through. He couldn't take it (Ewan *et al.*, 1991).

Convincing others: work colleagues

Convincing work colleagues that symptoms are genuine may also be important, particularly if a paid worker is to receive time off to visit the doctor or even to claim sick pay.

The notion of 'doing something' about the illness seems to be important in shaping people's attitudes towards the sufferer's condition. According to Ewan *et al.* (ibid.), an RSI sufferer who worked in the chicken factory claimed that colleagues became more accepting of RSI if official treatment had been sought (that is, from a doctor) and given (for example, a surgical operation).

Convincing others: employers

Bellaby (1990) conducted a six-month study in a Staffordshire pottery. One issue examined was the negotiation of legitimate illness at work. Clearly workers, managers and doctors have to negotiate whether an absence from work is legitimate. One case in the factory highlights the struggle that sometimes takes place:

> Margaret is feeling aggrieved because of Don's (the manager) attitude over absences: sickness is not taken as a valid reason, she says. She was told when she was off with glandular fever some time ago, that anyone can get a doctor's note. In the course of her bed rest, she was asked by phone to come down to the factory, which she did (Bellaby, 1990).

Doctors appear to be in a powerful position through their ability to provide sick notes or withhold them. The issue of social control is an important consideration when examining doctors in society. An additional consideration is the perceived status of official medicine over, say, 'alternative' treatments such as homeopathy.

Exercise 4.3 Convincing an employer

[a] 1. What do you think an employer's attitude would be if an employee presented a sick note from an alternative health practitioner?

[a] 2. Why do you think there may be a difference of status between doctors and alternative health practitioners?

[a] 3. What other factors may determine whether employers believe that employees' symptoms are legitimate? Who else might it be important to convince that you have a genuine illness?

Labelling and the sick role

Being believed involves a number of social actors, each of whom makes sense of the illness, sometimes viewing the symptoms as genuine and in other situations denying the legitimacy of the illness label.

What critical questions could be asked about being believed? Would people readily accept symptoms as genuine if an alternative therapist had been consulted? What effects might the status of healing systems have on individuals' own choices of treatment? Might a worker's choice of health care be guided by colleagues' and bosses' notions of what constitutes genuine treatment? What effect might a multi-ethnic workforce have on the legitimacy of 'unofficial' health care systems?

Parsons' 'sick role'

Parsons, (1975) notion of the 'sick role' may be useful when examining the issue of convincing others that symptoms are genuine. Parsons argued that illness is just another form of deviance and that too much illness can be dysfunctional (have negative effects) for society's productivity. What might happen if workers simply claim they are sick and are given full pay until they are ready to go back to work? For Parsons illness is a label that can only be applied when the sick individual wants to get well, and therefore the individual should visit a health professional. Only when these criteria are met can the individual start to acquire the 'sick role'. Parsons believes people have to seek health care from their doctors and should also cooperate with the doctors' instructions. In this way society ensures that people are returned to the workforce supposedly fit and healthy.

A criticism of this perspective can be clearly illustrated by examining the issue of chronic sickness. Conditions such as arthritis are classified as chronic illness: a long-term (perhaps permanent) condition where patients are unlikely to return to work quickly. Because the medical establishment often finds it difficult to cure chronic conditions it appears that sufferers may therefore be unable to seek effective health care from traditional sources, that is, doctors and hospitals.

When Parsons talked of the 'sick role' it appears he was largely dealing with acute sickness that might be effectively treated by traditional medical means (that is, drugs or surgery).

What critical questions could be asked about Parsons notion of the 'sick role'? Can doctors accurately diagnose all illnesses? Can they treat all symptoms adequately? What might happen if alternative treatments are more suitable but are not recognised as 'legitimate'? Can some people acquire the 'sick role' more easily than others by being more able to convince doctors that their condition is genuine? In whose interests is it that people are returned to work fit and healthy: bosses or workers?

Exercise 4.4   Being believed

 1. Imagine you feel ill (perhaps you believe it to be flu). Who is it most important to convince that you are genuinely ill? Explain your answer.

 2. In what ways would you convince a doctor you are ill? (Hint: dress, body posture, mood, behaviour, appetite?)

Coping with changes in material circumstances

A further problem to be confronted during and even after illness is the issue of financial hardship. In the UK statutory sick pay is paid to most employed people who are sick or disabled and therefore unable to work. The payment reflects your income – the more you earn the more sick pay you receive. Obviously those on low incomes stay on low incomes and are deprived of earning any of the overtime that previously may have increased their income. Until 1991 the government reimbursed employers for any statutory sick pay they gave to their workers, but in 1991 the government subsidy was reduced to 80 per cent, and since 1994 most employers have had to pay the whole cost of statutory sick pay. (What effect might this change have on employers' attitudes towards employee sickness or the employment of new staff whose application form shows they have previously had health problems?)

After 28 weeks individuals can be assessed for Invalidity Benefit, which is paid at a flat rate. Throughout the 1980s the number of people on Invalidity Benefit increased substantially, resulting in new regulations designed to limit the number who are eligible for benefit.

Exercise 4.5   Poverty and ill health

Imagine yourself in the following situation. You earn £20 000 a year as a self-employed plumber. You have a mortgage and two children. While driving to a job on a cold winter day your car skids on the ice and you suffer a serious accident that places you in hospital for four months. You are unable to work for a further three months.

1. Outline the financial problems you are likely to have throughout the period of illness.

2. What types of occupation might prevent people suffering from severe financial hardship during prolonged illness?

3. Why might there be social class differences in the extent to which employees suffer financial hardship when ill?

Some of those who have to give up work because of a work-related illness receive compensation. In the study of RSI respondents by Ewan *et al.* (1991) the highest lump-sum payment divulged to the interviewers was $25 000 (about £13 000). Virtually all the respondents had experienced financial hardship due to their loss of paid income. Many expressed doubt about actually receiving any compensation. Many women claimed they would prefer to return to work and start earning a regular income than rely on a compensation payment that would only last for a limited period of time.

Dealing with life disruption

The extent to which people's lives are disrupted by illness depends on a number of factors, including their emotional and psychological state, their financial circumstances, the severity of the illness/problem, the duration of the symptoms and the support and health care available. Some of the problems that might need to be confronted and successfully overcome include learning new skills to deal with the disorder, disruption of home life as new patterns of behaviour are required, dealing with social relationships, returning to work or finding new employment. These areas of life disruption can be clearly illustrated by focusing on individuals who have undergone radical surgery.

Kelly (1992) interviewed forty-five people who had undergone a panproctocolectomy – an operation whereby the entire bowel and rectum are removed. An ileostomy or false anus is then surgically formed in the lower right-hand quadrant of the patient's abdomen. Kelly explains that the patients could no longer open their bowels, but were forced to kneel in front of the toilet bowl to empty the waste products from a collection bag attached to the stomach opening. The patients' lives involved disruptions such as:

• Learning new skills: 'The [nurse] came in . . . she went "We'll change your bag now" . . . I looked at this and I thought "God, do I have to go through this every time?" . . . She showed me because I had no idea what was involved' (Kelly, 1992).

- Disrupted home life: 'Three times it's burst, or come off in bed and that's terrible . . . oh the smell . . . that's why I dinna go to bed early. I'm frightened to go. I mean its always after midnight before I go to my bed' (ibid.)
- Disrupted social relationships: 'I says to my pal, "How could I be going out wi' somebody for a couple of weeks and then say I've got something to tell you?" I think I have a fear of somebody turning round and saying "Oh yeah" and going out the door and never coming back, cos I think if somebody done that, it would really hurt you' (ibid.)
- Disrupted employment: 'I've started work three days a week just now, just to break myself in' (ibid.)

People may have to cope with a host of disruptions, particularly after severe or radical surgery or throughout chronic sickness and disability. The extent of the disruptions will depend on individual circumstances, the type and quality of existing and new social relationships and the severity of the symptoms.

Dealing with self-identity

Much traditional work in the sociology of health and illness has tended to focus on the stigma associated with certain illnesses, for example 'mental illness'. However some postmodern sociologists are more concerned with the way self-identity is affected by illness. Charmaz (1983, p. 168) argues that chronically ill people frequently experience 'a crumbling away of their former self-images'. Other postmodernists applaud the way Charmaz examines the issue of self-identity but are very critical of the way the 'self' is treated as an inactive product that can simply 'crumble away'. The 'self' can be remolded, reshaped by the individual within the constraints of the wider society and others' reactions towards the sufferer (Bury, 1991; Kelly, 1992).

What is self-identity?

The notion of self can be traced back to the works of William James (1892), Charles Cooley (1902) and George Herbert Mead (1934), who claimed that the way people view themselves is shaped by the way they believe others see them. Notions of self are therefore affected by both agency – that is, individual interaction with others – and structure, that is, overall established power relations in society such as racist power relations, sexist power relations, ageist power relations, social class and occupational power relations, and 'body power relations'. The latter term describes the way notions of the body (slim, tall, physically able, hearing, sighted, with all limbs) are taken to be the norm and those that deviate from expected appearance or ability may be viewed by some as deviant. The effects of being perceived as deviant or an 'outsider' (Becker, 1963) include reduced chances of getting a job and greater difficulties in establishing relationships as well as the psychological effect of altering self-identity. Although a physical set of symptoms may be regarded as simply a biological condition, from having flu to experiencing cancer, illness is also a social label that confers particular meanings. These meanings are sometimes very negative, particularly those conferred on individuals with psychological disorders such as schizophrenia. The perceived social reactions of people around the sufferer may well affect the individual's self-identity.

Why is self-identity affected by illness?

'Why cannot illness be just illness?' asks Sontag in her work *Illness as Metaphor* (1991) and applies to a contemporary example in her *Aids and its Metaphors* (1991). Sontag argues that illness may well be a set of physical symptoms caused by bacteria (for example food poisoning), a 'faulty' gene (for example cystic fibrosis) or even, though Sontag does not claim this, bodily reactions to the environment (for example stress-related disorders). However the experience of illness is shaped by people's reactions to it. Thus tuberculosis in the past and cancer today, along with AIDS, are 'mystified' into something strange or unusual. With any mystery people create images out of the condition (or in Sontag's case, people create 'metaphors'), which are expressed in thought-provoking and thought-shaping language (or discourse). AIDS is a 'plague', cancer is an 'enemy', and in *Nicholas Nickleby* Charles Dickens described tuberculosis as the 'dread disease'. Both cancer and TB have been said to 'consume' the body. Sontag goes on to describe the way literature uses language to build up metaphors about TB, thus shaping people's perceptions of TB sufferers.

To be ill is not just to be ill; the symptoms carry with them a 'discourse'. A discourse is language combined with power. To use particular words more than others is to shape people's understanding – for example the words 'bad' and 'evil' are both negative, however 'evil' conjures up more negative associations than 'bad'. Language is therefore a powerful tool that shapes the way we think and perceive the world in general and illness in particular. Illness, then, is not just an illness. Societal reactions to symptoms are likely to affect the sufferer's self-identity.

Exercise 4.6 *The meaning of illness and self-identity*

1. Look at the following illnesses and rank them according to the extent you believe they would affect the way you feel about yourself.

2. Explain your choice of the top three.
    - Anorexia nervosa
    - Multiple sclerosis
    - Schizophrenia
    - Measles
    - Depression
    - Alcoholism
    - Lung cancer
    - Breast cancer
    - Herpes
    - HIV positive
    - Flu
    - Amputated limb

3. What does this exercise suggest about the way illness may affect self-identity?

Changes in self-identity

As discussed above, Kelly (1992) examined the effect of a type of radical surgery that alters body form: having an artificial anus surgically placed in the lower abdomen. Kelly said that those who had undergone the ileostomy operation voiced concern about a change from their former 'self' to a 'new self'. The comments betrayed an awareness that their new physical difference would be perceived by others as undesirable. This concern became more obvious or 'salient' when the person was in pain or emotional trauma. Simply going to the toilet, an act that many take for granted, served as a reminder that they were now different: 'Oh the first time I looked at my scar, I promptly just keeled over. I mean it was such a shock. . . . I went through a period when I was really down' (Kelly, 1922).

Depression was not the only psychological effect; denial and rejection were common experiences: 'Oh I don't want to touch it, I don't want to er, er, er. . . . I couldn't understand why it was green, but no its alright, its there, I can take it, so long as I don't have to touch it' (ibid.)

Out of hospital the patient's problems took a different form: 'when I came out, and I started to go out and about again with my friends, I felt a bit different. . . . I thought it wasn't fair. . . . You feel jealous somehow . . . why did it happen to me, and not to them?' (ibid.)

However self-identity can be legitimated, rationalised or explained in ways that shore up feelings of self-worth. One patient was very positive about his situation: 'I'm happy that I'm healthy and that, again, terrific, and it's great I can still do the sports I want to do' (ibid.)

The role of self-help groups and self-identity

Self-help groups such as Action for ME not only provide practical and political support for sufferers, but also allow a more positive reshaping of self-identity through contact with other sufferers.

A more critical view of self-help groups examines the way in which by mixing with patients who are sicker than oneself one can develop a more negative sense of self; one can become more pessimistic about the chances of a recovery and, through contact with others, can even become aware of new symptoms associated with the illness.

Private self and public identity

Rather than viewing self-identity as a relatively stable phenomenon – a view of self that is relatively consistent throughout a period of life – sociologists have examined the ways in which self-identity can change depending on the context in which people find themselves. Kelly (1992) examined the way the post-operative ileostomy patients reacted when they emerged from hospital, a relatively private arena, into a more socially interactive environment where public identity becomes a private concern. A change in body structure (for example having a false anus constructed in the lower abdomen) is a biological fact but also a social category because it affects the way we view ourselves and the way others view us.

Mead (1934) claimed our self-identity has much to do with the way others view us. In other words people ask themselves 'how do others see me?' Indeed people are capable of changing their appearance (clothing, looks) or their accent or demeanour in the hope that these changes in 'self-presentation' will alter the way others perceive them. People who have undergone radical surgery where their body is altered may appear 'normal' but physically they are 'different'. Private self versus public identity therefore becomes a concern. Do people with ileostomies openly declare themselves as such and risk the stigma associated with the social definitions people impose on them: 'sick' or 'non-normal'? The issue of labelling social categories as deviant is similar to other areas of sociological interest, for example 'ex-criminal', 'homosexual', 'troublemaker'.

Much work on changing identity is presented as if the 'self' is in crisis, undergoing a change of identity that is relatively irreversible and largely determined by the reactions of others.

Exercise 4.7 Note-taking guide for self-identity and illness

Use the following questions to help you summarise some of the key points from the preceding text:

[i] 1. What is meant by 'self-identity'?

[a] 2. Why is self-identity a sociological consideration?

[i][a] 3. How does Sontag's work on AIDS illustrate the notion that 'illness is not simply an illness'?

[i] 4. Briefly summarise the main changes in self-identity that Kelly suggests in his examination of people with radical surgery.

5. What is the difference between 'private self' and 'public self'?

6. Mead (1934) claims self-identity has much to do with the way we believe others see us. How might you use Sontag's work on illness as a metaphor (for example AIDS) to illustrate Mead's point?

Models of changing self-identity

The Crisis Model

Gerhardt (1989) considers there are two models that are relevant to illness and illustrate changing self-identity. The crisis model has its roots in the ideas of interactionist sociologists such as Lemert (1962) and Becker (1963). The model views changing identity in a rather deterministic manner, with the individual simply responding to the way others see him/her by 'absorbing' any negative (or positive) reactions or comments.

In his study of people who had undergone an ileostomy, Kelly (1992) presents the issues of self-presentation and self-identity in a way that subscribes to Gerhardt's crisis model of self-identity, as shown by the following statements by three of those interviewed: 'I was worried about meeting people for the first time. I thought it was as if I had two heads. I felt it was a very obvious thing. I felt I couldn't walk along the street, but everyone would see this large bump and realise I had a bag'; 'I thought nobody will ever look at me again. I'm a freak'; '[A friend] came round just after New Year, from my work. . . . I was in on my own. . . . He says "What was wrong with you anyway?" I told him. . . . He backed off, virtually ran out the door' (Kelly, 1992).

These quotes show how the people concerned accepted others' reactions to their new condition. However people can resist and challenge such perceptions.

The Negotiation Model

Gerhardt (1989) suggests there is also a negotiation or interaction model, which takes account of interaction and resistance between the individual and other social actors. This model is illustrated by the works of Bury (1982) and Williams (1984). Sociological work in health and illness has shown that people are able to resist the labels and social definitions associated with illness.

Although many people are able to defend their self-identity or change it in ways that preserve their self-esteem and confidence, perhaps both models are useful during an individual's life span: at times we may feel able to resist the reactions and labels of others; at other times we may react according to the way others see us – the so-called self-fulfilling prophecy.

People have the power to resist and challenge others' reactions, illustrating Gerhardt's negotiation model of self-identity. As two of the ileostomy patients interviewed by Kelly (1992) put it: 'I've no regrets what I have got now y'know, I've got it, and that's it. You must accept it, you must get on with life. It's as simple as that', and 'Well, y'disfigured. And er, I mean my husband. He's the type that, he says, "Well, its better having y'here, because if y'didn't have that you wouldn't be here". He's right down to earth and he's very good for me'. These quotes suggest that people can reject dominant perceptions of a bodily condition without it appearing to maladaptively (negatively or harmfully) affect self-identity.

Exercise 4.8   Applying Gerhardt's two models of self-identity

[i] 1. Refer to your answers to Exercise 4.6 and write down the three conditions you thought might alter your self-esteem most.

[a] 2. Examine Gerhardt's two models of the way people react to the meaning others impose on illnesses. How would you react to the three conditions you have chosen – would you simply accept other people's negative notions about your condition or would you resist?

Self-identity and intimate relationships

Feelings are mixed as people's unhappiness at their changed bodily form is coupled with recognition that they have been released from a major debilitating illness. However people who have had an ileostomy, along with others who have suffered a changed body form or changed physical ability, confront a public world in which shared (and unshared) meanings are attached to such body form and body function. In Kelly's study particular concern was voiced about intimate relationships:

> I had this boy, this boy before [the operation], and er, I'd just been out wi' him a couple of times right. . . . So I told him. And he says 'God what does that matter? He says, er, I mean, he says 'to tell you the truth my Grandad's gone through the same operation'. And I thought he was really genuine and everything. The next time he saw me, he never spoke to me or anything, and that sorta put me off, y'know, telling anybody, cos he seemed really genuine about it (Kelly, 1992).

Kelly points out that fear of rejection, loss of confidence and damaged self-esteem are particularly pertinent where sexual relationships are concerned. The identities that can be conferred on people with ileostomies are those of 'being sick', 'non-normal' and not a legitimate sexual partner. It is important to point out that at a time when a relationship appears to be less stable, and the prospect of being on one's own grows, then the opportunity to meet new intimate partners becomes a very real concern.

Exercise 4.9 Intimate relationships, self-identity and illness

[i][a] 1. Use the section on self-identity and intimate relationships to write a paragraph on how consideration of self-identity is an important issue for individuals as well as sociologists. (Hint: think about who should know about the effects of radical surgery on intimate relationships – doctors, patients, nurses, relatives.)

[a] 2. What services might need to be provided to help people come to terms with changes in self-identity?

[e] 3. Should changes in self-identity be the individual's problem?

Role negotiation

With illness sometimes comes a change in the roles that one normally performs. When a person has a cold they may decide to stay off paid work for a period of time, or decline to do any housework, shopping or cooking. People will vary in the extent to which they can renegotiate these roles. Some people may desperately need to earn money and therefore struggle into work. Others claim they do not have time to be ill because they need to look after their children. Some may have family or friends to help them during illness whilst others may lack this informal support.

Exercise 4.10 Costs and benefits of the sick role

[a] Copy and complete the following table, which requires you to suggest the costs and benefits of being defined as ill.

Advantages	Disadvantages
Time off work	Wages might be reduced

Certainly in longer-term and more severely restricting illness the need to renegotiate roles will become imperative. In Ewan, Lowy and Reid's (1991) study of people with repetitive strain injury role changes were a key feature of the condition. Many of the all-female respondents claimed that their partners and families were sympathetic to their illness. Some reported the benefits of renegotiated roles, for example concerning household chores: 'My family's been marvellous. Sisters-in-law. They come here. They do my work. And as you know, I've got my mother living with me'.

However, to what extent do these newly negotiated roles depend on traditional female domestic labour as opposed to a more equitable distribution of household tasks between men and women? Some of the female respondents treated the redistribution of work as an additional emotional and psychological burden, wanting to carry on as usual, even though to continue with housework caused intense pain and sometimes annoyed other family members:

> I can remember once the shower recess needed cleaning. . . . No one else knows how to clean it. So I got stuck into it and cleaned it. Well, I couldn't move. It was absolutely agony when he got home. When [my husband] came home he went off his brain. 'You stupid woman!' he said . . . 'All you had to do was ask'. I said 'I don't consider that I should have to ask'. And that was a time when things got a little strained (ibid.)

Role negotiation and time scale

The issue of time scale is also an important consideration. Whilst family members and others may 'help' (Whose role is it to do the housework? Whose role is it to earn an income?) with domestic chores or even do paid work to support the family, how long will the support continue? Some of Ewan *et al.*'s respondents commented on the way support over time seemed to be resented by other family members. What is interesting is the way that many of the women viewed domestic chores as their domain and, when housework had been unequally divided, did not see illness as the time to be liberated from such chores.

Exercise: 4.11   Gender, paid roles and illness

 1. To what extent might men view it as their domain to provide an income?

 2. How might a person's inability to carry on with paid work affect conjugal roles?

Dealing with certainty and uncertainty

Along with pain, disbelief, disrupted lives and changing self-identity, people may well have to deal with uncertainty: the inability to predict when symptoms may reappear or when the pain will start again. For instance people suffering from RSI complained of disruption to even routine activities (for example shopping) because of an inability to predict when debilitating pain would appear. Pain in particular was viewed as beyond the sufferers' control: 'It just starts up. . . . It will ache and you think 'There it goes again' . . . but last night I honestly don't know what I've done to aggravate it. . . . It's a mystery the whole way round. I don't care what anyone says' (Ewan *et al.* 1991).

People with illnesses such as RSI, arthritis, rheumatism, multiple sclerosis, ME or cancer, as well as many other conditions, may well have to come to terms with a lack of certainty. Medicine and medical diagnosis cannot always relieve the symptoms adequately, nor can it provide definite control and certainty over the future. Some illnesses may offer the hope of future remissions (for example MS), complete recovery or improved treatment with future medical advances. Others may leave sufferers with a reduced and/or uncertain life expectancy, with the possibility of the disease recurring in the future. And instead of facing *uncertainty*, some people may have to deal with the *certainty* that their condition will continue and will deteriorate further.

Structured exam questions

Complete the following exercises to practise some of the issues and skills presented in this chapter.

Question

1. Critically examine the view that the 'experience' of illness is as much determined by a physical or mental set of symptoms as by the reactions of others towards the sufferer. (*25 marks*)

(a) Use the following key words to fill in the gaps in the essay below: community, intimate, Gerhardt, reactions, work, identity, stigmatisation, positive, Sontag.

(b) Using the hints provided in the skills comments, try to write a better answer to the essay question than the one shown here.

Student answer

> The medical model tends to deal with the physical and mental problems the sufferer reports. However, for some people the illness experience is determined not just by the physical and mental symptoms but also by the . . . . . . of others.
>
> **Comment** *Interpretation and application: as an introduction you could briefly summarise the social actors who may be involved in shaping the illness experience of others, for example intimate partners or colleagues. You might mention some conditions that could create a stigma, for example AIDS. Sontag (1990) claims that 'Illness cannot simply be an illness' – you could explain what she means by this*

statement by examining the section in this chapter on self-identity. By doing this you will also gain marks for knowledge and understanding. Evaluation: you could mention that the experience of illness cannot be generalised because some people may not accept a stigma in the same way as others. Some symptoms are not stigmatised in the same way as others, for example having measles is not treated the same as being HIV positive.

Although people may feel ill due to the physical or mental symptoms from which they are suffering, the reactions of others may add to the experience of their illness. One issue worth examining is possible changes to self . . . . . . This has been examined by Kelly (1992) in his work on people with ulcerative colitis.

Comment   *Some knowledge and understanding is shown in the paragraph. Interpretation and application: relevant points from the work by Kelly could be applied to show how sufferers were found to be subjected to the stigmatising behaviour of others. Evaluation: it is worth pointing out that not all illnesses are stigmatised: therefore the reaction of others will not affect all experiences of illness. However there are other illnesses that might be stigmatised – can you think of any?*

The experience of illness may depend on individual circumstances and the social situations in which people find themselves. Kelly (1992) studied sufferers of ulcerative colitis and found that the context of . . . . . . relationships was one area in which any complication tended to be caused by people's reaction to the sufferers' condition, not the illness itself.

Comment   *Some knowledge and understanding is shown in the paragraph. Evaluation: by stating that not all people's experience of illness will be shaped by the reactions of others marks for evaluation could be gained as well as relating the point to the essay question. Interpretation and application: use the work of Kelly on ulcerative colitis to show how intimate relationships are affected by the reactions of others. Evaluation: note that not all the intimate experiences outlined by Kelly were negative, so it is difficult to generalise the issue.*

People do not have to adopt the negative labels others apply to their condition. . . . . (1989) refers to the way people may resist changes to self-identity as the 'negotiation-model' of self-identity.

Comment   *Increase your marks for knowledge and understanding as well as gain marks for interpretation and application by outlining* *and applying Gerhardt's model to the question. Evaluation: using Gerhardt's negotiation model as a starting point, state that negative labels might not affect all sufferers in the same way – some people might resist labels. Thus to assume labelling will affect the experience of illness is rather too deterministic.*

The role of labelling is an important consideration in the experience of illness. The issue of . . . . . . (applying a negative label) is particularly important and can be applied to the experience of mental illness.

Comment *Interpretation and application: use the information on labelling in Chapter 9 to show how the experience of mental illness may be shaped by the way others react to the condition. You could examine the implication of community care in Britain since more mentally ill people will be 'cared for' in the community and sufferers are therefore more likely to come into contact with lay people who may stigmatise their condition. Evaluation: you could raise the point that not only might the experience of mental illness be shaped by the reaction of others, but also the definition of mental illness is determined by others, for example psychiatrists. You could then criticise the view that 'mental' illness and indeed 'physical' illness can be easily defined and show that the experience of these illnesses is determined by powerful social actors such as doctors and psychiatrists who help determine which symptoms are defined as an illness.*

Self-help groups for certain illness sufferers may provide a means of making the experience of illness more . . . . . .

Comment *Interpretation and application: outline the ways in which the reactions of self-help groups may make the experience of illness more positive. Evaluation: self-help groups may also cause sufferers to view their condition in more negative ways.*

Most of this essay has examined the way people's symptoms are stigmatised, however for some people their illness experience is shaped by the refusal of others to view their condition as legitimate. Their experience of illness may depend on the way doctors react to the condition. If doctors deny that a set of symptoms is legitimate, then the sufferer may experience problems in taking paid absence from . . . . . . The case of repetitive strain injury is worth examining to illustrate the issue of being believed.

Comment *By outlining the case of RSI you could gain marks for knowledge and understanding. Interpretation and application: use the section on 'Being believed' in this chapter to help you make relevant comments on which social actors' (for example employers')* *reactions to a condition are important and why. Evaluation: some employees have more time off work through ill-health than others (without loss of pay or job insecurity), thus the reaction of employers to the illness are more important for some workers than others.*

In conclusion, the issue of reactions of others to an illness is an important consideration because, as Sontag (1990) states, 'illness is not simply an illness'; thus symptoms are perceived in different ways by the sufferer and other social actors such as employees. The medical model tends to focus simply on the direct symptoms of a condition, yet for many sufferers the reactions of others remains an important experience of the illness, as Kelly's (1992) work with ulcerative colitis sufferers shows. The work on mental illness and stigmatisation is also an issue to consider, particularly because more mental illness sufferers are likely to depend on people within the . . . . . . since the recent promotion of the community care programme in Britain. However it is difficult to generalise because not all illnesses are stigmatised in the same way or to the same extent and not all sufferers react to stigmatisation in the same way.

Comment *Interpretation and application: the conclusion provided deals specifically with the essay question and attempts to apply the main points of the essay to the question. The conclusion also refers to the implications of the community care programme. You could add some points of your own. Evaluation: the fact that not all sufferers will react in the same way to stigmatisation has been mentioned as well as the point that not all illnesses are stigmatised (or not to the same extent). You could add any further points about the reaction of others that could help evaluate the role reactions play in determining illness experience. Knowledge and understanding are displayed in the conclusion by dealing with and extending the information on community care and Sontag's work.*

Questions

2. Answer the following specimen examination questions:

(a) How might a sociological consideration of self-identity provide an understanding of how individuals may respond to illness? (*25 marks*)

(b) Assess the role that social actors may play in determining whether an illness is 'legitimate'. (*25 marks*)

Summary

This chapter has examined the ways in which people respond to illness. The type of response will depend on the individuals concerned, the nature of their illness and the circumstances in which they find themselves. The responses explored in this chapter were selected from sociology books and articles examining the effects on people of radical surgery and severe illnesses. Responses included the need to understand more about the nature of the medical condition. Further knowledge of an illness can be gained from a variety of sources, such as health journals and magazines. Self-help groups may play a role in spreading information.

A further response was sufferers' need to have their condition accepted as legitimate, especially by employers, doctors, family and friends. There may be negotiation in the way in which some illnesses are regarded as legitimate and others are not. Issues of life disruption and financial problems were explored, followed by the effects of illness on self-identity. Sontag's (1990) work on AIDS was important in that illness was claimed to be 'more than just an illness' as people conferred on the illness additional (negative) meanings that could affect a person's self-identity. Further issues examined included the need to renegotiate certain roles (for example chores within the home). Finally the area of certainty and uncertainty was explored, which raised the issue of how people deal (or fail to deal) with the future implied by the condition.

One further issue to consider is the notion many postmodernists would wish to present, which deals with the nature of scientific knowledge. Knowledge is 'fabricated' (socially invented), thus the variety of responses to an illness raised in this chapter present only some ways of examining the issue. From your experience, or the experiences of friends and relatives, what issues do you think have been neglected in this chapter?

5 The relationship between social class and health

> By the end of this chapter you should be able to:
> - understand why measuring social class is problematic;
> - understand the problems of studying the relationship between class and health;
> - interpret the social class patterns of health and illness;
> - apply and evaluate different explanations of these patterns;
> - assess the health issues that particularly affect the unemployed and the homeless.

Introduction

This chapter begins by examining the problems involved in measuring social class. Despite the difficulties of operationalising the concept, evidence is examined to show that, in general, those in lower social classes experience worse health and have a shorter life expectancy than those above them in the social hierarchy.

Various explanations for the apparent link between class and health are discussed. The artefact explanation suggests the inequalities shown in the statistics do not exist in reality. Other explanations that do accept the existence of class inequalities focus on 'social selection' (with unhealthy people slipping down the social scale), on cultural and behavioural differences between classes (for example smoking habits), on material and structural inequalities (for example poverty as a cause of smoking) and on inequalities in health care (with poorer areas having less adequate services). These competing explanations have implications for social policy. Different explanations (for example cultural/behavioural) are seen to favour different social policies (for example anti-smoking campaigns).

The links between health and occupation, unemployment and locality are also examined in this chapter, as are health issues that relate specifically to the growing number of homeless people.

What is meant by 'social class'?

Just as rocks are stratified (arranged in layers or 'strata' one above another), so are groups in society. The term 'social stratification' draws attention to the fact that within societies there is usually a hierarchy of unequal social groups. Social class is a form of stratification based mainly upon economic differences between groups. For Karl Marx these differences were caused by elite ownership of the means of production (for example the land, factories or businesses). In capitalist society Marx distinguished two classes: the bourgeoisie, who own the means of production, and the proletariat, who sell their labour in order to earn a living. Max Weber drew more attention to the economic differences that exist among those who go to work: people bring different qualifications, skills and bargaining power to the job market and as a result they are unequally rewarded.

The Black Report (Townsend and Davidson, 1982) identified patterns of ill health and regarded social classes as 'sharing broadly similar resources, broadly similar styles of living and (for some sociologists) some shared perception of their condition'.

Why study social class and health?

The concept of social class has been central to much sociological research. However in recent years some politicians have called Britain a 'classless society' and sociologists have become increasingly concerned with other aspects of social inequality apart from class: in particular gender and ethnicity, but also age, sexuality and disability.

Postmodernists argue that postmodern society is characterised by increasing uncertainty, fragmentation and diversity, and that analysis of distinctive class subcultures (for example working-class subculture) is less relevant now that people have the opportunity to create their own lifestyles and self-identity. Willis (1990) points out how the media presents us with a multitude of different images (for example slim equals beautiful) and views, while the economy offers us an enormous range of consumer goods (for example cream cakes, slimming products and cosmetic surgery); the postmodern emphasis on 'agency' stresses the opportunity for individuals to select from the choices offered and be creative about lifestyle (for example, do I exercise? Do I purchase private health care?), rather than seeing behaviour (and health) as a product of one's position in the social structure and social class background. Postmodernists are also critical of the ability of grand or 'metatheories' (such as Marxism) to provide any superior form of understanding of postmodern society; they are simply one way of seeing the world.

This raises the question of whether it is still relevant to study the relationship between social class and health. Westergaard (1996) stresses the continuing importance of social class. He points out how inequalities between classes, far from disappearing, have in fact grown during the 1980s and 1990s. Whilst the top 10 per cent have seen their real income rise by 60 per cent, the poorest 20 per cent have seen only a negligible increase. There is well documented evidence that a 'health divide' (Whitehead, 1992) remains between the social classes, and recent research suggests that between 1981 and 1991 in poor areas in the north-east the death rate has actually been rising (Phillimore *et al.*, 1994). As Jones (1994) points out in response to postmodernists, even if 'the class structure does not have a reality beyond our perceptions of its existence, then it is certainly real in its effects (on health)'.

There is a strong argument for investigating in more detail the link between class and health. In order to do this researchers must make decisions about how to operationalise (measure) both class and health.

Is measuring social class problematic?

A social class system can lack clear boundaries between classes and clear criteria for class membership. In a social class system questions such as 'how many classes are there?' and 'how do we identify the members of each class?' can be problematic.

Exercise 5.1   Problems of class measurement

Answer the following questions and, if possible, have a report-back session in class to see how much agreement/disagreement there is about class and how it should be measured.

[a] 1. How many social classes are there in Britain today?

[a] 2. What do you call these different classes?

[i][a] 3. What class would you say you belong to and why?

[a][e] 4. Would you put the other members of your immediate family in the same class or a different one? Why?

[a] 5. If you were doing a piece of research that required you to allocate people to social classes, what indicator(s) would you use?

[i][a] 6. If you were using occupation to allocate people to classes, in what order would you rank the following? How would you justify your decision?

- Train driver
- Hairdresser
- Clergyman
- Police inspector
- Judge
- Secretary
- Kitchen hand
- Telephone operator
- Bar staff
- Car park attendant
- Electrician
- Pilot

How does the registrar general measure social class?

In many studies occupation has been used as a convenient indicator of social class. Many researchers have used the registrar general's scale (RGS); this was first introduced in 1911 to analyse infant mortality, and it classifies occupations into six groups, initially on their 'standing within the community' but since 1980 on the basis of occupational skill, as shown in Item A.

ITEM A

Social class		Examples of occupations	Percentage of males, 1986 (economically active/retired)
I	Professional	Accountant, doctor, lawyer	5
II	Intermediate	Manager, teacher, nurse	18
IIIN	Skilled non-manual	Clerk, secretary, shop assistant	12
IIIM	Skilled manual	Bus driver, carpenter, coal miner	38
IV	Semi-skilled manual	Farm worker, bus conductor	18
V	Unskilled manual	Labourer, cleaner	9

(*Source*: P. Trowler, *Investigating Health, Welfare and Poverty*, Collins Educational, 1989.)

ITEM A   *Exercise 5.2   Occupation as a measure of social class*

|e| 1. How much does knowing someone's occupation tell us about that person? Is it a good guide to the resources they have available and their lifestyle?

|a||e| 2. Would you expect people in the same occupation to have very similar circumstances? Why might this not be the case?

|e| 3. The RGS system of classification has been used since 1911. Does this present advantages/problems?

|a||e| 4. Which members of society cannot be conveniently classified according to occupation?

What are the problems of using the registrar general's scale?

Sociologists have used the RGS for its convenience and because it does give *some* insight into working conditions, income, job security, standard of living, social relationships and level of education. It has, though, been subject to criticism.

Exercise 5.3   Criticisms of the registrar general's scale

|i||a||e| The nine bulleted points below are criticisms of the RGS. Complete each criticism by matching it with one of the statements numbered (1) to (9).

- A classification based only on occupation ignores another major inequality . . .

- The majority of the population do not actually have an occupation . . .

- Many children can be classified according to the occupation of the household head (though deciding the household head may be problematic) . . .

- People who are retired or unemployed can be classified according to their previous occupation (if they have had a job since leaving school) . . .

- When couples are married or cohabiting it is usually the man's occupation that is used to determine social class: women are therefore classified according to their partner's social class . . .

- The social classes are very broad groupings. Within each class there can be considerable variations in resources, experiences and lifestyle . . .

- Even within a single occupation, there can be significant variations in levels of income, work situation and lifestyle . . .

- The RG scale has had to include new occupations that have developed since 1911 (for example computer programmers) and also to reclassify others as their social status has changed (for example university teachers were moved from Class II to Class I in 1961) . . .

- If a decision about a person's class is made by someone who has constructed an occupational classification there is no opportunity for the subject to say which class he or she identifies with and belongs to . . .

1. . . . there is a problem with deciding how to classify people with no occupation.

2. . . .however, previous occupation might not give a valid indication of the resources they currently have available, especially if they have not worked for some time. Also, people's final full-time job before retirement can differ from the type of work they have been used to.

3. . . . caused by differences in the amount of wealth people have.

4. . . . the circumstances of a premier league professional footballer are very different from those of a player for a club at the foot of the third division.

5. . . . subjective feelings are not taken into account.

6. . . . the Birmingham University Institute of Occupational Health (quoted in *The Sunday Telegraph*, 19 March 1995) researched the effects of organophosphorous sheep dips on the health of 200 sheep farmers. The study suggests that there might be specific health risks among some Class IV farm workers that are very different from, say, the health risks among Class IV bus conductors.

7. . . . however, childhood mortality (deaths between 1 and 15 years) is highest among children in the 'unoccupied' category; Judge and Benzeval (1993) estimate that 90 per cent of these children are living with lone mothers who are economically inactive.

8. ... this creates problems when comparing social class data for different years and studying trends.

9. ... the RGS can be criticised for perpetuating the idea that a woman's social status is obtained through her male partner (Graham, 1984) and for underestimating the resources of the two-earner family.

Can measures of inequality be improved?

Some researchers have identified the need to improve the occupational measures of social class. For example Goldthorpe (1987) has used an occupational classification that is based more on the economic reward a job gives than on its social status. A new classification will need to incorporate recent changes that have taken place in patterns of employment and unemployment (for example the growing importance of women in employment).

Other measures of inequality have avoided relying on occupation alone: Whitehead (1992) considers that the social index used in the child health and education cohort study (Osborn and Morris, 1979) gave a sensitive measure of the social inequalities experienced by children. The social index included seven variables:

- Occupation of household head.
- Parents' education.
- A social rating of the neighbourhood.
- Housing type.
- Housing tenure.
- Crowding at home and bathroom availability.

What is the relationship between social class and health?

Is evidence available about the relationship?

The health chapter in *Social Trends* (1995) contains 31 tables and graphs on health and illness: which sociologically relevant variables are examined in these statistics? The table below shows the number of references to five key variables.

Variable examined	Number of tables/graphs
Gender	17
Social class	1
Age	10
Ethnic group	0
Locality (region or country)	5

An examination of *Social Trends* (1995) might lead to the conclusion that there is a negligible amount of evidence on health issues relating to social class (or ethnicity). The one table in *Social Trends* that does refer to social class shows an inverse relationship between social class and smoking: in other words, the higher the social class, the lower the percentage of males and females who smoke. We might ask 'why smoking?' Why not occupational diseases and injuries, for example?

In fact, considerable evidence on health and social class is available: the Black Report (Townsend and Davidson, 1982) and *The Health Divide* (Whitehead, 1992) are major studies that draw on existing secondary evidence: they bring together the findings of official statistics and other research. Various measures of inequality (for example, occupational class, housing tenure, education, car ownership) are related to the data on mortality (deaths) and morbidity (illness).

However the issue of social class and health does remind us that, as sociologists, we need to ask questions about the availability of evidence on social issues:

• In terms of official statistics, what factors influence decisions to collect (or not collect) and publish (or not publish) particular social indicators? Whitehead suggests that the problems with data collection that had been pointed out in the Black Report still remain. She also suggests there is a need for health statistics (for example those on hospital admissions) to include more data on social background, and for other social surveys to include more information on health; for example the General Household Survey asks people to report on their state of health, but it does not thoroughly measure family income/resources. *Publication* of information is also an important issue: the authors of the Black Report (set up by the Labour social services secretary in 1977) point out that in 1980 the new Conservative government initially released only 260 duplicated copies of the report.

• In terms of sociological research, why do some issues seem to stimulate far more research than others? (This in turn might lead us to ask why some issues are regarded as social problems. Problems for whom? Who funds the research and how much does this influence what gets studied? Are the findings of research readily available?) Whitehead suggests that the Black Report had the effect of stimulating more research into health and social inequality.

Exercise 5.4 Prioritising variables

1. Rank the following variables in what you consider to be their order of importance for research into the issue of health inequalities:

- Disability
- Housing
- Region

- Gender
- Sexuality
- Social class

- Ethnic group
- Age

2. Justify your choice (one paragraph).

3. How do you think the following would rank the variables:
    (a) A pressure group for the disabled?
    (b) A sociologist concerned about inequality?
    (c) A health minister in a government seeking to limit state expenditure?
    (Hint: which factors would require the least costly intervention?)

What is the relationship between social class and mortality?

Death certificates record the occupation of the deceased (or next of kin) and the cause of death. The Black Report (Townsend and Davidson, 1982) showed a social class gradient in mortality for infants (under one year old), children (1–14 years old) and adults (15–64 years old) of both sexes, with the gradient most marked in early life. Class I tended to have the lowest mortality and Class V the highest. The class gradient applied to a wide range of illnesses.

ITEM B

Standardised Cancer mortality rates, 1981 (men 20–64 years, women 20–59 years)

class	Cervical (female)	Melanoma (male)	Melanoma (female)	Lung (male)	Lung (female)	Breast (female)
I	29	133	118	43	48	109
II	60	126	107	63	69	104
IIIn	73	134	112	80	75	106
IIIm	112	85	107	120	115	101
IV	124	89	88	126	126	99
V	186	82	98	178	149	96

(*Source*: OPCS Occupational Mortality, Decennial Supplement 6, 1979/80, 1982/3, from The Health of the Nation, Variations in Health, Department of Health, 1995.)

ITEM B

Exercise 5.5 Social class gradients in cancer mortality

1. On squared paper, plot the social class mortality gradients for the cancers shown in Item B. Use different colours to indicate different cancers/gender. You will need a grid similar to this, but larger:

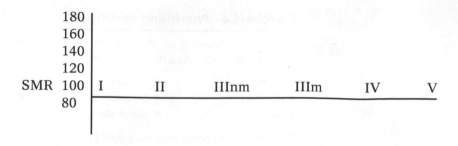

```
180
160
140
120
SMR  100 | I        II       IIInm     IIIm      IV        V
      80 |
```

[i][a] 2. Compare the social class gradients:
   (a) Which show an inverse/negative relationship between class and
        mortality (that is, lower class = higher mortality)?
   (b) Which show a positive relationship (that is, higher class = higher mortality)?
   (c) Which cancers show the steepest class gradients?

[a] 3. Name one lifestyle factor that might help explain the class gradient in lung
   cancer mortality.

[a] 4. Earlier menarche and delayed childbearing appear to increase the risk of
   breast cancer; how could these factors be linked to higher breast cancer
   mortality in higher classes?

More recent studies (for example Whitehead, 1992) confirm the class gradient in mortality. The OPCS longitudinal study followed a 1 per cent sample from the 1971 census and found that mortality in Class V was double that in Class I for respondents of working age, and 50 per cent higher for those who were retired. Studies of single occupations such as Marmot's (1984, 1991) longitudinal study of 17 500 London civil servants show very steep gradients: the death rate among the lowest grade of civil servants was three times that of those in the highest grade.

The Department of Health's Report on Variations in Health (1995) points out that:

- Life expectancy is seven years longer for a child born in Class I than for a child in Class V.
- A child in Class V has four times the chance of accidental death than a child in Class I.
- Of 66 major causes of death for men, 62 were most common in Classes IV and V.
- Of 70 major causes of death for women, 64 were most common in women married to men in Classes IV and V.

Other measures of inequality confirm the social class gradient in mortality: this can be seen in Item C below. Items B and C refer to the standardised mortality rate (SMR). This compares the mortality rate for the whole population with that of a particular group within the population. It is expressed as a ratio, 100 being the average mortality and any figure above 100 indicating higher than average mortality.

Standardised mortality ratio of 15–64 year olds, 1971–81

		Males	Females
Home:	Owner occupied	84	83
	Privately rented	109	106
	Local authority	115	117
Education:	Degree	59	66
	Other higher education	80	78
	A levels	91	80
	None/not stated	103	102
Access to Car:	One or more	85	83
	None	121	135

(*Source*: P. Goldblatt, 'Social Class and Alternative Classifications', in P. Goldblatt, Longitudinal Study 1971–1981, OPCS LS Series No. 6, 1990.)

ITEM C **Exercise 5.6 Alternative measures of inequality**

i 1. Which three indicators of social class were used in Goldblatt's study?

i 2. Describe the mortality trends for males and females according to the three measures of social class.

i 3. Identify the measure of social class that revealed (a) the highest mortality ratio and (b) the lowest mortality ratio for males and females.

a 4. What does the variation in mortality according to each measure tell you about:
   (a) the validity of such research (accuracy);
   (b) the problems that might arise when comparing different pieces of research?

The Black Report (Townsend and Davidson, 1982) and *The Health Divide* (Whitehead, 1992) indicate that members of the lower classes have continued to experience higher mortality rates. These studies suggested that a considerable number of deaths could be prevented each year if all classes shared the advantages of Class I.

Critics, however, have pointed out that the number of people in Class V is shrinking, and with the general increase in life expectancy it is now relatively uncommon for people to die in infancy, childhood or early adulthood.

What is the relationship between social class and morbidity?

If people are, on average, living longer it becomes more important to ask about their quality of life. To what extent are members of different social classes likely to experience illness and disability?

The Black Report (Townsend and Davidson, 1982) found limited data on social class and morbidity, and expressed concern about the validity of some data (for example data from consultations with doctors measures not simply 'illness', but the willingness of different individuals to define themselves as ill and seek medical attention).

ITEM D

1992 General Household Survey

Socioeconomic group of household head	Chronic illness (%)		Limiting long-standing illness (%)		Av. no. of restricted activity days per year	
	(m)	(f)	(m)	(f)	(m)	(f)
Professional	27	28	12	13	16	23
Employers/managers	28	30	15	17	17	24
Intermediate non-manual	29	34	15	20	17	25
Junior non-manual	27	37	14	21	18	33
Skilled manual	35	32	21	19	24	26
Semi-skilled manual	35	38	21	24	25	37
Unskilled manual	37	41	23	26	24	34

(*Source*: adapted from General Household Survey, London, HMSO, 1992.)

ITEM D   *Exercise 5.7   The General Household Survey, social class and morbidity*

Since it began in 1971 the General Household Survey (GHS) has collected information from respondents on their health. The GHS asks people whether they suffer from chronic illness (that is, a long-standing illness, disability or infirmity) and if so whether it limits their activities in any way ('limiting long-standing illness'); it also asks about acute illness, (that is, whether normal activities have been restricted in the last two weeks as a result of illness or injury, and the average number of days of restricted activity per year.

[i]   1. Describe the relationship between social class and the three measures of illness shown in Item D.

[e]   2. Why is it important to distinguish between males and females?

[i] [e]   3. Write a paragraph evaluating the use of subjective measures of morbidity. Hint: you could include, in a suitable order, some of the following ideas:

- Differences over time may be influenced by peoples' changing expectations about health, rather than by actual changes in health; the GHS figures show a steady increase since 1972 in the percentage reporting chronic illness.
- People's subjective views about their health may give a useful guide to their likely demand for health care.
- Whether people describe an illness as 'limiting their activities' will depend on their views about what counts as 'normal activity' (for example, sitting by the fire, working on a building site).
- Objective measures of health (for example blood pressure measurements) do not indicate how people feel about their health.

- Differences between groups may be influenced by their expectations about health, as well as their willingness to admit to an interviewer that they are ill.
- Subjective measures of health do not distinguish between a person who is genuinely ill and a hypochondriac.

Recent research has often attempted to combine subjective measures of morbidity with more objective information. The Health and Lifestyle Survey (1990) measured health through medical examinations (for example blood pressure, lung function) and interviews: both measures showed marked class differences: 36 per cent of Class V men described their health as 'fair' or 'poor', but only 12 per cent of Class I men did so (Blaxter, 1990a). Marmot *et al.*'s second study (1991) of civil servants showed higher morbidity in the lower grades, measured by medical examination and the respondents' own perception of their health. Whitehead's (1992) conclusion was that (with the possible exception of adolescence) far more illness is experienced in the lower occupational classes.

Why is explaining the relationship between social class and health problematic?

Social class is an 'umbrella' variable

Research shows convincingly that there is a relationship between social class and health. But can we determine the actual cause of this relationship? Social class is an 'umbrella variable', and the problem researchers face is establishing which variables beneath this umbrella are significant. How important is diet? For which diseases? Diet in infancy, or childhood, or later life? How important is housing? Which aspects of housing? For which diseases?

The influence of extraneous variables

Extraneous (or extra) variables can also cause difficulties. Social class is not the only variable influencing our health; additional variables such as age, ethnicity, gender or locality can complicate the relationship between social class and health – it might be healthier to be working class in a rural area rather than in an urban area. Chapter 7 explains that ethnicity is a factor in variations in health and that some ethnic groups are concentrated in certain social classes.

Standardised mortality rates in different regions, by class and gender				
Region	I & II male	IV & V male	I & II female	IV & V female
North	81	152	80	136
South East	67	112	71	100
South West	69	108	70	96
East Anglia	65	93	69	81

(*Source*: M. Whitehead, *The Health Divide*, Harmondsworth, Penguin, 1992.)

ITEM E   *Exercise 5.8   Mortality patterns by social class and region*

i 1. In Item E, in which region is mortality (a) highest and (b) lowest for each social class?

i 2. In which region is mortality (a) highest and (b) lowest for each gender?

i 3. In which region is the mortality difference between the social classes (a) greatest and (b) least?

a 4. Can you think of any reasons for regional differences in health? (Hint: might any of the following be relevant):

- Cultural factors (for example diet).
- Amount of unemployment.
- Levels of income/poverty.
- Access to and use of health services.
- Types of employment available.
- Environmental factors (for example pollution).
- Housing conditions.

Social change affects all classes

Change is a further problem: the relationship between social class and health has persisted, but in many ways all social classes have experienced changes in their working and living conditions and in the medical care that is available to them, and explanations need to take account of these changes. For example increases in unemployment, the employment of married women and car ownership might all have implications for health and illness.

Delay in the onset of disease

Explaining the link between class and health is complicated by the fact that some diseases only appear years after exposure to the conditions responsible for them. Exposure to the cold virus can lead to the rapid development of the uncomfortable symptoms of a cold. However this is not true for all diseases: a disease experienced today might have its origins in earlier life experiences. The Health and Safety Commission (1994) points out how work-related past exposure to substances such asbestos, coal dust and silica continues to cause ill-health today; pneumoconiosis (a lung disease associated with mining, quarrying, foundries and potteries) normally develops 15–30 years after exposure; among asbestos workers there can be a delay of up to 60 years between exposure to asbestos and the onset of lung cancer and mesothelioma. The long latency period associated with some diseases helps to explain the current uncertainty as to whether the epidemic of bovine spongiform encephalopathy (BSE) ('mad cow disease') presents a future threat to health by increasing the incidence of the human brain disease Creutzfedt–Jacob disease (CJD).

ITEM F

Area of Manchester	Low-weight births (%)	Household heads in Class V (%)	Household on housing benefit (%)	Household without a car (%)
North A	8.4	7.6	38.0	56.0
North B	8.0	8.4	42.0	60.0
North C	10.3	9.5	54.0	69.0
Central A	10.1	12.0	58.0	76.0
Central B	10.1	7.5	41.0	59.0
Central C	8.1	6.4	32.0	54.0
South A	8.7	5.1	32.0	46.0
South B	7.5	3.8	26.0	41.0
South C	7.8	9.3	40.0	50.0
South D	8.6	10.6	53.0	61.0

(*Source*: R. Stevens, ed., *Health Inequalities and Manchester in the 1990s, Manchester Health For All Working Party*, Manchester City, 1993.)

ITEM F   *Exercise 5.9   Recent research into health inequalities: low weight births*

According to the Manchester 'Health For All' report (Stevens, 1993), 9 per cent of babies in Manchester are of low birth weight compared with the average of 7 per cent in England and Wales. Low-weight births are associated with poor infant health as well as poor maternal health and nutrition. There is increasing evidence that the disadvantage conferred by low birth weight might extend beyond infancy to ill-health in adulthood and premature death.

i 1. According to Item F, which areas of Manchester have the (a) highest and (b) lowest rates for low-weight births?

e 2. How useful do you consider the other three columns of data as measures of social inequality in Manchester?

a 3. Choose a suitable method of data analysis (for example scatter diagram, correlation coefficient) to see whether there is a relationship between the percentage of low-weight births in each area of Manchester and the other variables.

i *a* 4. Comment on your findings. (Hint: is there a relationship between the variables? If so, how close is it? What could explain a relationship? For example chance? Cause and effect relationship? Some other factor? Would any additional data be useful? For example the percentage of smokers, or mothers who smoke? Why?)

What are the explanations for the relationship between social class and health?

It seems unlikely that, having divided the entire population into about six large social classes, a single explanation would account for all the health differences between them. Five main explanations will be examined:

- Artefact
- Social selection
- Culture
- Material/structural
- The health services

The artefact explanation

This suggests there is no 'real' problem to explain: social class health inequalities do not exist in reality: they are simply a product of the methods researchers have used to measure social class and health inequality.

The measures used do make a difference: Wagstaff *et al.* (1991) point out that class gradients are steeper if 'years of potential life lost' rather than 'standardised mortality rates' are compared. Also, researchers who focus on the health differences between Class I and Class V could be accused of selecting two relatively small classes at the extremes of the social scale, and therefore exaggerating class differences.

However there is no convincing support for the view that the artefact explanation can simply explain away class differences in health. Acceptance of the artefact explanation would require us to ignore the fact that different measures of social inequality (for example occupation, housing tenure) show a fairly consistent social class gradient: the lower the social class, the more health deteriorates and life expectancy decreases.

Accepting the artefact explanation means that no social policies would be needed to deal with this (non-existent) problem.

The social selection explanation

This explanation suggests that good or bad health causes social mobility (movement up or down the social class hierarchy):

- The selection process: healthy people tend to be upwardly mobile (or stay in the highest class); unhealthy people tend to move down into lower classes (or stay in the bottom class).
- The effects of social selection: higher classes appear healthier because they select healthy people from all classes; lower classes seem less healthy because the unhealthy from all classes enter them.

There are a number of avenues towards upward social mobility, including winning the lottery, inheriting wealth, building up one's own business, developing a career (through some combination of talent/hard work/good luck/educational success) or marrying into a higher class. Similarly there are a number of causes of a fall down the social scale (for example business failure). The social selection hypothesis argues that people move down the social scale due to ill health. The working class appears to be relatively unhealthy simply because people in higher classes who suffer serious ill health move down into the working class.

Exercise 5.10 Evaluating the social selection hypothesis

|a| 1. What do you consider are the main methods by which people become socially mobile?

|a| 2. In what ways do you think (a) good health could improve peoples' chances of upward mobility and (b) poor health could increase the likelihood of downward mobility? (Hint: could there be effects on educational achievement, employability, career progress, marriageability?)

|e| 3. Do you see any problems with the hypothesis that the class differences in health are caused by social selection? (Hint: does health really affect social mobility? Might living in a lower class actually be less healthy than living in a higher class? Why?)

There is some supporting evidence for the social selection explanation. Wadsworth (1995) suggested that boys who had experienced serious illness in childhood were more likely to be downwardly mobile by the age of 26. Connelly and Crown (1994) in the Royal College of Physicians report on homelessness and ill-health and suggest that schizophrenics are overrepresented among the homeless because of social selection: it is not homelesssness that causes schizophrenia, rather schizophrenia puts one at risk of becoming homeless.

There are, however, a number of limitations to the social selection hypothesis:

- Ill health (particularly in a competitive job market where many companies have reduced their labour force) may lead to unemployment rather than a move into lower-status employment. Lower-status jobs might make as many health demands as high-status ones, reducing the likelihood of the unhealthy becoming downwardly mobile.

- Good health might be a *necessary* factor for upward mobility, but it is by no means a *sufficient* factor on its own in a job market that increasingly demands appropriate qualifications and experience.
- Illness does not necessarily lead to downward mobility. Some illnesses are fatal very soon after their onset, and therefore there might not be sufficient time for the selection effect to operate. On the other hand, some people are able to adapt to illness and continue with their career without experiencing downward mobility.
- The selection hypothesis is not a complete explanation of the greater health problems in Classes IV and V. In the case of illness among infants and children in lower classes, there has been no opportunity for them to experience social mobility. Nor can the selection hypothesis explain health problems that develop after retirement age.

The health selection effect cannot be ignored. The distress of illness (one's own or a family member's) is likely to be compounded if it is accompanied by economic uncertainty and declining living standards.

The social selection explanation has some implications for social policy:

- Should action be taken to preserve the living standards of those who become ill?
- If so, who should be responsible for preserving living standards (for example the state through benefits, the individual through private insurance, or employers through more generous provisions for employees who become ill or disabled?)

Link Exercise 5.1 *The costs of ill health*

 Those who are sick or disabled are overrepresented among the poor: illness or disability can increase expenses and at the same time reduce income. Review Exercise 4.5 (page 59) and briefly explain the key factors that will influence the severity of the financial effects of illness. Points to consider are:

- Nature of the illness.
- Care/treatment needs.
- State benefits.
- Savings.
- Employment (for example self-employed v. employed; contract of employment and benefits).
- Duration of illness.
- Support available (for example immediate family, relatives).
- Private benefits (for example critical illness insurance).
- Expenditure (for example mortgage, school fees).

However, since the health selection effect can only explain a small amount of the social class inequality in health, other explanations must be considered.

The cultural explanation

Culture is the shared and learned way of life of a group of people. The cultural explanation suggests that different social classes behave in different ways; the poorer health of the lower social classes is caused by their behaving in ways that are more likely to damage their health. On the other hand the culture of the higher classes (their knowledge, social norms, values and beliefs) leads to better health and a longer life expectancy. This explanation is sometimes called 'blaming the victim' because it suggests that the solution to ill-health depends largely on the willingness of the working class to adopt the more enlightened and responsible lifestyles associated with the middle class.

Graham (1985) points out that victim-blaming theories of ill-health (and poverty) have a long history – they were particularly influential during the industrial revolution and have again become popular. She compares the view of a chief medical officer in 1906 who suggested that infant mortality was largely due to ignorance and negligence, with a 1977 DHSS report that argued that unwise behaviour and overindulgence was responsible for much illness in Britain.

The recent emphasis on cultural explanations of illness (and poverty) is associated with the growing influence of the New Right since the 1980s. The New Right stresses the responsibility of individuals for their own and their family's wellbeing; expensive state provision for health and welfare is seen as undesirable, especially if it creates a 'dependency culture' in which sections of the population become less self-reliant because they expect the state to meet their needs (see Marsland, 1989).

The New Right's preference for a society in which market forces are able to operate without undue state interference means that policies to improve health through, for example, a major redistribution of income from rich to poor are considered inappropriate. On the other hand, policies that promote healthier lifestyles are seen as desirable because they are based on individuals taking responsibility for and making choices about their own lifestyle.

Exercise 5.11 Testing the cultural explanation

 To see whether the cultural explanation can explain class differences in health it is necessary to decide which aspects of culture are likely to affect health. Make a list of 'bad health habits' that you think might increase one's risk of illness and/or premature death.

Whitehead (1992) examined four aspects of culture: smoking, drinking, eating and exercise.

Smoking and social class

The government (*Social Trends*, no. 25, 1995) considers smoking to be the greatest cause of preventable death in this country in view of its association with illnesses such as lung cancer, respiratory disease and heart disease. The social class gradient in smoking is shown in Item G.

ITEM G

Cigarette smoking by gender & socioeconomic group (percentages)

	1982		1992	
	Female	Male	Female	Male
Professional	21	20	13	14
Employers and managers	29	29	21	23
Intermediate/junior non-manual	30	30	27	25
Skilled manual	39	42	31	34
Semi-skilled manual	36	47	35	39
Unskilled manual	41	49	35	42

(*Source*: Social Trends, 25, London, HMSO, 1995.)

ITEM G   *Exercise 5.12   The relationship between smoking and social class*

i 1. From Item G, identify the trends in smoking for (a) professional males and unskilled males and (b) professional females and unskilled females.

i *a* 2. Compare the trends in smoking for males and females.

e 3. What useful information is missing from the table?

Although the table in Item G does not explain how a 'smoker' was defined or distinguish between heavy and light smokers, it does show a marked *class gradient* in smoking, a *decline* in smoking in all socioeconomic groups between 1982 and 1992, and some *gender differences* in smoking. It shows that smokers are a minority in every class, but that only one class has reached the government target for the year 2000 (20 per cent of the population smoking). The Manchester Health Needs Survey (1992) showed that heavy smoking (defined as 15+ cigarettes a day) was more common among manual workers than non-manual workers; the survey also showed regional variations in smoking in 1992:

	Non-manual	Manual
Percentage of smokers in Britain	22	36
Percentage of smokers in North Manchester	31	46

(*Source*: Manchester Public Health Resource Centre, 1992).

There is certainly a class gradient both in smoking and in mortality from smoking-related diseases (lung cancer, respiratory disease and heart disease). Smoking can affect the health not only of the smoker but also of other family members (this might link with the low-weight births discussed earlier).

Alcohol and social class

The link between alcohol and class is far less clear. The General Household Survey (1992) points out that it is difficult to obtain valid data on drinking: surveys generally record levels of drinking that are lower than those suggested by the sale of alcohol. Women drink less than men, and research generally shows a clear social class gradient in their drinking patterns: that is, women in higher social classes and with higher incomes are more likely to consume more than the recommended amount of alcohol per week. For men there is no clear occupational class gradient. Higher income is linked with heavier drinking for men (but it must be remembered the General Household Survey excludes from its sample the homeless and those living in institutions, some of whom might drink heavily). In Manchester 'high-risk drinking' is largely a male problem, and also more of a working class problem, even for women:

High-risk drinkers	Non-manual (%)	Manual (%)
female	0.8	2.4
male	6.8	7.9

(*Source*: Manchester Health Needs Survey, Topic Report 2, Alcohol, Manchester Public Health Resource Centre, 1993.)

It is recognised that excessive drinking can lead to a range of physical problems (including liver damage, some cancers, high blood pressure and stroke) and social problems (for example family breakdown, domestic violence). But there are still a number of questions to ask about the link between alcohol and health: to what extent is some alcohol consumption beneficial to health? Is regular drinking or binge drinking more damaging to health? Since alcohol may damage other peoples' health (especially through violence and accidents), is this more likely to happen in certain situations/social classes?

Diet and social class

Diet affects growth and resistance to infection, and it can cause specific problems (obesity, heart disease). Whitehead (1992) concludes that although the top income group continues to have the 'best' diet, all classes are now eating better: more wholemeal bread and potatoes and less lard, butter and sugar are now being consumed. However low-income households still eat more sugar and less fruit, vegetables and high fibre food than better-off families. These differences could be explained by cultural factors. For example working-class families might lack knowledge about healthy diets, budget and shop less efficiently and prefer less healthy foods. However evidence from the National Food Survey (1989) suggests that low-income families obtain food more cheaply and more nutrients per £1 spent than high-income families. Therefore a non-cultural explanation for the poorer diet of disadvantaged groups might be necessary.

The importance of early nutrition has been stressed by Greenhalgh (*The Times*, 24 August 1995), who points out that there is increasing evidence 'that *under-nutrition* in the foetus, infant and toddler is a serious risk to health, not just at the time but for 50, 60 and even 70 years afterwards'. She quotes research that has traced 16 000 people born between 1911 and 1930 in Hertfordshire and for whom detailed birth and infancy records were kept. The research found that those who had weighed less than 5.5 lbs at birth (due to poor growth, not prematurity) are today twice as likely to suffer from coronary heart disease than those who had weighed more than 9.5 lbs. Nutrition in the first year of life is also very important: infants who had weighed less than 17 lbs when they were one year old had four times the incidence of heart disease 50 years later than those who had weighed 28 lbs or more.

Exercise and social class

Exercise can have a beneficial effect on health. The General Household Survey (1990) shows a marked class gradient in leisure exercise (for example the professional class has the highest rate for walking and swimming). But Whitehead (1992) points out that in all classes only a minority have 'adequate' exercise, and that working-class people are more likely than middle-class people to have jobs that are physically demanding.

Exercise 5.13 *Policy implications of the cultural explanation*

1. Select five policies from the following list that you think would most encourage people to behave in a healthier way. For each policy you select, identify an illness that could be reduced:

   • An anti-smoking campaign.

- Introduction of a minimum wage for low-paid workers.
- The promotion of safer sex.
- Drug awareness lessons in school.
- Higher levels of income support.
- Encouraging people to exercise more.
- Stricter controls on levels of pollution.
- Healthy-eating leaflets in supermarkets.

[a] 2. Suggest one other campaign that could promote healthier behaviour.

[e] 3. Do you think policies to encourage healthier behaviour could lead to the elimination of class differences in health? Explain your answer in a paragraph. (Hint: does the working class show less healthy behaviour than the middle class? Are campaigns to change behaviour effective? Is changing behaviour all that is needed to remove class inequalities in health?)

[i][a] 4. Select one policy from the list above that is unlikely to appeal to the New Right and explain why.

What are the limitations of the cultural explanation?

Do the cultural differences in smoking, alcohol consumption, diet and exercise explain the poorer health of those in lower social classes? There is certainly some evidence that the most disadvantaged groups in society are least likely to have a healthy lifestyle. A class gradient in smoking is particularly noticeable. Other aspects of class cultures (for example social norms about child rearing or gender roles) might also have implications for health.

The cultural explanation has the following limitations:

- There are significant cultural variations within each social class (for example different ethnic groups may have differences in lifestyle, even if they belong to the same social class). There is also a considerable cultural overlap between different social classes: Blaxter (1990a) suggests that most people have a lifestyle that combines healthy and unhealthy behaviour as far as smoking, drinking, diet and exercise are concerned.
- Peoples' lives are likely to be affected by their culture *and* by their position in the social structure; it can be difficult to separate these factors. If the poor behave differently from those who are better off it is not necessarily because they have internalised a different culture – they might simply be responding in a rational way to the situation they find themselves in. Their position at the bottom of the social structure limits the choices they can make – they face 'situational constraints'. This view suggests that if they moved into the middle class they would soon change their behaviour in response to their new situation. Blackburn (1991) argues that whilst it is true that diet and child care practices among the poor appear

to be different, when we take into account their preferences (what they would like to do) and their goals, social class differences are much reduced. She argues, for example, that improving household income is a key factor in improving the eating patterns of low-income families. The Department of Health (DoH, 1995) recognises that 'personal, social and economic circumstances' might make it difficult for some groups to change behaviour that could be health damaging.

- McKinlay (1984) points out how capitalism generates profits by producing commodities for sale (such as cigarettes). Thus from a Marxist perspective it is not the purchase of these products that is the cause of ill-health; rather it is the production and promotion of health-damaging products. (If BSE in cattle is shown to be linked to CJD in humans, there is an important issue about who is responsible for the illness: the state, the consumer or those involved in beef production.)

- Phillimore *et al.* (1994) criticise the recent preoccupation of researchers with cultural/behavioural explanations of health inequalities. Their research into mortality rates between 1981 and 1991 in the north of England suggest a very close relationship between the mortality rate and the level of material deprivation in the 678 wards they studied.

Link exercise 5.2   Smoking: are you really free to choose?

 In one paragraph and using Item C in Chapter 6 (page 145), explain how individuals' decisions about smoking might be influenced by their position in the social structure.

The material/structural explanation

The material/structural explanation suggests that social class differences in health are caused by the different working and living conditions of the different social classes. Researchers such as Blackburn (1991), and indeed the Black Report (Townsend and Davidson, 1982) and Whitehead (1992), argue that this explanation is crucial to an understanding of social class differences in health.

Exercise 5.14   Paid work and ill health

 1. Make a list of factors associated with the working environment that might have a harmful effect on health. For each factor you mention, suggest what the health effects are likely to be.

 2. What types of occupation would you associate with greater health risks? Would you expect a link between the social class of an occupation and its health risk?

What is the relationship between employment and health?

Employment and health: do occupations vary in their health risks? Lower-status jobs do appear to be associated with higher rates of morbidity and mortality. Industrial accidents (for example in the construction or fishing industries), exposure to toxic substances (for example in furnace and foundry work) and long and unsocial working hours are more often features of manual work. Non-manual workers also experience health risks, but Marmot *et al.*'s study (1991) of Whitehall civil servants showed that the lower the grade, the higher the mortality (from administrative to professional/executive, to clerical and office support). It is likely that the explanation in part lies in differences in the work situation of the different grades.

Mullen (1992) felt it important to look at the health effects of specific occupations rather than divide workers into broader social groupings. There are significant variations between occupations:

Occupation	Standardised mortality ratio (men 15–64)
University teachers	49
MPs	61
School teachers	66
Architects	74
Doctors	81
Postmen	81
Coal miners	141
Steel erectors	164
Fishermen	171
Policemen	209
Bricklayers' labourers	274

Macran *et al.* (1994) looked at data on women in employment. Previous studies had shown a social class gradient for married women with regard to mortality and limiting long-standing illness when they were classified by their *partner's* occupation (obviously in many families the husband's income is a major determinant of the living standard). For their study Macran *et al.* took data from the first Health and Lifestyle Survey (1984–5), which had asked women: 'Would you say that for someone of your age your general health is: excellent, good, fair, poor, don't know?'

The women's subjective assessment of their health was then compared with their (present or last) occupation. Instead of using the registrar general's five social classes, Macran *et al.* used 15 different occupational categories. They found a link between a woman's occupation and her self-assessed health: those in some occupations (especially the higher-status ones) appeared to be considerably healthier. However they also found differences between occupations that are often placed in the same social class, for example teachers and nurses are both in RG Class II; retail workers are often placed in the same class as clerical workers.

ITEM H

Self-assessed health status (percentages)

Occupational group	Excellent	Good	Less than good
Professional	27	59	14
Nurses	24	52	24
Teachers	23	60	16
Clerical	23	58	19
Retail	18	49	33
Catering	19	53	28
Semi-skilled	16	48	36
Unskilled	15	50	35

(*Source*: S. Macran *et al.*, 'Women's Socio-economic Status and Self-assessed Health', *Sociology of Health & Illness*, vol. 16, no. 2, 1994.)

ITEM H *Exercise 5.15 What is the link between self-assessed health and occupation?*

[i] 1. Which categories are associated with (a) the best and (b) the worst health?

[i][a] 2. What do you notice when you compare the health of (a) teachers and nurses and (b) clerical workers and retail workers?

[a] 3. Suggest two reasons why some of the occupations seem to be associated with better health/worse health?

Employment and health: are workers aware of the health risks of employment? Mullen (1992) interviewed 70 men aged 30–49 in Glasgow with manual or non-manual jobs. Each interview lasted between one and two hours and used an ethnographic approach: there was no strict order of questions and each topic discussed was explored in depth. Mullen wanted to investigate the respondents' views about the effects of their work on their health, and how they coped with this. On the one hand work was seen to benefit both mental and physical health, especially when compared with unemployment: 'Ah think working hard has a good effect; it hasn't done me any harm; you're using your muscles all day long...' 'I have a job. I suppose that is a big help to your mental state. At least you have somewhere to go every day. Different surroundings from home...' (Mullen, 1992). On the other hand, employees were well aware that work can cause mental and physical damage: 'I think a lot of the illness is inflicted through the style of life of the occupation or the environment... people who are working in industries where there are a lot of fumes, dangerous chemicals, things like that.' (ibid.)

A wide range of health hazards at work were mentioned: smoke, dust, dangerous machinery, noise, shifting from hot to cold areas and lack of exercise due to sitting behind a desk or at the wheel of a car. Mental stress was most often caused by pressure of time (either too much to do in the time available, or having to work very long hours); stress was also linked to the type of work people were doing (for example problems of dealing with other people), fear of redundancy, having to work away from home and having too much responsibility. Stress was mentioned especially by self-employed respondents, but both manual and non-manual employed workers were concerned about stress. The respondents associated stress with the risk of heart disease in particular, but also mentioned migraine, exhaustion and problems with sleeping.

Employment and health: do workers respond to the health risks of employment? Mullen (ibid.) found that the workers did not passively accept the damaging health influences of their occupations. One response was compensation. This could involve putting some distance between themselves and their work, (for example taking a break, refusing to get too involved in the job). Taking exercise or paying attention to diet were ways of compensating for jobs that involved a lot of sitting around.

Mullen also found that the workers actually tried to change the work in some way to make it less damaging. However the respondents generally did not seem to have been very successful at this as individuals (only one respondent mentioned the use of collective action – the setting up of a self-help group for church ministers): 'As a welder I am out in the open but some of the fumes I swallow is unbelievable you know. So what do I do? Chuck my job because of the fumes . . .' (ibid.) A number of respondents had changed their jobs as a way of improving their work situation, but the concept of situational constraint might again be relevant here: some employees might have fewer opportunities than others to change to a healthy working environment.

Exercise 5.16 Glasgow workers' response to health risks

[i] In your own words write a paragraph summarising Mullen's findings on the Glasgow workers' views on and responses to health risks in the workplace.

Employment and health: do employers respond to the health risks of employment? Employers' control over the working environment gives them a key role in influencing the health risks of employment. Doyal and Pennell (1979) present a Marxist argument that capitalist production is unhealthy because the pursuit of profit takes place at the expense of work safety, job security and a fulfilling working environment. In other words there is an incompatibility between maximising profit and promoting good health. Doyal and Pennell suggest that interference with the production process is minimised by the development of a health care system that is geared towards curing illness rather than taking action to prevent it in the first place. Dobraszczyc (1989) agrees that employees' health might be sacrificed in the interests of production, and that they may receive compensation rather than protection (and only if they can establish conclusively that a particular feature of the work environment was responsible). She refers to the examples of the chemical leak from the Union Carbide factory in Bhopal and the dangerous working practices that were associated with asbestos production.

Navarro (1979) suggests that doctors act as servants of capitalism by reinforcing the message that responsibility for ill health lies with individuals and their unhealthy lifestyle, rather than with the capitalist production process. Critics (for example Hart, 1985) suggest that the Marxists have used evidence rather selectively in order to support their theory. The critics highlight the health problems associated with production in socialist societies, and the significant health improvements that have occurred in capitalist societies. They also question the extent to which doctors passively serve the interests of capital (see Bellaby, 1990).

Exercise 5.17 Health and safety at work

1. Find out at least three details about legislation affecting health and safety in the workplace (for example the 1974 Health and Safety at Work Act). You may need to consult a business studies book.

2. Watterson (1994) expressed concern at:
- The 2.6 per cent budget cut in 1994–5 for the Health and Safety Commission and Executive.
- Staffing levels: 1400 HSE inspectors for one million workplaces.
- Proposals for deregulation (that is fewer regulations on health and safety).

(a) How might these factors influence health and safety at work?

(b) Do you think health and safety legislation is necessary if workers are to have a safe working environment?
(Hint: would 'market forces' encourage businesses to provide high or low standards of safety at work? Why? The economist Adam Smith argued that workers doing dangerous work would expect such high wages that employers would develop safer working condition in order to reduce the cost of wages; Watterson challenges this view, and suggests that relying on market forces and voluntary action by employers does not generally produce high standards of health and safety. Do you think multinational companies are likely to be attracted to countries with strict or limited health and safety regulations?)

Employment and health: is occupational disease contested? The extent to which the dangers of work are essentially contested is relevant here. In 1994 the Health and Safety Commission (HSC) pointed out that whilst some diseases (for example asbestosis) are unquestionably work-related, there are many others that have a number of causes, of which the working environment may be one.

This issue is well illustrated in a study by Ewan *et al.* (1991). They interviewed 52 Australian women suffering from repetitive strain injury as a result of working either as telephonists or in a chicken processing factory. RSI affects the hand, arm and neck and is associated with repetitive movement, often from an awkward position: 'there were three of us and we were averaging 28 000 to 30 000 chickens a day ... we were doing 78 birds a minute and we had a timekeeper on us all the time' (ibid.) The effects of this painful and limiting disability included 'unemployment, reduced capacity to do housework, disruption of family relationships and future plans, financial hardship, emotional distress, loss of sleep, an erosion of self-esteem and involvement in leisure activities' (ibid)

Research has pointed out the contested nature of RSI as an occupational disease. According to Ewan *et al.*, 'the debate about RSI, the medical uncertainty about its status, and the attempts by employers and insurers to contain their liability for compensation payments by discrediting sufferers created an environment which was often felt as hostile'; one respondent's account given by them of a consultation with a surgeon has already been quoted above (p. 56).

Currently contested are the illnesses suffered by members of the armed forces ('Gulf War Syndrome') since their return from the Gulf War, and by sheep farmers, allegedly as a result of using organophosphorous sheep dips. It is clear that when people believe their health has been damaged by their working environment they might face considerable difficulty in having their claim recognised by their employers and others.

Link exercise 5.3 Being believed

Review the section in Chapter 4 on 'being believed' (pages 56–9) and write a paragraph to explain why employees who believe their job has made them ill may find it difficult to convince their employer of this. (Hint: why would employers be reluctant to admit liability? Is it always clear what causes illness?)

Employment and health: are the statistics for occupational disease valid? The contested nature of occupational diseases might lead us to question the validity of statistics on workplace ill-health.

Morbidity statistics are socially constructed – this was shown in Bellaby's (1990) study of absenteeism in a Staffordshire pottery. The management, fellow workers and the medical profession all had a role to play in the creation of 'genuine sickness' at work. The employees themselves shared the norm of being expected to put on a brave face if they were in pain or under stress at work. GPs, on the other hand, would sometimes word medical certificates in such a way that the sufferer qualified for company sick pay, (for example hyperemesis rather than morning sickness and 'anxiety state' rather than caring for a sick relative).

In the case of accidents at work the Health and Safety Commission (HSC, 1994) estimates that nearly all fatal accidents are reported and recorded. However, although employers are required to report major injuries and injuries that result in more than three days' absence from work, the HSC estimates a low rate of overall reporting (below 40 per cent), with wide variations between industries.

Employment and health: what are the likely effects of recent changes at work? It is important to take account of changes at work. For example the threat of RSI has been reduced by the spread of automation. In terms of accidents at work the HSC (1994) points out that the fatal injury rate of 1.2 per 100 000 employees is a quarter of the rate in the 1960s and less than half the rate in the 1970s. (However it must be remembered that the traditionally most dangerous sectors, such as agriculture, coal mining, construction and manufacturing, have been employing fewer and fewer people while the safer service sector has grown).

Details from the HSC about action taken to deal with breaches of health and safety legislation must be interpreted with caution: they might tell us more about changes in enforcement practices than changes in the working environment. Between 1981 and 1993 the number of health and safety enforcement notices issued increased from 15 000 to nearly 40 000. However the number of actual prosecutions fell from over 2600 in 1989 to about 1800 in 1993.

However many employees are experiencing changes in their market situation (for example job security, type of contract) and work situation (for example responsibilities, pace of work) as businesses seek to reduce costs and become more adaptable and competitive.

Some sociologists point out that since the 1970s Fordism has been replaced by post-Fordism. Fordism refers to the system where standardised goods are mass produced using assembly lines and large numbers of relatively low-skilled employees, each specialising in a particular part of the production process. Post-Fordism is associated with:

- Developments in technology that allow frequent modifications in products.
- Markets that demand smaller batches of goods, delivered promptly.
- More highly skilled and flexible workers who are willing and able

to switch to whichever activity is a priority at the time. The multiskilling of employees makes them more flexible in terms of what work they can do; and contracts of employment that, for example, specify annualised hours or zero hours (i.e. no specified hours per week) allow greater working-time flexibility.

- A desire to minimise costs in order to compete effectively. In terms of goods this means minimising the cost of holding stock and operating a 'just-in-time' delivery system. In terms of staff, costs are reduced by reducing the size of the core labour force (that is, key employees who have relatively well-paid and secure full-time employment). Other staff, the 'peripheral' workers, are less securely employed; and some will be directly employed by the company (perhaps on part-time, temporary or zero-hour (no-specified hours) contracts) whilst others might be brought in from agencies as required.

Postmodernists emphasise that post-Fordist firms operate in a global economy. One aspect of globalisation is the relative ease with which multinational companies can switch production from one location/ country to another; this creates increased uncertainty for employees.

Although it is dangerous to make sweeping generalisations about the changes affecting firms, it is clear that many employees have experienced significant changes in their market and work situation. In addition to the uncertainty felt by employees (particularly in organisations that have made redundancies through 'downsizing' or 'delayering'), Thompson (1993) suggests that many employees are now experiencing a greater intensity of work, with more pressure and often additional monitoring of performance.

Occupational psychologists have suggested that the increasing level of stress in the post-Fordist workplace (affecting white collar as well as manual workers) may well have a harmful effect on employees' health. In other words the 'casualties' of occupational change may include those who are *not* made redundant, as well as those who are. It has been suggested that 'presenteeism' (feeling obliged to put in long hours at work) is a new and potentially damaging adaptation to the working environment. Clearly more research is needed.

Exercise 5.18 Investigating the impact of change at work

 Interview one employed person (for example a family member or friend) who has been working for at least three years. Ask them about recent changes at their workplace: you will need to decide on a number of topics you wish to cover, though they might suggest others: for example a change in technology, staffing levels, organisation of work, pace of work, management style and supervision, health and safety, contract of employment. Also ask them whether they feel that the changes at work are having any effect on their (or their colleagues') health.

What is the relationship between unemployment and health?

The reappearance of high levels of unemployment in the 1980s and 1990s makes the investigation of the complex issue of the relationship between unemployment and health increasingly important. There is growing evidence that mortality and physical and mental illness are greater among the unemployed; there is also evidence that this extends to the children and partners of the unemployed. In addition there is the issue, raised above, of the extent to which the health of those who have work is adversely affected by changing working conditions and the threat, if not the fact, of unemployment during periods of recession.

The link between unemployment and ill health could of course be an artefact: the unemployed may have more time and motivation than the employed to have themselves defined as 'ill', and social class might be operating as an extraneous variable – the unemployment rate is higher among those in lower social classes, and it has already been established that ill-health is greater in lower social classes. Social selection could also be a factor: ill-health could be the cause rather than the result of unemployment. However evidence from longitudinal studies (for example Morris *et al.*, 1994) suggests that unemployment actually does cause ill-health. A range of factors are likely to be involved here: the material effects of unemployment are likely to be significant, especially if unemployment is prolonged, contributing not only to the physical problems of poverty (for example diet and housing) but also to higher levels of stress and demoralisation. Being unemployed is disruptive of social routines and social contacts and can undermine self-worth and sense of purpose. The behavioural patterns adopted as a response to unemployment may themselves be health damaging (for example less exercise, more smoking).

What is the relationship between loss of employment and mortality?

Morris *et al.* (1994) studied a sample of 6191 men aged 40–59 in order to examine the link between unemployment and early retirement and mortality. The men were chosen at random from one general practice in 24 towns. Initial information was collected from the sample and five years later a postal questionnaire was distributed. This provided information on employment, social class, health and lifestyle (for example smoking, drinking). Over the next 5.5 years any deaths among the members of the sample were recorded.

During the 5.5-year follow-up period 379 of the sample died. What was noticeable was the higher mortality rate for those who had been unemployed or had retired during the study compared with those who had been continuously employed. This difference remained when the results were adjusted to take account of confounding variables (for example smoking, drinking, social class, pre-existing disease, age):

Employment status	Sample	Deaths*	Relative risk of dying
Continuously employed	4412	174	1.00
Unemployed, not due to illness	923	68	1.47
Retired, not due to illness	479	59	1.86
Unemployed/retired due to illness	377	78	3.14

* The majority of the deaths related to heart disease and cancer.
(*Source*: Adapted from J. K. Morris, D. G. Cook and A. G. Shaper, 'Loss of employment and mortality', *BMJ*, vol. 308, 1994, p. 1135.)

This study suggests there is a causal relationship between unemployment/early retirement and increased mortality in men. The relationship cannot simply be explained by social selection (those who were unemployed/retired because of illness are considered separately in the final row of the table). Nor can the relationship easily be explained by the unhealthy lifestyle of the unemployed/retired: the study took into account the smoking and alcohol consumption of sample members. With regard to retirement, the study did not distinguish between those who were happy to take retirement and those who were pressured into retirement by their employer.

Morris *et al.* conclude that loss of employment (through unemployment or retirement) for reasons unrelated to ill health appears to increase the risk of dying, even when adjustment is made for smoking and drinking behaviour.

Exercise 5.19 The relationship between loss of employment and mortality

[i] 1. What evidence is there in the above study that social selection partly explains the higher mortality of the unemployed/early retired?

[i] 2. According to the study, was the risk of mortality greater for those in employment or for those not in employment?

[e] 3. Unhealthy lifestyles could contribute to the mortality of those who are not employed. How far do Morris *et al.* allow for this factor?

[a] 4. Can you suggest any other possible explanations of the mortality of those who were not employed?

[e] 5. In what ways could this research be extended? (Hint: which age group was studied? Which gender? Might ethnicity be an important variable? Did the study focus on morbidity or mortality? Which members of the family might be affected by unemployment? Might the health effects of retirement be different for those who wish to retire compared with those who are forced to retire?)

Further questions remain to be answered if we are to understand fully the relationship between unemployment and ill-health. In particular we might ask: who becomes ill as a result of unemployment and who doesn't? What are the key causes of deteriorating health? What strategies and interventions would be most effective in reducing the health-damaging effects of unemployment? As the 'full employment' associated with the 1950s and 1960s is unlikely to return in the foreseeable future, these issues are of vital importance.

What is the relationship between income and health?

Inequalities in income are also linked to social class differences in health. Here we need to take into account the amount of income, its regularity and how it is distributed among household members. Whilst income can come from a variety of sources (rent, interest and dividends, social security benefits) it is income from employment that decides for most of us whether we have an acceptable standard of living. Furthermore the inequalities we experience during our working lives are likely to continue into retirement, as better-paid jobs are likely to have better pension provision.

The Rowntree Report on Income and Wealth (1995) has shown that:

• The gap between those on high and low income widened significantly during the 1980s.
• Increasing numbers became dependent on income support.

For those in employment:

• The 'real' value of wages for the lowest paid did not change between 1975 and 1992.
• Those with median incomes saw a 35 per cent increase in 'real' value.
• Those with the highest incomes saw a 50 per cent increase.

Blackburn (1991) suggests that low income has a damaging effect on health in three ways: (1) the lack of resources (for adequate food or shelter) can make one vulnerable to physical illness; (2) the lack of control over one's circumstances can be psychologically damaging; and (3) the coping strategies adopted by those on low income may lead to behaviour that damages health. She suggests that smoking by mothers may be seen as a mechanism for coping with the tensions of bringing up children in poverty.

Income is an important influence on diet. Studies of low-income groups (who spend a larger *proportion* of their income on food than the better off but less in *absolute terms*) show that lack of money limits the type and amount of food consumed. The National Children Homes' (1991) study of 350 poor families showed many would buy healthier foods (for example fruit, lean meat, vegetables) if they had more money, and that 20 per cent of parents had gone hungry in the month before the survey because they lacked money for food.

Studies of low-income families suggest they are not simply part of 'a culture of poverty'; rather their behaviour can be seen as a rational response to the 'situational constraints' that they face: Graham (1984) suggests that a mother who decides not to visit a clinic but instead to spend the fare on food can be making a rational decision, even though an outsider might interpret this as irresponsible behaviour.

Link exercise 5.4   Gender and smoking

 Examine Item C in Chapter 6 (page 145) and write a paragraph to explain why it is important to consider not just the link between income and smoking, but the link between gender, income and smoking.

Phillimore *et al.* (1994) examined mortality rates between 1981 and 1991 in 678 wards in the north of England. They constructed an index of material deprivation (based on unemployment, car owner-ship, housing tenure and household overcrowding) as a way of meas-uring deprivation in each ward. The results showed a close relationship between material deprivation and mortality, and that between 1981 and 1991 (a decade of widening inequalities in income) there was a widening of health inequalities. In particular, in poor areas there was a substantial increase in the mortality of men aged 15–44:

| | Standard mortality rate | |
	1981–3	1989–91
Most deprived decile	145	158
Least deprived decile	84	81

(*Source*: Adapted from P. Phillimore, A. Beattie and P. Townsend, 'Widening inequality of health in northern England, 1981–1991', *BMJ*, vol. 308, 1994, p. 1126.)

What is the relationship between housing and health?

The specific problems of the homeless are examined later. Neverthe-less there are many other aspects of housing that can affect health: the location of housing brings in aspects such as noise level, atmos-pheric pollution and the availability of services such as shops and transport; the design and maintenance of housing brings in aspects such as the level of crime, vandalism and noise, the availability of safe play space, the cost of heating, the incidence of damp, conden-sation and insect/rodent infestation, and the risk of fire. Those on low incomes are more likely to be exposed to these risks since a lack of resources is likely to limit their choice of housing. For example Acheson (1990) suggested that houses in multiple occupation could be especially dangerous where families have to share bathrooms, toilets and kitchens and where services such as sanitation and fire escapes are overburdened.

Social policy and material/structural explanations of ill-health

There is clearly an interrelationship between the cultural explanation examined earlier and the material/structural explanation of social class inequalities in health. The way people choose to behave cannot be divorced from their social circumstances: those in deprived circumstances may find their choices severely limited and the choices they do make are directed more by the need to cope with immediate problems rather than to plan for the long term.

Acceptance of the material/structural explanations of class inequalities in health leads to a consideration of social policies that would change the social structure in some way. In the case of Marxists, these proposals may be dramatic (that is, the removal of capitalism); the Beveridge Report (Beveridge, 1942), with its proposals for the establishment of the welfare state, identified the need for more modest policies to tackle the five social evils of idleness, want, squalor, ignorance and ill-health. Much of the recent research into health inequalities emphasises the need for policies to reduce social inequalities (for example Phillimore *et al.*, 1994).

Exercise 5.20   *Social policy and material/structural inequality*

1. Copy the table below, and in the right-hand column suggest social policies that might help tackle the structural problems listed in the left-hand column. (Hint: insert the following suggestions in the appropriate place:

   - Local authority funding for the construction of high-quality council housing.
   - Financial incentives to companies to take on more staff.
   - Introduction of a minimum (and maximum?) wage.
   - Adoption of European health and safety regulations.
   - An uprating of welfare benefits such as income support.

Structural problem	Possible social policy
Unhealthy working environments	
Low-paid employees	
High levels of unemployment	
Poor-quality housing	
Poverty among welfare claimants	

2. The New Right may not support the sort of policies listed in your table. Match up the two halves of the following sentences to identify some of their likely criticisms; you can also add some of your own:

- Reforms that would require tax increases . . .
- If market forces are left unrestricted . . .
- More generous welfare benefits . . .
- There are already too many regulations affecting businesses . . .
- A big differential between those on high and low pay . . .

(a) which raise costs and make our businesses less competitive in the global market.

(b) eventually everyone will benefit as prosperity trickles down.

(c) is necessary if people are to have the incentive to work harder.

(d) would not be accepted by the electorate and would reduce people's choice about how to spend their money.

(e) will encourage irresponsible behaviour and create a dependency culture.

The role of the health services

Social class differences in morbidity and mortality might, in part at least, be explained by the role of the health care system. The intention of the NHS was for health care to be available to all on the basis of need, not social class. It is therefore important to question whether different social classes have similar access to care, whether the use they make of the services reflects their health needs and whether the quality of care and treatment received is similar. Cultural factors (for example people's knowledge about and attitude towards health care) and structural factors (for example the availability and cost of medical services) might both be important.

Access to care

Not all social classes have equal access to health care. Factors such as where you live, your income, car ownership, working hours and knowledge can affect your access to care.

Link exercise 5.5 Social class and access to private health care

1. Look at the table in Exercise 10.14 (page 278) and the paragraphs that follow, then write a paragraph summarising the link between class and private health insurance.

2. Briefly explain the pattern you have just summarised.

3. List the reasons why people use private medicine.

The 'inverse care law' (Tudor-Hart, 1971) suggests that 'the availability of good medical care tends to vary inversely with the needs of the population served'. In other words, more prosperous areas tend to be better provided with medical services (that is, better funded and more attractive to medical personnel). Skrimshire (1978) concluded that at the time of his study working-class people had better access to medical care if they lived in a socially mixed area rather than a predominantly working-class area. Rather than the 'inverse care law', we should perhaps talk about the 'inverse care hypothesis'; this would indicate the need to retest it to take account of the effect of changes in the funding and organisation of the health services.

The introduction in 1976 of a national formula for allocating resources for hospital and community health services according to local need did tackle the issue of health spending per head; it had been about 30 per cent higher in the most prosperous regions compared with the poorest. However a change in the formula in 1991 led to a reversal of this pattern, with funding tilting back in favour of the more prosperous south (Whitehead, 1994). In 1994 the government asked economists and statisticians at the University of York to develop a new formula for allocating resources for health care so that they would be directed to the areas of greatest need. The formula took account of levels of unemployment and the number of elderly people living alone in different areas. If implemented fully it would have had the effect of redistributing resources from the south to the north and from the shire counties to the inner cities. Critics now suggest that because the formula was only partially implemented it had the effect of increasing resources to the more affluent south-east, and reducing them to areas of greater need such as Manchester and Liverpool.

The reduction in the number of dentists providing NHS (rather than private) treatment, the withdrawal of free eye tests, and even the ability of GPs to remove patients from their lists, might all limit access to care for those in the lower social classes.

GP attacked for removing 60-a-day smoker from list

'A GP who does not like the smell of cigarettes, and is refusing to treat an elderly arthritis patient who smokes up to 60 a day, has been roundly criticised by fellow doctors and patient groups.

The GP wrote to Elizabeth Pratt, 75, informing her that her name has now been removed from his patient list. The letter states: "I find that I am unable to tolerate the environment within your home. I am a non-smoker, and I find the heavy odour of cigarette smoke in your flat makes my eyes water, my chest feel tight and my clothes smell."

Last night, Mrs Pratt's daughter, Janet King, with whom Mrs Pratt lives, reacted furiously to the doctor's actions. "At 75 you have earned yourself a doctor, surely," she said. "This could open the floodgates (...) to doctors being selective about their patients."

The GP's actions have renewed fears about the creation of a group of NHS patients whose social behaviour or moral beliefs are limiting their chances of treatment. A GP in Presteigne, on the Welsh border, came under fire last year after removing eight children from his patient list because their parents did not want them immunised.

The Patients' Association has said it is increasingly concerned about the number of patients being struck off GP's lists for apparently superficial reasons. In some cases cost is thought to be a factor with chronically ill patients who require expensive drugs, although hard evidence of this is scarce.

The British Medical Association said that a dislike of cigarettes was "insufficient reason" for a GP to strike off a patient.

An estimated 85 000 patients were removed from GP's lists in 1993–94. An attempt to have the law changed so that GPs could only remove a patient under clearly defined circumstances, such as violent behaviour, failed last year.'

(Source: Liz Hunt, Independent, 26 February 1996.)

ITEM I   *Exercise 5.21   Patient lists*

i   1. In Item I, what reasons are mentioned for the possible removal of patients from GPs' lists?

a   2. What other reasons do you think might lead a GP to wish to remove a patient?

a e   3. If there was evidence that patients were removed from lists on the grounds of (a) an unhealthy lifestyle and (b) the need for expensive treatment, would this affect some social classes more than others? Why?

i   4. Refer to the section in Chapter 10 headed 'What are the criticisms of GP fundholding?'; criticism (5) is called 'cream-skimming' (page 272). Read this criticism and write a paragraph to summarise the evidence on whether or not GP fundholders 'cream-skim' the healthier (cheaper) patients.

Use made of medical services

The Black Report (Townsend and Davidson, 1982) showed that at the time of the report the middle class made greater use of a range of services, including ante- and post-natal care, family planning, dentistry, immunisation and cancer screening. Whitehead (1992) agreed that 'there is plenty of evidence lower occupational classes make less use of preventative services for themselves and their children'. Recent research suggests that underusage of services by the working class remains an issue.

ITEM J

Dental attendance and socioeconomic group: Manchester Health Needs Survey, 1992

Time since last visit	Non-manual (%)		Manual (%)	
	Male	Female	Male	Female
Less than 6 months	38.4	46.6	25.8	33.6
6 months–1 year	18.5	22.7	17.2	19.8
1–2 years	15.1	11.4	15.4	17.7
Over 2 years	27.9	19.1	41.3	28.7

(Source: Manchester Health Needs Survey, Manchester Public Health Resource Centre, 1993, Topic Report 3, Dental Health, 1993.)

ITEM J **Exercise 5.22 Social class and under usage of dental services**

[e] 1. This data was collected by postal questionnaire. What factors might affect the validity of data collected from a postal questionnaire?

[i] 2. What social class and gender patterns are shown in Item J?

[i] 3. What proportion of people in the groups shown are meeting the British Dental Association recommendation of a check-up every six months?

[a] 4. What factors might explain low dental attendance? How could they be tackled? (Hint: for example by the government.)

Only a minority of men and women are meeting the target of six-monthly check-ups, with men and the working class being least likely to attend. Why is this? According to the Manchester Health Survey (1993) many people in Manchester said they did not see any immediate need for dental treatment, but this was not the only reason for non-attendance: in fact 47 per cent of those who had not visited a dentist for over two years felt they needed dental treatment. Other reasons mentioned in the study included the relatively low number of dentists per head of population in Manchester, fear of the dentist, the image of the practice, the cost of treatment and difficulty in getting to the dentist (for example because of work or disability). Cost (with rising NHS dental charges and more dentists concentrating on private treatment) is clearly one (but only one) factor in improving dental health and reducing social class inequalities. In Manchester 11 per cent of non-manual and 23 per cent of manual workers had no natural teeth, statistics that suggest there is scope for improving the dental health of manual workers in particular (ibid.)

The General Household Survey (1992) reported that 36 per cent of professional respondents had had an eye test in the 12 months prior to the survey; this figure fell to 27 per cent for unskilled manual workers. Interestingly, despite these figures women in the professional group were less likely than women in the unskilled manual category to wear glasses – 81 per cent of the professionals had paid for their eye test, whereas only 51 per cent of the unskilled manual workers had done so.

What about visits to the doctor? The General Household Survey (1992) showed that members of the working class were slightly more likely than the middle class to have consulted their GP in the previous 14 days, but this would be expected in view of the higher level of reported illness among the working class. The difficulty here is for researchers to relate the number of visits to a GP for each social class with the amount of illness people in that class experience: in other words, to relate need for a GP with use of a GP.

Exercise 5.23   The cost of health care

Cost might limit the use of health services, especially among the working class.

1. When the NHS was established it was free of charge; list some of the charges that are now made for health care. (Hint: examine the previous three paragraphs.)

2. Find out which groups are exempt from these charges (for example, ask a pharmacist.)

3. Are there any other 'costs' involved in the decision to seek health care (for example if you are employed?) Why might these affect working-class patients more? (Hint: you could check Graham's (1984) example in the earlier section of this chapter on 'the relationship between income and health'.)

Quality of care

A number of studies that have looked at consultations with GPs have noted social class differences. For example Cartwright and O'Brien (1976) suggested that middle-class patients are given longer consultations, during which they ask the doctor more questions and discuss more problems than working-class patients. The Black Report

(Townsend and Davidson, 1982) concluded that middle-class patients tend to receive better care from their GP.

Boulton *et al.* (1986) investigated the influence of patients' social class on consultations with GPs. The 328 patients taking part were divided into service, intermediate and working classes using the Hope–Goldthorpe classification of occupations. Their consultations were tape recorded and later transcribed; the patients were also interviewed at home within a week of the consultation.

During the consultation it was found that middle-class patients tended to adopt more active strategies (for example giving their own lay diagnosis of the problem, or asking the doctor for further explanation). However there was no social class difference in the duration of the consultations, nor in the amount of explanation the doctor actually gave to the patients – in fact the doctor often controlled the conversation in such a way that the patient's request for more information was not met. There was some class difference in terms of whether the patient misunderstood and/or rejected the doctor's advice:

	Social class (%)		
	Service	Intermediate	Working
Misunderstood at least one important element	30	34	42
Rejected at least one important element	15	18	13

(*Source*: Adapted from M. Boulton *et al.*, 'Social Class and the GP Consultation', *Sociology of Health & Illness*, vol. 8, no. 4, 1986.)

Boulton *et al.* concluded that middle-class patients do not get a better GP service than working-class patients, but they point out that their study did not measure whether middle-class patients were more successful in obtaining tests, referrals to consultants or prescriptions. They suggest that future research should focus more on the outcome of consultations rather than what goes on in them. Their sample was drawn only from the south-east of England; could this make a difference? One social class difference in outcome of consultations is shown by the General Household Survey (1992): manual workers are more likely to be issued with prescriptions than non-manual workers.

A study by Crombie (1984) indicated that GPs were more likely to arrange repeat appointments for patients in Class V, suggesting that doctors felt Class V patients needed more help with coping with illness than patients from other classes.

One important decision GPs have to make is whether it is necessary to refer patients for tests and/or to a consultant. Findlay *et al.* (1991) looked at 500 patients who were eligible for a test for heart disease (coronary angiography). The patients were given a social deprivation score (based on social class, car ownership, overcrowding and unemployment). It was found that patients with the lowest deprivation scores (that is, those least likely to suffer from heart disease) were more likely to be referred for an angiography than those in the most deprived group, which had a higher mortality rate for heart disease.

The 'professional control' view suggests that doctors' control over consultations ensures that all patients, regardless of social background, are treated similarly. Findlay's study seems to challenge this view: perhaps more knowledgeable and articulate middle-class patients are able to influence the doctors' judgment, or perhaps the doctors' own judgments are leading to some form of class bias. On the other hand, the General Household Survey (1992) showed no social class differences for males in hospital referrals: 14 per cent of both non-manual and manual male workers who had visited their doctors in the 14 days prior to the survey were referred to a hospital. For females there was a small class difference: 15 per cent of non-manual and 12 per cent of manual female workers were referred.

There is some evidence to suggest that patients from higher social classes have a relatively better chance of surviving a serious illness. For example the incidence of breast cancer is considerably higher in Class I (registration ratio: 121) than in Class V (registration ratio: 78); however the mortality ratios are fairly similar: in Class I the standard mortality rate (SMR) is 109, in Class V it is 94. Quality of treatment received could be a factor: perhaps middle-class patients are more likely to 'win' in what has been described as a cancer care 'lottery' (*Guardian* 25 April 1995) owing to variations in the treatment offered by different hospitals. (A 1989 survey by the Royal College of Radiologists revealed 51 different ways of treating 45 year old women with localised breast tumours, as suggested by the sample of 170 consultants questioned: *Guardian* 25 April 1995). Obviously other factors, such as how early a patient presents for treatment, will also affect the outcome of treatment.

What is the relationship between locality and health?

It is not surprising to find a relationship between locality (that is, where one lives, works or spends one's leisure time) and health. This can be seen on a global scale, with developing countries generally having higher rates of mortality and morbidity than industrialised societies, but there are also noticeable health variations between industrialised countries. The figures for maternal mortality are informative: Worldwatch estimated that the rates are often 100 times higher in developing countries as a result of illiteracy, poverty, poor nutrition, large families and limited health services (*Guardian* 3 January 1992); the rate in Britain, at just over six maternal deaths per 100 000 births, contrasts with four in Sweden, 11 in France and 15 in Hungary (1986–88, Social Trends, no. 22, 1992).

Are definitions of locality problematic?

If we are trying to identify links between health and locality in Britain, how we operationalise the word locality is crucial. A north–south health divide can be identified if one divides the country into regional health authorities (there are 14 in England). Mortality from heart disease and stroke is higher in the north, a factor that has been linked to lifestyle factors (for example heavier smoking, fattier diet), although Variations in Health (DoH, 1995) argues that much of the variation between north and south is still unexplained.

Data from the 14 RHAs, however, shows a more complex picture than a simple north–south divide. For one thing a number of diseases (for example breast cancer, skin cancer) are considerably more prevalent in the south. Secondly, within the broad categories of 'south' and 'north' there are marked variations between one area and another: for example the SMR in 1992 for cervical cancer was 65 in the South West Thames Area but 108 in South East Thames.

If the country is divided into slightly smaller areas (as has been done in the Medical Research Council's Atlases of Mortality), the variations between adjacent areas are intriguing: why should the mortality rate for testicular cancer be so much higher in Dorset than in the neighbouring county of Somerset, which in turn has a higher mortality rate for skin cancer? Phillimore *et al.* (1994) took an even smaller unit of analysis (678 wards in the north of England) and found that mortality was highest in the most materially deprived wards (measured by unemployment, car ownership, housing tenure and household overcrowding).

An OPCS study (1995) divided England into 366 districts and examined the death rates between 1989 and 1993. It found that Manchester was the least healthy place in England for males, with Corby the least healthy for women. Again material factors appeared to be important as the healthiest areas tended to be in the south; however some of the least healthy areas were in the less affluent parts of London (for example Hammersmith, Fulham, Lambeth).

Some illnesses may be very localised and therefore patterns will only be discovered if small areas are analysed. For example clusters of non-Hodgkins lymphoma and leukaemia have been identified (though as yet not fully understood) near Sellafield and two other nuclear plants. Research into the 'sick building syndrome' attempted to identify features of specific buildings that were detrimental to health.

Link exercise 5.6 Low-weight births in Manchester

Look again at Item F (page 87).

| i | 1. How were low-weight births distributed across Manchester (Hint: were they higher in some areas than others?)

| i | a | 2. Can you find any link between low-weight births and social inequality in Manchester?

The distribution of some diseases may not conveniently match administrative boundaries. A current area of research is the possible health implications of living near power transmission lines. If pollution from vehicles has harmful effects, then these might be most noticeable among those living closest to busy roads. The difference between rural and urban areas might be significant for certain illnesses.

Are explanations of the link between locality and health problematic?

Extraneous variables must be considered when trying to explain local variations in health. The patterns we identify might be largely caused by factors considered elsewhere in this book:

- Social class differences: some areas may be predominantly middle class (or working class); the cultural (for example smoking) and material (for example housing) factors associated with social class might therefore explain differences in health between areas.
- Age differences: some areas have a younger population than others, and one would expect to find a different pattern of morbidity and mortality in a retirement area such as Eastbourne than on a university campus.
- Ethnicity: ethnic minorities are overrepresented in certain localities (for example Brent in London), and ethnicity can affect health patterns.
- Differences in unemployment rates: the link between unemployment and ill-health has already been established, and unemployment rates vary across the country.

Even if these variables are controlled, other factors may need to be considered to account for variations in health between one area and another:

Link exercise 5.7 Regional differences and extraneous variables

| i | Look again at Item E (page 86). Was the higher mortality rate in the north explained by the variable of class, or was the higher mortality still apparent when Classes I/II and IV/V were studied separately?

Additional factors that might explain the link between locality and health

- Regional differences in culture and lifestyle (for example diet, alcohol consumption).
- Differences in the type of work available (and its associated health risks) in different areas.
- Differences in environmental risks (for example air pollution, climate).
- Differences in the quality and availability of housing.
- Differences in the availability, use and quality of health care (for example GP fundholding, hospital waiting lists).

Link exercise 5.8   Distribution of GP fundholders

Turn to Chapter 10, Exercise 10.8 (page 270).

[i] 1. In your own words, summarise the information provided in the table about the regional distribution of GP fundholders.

[e] 2. Why might this be important?

Exercise 5.24   Health in your locality

[a] 1. Identify factors in your locality that might affect how healthy or unhealthy the area is.

[a] 2. How do the factors listed above influence your area? You could consult various sources of secondary information (for example local newspaper articles, local census data) or speak to a health professional to help you identify important factors.

What is the relationship between homelessness and health?

The question of whether a distinctive underclass has developed in Britain (and America), and if so, what has caused its emergence, has led to a debate between the New Right and the Left in the 1980s and 1990s. The underclass is distinguished from the rest of the working class according to various criteria. Economic marginalisation (that is, few resources because of dependency on low-paid, insecure work or welfare benefits) is a central theme. On the right, Murray (1984) explains the underclass partly in cultural terms (that is, its members have developed a lifestyle and set of attitudes that prevent them from competing effectively in the job market), but he also blames the welfare state for providing the benefits that allowed a dependency culture to develop. On the left (for example Dahrendorf, 1987), the explanation focuses more on structural changes in society, especially in the labour market, which reduce employability and thus help to create a jobless underclass.

If a recurrent theme in the underclass debate is the issue of marginalisation, it is clear that the homeless lack what is a basic necessity as well as one of main symbols of economic success: a home of their own.

Why study homelessness?

Social class is a socially constructed way of dividing a population into groups. One group of people who have very different life and health chances are the homeless, the number of whom is increasing. Their experience of homelessness is likely to have an impact on their health, yet research evidence is limited. If we divide the population into broad social classes the homeless are likely to become invisible. Likewise occupational classifications of social class are of limited value when studying the homeless, since most are not currently employed.

Graham (1995) has pointed out that the homeless are particularly likely to be omitted when official statistics are collected. For example the General Household Survey, the Family Expenditure Survey and the Annual Health Survey for England take as their sampling frame private addresses on the postcode address file. Therefore rough sleepers and those living in hostels or bed and breakfast accommodation lack private addresses and are excluded from these studies.

Exercise 5.25   Quantifying rough sleepers in Britain

The 1991 census produced the following information on the number of people sleeping rough in Britain:

	England	Scotland	Wales
Male	2243	124	30
Female	407	21	2

(*Source*: Adapted from: Communal establishments, Census 1991, London: HMSO, 1993.)

e 1. Outline the problems census enumerators would face in trying to produce accurate figures for rough sleepers. (Hint: is locating rough sleepers a problem? Are they likely to stay in the same location? Why might some wish to conceal their location? Will all wish to be included in the study? Are the eventual results likely to underestimate or overestimate the problem?)

e 2. Census data is a 'snapshot' taken once every ten years (April). Why does this limit the value of the evidence to sociologists? (Hint: are there likely to be variations in the number of rough sleepers from day to day, seasonally, or from year to year?)

The Royal College of Physicians' report *Homelessness and Ill Health* (Connelly and Crown, 1994) attempted to bring together the available evidence on this group, as follows.

How is homelessness defined?

The *official homeless* are those legally recognised as homeless by local authorities under the 1985 Housing Act and placed in (often temporary) accommodation.

The *unofficial homeless* are not officially regarded as homeless; they sleep on the streets or find themselves places in night shelters, hostels or bed and breakfast (B & B) hotels.

Who are the homeless?

The *official homeless* are mainly couples with children, single parents, pregnant women or people who are vulnerable (for example because of mental illness or disability). In 1992, 170 000 households in Britain were officially homeless, an increase of 80 000 since 1982.

The *unofficial homeless* are mainly single, white, 18–59 year-old males who are not in employment. The majority have no educational qualifications and many have spent time in residential institutions such as children's homes, prisons and general or psychiatric hospitals (Anderson *et al.*, 1993).

What is known about the health of the homeless families?

Case reports by health professionals (for example health visitors) indicate higher levels of mental and physical illness among those in B & B accommodation. Connelly and Crown (1994) conclude that 'the social and financial disadvantages of homeless families make healthy lifestyles unattainable in most instances'. However 'the health of some people may be poor before they become homeless, especially political refugees and those recently arrived from abroad'.

Exercise 5.26 Health and homelessness

Refer to the next three paragraphs to help you answer these questions:

[i] 1. What variables associated with living in bed and breakfast accommodation might affect physical or mental health?

[i][e] 2. Is time likely to be an important variable in examining the health effects of B & B accommodation?

Connelly and Crown (1994) state that there are difficulties associated with hygiene when a family lives, sleeps and eats in one room (possibly leading to higher levels of infection such as gastroentiritis), and poor nutrition if inadequate cooking facilities/frequent take-away meals/low income/limited knowledge about nutrition are involved. Lack of safe space for children to play leads to high accident rates and hinders their development. The stress caused to parents and children living in a confined space with limited income, status, activities and social contacts can damage relationships and mental health. Behavioural problems and delayed development in children have been noted, which cannot be helped by the fact that children in B & B accommodation can face frequent changes of school.

Time is likely to be an important variable in assessing the health effects of B & B accommodation on families. Firstly, a short period of residence might have fewer effects than a longer period. Secondly, the effects on children might depend on their age. Thirdly, some effects might be short term and relatively easy to identify, but long-term health effects (for example, if children suffer increased ill-health later in life) would be difficult to identify without adequate longitudinal studies.

To know whether living in a B & B actually makes people less healthy, researchers would need (a) to know how healthy the people were when they became homeless, and (b) to compare homeless people with a control group who are not homeless.

Exercise 5.27 The Parkside survey

The Parkside survey (Victor, 1992) compared 319 homeless families with a sample of inner-city residents in the Parkside Health Authority in London and other residents in the North-West Thames region. As three quarters of the homeless were in the 16–34 age group, age was an extraneous variable that had to be taken into account. The results of the survey were as follows:

Health indicator	Rates for homeless/control
Chronic limiting illness/disability lasting 1 year+	Double among the homeless (34%)
Acute illness in last two weeks	Higher among the homeless
Hospital admission rate for children	Double among the homeless
Mental morbidity (based on 12-item general health questionnaire)	More than double among the homeless (45%)
Smoking	Higher among the homeless
Regular alcohol consumption	Lower among the homeless
Participation in vigorous exercise	Lower among the homeless
Daily intake of fresh fruit and vegetables	Lower among the homeless
Preventative health: cervical smear takeup	Similar
child immunisation	Slightly lower among the homeless

(*Source*: Adapted from C. Victor, 'Health status of the temporarily homeless population and residents of North West Thames Region', *BMJ*, vol. 305, 1992.)

 1. Explain why we have to consider the variable of age when comparing the health of homeless families with those who are not homeless.

2. Using the table above, write a clear comparison of the homeless with the control group, referring to:
   (a) The health of the two groups.
   (b) Their lifestyle.
   (c) Their use of preventative health services.

What is known about the health of the (unofficial) single homeless?

Is useful evidence available?

Ideally evidence should be representative of the group being studied. The absence of a complete sampling frame of the unofficial homeless means that the samples used in studies might be biased (for example some studies look at the health of those attending clinics for homeless people: could they be less healthy than non-attenders?) Secondly, the method of data collection should give information that is as complete as possible about mortality and morbidity (for example few studies involve a clinical examination of the homeless). Thirdly, a control group is needed to enable the health of the homeless to be compared with the rest of the population, taking into account the effect of extraneous variables such as gender and social class. Connelly and Crown (1994) conclude there have been no ideal studies of the health of the homeless in Britain.

What does the available evidence suggest?

Connelly and Crown (1994) compared 19 studies conducted in Europe and the USA and found considerable similarities. Higher mortality was linked particularly to an excess number of deaths due to violence, suicide, accidents, alcohol-related diseases and respiratory disorders. Single homeless people were also found to have higher rates of morbidity for a wide range of physical illnesses, for example respiratory illness (including pneumonia and tuberculosis), foot problems and skin infections.

Why do the single homeless experience worse physical health?

* Physical illness can cause homelessness: the selection effect suggests that illness can reduce ability to maintain income and a home, and those who are ill are not always allocated housing on grounds of medical priority. Epilepsy might be more a cause of homelessness than an effect of homelessness.
* Homelessness can cause physical illness: for example lack of adequate shelter can increase the risk of illness through exposure to

the elements, poor facilities for personal hygiene or lack of security. Foot problems can be linked to shoes that are often badly fitted, often subjected to wet conditions and often worn 24 hours a day to prevent theft.

- Homelessness can prolong physical illness: for example the homeless might have poor access to health care and find it difficult to follow the treatment suggested; this could be a reason for the development of drug-resistant TB among the homeless.
- The lifestyle of the homeless can damage physical health: for example those homeless who abuse alcohol or other drugs or are involved in prostitution are exposed to additional health risks. Heavy smoking among the homeless could be linked to respiratory problems.

Exercise 5.28 Physical illness and homelessness

 Copy the following table and in the right-hand column suggest reasons why the physical illnesses listed are more common among the single homeless.

Illness	Possible causes
Respiratory illness	
Foot problems	
Neurological problems, including epilepsy	
Alcohol-related diseases	

Why do the single homeless experience worse mental health?

Evidence suggests that mental disorders, including major disorders such as schizophrenia, are more common among the single homeless. However there is little evidence that homelessness causes schizophrenia. Connelly and Crown (1994) suggest a health selection effect; in other words, schizophrenia increases the likelihood of entering the homeless category. To appreciate how this happens it is necessary to consider (i) the effects of illness on the patient and (ii) the social context which confronts the patient.

(i) Possible effects of schizophrenia:

- Poorer social skills reduce the ability to support oneself.
- Socially unacceptable behaviour can lead to rejection by others.
- Secondary problems, for example depression, increase difficulties.
- Lack of insight into their own problems can lead patients to reject assistance and medication.

(ii) Social context of schizophrenia:

- Limited employment opportunities and a shortage of low-cost housing.
- Loss of contact with family/friends means little support is available.
- Negative attitudes towards the mentally ill in the wider society.
- Problems in providing adequate psychiatric care: 'a shortage of community psychiatric nurses, bureaucratic barriers prevent . . . prompt assistance, failure to follow patients who do not attend appointments, concentration of resources on the less severely ill. Emphasis on patient autonomy . . . meant health workers were unwilling or unable to deflect some patients from action that will make homelessness inevitable' (Connelly and Crown, 1994).

Thus Connelly and Crown suggest that when a 'housing crisis' occurs for a schizophrenic they are unlikely to have the resources to resolve it and are likely to become homeless, frequently ending up in hostels for the homeless where medical support is limited.

Structured exam questions

To help you practise some of the issues and skills learned in this chapter, carry out the following exercises.

Questions

1. Outline and assess different sociological explanations of the continuation of social class inequalities in health and health care. (*25 marks*) (AEB, June 1993)

(a) Read the following student answer to the essay question:

Student answer

(a) There are four main explanations put forward to deal with the continuation of social class inequalities in health. The first of these four explanations is the artefact explanation which states that the number of people in social Class V, where most inequalities in health occur, is declining and therefore the problems of health inequalities are also declining as fewer people are subject to a higher frequency of illness. This approach suggests that health inequalities can be reduced when the numbers within social Class V decline yet further. However there are also social class inequalities between social Class I and social Class IV so the inequality will not necessarily disappear.

(b) An alternative explanation, which is similar to the artefact theory in the sense that no social policy is required to deal with the health inequality, is the social selection explanation, which suggests that people fall into lower classes because they are ill rather than becoming ill because they are in a lower social class. Again according to people who support the social selection explanation there is very little that can be done about health inequalities.

(c) The third explanation is the cultural/behavioural explanation and this was the explanation taken up by Edwina Currie during her time as a minister for health. This explanation states that ill health is due to the unhealthy lifestyle people choose to adopt, for example eating fatty foods and smoking and drinking too much. Working-class people were claimed to lead unhealthy lifestyles and thus they were to blame for their poorer health record.

(d) Finally, the structuralist explanation states there are four main factors affecting health chances: poorer housing, more dangerous and less healthy working conditions, unhealthy lifestyle and unemployment. Poor housing, for example damp and overcrowded, may cause more illness such as respiratory problems. The type of work people do may affect health chances because if a job is more dangerous workers may suffer higher rates of industrial accidents. Unemployment may cause people to have poorer diets and increase in stress levels, which may lead to ill health. The social policy implication of the structural explanation is that the way society is organised needs to change: improve poorer housing, make working conditions safer, reduce unemployment and reduce levels of poverty.

This essay was awarded the following marks:

- Knowledge and understanding: 4/9
- Interpretation and application: 4/9
- Evaluation: 4/9
- Total mark: 12/27

(b) Below is a list of skills comments on how to improve the essay. Link each section (1, 2, 3, 4) on skills to the appropriate paragraph (a, b, c, d) in the essay. Then carry out the improvements to produce a response that applies more recent information to the essay title and applies theories of social class inequalities in a more detailed and relevant way. Suggestions are also made about how to improve the evaluation mark awarded for the essay.

Comment

(1) Knowledge and understanding: the marks gained could be increased by providing relevant detail on social selection and social mobility. Interpretation and application: remember there are two features to the question:

health and health care. The social selection theory is not really related to the question about continued class inequality. The answer might have mentioned that if we accept the social selection theory then continued health inequality between the social classes might be due to increasing downward social mobility. Evaluation: no evaluation was presented of the social selection theory, for example the information on homelessness and social selection in Chapter 5 could have been used to provide evidence of social selection. Evidence against social selection can also be found in Chapter 5.

(2) Knowledge and understanding: more marks could be scored by providing relevant detail about the link between social class and illness as well as social class and health care to address the second part of the essay question, for example the inverse care law proposed by Julian Tudor-Hart (1971). In addition, use Chapter 10 to find out more details on social class and health care inequality. Interpretation and application: to address the issue of continued social class inequality why not mention the recession of the late 1980s and early 1990s, which might have influenced the health chances of the unemployed, for example. You could also use the postmodern debate of globalisation, that is, that goods can be produced all over the world, thus contributing to the decline in manufacturing in Britain in the 1980s, which may have caused the increase in unemployment in the manual job sector. This increase in manual sector unemployment may have contributed to the health inequalities of the working class. Recent evidence in support of the materialist/structural explanation would be useful. Evaluation: criticisms of the structural explanation such as the issue of lifestyle choice being important should be included. The materialist explanation could also be contrasted with the artefact explanation. A conclusion might readdress the issue of gender variations and ethnic and regional variations, of all which contribute to differences in health chances so social class as an isolated variable may be an inadequate focus of an essay on health inequality.

(3) Interpretation and application: the essay should start by interpreting the question carefully, so evidence of social class inequality should be briefly outlined by addressing inequality in the past and present in order to deal with the continuation of social class inequality. Use the information from the Black Report (Townsend and Davidson, 1982) and more recent evidence, for example Whitehead (1992), to suggest that social class inequality in health may still exist. By providing relevant evidence you may also score marks for knowledge and understanding. Evaluation: the candidate could point out that examining social class is problematic because of additional variables, for example gender, ethnicity, age and region. The actual measurement of social class is also problematic, for example the problems involved in using occupational measures of social class (see the section in Chapter 5 on the registrar general's scale) or alternative measures of material deprivation (for example car ownership, housing tenure).

(4) Interpretation and application: claiming that a theory offers a third explanation suggests that no real link to the question is being made. Why not state that a contrasting theory to explain continued social class inequalities in health is the cultural/behavioural theory. Apply evidence in support of this theory to show how it might explain continued social class inequality. Knowledge and understanding: more marks could be gained by outlining evidence on the continuation of social class inequality. More evidence of lifestyle differences between social classes might be used, for example smoking and alcohol consumption. Evidence of visits to doctors by social class might also be examined. Evaluation: provide some criticisms of the cultural explanation, for example people may choose to smoke cigarettes but their material position in society, such as being poor, may influence that decision. (Hint: use the Hilary Graham article on gender and smoking in Exercise 6.9, Chapter 6).

Questions

2. Improve your essay skills by answering the following examination questions:

(a) 'The culture of poverty thesis attempts to explain the poorer health of less advantaged groups in terms of their values and lifestyles.' Assess the evidence for and against this view. (*25 marks*) (AEB, June 1995)

(b) 'The artefact view of health inequalities asserts that the apparent differences between social groups are simply the result of the inability to measure a complex phenomenon such as health.' Critically examine the sociological arguments for and against this view. (*25 marks*) (AEB, November 1995)

Summary

This chapter has highlighted the difficulties of studying the relationship between social class and health; there is a problem of measuring class and a need to control for other variables that affect health (for example locality, gender, ethnicity).

Research has convincingly shown that there is a relationship between social class and both mortality and morbidity. Little support was found for the attempt to explain this away as an 'artefact'. Social selection, cultural and behavioural differences, material and structural inequalities and inequalities in the health care system itself all contribute to an understanding of health inequalities associated with social class. Each explanation was seen to have implications for social policy.

Health inequalities appear to be remarkably persistent. The inequalities identified in the Black Report (Townsend and Davidson, 1982) were echoed by Whitehead (1992); Phillimore *et al.* (1994) suggest they are widening. These researchers favoured material/structural explanations and proposed policies to reduce social inequality. The political climate in the 1980s and 1990s has not favoured the introduction of such policies, although the Department of Health recently published a report on variations in health (DoH, 1995), including class variations. Indeed, widening social inequality, rising unemployment and homelessness, and the introduction of post-Fordist working practices may well be exacerbating health inequalities.

This chapter has stressed the influence of structural inequalities and the way they can influence lifestyle and health. The postmodernists, on the other hand, have emphasised the opportunity for people to make choices about (healthy or unhealthy) lifestyles and have shown that self-identity (including gender and ethnicity) has an impact on health. In the following chapters the relationship between health and gender, ethnicity and age will be examined.

6 The relationship between gender and health

By the end of this chapter you should be able to:

- define 'sex' and 'gender';
- compare the patterns of ill-health for men and women;
- assess the explanations of these patterns;
- evaluate the problems of studying gender and health.

Introduction

This chapter examines the differences in the mortality (death) and morbidity (illness) rates between men and women. It encourages the reader to realise that gender cannot be isolated from issues of social class, ethnicity and age; for example women cannot be treated as a single group of people who share a similar lifestyle: there are social class differences that make women's health experiences extremely varied.

One pattern examined is mortality: on average women appear to survive longer than men. Reasons are offered to explain this phenomenon. A discussion is also provided of the morbidity pattern whereby women visit the doctor more frequently than men. The explanation of the gender difference in morbidity takes into account genetic differences, behavioural and cultural differences, the material and structural causes of ill-health, and problems with the treatment women receive from the health service.

The chapter encourages the reader to be critical of morbidity figures that indicate more women than men visit doctors. This pattern might be reversed if female visits for reproductive reasons are excluded from the GP figures. Therefore men may suffer more illness than women. The reader must view patterns of illness for men and women as problematic.

What is the difference between 'sex' and 'gender'?

Sex refers to the biological characteristics (for example reproductive organs) associated with being male or female. Gender refers to the way men and women think and behave as a result of learning in society. Gender is 'socially constructed' through socialisation (for example by family, friends, television) to create what it is to be a 'man' (masculinity) or a 'woman' (femininity). Gender patterns are likely to vary within and between societies. Gender roles are the parts society expects men and women to play, for example bread-winner and/or housewife.

Some references to men and women use the term 'sex' because they are simply referring to males and females. Others use the term 'gender' to remind us that patterns and explanations of men's and women's behaviour are not necessarily natural but are influenced by society.

Why study the issue of gender and health?

Sociologists often concern themselves with detecting patterns in society, for example do men commit more crime than women? Do working-class pupils perform as well as middle-class pupils in examinations? Do particular ethnic groups suffer higher rates of unemployment? This chapter explores the different male–female patterns of health and illness that researchers have discovered. The fact that health and illness is not distributed evenly between men and women is worth investigating.

Health is an important sociological issue when examining 'life chances': your own health can determine your progress in education and employment; giving up your job due to ill health is likely to affect your income, and in due course the quality of your housing, diet and possibly your children's life chances.

What methodological problems arise when studying gender and health?

The problem of (extra) extraneous variables

A person's health/ill-health is likely to depend on a variety of factors working together. For example a person may be a *young, rich, middle-class, Chinese, woman*: which of these five variables (factors) is most important in determining her health chances? A factor such as very low income may be an important cause of illness for one person but not for someone with an inherited blood disorder. Thus when examining gender and health we must acknowledge that other contributory or even just coincidental factors may play a role. Factors that are coincidental or contributory are called extraneous variables. To help avoid extraneous variables we should ask further questions about men and women, such as whether we should treat them as two single homogeneous groups.

Exercise 6.1 Chronic sickness and gender

The General Household Survey defines a 'longstanding' illness as an illness, disability or infirmity that has been experienced in the past and is likely to persist in the future:

The prevalence of reported longstanding illness by sex, age and socioeconomic group (per cent)

Head of household	Males				Females			
	0–15	16–44	45–64	65+	0–15	16–44	45–64	65+
Non-manual worker	17	21	35	57	14	24	40	61
Manual worker	18	24	47	64	16	24	46	64

(*Source*: General Household Survey, London: HMSO, 1992.)

[i] 1. What definition of socioeconomic group was used in this study?

[i] [e] 2. Does this method of gauging socioeconomic status have any problems? Refer to Chapter 5 to help with your answer.

[i] 3. What pattern seems to exist between the manual and non-manual workers and reported sickness?

[i] 4. Does the evidence show any clear gender differences?

[e] 5. Can gender differences be studied in isolation from social class? Explain your answer.

[a] 6. Identify some additional social factors that might also affect health chances. (Hint: housing and ethnicity.)

Should we treat all men and all women as single groups?

Another problem with studying gender and health is the issue of treating men and women as single groups, all the members of which face similar circumstances and behave in similar ways. We need to break men and women down into smaller groups to compare, for example, the experiences of those who are young with those who are elderly. So when we speak of men and women we need to ask 'of what age?' 'from which social class?' and 'from which ethnic group?' Questions that try to break down a group into smaller components may be called 'pinpointing questions'.

Exercise 6.2 Gender and 'pinpointing questions'

 Try asking a set of pinpointing questions that attempt to break down the groups mentioned in each of the following statements:

1. Females perform better than males at GCSE level (for example from which social class, from single-sex schools or mixed schools, from which ethnic groups?)

2. Males commit more crime than females.

3. Religious membership has decreased over the last fifty years.

4. On average, women live longer than men.

Are the mortality figures valid?

Mortality figures are recorded by doctors, who provide a death certificate stating cause of death when they have examined a recently deceased person. The problem with mortality figures is similar to the problem with suicide figures as they both rest on the doctor's or coroner's diagnosis of the cause of death. Doctors can not always tell how somebody died and the recorded cause of death is not always the underlying disease that has led to death. For instance AIDS victims do not die of a severely damaged immune system as such but of an illness (for example pneumonia) their immune system has been unable to fend off. The play 'A Normal Heart' by Larry Kramer shows how doctors in the early 1980s in New York failed to recognise that many premature homosexual deaths were the result of a single cause, and instead recorded the more obvious symptoms as the official cause of death.

However mortality figures do have advantages and they can provide a wealth of information about the cause of death. Nearly all deaths are registered so the mortality figures are fairly complete, and unlike the figures for illness, mortality figures do not depend on people interpreting their own symptoms and declaring themselves ill.

Are the morbidity figures valid?

Morbidity figures share a common problem with crime figures: they both depend on incidents that have been reported to official recorders: the police in the case of crime and doctors in the case of illness. In both cases the figures depend on the officials recording what has been reported to them. Perhaps women as a group *appear* to be less healthy because they report more of their symptoms to the doctor, whereas men actually suffer more 'illness' despite fewer consultations with their doctor. Statistics on illness can also be obtained from absence from work figures, although these too may suffer from problems of validity: the 'sickness' employees report might not always be genuine. On the other hand some people may attend work when they should really report their symptoms to a doctor.

Nonetheless the morbidity figures are valuable – they inform us of doctors' consultation figures on the absence of health. There is more to ill-health than the extreme end products of fatalities: it is important to know how much and what type of illness people experience during their lives.

What is the relationship between mortality and gender?

There appear to be significant differences between men and women in terms of average life expectancy and cause of death.

What was the situation in the past?

In 1846 the mortality risk was fairly similar for men and women (most people died of infectious diseases such as tuberculosis), but since then it has diverged and women now tend to survive longer than men. This change in a relatively short period of time suggests that social factors rather than genetic factors are likely to be responsible. One possible explanation is the changing nature of the mother/housewife role, which has resulted in women having fewer children than in the past. This in turn has reduced the risks associated with pregnancy and childbirth. Thus the risk of mortality for women has reduced more rapidly than the risk for men. Further explanations of the widening mortality gap between men and women have focused particularly on the role of men's paid employment (accidents at work, work-related illness), as well as gender differences in health decisions on matters such as diet, smoking, alcohol consumption and exercise.

What is the situation today?

Though the causes of death for men and women still differ, they have become more similar recently, for example more women are likely to die of lung cancer than ever before. This might make us think about recent changes in gender roles in society, for example in the 1990s there are more women in paid employment than there were in the 1960s, and this might result in converging health problems as women adopt similar life styles to men (for example smoke more). A recent survey revealed a growing percentage of teenage female smokers (General Household Survey, 1992).

Data showing selected causes of death of men and women provide a useful indicator of sex and health chances today:

Mortality and gender, selected causes of death: by age and sex, 1992 (per cent)

	0–1	1–14	15–39	40–64	65–79	80+
Males:						
Infectious diseases	4.8	5.1	0.7	0.7	0.4	0.3
Cancer	1.0	17.3	13.5	34.3	31.6	20.9
Circulatory diseases	4.0	4.0	10.7	43.8	48.2	47.3
Respiratory diseases	11.9	5.1	3.4	5.3	10.3	16.7
Injury and poisoning	17.6	34.2	52.7	6.6	1.3	1.2
All other causes	60.8	34.2	18.0	9.3	8.3	13.5
Females:						
Infectious diseases	4.3	4.8	1.9	0.6	0.4	0.3
Cancer	1.5	18.0	33.3	51.8	30.6	14.2
Circulatory diseases	5.6	4.4	10.7	26.7	46.6	52.3
Respiratory diseases	10.6	5.6	3.4	5.8	9.2	13.7
Injury and poisoning	16.8	25.8	28.9	4.0	1.4	1.4
All other causes	61.3	41.4	21.8	11.1	11.8	18.0

(*Source: Social Trends*, no. 24, London: HMSO, 1994.)

Exercise 6.3   Gender and mortality: the situation today

Examine the table above, then answer the following:

[i] 1. What is the most common cause of death of males in each of the age groups?

[i] 2. What is the most common cause of death of females in each of the age groups?

[i] 3. Describe the main differences in cause of death between males and females.

[a] 4. Why do you believe there is a difference in cause of death between males and females?

What is the relationship between life expectancy and gender?

Do mortality figures inform us of men's and women's respective 'health chances' throughout their lives? Have these health chances changed over time? Life expectancy is a useful measure of health chances because it shows how long, on average, men and women can expect to live. Using birth and death records we can compare life expectancy, say, 150 years ago with today's life expectancy:

Life Expectancy by gender

Year	Male	Female
1838–54	39.9	41.8
1891–1900	44.1	47.8
1950–52	66.5	71.5
1996*	74.4	79.7

(*Source*: Adapted from N. Hart, *The Sociology of Health & Medicine*, Causeway Press, Ormskirk, 1985; *Social Trends*, 1995, p. 116.)

Exercise 6.4 Gender and life expectation

Examine the table above, then answer the following:

1. Describe the trend (pattern over time) of the life expectancy of males and females between 1838 and 1996.

2. Examine the list below the following table. The items in the list explain (a) why the life expectancy of men and women has increased over time, and (b) why on average, women appear to survive longer than men. Copy the table headings then match the reasons with the two trends in life expectancy for males and females (two examples are provided).

Reasons for increased life expectancy of men/women	Reasons for differences between the life expectancy of men and women
1. Scientific and medical advances	1. Genetic differences between men and women

- Scientific and medical advances.
- Gender differences in smoking.
- Men may live more dangerous lives (take more risks).
- Better hygiene.
- Better food and food technology.
- Safer and healthier working conditions.
- Improved education and health awareness.
- Men have been retiring later, which may be harmful to health.
- Improved health care.
- Genetic differences between men and women.
- Inequality in health care provision between male and females.
- Men may be more likely to work unsociable hours, long hours are harmful to health.
- Gender differences in responding to health advice.
- The welfare state.
- Higher living standards.
- Gender differences in exercise and diet.

What is the problem with the life expectancy figures?

Although health chances seem to have improved for both sexes, on average women survive longer than men. However we should treat these figures with caution. The problem with life expectancy figures is the question of averaging out the ages at which men and women die. Not all women share an equal life expectancy, and women's mortality seems to be affected by social class. According to Le Grand (1982) women in Class V (unskilled manual workers) have a shorter life expectancy than males in Class I. Le Grand also argues that among women in Class V the rate of serious longstanding illness is three times that of men in Class I. The differences in illness rates cut across social class and gender, resulting in differences in life expectancy between women from different social backgrounds. Therefore we must not treat men and women as large, homogeneous (undifferentiated) groups because we also need to examine the patterns among males and females of, for example, different social classes.

What is the relationship between morbidity and gender?

The consultation figures of NHS GPs indicate that women visit their doctors more often than men, suggesting that women suffer more illness than men. However some researchers point out the contradiction that although women seem more likely to define themselves as ill, on average they survive longer than men. Could visiting a doctor more regularly mean that women are more likely to prevent serious illness, and as a result live a longer life? Or do the figures need to be examined more carefully: do women really visit their doctors more often than men?

All age groups have become more likely to visit a doctor since 1972 (although this does not necessarily mean we have become less healthy). There seems to be little gender difference among the under 15s or over 65s (and don't forget that the latter group includes a significant number of very elderly women). Among adult women we need to ask whether higher consultation rates mean women experience more illness, find it easier to take on the 'sick role' and talk about health worries, make more use of preventative services (for example cervical cancer screening) or visit more often on behalf of others in the family.

Exercise 6.5 Gender and visits to the doctor

Examine the following table:

Trends in consultation with an NHS GP 14 days before being interviewed, 1972–1992 (percentage consulting GP)

	Ages	1972	1982	1992
Males	0–4	13	21	22
	5–15	7	9	10
	16–44	8	8	9
	45–64	11	13	13
	65+	31	34	40
Females	0–4	15	20	22
	5–15	6	10	11
	16–44	15	16	18
	45–64	12	16	18
	65+	35	35	42

(*Source*: Adapted from General Household Survey, London: HMSO, 1992.)

[i] 1. According to the table, since 1972, have people become more or less likely to visit a doctor?

[a] 2. What are the possible explanations of this change? (Hint: attitudes to health, perceived benefits of GP health care, availability of health care.)

[i][a] 3. Compare the male and female consultation rates for all the age groups in the table. Why might more women than men in the 16–44 age group visit the GP? (Hint: for example reproductive reasons.)

[e] 4. Why might the '65+' category be inadequate if we wish to explore the extent to which the elderly consult the doctor? (Hints: is this age group rather too broad? Is it treating all over 65s as a single group?)

Are there alternative ways of measuring illness figures with regard to gender?

There are alternative ways of measuring morbidity (earlier we mentioned absence from work statistics). Surveys can be carried out that attempt to generalise the extent of illness and gender differences by questioning a sample of men and women. For example the organisation Action for Myalgic Encephalomyelitis and Chronic Fatigue (ME can cause muscle fatigue and disturbances in cognitive functioning) asked its members to complete a questionnaire. The study shows very marked gender differences (Item A), but also indicates the limitations of the data. Overall the evidence on gender and morbidity is far less straightforward than that on mortality.

ME and the pattern of morbidity

(Percentages of those taking part in the survey.)

Sex:		Employment:	
male:	23%	Full or part-time by choice:	16.5%
female:	77%	Part-time due to ME:	6.5%
		Sick leave due to ME:	26.0%
Age:		Unemployed/retired due to ME:	
0–18:	1.3%	Student:	38.0%
18–30:	9.1%	Housewife:	6.5%
31–40:	12.3%		4.5%
41–50:	14.4%		
51–60:	7.9%	Employment before ME:	
over 60:	55%	Professional:	57.0%
		Manual:	9.9%
		Student:	7.7%
		Housewife:	15.8%
		Unemployed/retired:	9.6%

'3,115 membership surveys have been completed so far. When considering these statistics it is important to remember that, in the final analysis, all they measure is those who were prepared to reply to our questionnaire. Not every member has replied. It may be that more older people and more women than men complete postal questionnaires. As more respondents complete and return their membership surveys the figures will become increasingly likely to mirror reality.

[An additional issue is whether] there are certain types of people who tend to join patient organisations like "Action for ME". Other surveys of people with ME confirm that, after the age of 25, up to three times as many women as men get ME. But this does not tell us anything for certain. It may simply be that more women than men admit to illness, that more women join self-help organisations or that more women than men take responsibility for the family's health. It might also be that there is a hormonal factor making women more susceptible or that there are more women than men working in ME "high risk" occupations such as nursing, teaching or social work: jobs with high exposure to viruses where loyalty encourages the worker to push through an illness rather than let down patients, pupils or clients.'

(Source: Interaction, Journal of Action for ME, no. 16, Summer 1994.)

> [i] Explain why Action for ME (Item A) is cautious about accepting its survey results at face value.

Why are there gender differences in morbidity and mortality?

Explanations of the different patterns of morbidity between men and women largely focus on the following:

- Genetic/biological explanations.
- Cultural/behavioural explanations.
- Material/structural explanations.
- Unequal treatment by the health service.

Each of these explanations might explain why women seem to suffer more ill-health and why men tend to have shorter lives than women.

The genetic/biological explanation

This explanation tends to focus on the ways that women suffer from certain biological conditions related to:

- Pregnancy and childbirth.
- Contraception and abortion.
- Menstruation and the menopause.
- Cervical, ovarian and breast cancer (although the last also affects *some* men).

Because women live longer than men they are more likely to suffer degenerative diseases, although women of course do not suffer from the specifically male cancers (testicular and prostate).

To what extent are the differences in health between men and women simply a result of sex differences? Some biological factors (for example the ability of women to produce children) are obviously subject to cultural influences (for example ideas about the age at which women should become mothers, contraception, the number of children that should be produced, how mothers should be treated during pregnancy and childbirth). It is therefore important to recognise the influence on health of socially constructed gender differences in addition to the purely biological differences.

Link Exercise 6.1   Gender and iatrogenesis (doctor-caused illness)

 Examine the section on 'Unequal treatment by the health service' on page 147 and find two examples of the way the medical profession can cause women harm.

The problem with the genetic/biological explanation is that it deals with only a proportion of illnesses and is therefore limited. The focus is now shifting to explanations that stress the influence of gender differences. Gender roles have a cultural dimension as well as a structural dimension (for example on average men have earned more than women, and women's traditional housewife role may have been shaped by an economic system that created a cheap way of caring for male workers and children).

The cultural/behavioural explanation

Women suffer ill-health because of their behaviour

Women might suffer from ill-health because of behavioural aspects of their life. By accepting the mother/housewife role and taking on too much responsibility (paid employment in addition to child care and housework) women might increase their chance of becoming ill and therefore of visiting a doctor. The pressure on women (and perhaps men, now) to be slim can contribute to eating disorders such as anorexia and make young women who smoke reluctant to give up the habit, increasing the risk of smoking related disease later in life. Women of all ages are far less likely than men to take regular physical exercise (defined as 20 minutes of vigorous exercise three times a week) and this might have harmful consequences for women's health.

However, although the morbidity figures show women visit the doctor more frequently than men, some researchers believe that women might be socialised into being more aware of health than men (for example brought up to take better care of themselves and others, and to talk more openly about problems). This might lead women to define themselves as ill more often, to report more illness to their GP and to adopt the 'sick role' more than men. It might be more socially acceptable for women than men to admit they are ill.

Women also visit the doctor on behalf of others, for example their children (Graham, 1984); this gives them more contact with doctors and health care services and provides them with more opportunities to report symptoms.

On the other hand women might occupy roles in society that limit the extent to which they can visit a doctor. It should be noted that when Tuckett (1976) asked women to keep a diary of symptoms experienced and consultations with doctors, he found that only one in 37 symptoms led to a visit to a GP. Thus it appeared that women did not report many of the symptoms they experienced. A similar diary for men would be useful in order to compare the rate of reporting between men and women.

Research does suggest that some women find it difficult to visit their GP. Pill and Scott quote evidence from working-class women who said their domestic role did not allow them to define themselves as sick very easily: 'I think with a family you can't afford to be ill. You think, well, you'll be ill after you've cooked the tea' (Pill and Scott, 1982).

Men suffer ill health because of their behaviour

There is considerable evidence of men adopting a less healthy lifestyle than women. Two examples are smoking and drinking, as shown in the following table:

Heavy smoking and alcohol consumption by sex, 1990 (per cent)

	Males	Females
Smoking: 20+ cigarettes per day	14	9
Drinks per week: 22+ units (males)		
15+ units (females)	27	11

(*Source: Social Trends*, no. 24, London: HMSO, 1994.)

Although it appears that men do not visit their GPs as often as women do, men might in fact be suffering more ill health than women. Men's behaviour seems to be less healthy (for example too much alcohol and smoking, a fatty diet, dangerous leisure activities), which leads to a higher male mortality rate. If men are reluctant to visit a doctor, this might lead to a lower *detected* morbidity rate but a higher mortality rate.

Matthew Parris, an MP for seven years, asked 589 male MPs (there are 650 MPs in total) to take part in his survey on men and health. Only 137 agreed to participate by returning a questionnaire and some agreed to be interviewed by Parris. The results showed that:

On going to the doctor:

- 67% 'put off going to a doctor'.
- 43% 'were too busy' to visit a doctor.
- 10% felt it was 'not important enough'.

On knowledge of and precautionary behaviour towards male cancers:

- 27% examined themselves for testicular cancer.
- 33% did not know the function of the prostate gland.
- 78% underestimated male death for prostate cancer.
- 63% did not know that cancer kills twice as many men as it does women.

(Source: M. Parris, 'To be a Man', feature in 'Pulse', Channel 4, January, 1995.)

ITEM B   *Exercise 6.7   'To be a man': a study of male MPs' health, lifestyles and attitudes to being men*

|i||a| 1. What percentage of male MPs replied to Matthew Parris' request to participate in the survey?

|i||e| 2. Did a sufficient proportion of MPs participate to justify making generalisations from the survey results?

|e| Are MPs a representative sample of the male population?

|i||a| 3. What do the results suggest about men's use of doctors?

Macfarlane (1990) claims that more men than women visit their doctors. By excluding visits necessitated by pregnancy or menstruation for women between the ages of 15 and 44, it appears that men actually visit their doctors more than women. Thus it might be that men are less healthy than women; in part their lifestyle might be responsible for this.

Exercise 6.8   Evaluating the cultural/behavioural explanation

|i||e| Using the key words listed below the text, fill in the gaps in the following:

The focus on behaviour and culture is an important consideration because people's lifestyle is likely to have an affect on their . . . . . . However one of the problems with this explanation is deciding which gender suffers more . . . . . . Women may suffer more illness than men and this may be related to their lifestyle. However men may appear to suffer less illness because (for example through . . . . . .) they visit their doctors less often than women. Just which sex leads the most unhealthy lifestyle is also difficult to assess, because whereas more men . . . . . . than women, women may suffer ill-health because of the pressures of their traditional domestic role, for example . . . . . . There are also widespread . . . . . . in lifestyle between men and women of different social classes, ... and . . . . . ., so generalisations are difficult to make.

Key words: socialisation, age groups, smoke, health, illness, ethnic groups, child care, individual differences.

The material/structural explanation

Women suffer ill health because of material/structural factors

Women's role as carer (of children, partner, relatives) causes ill health. Graham (1985) suggests that up to 80 per cent of handicapped adults who live at home are looked after by mothers. Parker (1980) found that a principal reason for the early retirement of women was the health of other family members. This caring and domestic role may make women feel isolated, lonely and depressed, and may result in illness.

Link Exercise 6.2   Women as carers

Examine the section in Chapter 10 on informal care (page 294) to find out more about the issue of gender and caring, then answer the following questions:

*i**a* 1. How might women's 'caring role' affect their health chances? (Hint: the effect of depression, restricted paid work opportunities and financial difficulties.)

*i**a* 2. How might women's 'caring role' cut across social class? (Hint: might some women be able to pay others to do the caring?)

Women's poor health may be due to poor employment conditions. A large percentage of women in paid employment do part-time work, which tends to be poorly paid and have fewer perks (for example sick pay), and this may force women into poorer living conditions. Poor pay may lead to poverty (with inadequate diet, unsatisfactory housing, stressful living conditions) as well as limiting occupational pension provision in old age.

Link Exercise 6.3   Women and RSI

*i**a* Turn back to Chapter 4 and examine the section on 'Coping with changes in material circumstances' (page 59, which describes the financial hardship borne by some sufferers of repetitive strain injury (RSI)). Given the large increase in the number of women employed in the service sector (for example typing for many hours on computers), complete the following table to examine why, and for whom, the employment of women might be a health issue.

Group or organisation	Why the employment of women is a health issue for this group or organisation
Women workers Employers Government Health Service Families	

Women's poor health may be due to greater exposure to substandard housing. Housewives may spend more time in the house than their working partners and therefore be more exposed to the harmful effects of, for example, damp housing conditions. As the male unemployment rate increases men may also be exposed to these health risks in the same way as housewives and unemployed women have traditionally been.

Women may suffer more exposure to poverty. Two groups in which women are overrepresented – single parents and the elderly – have an increased risk of poverty. Low-paid (part-time) work contributes to poverty, as does dependence on a husband's pay, which may not be distributed evenly among family members. Pahl (1983) has undertaken research into the distribution of and control over financial resources within households, and notes that members of the same household may not enjoy the same standard of living as one another. Graham (1986) conducted a survey of women in low- and middle-income households and found that female-headed, single-parent households were sometimes materially better off than they had been during 'marriage', even though they were sometimes on lower incomes than two-parent families. This was because all income went directly to the mother, whereas previously it had been unequally distributed.

Bernard (1982) takes the view that women may suffer more ill health because of marriage. In her study, 'The Wife's Marriage', Bernard states that married women are less healthy than single women and housewives are less healthy than paid working women. Giving up work and becoming a housewife may lead to depression, insomnia and nervousness. Marriage is unhealthy for women, claims Bernard, although married men are more healthy than single men. But how was 'healthy' measured? By the number of visits to a doctor? We already know the problems with such figures.

Women's smoking: government targets and social trends

'In 1992, The Health of the Nation laid down a new target for the reduction in smoking prevalence in England. The target represented a 31 per cent reduction in smoking prevalence among women in England between 1990 and 2000.

The Patterns of Women's Smoking

There has been a steady decline in the prevalence of women's smoking in Britain. But this decline has been accompanied by a rapid change in the social distribution of cigarette smoking and has been less steep for women than men. Cigarette smoking in Britain is becoming increasingly linked to being a women and to being working class.

Gender and Smoking

Looking at the gender patterns of smoking it is clear smoking began in Britain as a male habit. The male identity of cigarette smoking was still very clear in the 1950s when a significantly higher proportion of men (65 per cent) than women (40 per cent) were cigarette smokers.

Among adolescents and young adults, the gender difference has now been reversed. Smoking prevalence among young secondary school children is higher among girls than boys. Most

of the young women recruited into smoking are white: smoking prevalence among Asian and African-Caribbean women is significantly lower than among the majority white population. These differences are likely to reflect the cluster of religious and cultural influences that shape ideas of what is appropriate behaviour for women. However, it is important to recognise that smoking behaviour is not a fixed cultural trait, a habit found among white but not black women. The international evidence on cigarette smoking underlines the diverse and rapidly changing ways in which ethnic identity and smoking status are linked, both for women and for men.

Social Class and Smoking

The decline in smoking prevalence among women has been associated with a rapid shift in social class distribution. Smoking prevalence has fallen among women in all social classes. However, the rate of decline has been highest among those in non-manual households. Among the factors explaining the gender and class differences in smoking, ignorance of its harmful effects is no longer considered to be a major factor. Most smokers are aware of the health-risks of smoking both for themselves and for their children.

Why Women Continue to Smoke

Studies suggest that among white women cigarette smoking is linked to having heavy caring responsibilities and to living in materially-disadvantaged circumstances. Prevalence rates are high among some groups of nurses, including psychiatric nurses and nursing auxiliaries. Married and cohabiting women with dependent children are more likely to smoke than those without dependent children. The difference in smoking prevalence is at its sharpest among younger women. Among married women aged 16–24 without children, one quarter (26 per cent) are cigarette smokers. Among those with children, the proportion rises to over a third (37 per cent).

Smoking among white women is not only associated with more caring responsibilities, it is also associated with living on less income. . . . Few studies have asked women about why caring for others and living in poverty makes it harder to give up smoking. The limited evidence suggests that cigarette smoking is deeply woven into the strategies women develop to cope with caring and to survive in circumstances of hardship. For women in paid work, cigarette smoking can similarly provide a way of structuring time and coping with the stresses and pressures of the job. 'I smoke when I'm sitting down, having a cup of coffee. It's part and parcel of resting' [comment from a mother].

In talking about smoking in the context of poverty, material hardship gives them and their children little opportunity to take part in the lifestyles that others take for granted. They are unlikely to be able to afford either major household items like cars, telephones and holidays or more everyday experiences like buying new clothes or travelling out with their partner. In a lifestyle with little style left in it, smoking cigarettes can be the only item of personal spending and the only luxury. 'I try to cut down on cigarettes to save money but cigarettes are my one luxury, and at the moment they feel a bit of a necessity' [a mother]'.

(Source: Hilary Graham, Health Visitor, vol. 66, no. 3, 1993.)

ITEM C

Exercise 6.9 Gender, smoking and material circumstances

1. In no more than 100 words use Item C to show how an individual's decision to smoke might have its roots in material circumstances. (Hint: poverty.)

2. What other social factors apart from gender are examined in Item C? (Hint: ethnicity.)

Men suffer ill health because of material/structural factors

In a segregated labour market, men's health has been more likely to be adversely affected by the risks associated with certain occupations, for example construction, mining and quarrying or working with asbestos. The General Household Survey (1992) shows that men are more likely to suffer accidents than women, and that accidents affecting men are more likely to occur in the workplace. Structural changes in the economy have increased the risk of, in particular, male unemployment, and unemployment is associated with increased morbidity and mortality. However, with the decline in traditional manufacturing jobs and mining the number of industrial accidents and the incidence of occupational diseases associated with these types of work may also decline.

Although suicide accounts for only a small proportion of deaths, of considerable concern is the steady rise in the 1970s and 1980s in the suicide rate for males aged 15–44; there was not a similar increase in female suicide. What could account for this change?

Exercise 6.10 Applying the structural explanation

Below is a list of illnesses. Identify which illnesses may be caused by the structural and non-structural factors outlined above and insert them in the table on p. 146. Then record whether the factors have a greater effect on men or women and justify your answer in the final column.

Lung cancer, repetitive strain injury, asbestosis, industrial accidents, asthma, leukaemia, bronchitis, tuberculosis, depression.

Structural factors may cause:	Non-structural factors may cause:	Men/women worst affected	Justification

---

Exercise 6.11   Evaluating the structural/materialist explanation

 Copy the table and complete by sorting and listing the strengths and weaknesses of the materialist explanation provided below:

Strengths	Weaknesses

- There is a substantial amount of evidence to support the view that material circumstances are related to illness.
- The material basis of ill-health may inform social policy so housing and poverty can be addressed.
- If the material explanation is accepted then it leads to an expensive set of social policies, for example to improve housing and reduce poverty.
- Individual lifestyles must have an effect on health and cannot be ignored.
- Individual lifestyle can be associated with material position, for example working-class males and females may tend to smoke more than their middle-class counterparts.
- Not all poor men and women will suffer a greater amount of ill-health. The materialist explanation does not explore why some poor men and women suffer more ill-health than others in similar circumstances.
- The materialist explanation appears dated because gender roles are shifting, the explanation deals with traditional gender roles rather than issues relating to men and unemployment and women and paid work.

Unequal treatment by the health service

Women and the health service

Graham (1985) points out that only 13 per cent of hospital consult-ants are women, whilst 90 per cent of nurses and 75 per cent of ancillary workers are female, and that black women account for a large proportion of the lowest tier. Although most paid care seems to be done by women, they are under the control of male doctors and consultants. If men have a virtual monopoly over the control of health care this may result in treatment that is inappropriate for women. It certainly appears that women are more at risk than men from clinical iatrogenesis (disease caused by medical treatment); for example the increased risk of cancer or heart conditions associated with contraceptives such as the pill.

Abbott and Wallace (1990) claim that men's control over women's health has been deliberately evolved: in professionalising health care, men have assumed control over nearly all aspects of health, including gynaecology and childbirth. The evidence includes the following:

- In Britain doctors recommended as safe the contraceptive Depo-Provera, which was known to have damaging side effects on women (particularly black women) and was banned in the USA. This illustrates male ideology (male views) being imposed on women's health care.
- A similar example of male ideology influencing female health care is shown by the side effects (iatrogenesis) of prescribed drugs, for example Valium for depression, and the contraceptive pill.
- Men may also see themselves as the norm by which women should be judged. Indeed some feminists argue that male doctors still hold very inadequate notions of female health, and this leads to a failure to take female problems seriously, for example depression has sometimes been viewed as an example of female weakness – an inability to cope with children and/or housework. Scully and Bart (1978) claim that some doctors blame female emotional problems on their reproductive tract rather than on the problems they face in society and the home.
- Oakley (1993) claims that 69 per cent of first-time mothers feel they have little control over their childbirth and argues that the practice of Caesarean section (carried out by surgeons) is of doubtful benefit to both mother and child. Oakley also concludes that doctors and mothers view childbirth very differently: what one sees as a medical problem, the other sees as natural. Women have also complained of difficulty in communicating their views during childbirth. This is further evidence of male ideology controlling women's health care.
- It has been argued that because heart disease has been seen as a 'male disease', women with such symptoms have been less likely to receive appropriate investigation and treatment.

Whilst critical views have pointed out ways in which health services may fail to meet women's needs, it is also important to ask: in what ways have health services improved the quality of life for women?

To what extent can the fall in, for example, maternal mortality (and indeed infant mortality) be attributed to medical intervention?

Men and control of the health service

Although some feminists have claimed that men exercise control over the health service to the detriment of women, it is relevant to ask: to what extent have men benefited from their control of medicine? After all, women's life expectancy remains significantly greater than men's. In 1992 male deaths from prostate cancer (10 000) were over five times higher than female deaths from cervical cancer. Breast cancer (which claims 15 000 victims annually) attracts the most funds of all research into sex-specific cancers (Kossoff, 1995). In addition, whilst screening is available for cervical and breast cancer there is no equivalent NHS programme for prostate cancer; this might be explained by the currently limited ability to provide effective treatment for the disease. Screening might, of course, be particularly relevant for men in view of their apparent reluctance to consult a doctor and their generally limited knowledge of male diseases such as prostate cancer. How many readers of this book, male or female, are aware that men too can suffer from breast cancer? Two hundred men died of breast cancer in 1994 ('Pulse', Channel 4, 1995). Thus it is important to ask who benefits from the health service and to examine the extent to which the health service meets the health needs of both men and women.

Exercise 6.12   Evaluating the treatment by the health service

Below are two lists. Complete the sentences in the first list by choosing the appropriate ending from the second, then add each of the points to your notes.

List 1:

- There is mounting evidence that the health service does not meet men's needs . . .
- There is considerable evidence that women suffer from illnesses caused by the medical profession . . .
- The genetic, cultural and material explanations simply deal with the causes of illness . . .
- Despite the issue of clinical iatrogenesis (for example side effects) the health service . . .
- Instead of viewing the unequal treatment by the health service as an alternative to other explanations (for example materialist) . . .

List 2:

- for example the side effects of contraceptives such as the pill.
- it would be more appropriate to treat the explanation as complementary.
- is unlikely to cause the majority of illness, thus the alternative explanations deal more effectively with the issue of why certain groups suffer more illness.

- (for example in terms of screening for prostate cancer), thus a strength of the explanation is that it deals not just with the causes of illness but the subsequent treatment or lack of treatment, which is ignored by the alternative explanations.
- however further patterns may emerge if the treatment by the health service is examined.

Why do women live longer than men but appear to suffer more illness?

Data based on the number of visits to doctors suggests that women suffer more ill-health than men. However the mortality statistics show that women live longer than men. What can explain this pattern?

- Male ill-health may be more serious (for example heart disease), and therefore more likely to lead to sudden death. Evidence of gender and mortality supports this view. According to Whitehead (1992, p. 243) 'by middle age, circulatory diseases had assumed prominence for men while cancer claimed a high proportion of lives in women'.
- Men enjoy better health than women but are killed off by accidents and fatal diseases. Is there any evidence of this? In 1985 in England and Wales, 40 per cent of deaths of boys aged 1–14 were due to accidents and violence compared with 26 per cent of girls (Whitehead, 1992).
- Women suffer more ill-health because they live longer. Therefore throughout old age more women are likely to visit a doctor.
- Women may appear to suffer more ill-health simply because they are more likely to visit their doctors and take on the 'sick role'. Whether women really do adopt the sick role more easily will be examined below.

Macfarlane (1990) states that in old age women may visit their doctors more often, thus the morbidity figures will show that more females than men visit their GPs. There are fewer elderly men so the figures are likely to skew towards females. In addition Macfarlane finds little difference in the hospital admission rates for men and women aged 15–44, if admissions for reproductive reasons (for example childbirth or abortion) are excluded. However women are more likely to be admitted to mental hospitals than men, especially for depression, neuroses or senile dementia.

A number of questions need to be asked in order to establish the patterns of illness for men and women, including the following.

Firstly, is it easier for women to adopt the 'sick role'? Some researchers state that women's role as housewife allows them to adopt the sick role more easily than men, who are supposed to be the breadwinners. In addition women may be socialised to admit when they feel ill: to do so is not viewed as a sign of weakness.

Secondly, do women more easily define themselves as ill? When Zola (1966) studied illness behaviour he found that women tended to 'normalise' symptoms that others defined as an indication of illness, for example constant tiredness. This is supported by Pill and Scott (1982), who have already provided a quotation to illustrate the way women seem to accept many illness symptoms as an everyday experience to be expected (p. **141** above). Thus the traditional Western female role of 'carer' may explain why some women tolerate symptoms when others seek medical attention.

Tuckett (1976) found that the women only consulted their doctors for one in 37 symptoms recorded. This suggests that women do not adopt the sick role easily; however without comparative data for men it is difficult to draw conclusions about the extent to which males and females differ in reporting symptoms to their GPs.

Structured exam questions

Question

1. Critically examine the relationship between health and either gender or ethnicity. (*25 marks*) (London, now InterBoard, June 1993)

(a) Read through the following student response to the essay question:

Student answer

(a) When studying gender and health there are methodological problems which arise. The problem of extraneous variables is one complication (extraneous means extra variables), for example a person's health may not only be affected by gender but also by their social class, ethnicity and age. A similar problem with studying gender and health is the issue of treating men and women as entire groups. There may be significant variations within these groups such that middle class women may suffer less illness, on average, than working class women. Thus any essay about gender and health must ask whether further relationships exist, for example between women and their social class. Another problem which arises when studying gender and health is the validity of morbidity figures. Morbidity figures often depend on people reporting their symptoms to a doctor: not all illnesses will be reported to the doctor. It could be that because women visit the doctor more they appear to be less healthy, whereas men really suffer more serious illness despite fewer consultations with the doctor.

(b) When discussing gender and health it is worth comparing the patterns of mortality between men and women. In terms of their average life expectancy and cause of death, there appear to be significant gender differences. In the past mortality risk was relatively similar for men and women, however, since 1846 women have tended to survive, on average, longer than men. Today the causes of death for men and women vary, though with more women doing paid work they may also be adopting similar lifestyles to men, for example smoking. This pattern may cause a convergence of the causes of both illness and death. However, life

expectancy figures are expressed in averages and they may obscure differences in life expectancy for working class women and middle class women. The social class differences for women have been explored by Le Grand (1982) who stated that working class women have a rate of serious longstanding illness three times higher than that of men in social Class 1.

(c) It is also worth examining the issue of morbidity (illness) and gender. It is suggested that women suffer more illness than men as they visit the doctor more than men. One reason for women suffering more ill health is provided by a biological explanation: women may suffer more illness due to reproductive reasons. Women are also more likely to suffer degenerative diseases because on average they survive longer than men and are thus more likely to experience illness throughout old age. However, not all illness can be explained by biological factors. Individual behaviour and cultural lifestyles should also be examined. The cultural/behavioural explanation states that lifestyle affects health and illness. The traditional female caring role (eg. child rearing) may put women in situations where too much domestic responsibility is given to them and this may lead to depression. Another example of a cultural explanation of ill health is the pressure on women to be slim, which might contribute to the amount of anorexia. Men may be socialised to be reluctant to adopt the 'sick role' whereas women may adopt the sick role more easily and admit they are ill. Tuckett (1976) quotes evidence which asked women to keep a diary of symptoms experienced and consultations with the doctor and found that only one in every 37 symptoms led to a visit to the doctor. Thus women do not tend to 'over-report sickness' and adopt the sick role easily. A similar diary for men would have been useful to compare the extent to which men experience symptoms and report illness. There may be differences between women in the extent to which they adopt the sick role such as variations by social class. Pill and Scott (1982) claim that social class differences need to be examined: working class women felt their ability to define themselves as sick was restricted by their traditional gender caring role: they hadn't time to be sick because they felt they had to look after the children.

(d) Although women appear to visit their GP more often than men, thus suggesting that they suffer more ill health, evidence suggests that men adopt a less healthy lifestyle than women. In support of this view, an article in *Social Trends* on heavy smoking and alcohol consumption by sex shows that males are more likely to smoke 20 plus cigarettes per day and drink more alcohol per week than females. This may lead to higher male morbidity and eventually a high mortality rate. In addition, if men are reluctant to visit the doctor this might lead to a lower detected morbidity rate but a higher mortality rate. Macfarlane (1990) found that by excluding visits by women in connection with menstruation and pregnancy between the ages of 15 and 44, men actually visit the doctor more than women. Men's lifestyle might be responsible for them being less healthy than women.

(e) Men's and women's poor health may not only be due to cultural factors but may also be explained by material/structural factors. Women may suffer more ill health due to greater exposure to poor housing because housewives may spend more time in the house than their working partners and they are therefore exposed to the harmful effects of some poor living conditions, for example damp. However, as the male unemployment rate rises men may also be increasingly exposed to poorer housing.

(f) Women may suffer more exposure to poverty. Low-paid work contributes to poverty, so too does dependence on husbands' pay, which may not be distributed equally among family members. Jan Pahl (1983) conducted research into the distribution of and control over household finance and found members within the same household may not enjoy the same standard of living. Men may also suffer ill health due to material and structural factors. In a segregated labour market men's health may have been affected more by the risks associated with certain dangerous occupations, such as mining or working with asbestos. The General Household Survey found that men were more likely to suffer accidents than women and that accidents affecting men are more likely to occur in the workplace.

(g) An alternative explanation might be unequal treatment by the health service. Men may benefit more (or even less) than women from the health service. Men may lack the same screening services for male-related disorders such as prostate cancer whereas women are provided with a national breast cancer screening programme. Hilary Graham (1987) points out that men dominate the health service and this level of control may mean that more female conditions become medicalised by men because doctors may apply male values to female behaviour, resulting in a number of women being prescribed sedatives for depression when really the root cause of their depression is coping with childrearing. This type of argument suggests that patriarchy (male domination) is responsible for some illnesses as opposed to the economic structure of society. Ann Oakley (1993) states that many first-time mothers claimed they experienced a lack of control over their pregnancy and that mothers' and doctors' views were not necessarily the same – thus male control of the health service may produce some inequality.

(h) In conclusion the relationship between gender and health is complicated because only to consider the issue of gender is too limited. Further issues of social class, occupation, ethnicity and age as well as region or location need to be explored to provide a broader picture of gender and health, such as the impact of changing gender roles (for example more women working, becoming financially independent) because some paid working women may be adopting similar illness patterns to men, such as smoking more. Graham (1984) has shown that smoking amongst young women is rising, thus gender roles may already be changing: the impact on women's health may have to be measured in the future. Similarly the impact of unemployment on men may also be an issue to be examined in the future as more men are made redundant as the economic climate changes. The relationship between gender and health is one that is constantly changing.

This essay was awarded the following marks:

- Knowledge and Understanding: 7/9
- Interpretation and Application: 6/9
- Evaluation: 6/9
- Total mark: 19/27

(b) Now match the following skills comments to each of the paragraphs in the student essay above.

Comment

(1) Knowledge and understanding: sociological information relating to low pay and citing Pahl on the distribution of income within the household contribute to the marks awarded for knowledge and understanding. Interpretation and application: this paragraph adds to the material/structural outline. Could the reasons why men do certain dangerous jobs be associated with cultural factors as well, for example male employers only selecting men for dangerous jobs? Thus the material explanation may have a relationship with the cultural explanation rather than treating these explanations as distinctly separate. The use of the General Household Survey material may add to the application marks because the student has managed to apply appropriate evidence to support the argument. Evaluation: the student could state the material/structural explanation that poverty causes ill health – this point would add to the theoretical evaluation of the answer.

(2) Knowledge and understanding: the candidate has explained the effects that poor housing may have on health, though no sociological evidence is produced. Evaluation: the student has offered an alternative explanation to the cultural factors examined earlier. However the relationship between possible cultural factors (for example the traditional housewife role) could be related to structural factors (for example worse health due to poor housing). This relationship would add to the evaluation marks awarded thus far. Interpretation and application: the candidate has applied the issue of poor housing in a useful and relevant way. Evidence of a reasonable interpretation of the question is shown in the way that the candidate appears to be using (limited) information to relate to the essay question.

(3) Evaluation: the conclusion provides evaluation points by attempting to state that the relationship is more complicated because of other variables – however marks have already been awarded for this point in the introductory sentence. Knowledge and understanding: citing Graham (1984) adds to the marks awarded for knowledge, though the conclusion is rather repetitive. Interpretation and application: the candidate continues to offer material that relates to the essay question, though few new points are mentioned.

(4) Interpretation and application: both men and women are addressed in the two preceding paragraphs, which provides a more balanced answer than simply examining just men or just women. Thus the student has managed to interpret the question in a balanced fashion. Evaluation: marks would be awarded for criticising the evidence quoted by Tuckett (1976) and exploring the issues of social class and the sick role. Interpretation and application: the candidate has offered explanations of the gender differences in illness by exploring the biological and cultural explanations. Evaluation: there is no clear evaluation of the cultural explanation, although the candidate does examine the morbidity figures in Macfarlane (1990). Interpretation and application: there needs to be a more explicit link to culture, particularly for men. Male socialisation could be mentioned as a factor that might prevent men from adopting the sick role (if it is true that men do not adopt the sick role as easily as women). Knowledge and understanding: evidence from Social Trends on the smoking rates of men and women adds knowledge related to the question, as does the information from Macfarlane (1990).

(5) Interpretation and application: in the introduction the student has clearly shown that the issue of gender is the focus of the essay, not ethnicity. The answer, then, explicitly relates to the question. Evaluation: the student has started by offering evaluation points that relate to the problems of studying the area of gender and health. This has allowed the student to gain evaluation marks. Knowledge and understanding: an understanding of the question is clearly shown by the relevance of the points made. The discussion of the problems of studying gender and ill health suggest the candidate understands the essay question.

(6) Interpretation and application: mentioning the health service adds to the assessment of the relationship between gender and health. Evaluation: likewise, mentioning patriarchy adds to the theoretical evaluation of the answer. Knowledge and understanding: citing Oakley (1993) and Graham (1984) provides marks for knowledge and understanding. The material presented is accurate and relevant.

(7) Evaluation: the student has produced some sociological evidence by using the work of Le Grand (1982) to evaluate the notion that men and women cannot be treated as homogeneous ('entire') groups. Interpretation and application: relevant use of Le Grand (1982) – the candidate shows that a sound interpretation of the question has been adopted. Knowledge and understanding: very little sociological material is presented, although citing Le Grand provides some indication that sociological knowledge is being applied.

(8) Interpretation and application: the student has tried to gain marks for application by applying the notion that more women appear to be entering paid work, and thus patterns of ill-health may change. Evaluation: by criticising average figures the student is demonstrating evaluation skill. However the question of averages and treating people as homogeneous groups has also appeared in the first paragraph. Knowledge and understanding: there is little sociological evidence, though sound sociological enquiry is indicated by pointing out the problems of using 'average' figures.

Questions

2. Further essays to practise:

(a) Assess the view that men and women suffer different patterns of morbidity due to their behaviour. (*25 marks*)

(b) Evaluate the claim that unhealthy behaviour is rooted in the structural and material circumstances in which men and women find themselves. (*25 marks*)

(c) Assess the evidence and arguments that suggest women make greater use of health services than men. (*25 marks*) (AEB November 1993)

Summary

The issue of gender and health must be examined alongside data on other important variables such as social class, age and ethnicity, which might have a serious impact on health chances. Women appear to survive longer than men, yet this difference is complicated by variables such as social class. Women also appear to visit their doctors more often than men. However some research suggests that rather than actually experiencing more ill-health, they might define themselves as ill more easily than men. Research also suggests that men visit their doctors more than women do if female reproductive cases are excluded from the morbidity figures. Thus men might define themselves as ill more often than women or they might actually experience more ill-health than women.

As sociologists it is important to examine which illnesses tend to be unevenly distributed between men and women and which particular types of women and men suffer more/less from such illnesses, for example working-class men and women, men and women from ethnic minorities, men and women from particular age groups. Why is breast cancer more common in women in social Class I? Why do young Asian females have a higher suicide rate than white and Afro-Caribbean females of similar age? What genetic factors, behaviours and structural factors might explain different patterns of illness between men and women? In examining these questions sociologists need to be sensitive to the impact of changing gender roles on health.

Additional issues that might be explored include the way health services respond to illness: are there inequalities between men and women in the treatment they receive? How might treatment exercise social control over men and women, for example do some doctors define women's conditions differently from those of men?

7 The relationship between ethnicity and health

By the end of this chapter you should be able to:

- define 'race' and 'ethnicity';
- understand why measuring ethnicity is problematic;
- apply the different ways of measuring ethnicity;
- describe the patterns of ill-health among ethnic groups;
- evaluate explanations of these patterns of ill-health;
- assess the problems of studying morbidity and mortality patterns.

Introduction

This chapter examines the problem of defining both 'race' and 'ethnicity', as well as the problems involved in using demographic (population) figures (for example from the census) that provide data on the proportion of ethnic minorities within the population. Although the overall proportion of ethnic minorities is relatively small, some local areas (for example Brent in London) have a larger proportion than the national figures reveal. Particular health needs may have to be catered for when ethnic groups are concentrated in different geographical areas.

Some ethnic groups suffer from higher rates of mortality (death) and morbidity (illness) than others. Various explanations are offered for these patterns, including genetic causes (for example blood disorders), behavioural and cultural factors (for example smoking and diet), material and structural factors (for example poverty, which may influence smoking and diet), migration and racism, as well as unequal treatment within the health service. There are critics of the view that there are genuine differences in health and illness between ethnic groups: this is referred to as the artefact explanation.

What is meant by 'race'?

'Race' refers to a person's biological characteristics such as the colour of their skin (for example black/white). The notion that biological characteristics can be identified and grouped together is a socially created phenomenon – it is not a natural way of separating people.

Who decides which biological characteristics (for example colour of skin, build) separate groups of people? Further problems occur with the concept of 'race'. Firstly, the variation between individuals makes it very difficult to classify them into groups on the basis of physical appearance. Secondly, when distinguishing between groups of people it may be important to consider more than just their physical characteristics; for example the need to take account of people's traditions and religious beliefs means sociologists often use the word 'ethnicity' rather than 'race' to distinguish between different groups of people.

What is meant by 'ethnicity'?

Ethnicity refers to a person's culture (way of life) and sense of cultural identity. Members of an ethnic group share a common culture. Legal battles have extended the boundaries of ethnic groups to include Sikhs and Jews. Romany travellers are considered to be an ethnic group, but Rastafarians are not according to the definition used in the Race Relations Act 1976. Therefore what counts as an ethnic group may be problematic in itself. An ethnic minority may be defined as a group of people who share a common culture (language, religion, customs and traditions) that is not the majority culture. For instance black people in Britain are an ethnic minority but in South Africa they are an ethnic majority. Interestingly, when we refer to black or white people are we making reference to race or ethnicity? This is often not made very clear in sociological work. The word black may be used to describe people from the West Indies, yet 40 per cent of the population of Trinidad is of Asian origin. Terms used to label groups of people from different origins or cultures are therefore very problematic.

Ethnicity in Britain

The movement of populations, both emigrant and immigrant, has been a feature of Britain's history. Many of the earlier groups who entered Britain gradually lost their distinctive cultural identity. Identifiable ethnic groups in Britain today include those who have preserved their culture over several generations (for example Jews) and others whose migration to Britain has been more recent (most immigration from the black Commonwealth countries has taken place since the 1950s).

Exercise 7.1 Which are the main ethnic groups in Britain?

Examine the following data:

Ethnic groups as a percentage of the British population, 1991

Ethnic group	% of population
Black, Caribbean	0.9
Black, African	0.4
Black, other	0.3
Indian	1.5
Pakistani	0.9
Bangladeshi	0.3
Chinese	0.3
Other Asian	0.5
All ethnic minority groups	5.5
White	94.5

(*Source*: OPCS, 1991.)

a 1. What is meant by (a) race, (b) ethnicity, (c) ethnic minorities?

i 2. Who might have produced the information on population and ethnicity in the above table?

i 3. Which ethnic group forms the largest proportion of Britain's population?

i 4. According to the table, what is the total percentage of all ethnic minorities resident in Britain?

i a 5. Give examples of ethnic groups that have not been identified in the table. (Hint: have any white ethnic groups been omitted?)

Why is ethnicity and health an issue for sociologists?

Do different ethnic groups have different health problems?

The Office of Population, Census and Surveys (OPCS) found that nearly 6 per cent of the British population is made up of ethnic minorities (though quite which groups this figure includes is not made explicit). This figure seems quite small, so why have sociologists concerned themselves with the study of ethnicity and health? As in the case of gender and social class, different ethnic groups appear to have different patterns of health and illness. For instance Afro-Caribbeans suffer a higher rate of sickle cell anaemia (an inherited blood disorder). White Europeans suffer a higher rate of haemophilia (a blood disorder that prevents blood clotting). Small-scale studies show that Asians suffer a slightly higher rate of heart disease but have fewer cases of lung cancer, a common cancer in Britain today. Mares *et al.* (1987) identify another pattern: black communities suffer disproportionately from death due to accidents, poisoning and violence.

Are ethnic minorities concentrated in particular areas?

The study of ethnicity and health also appears important when we examine the *distribution* of ethnic groups in Britain because some areas – such Brent, an inner city authority in London – have a large proportion of ethnic minorities. Thus for some areas understanding issues relating to ethnicity is of crucial importance as we could be examining the health care needs of the majority of the local population.

ITEM A

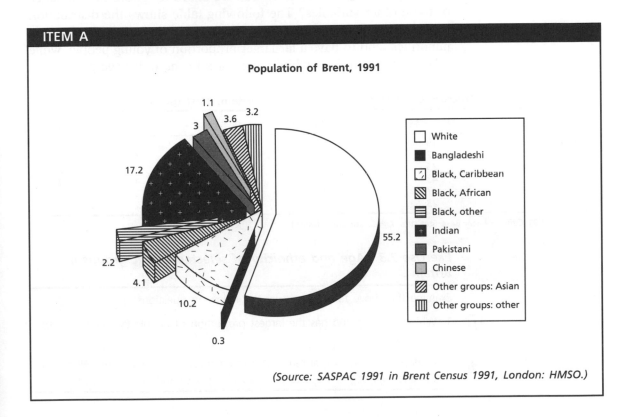

Population of Brent, 1991

Legend:
- White
- Bangladeshi
- Black, Caribbean
- Black, African
- Black, other
- Indian
- Pakistani
- Chinese
- Other groups: Asian
- Other groups: other

(Source: SASPAC 1991 in Brent Census 1991, London: HMSO.)

ITEM A | **Exercise 7.2 Ethnicity in Brent**

[i] 1. According to Item A, what is the proportion of whites in Brent?

[i] 2. What is the proportion of blacks in Brent?

[i] 3. Compare the proportions of ethnic minorities in Brent with the national figures in Exercise 7.1.

[a] 4. Why is it important to consider the proportion of ethnic groups in a local area rather than rely on the national figures, as in Exercise 7.1?

[a] 5. What are the proportions of ethnic minorities in your locality?

What are the problems of studying ethnicity and health?

Do extra (or extraneous) factors complicate the study?

Does a person's ethnicity matter more than their occupation (or lack of one), income level, gender, place of birth or age when understanding their state of health? Can we afford to ignore the influence of these other variables? The following table shows the distribution of ethnic groups in different age bands. It is clear that some ethnic minorities tend to have a far larger proportion of young people, while a larger proportion of white people are in the older age groups.

Age structure of selected ethnic groups in Britain, 1991 (per cent)

Ethnic group	Under 15	16–44	45–64	65–74	75+
Whites	19	42	22	9	7
Black, Caribbean	22	48	25	4	1
Black, African	29	59	10	1	0
Pakistani	43	43	12	1	0
Bangladeshi	47	38	14	1	0
Chinese	23	59	12	2	1

(*Source*: 1991 Census, Local Base Statistics, OPCS, London: HMSO.)

Exercise 7.3   Age and ethnicity of selected ethnic groups in Britain

Examine the above table to answer the following questions:

[i] 1. Which ethnic group has the largest proportion of people (a) under 15, (b) 60 or over?

[a] 2. By examining age we are including more cross-cutting variables. What other variables might you need to consider along with age and ethnicity?

Is there much evidence on ethnicity and health?

There are very few studies of ethnicity and health, and except for the census few studies provide extensive information on the proportion of ethnic minorities in Britain. It was not until 1991 that the census included a question on ethnicity, enabling us to study accurate data on ethnic minorities, including the proportion living in different areas, household size and composition, birth rates, age structure and unemployment rates.

Is measuring 'ethnicity' problematic?

Although we defined the term 'ethnic group' at the beginning of the chapter, no suggestion was given about how to measure ethnicity.

Researchers who wish to collect data on ethnicity have to decide how they will operationalise (make measurable) this concept. The decisions researchers make about how to measure things are likely to have a major effect on the results they produce.

Exercise 7.4 The problems of measuring ethnicity

Ahmad *et al.* (1992) studied white, Asian and Afro-Caribbean people's views on the causes of health and illness, using data from a survey carried out by other researchers. Ahmad *et al.* point out that the quality of the data was problematic because there had been no interview question about ethnicity. Instead the interviewers had been instructed to determine the respondents' ethnic groups by looking at them and then making up their own minds.

[i][a] 1. Would you consider this method of measuring ethnicity a valid one?

[i][a] 2. Would it be more likely to measure race than ethnicity?

[e] 3. What problems might there be in measuring race rather than ethnicity?

[e] 4. What problems might occur if you measured ethnicity using only these categories: (a) 'Asian', (b) 'White', (c) 'Afro-Caribbean'?

[i][a] 5. What category might a person place themselves in if their parents are of 'mixed race', for example a Bangladeshi mother and a white Irish father? (Hint: will the person be able to place themselves easily in a category?) What does your answer illustrate about the problems of defining ethnicity?

[a] 6. If we use birth certificates (that is, country of birth) to decide a person's ethnicity, then how would you classify a black British-born person whose parents were born outside Britain (for example in a Caribbean country)?

[a] 7. (a) What ethnic category might a person choose who has Indian-born parents but was born in Britain, has never been to India, knows no Asian languages and has no interest in India?

[a]   (b) Might the same or a different category be chosen by someone who also has Indian-born parents but is able to speak Hindi, has travelled to India several times and enjoys the distinctive cultural traditions their family promotes?

[e]   (c) What do the problems in 7a and 7b illustrate about the notion of ethnicity?

Can we compare the results of different studies?

When examining the results of different studies of ethnicity and health we may have the problem of lack of comparability because different studies have used very different measures of ethnicity. If the studies produce different results is this because they have found something genuinely different? Or is it simply that they have put the people in their sample into different categories?

Comparing the categories from research on health and ethnicity is very difficult because there are many ways of classifying ethnicity. The table below clearly shows the variation between the measures of ethnic group used by three studies of health and illness. Such variation makes it difficult to compare trends between ethnic groups.

Measures of ethnicity used in 3 main studies

Ahmad et al. (1992)	Townsend and Davidson (1980)	OPCS (1991)
Asian White Afro-Caribbean	India and Pakistan Europe (inc. UK and Eire) West Indies UK and Eire England & Wales	Bangladesh India Pakistan Caribbean Commonwealth Rest of Africa E. Africa Ireland Australia, Canada and New Zealand

Exercise 7.5 Classifying ethnicity

Examine the table above and answer the following:

1. State the number of ethnic groups identified in each of the three surveys.

2. What problems might arise if we used ethnicity data from the three sources? (Hint: given the variation in type and number of ethnic groups between the studies, could you usefully compare ethnicity data between the studies? Why? Why not?)

Ethnicity: what are the patterns of health and illness?

We have recognised that the topic of ethnicity and health is an important one for sociologists, despite the problems involved in researching any patterns of ill-health between ethnic groups. Item B shows some limited findings from research comparing different ethnic groups.

Patterns of illness and death

(1) Immigrant mortality study in England and Wales, 1984

The sample in this study consisted of people aged 20 and over born outside England and Wales. The findings are summarised below:

Africa	Higher rates:	strokes, high blood pressure, maternal deaths, tuberculosis, violence/accidents
	Lower rates:	heart disease, diabetes, lung disease
Indian sub-continent	Higher rates:	diabetes, tuberculosis, liver cancer, maternal deaths, accidents/violence, heart disease
	Lower rates:	cancer of stomach, breast cancer, lung disease
Caribbean	Higher rates:	strokes, diabetes, violence/accidents
	Lower rates:	lung disease
England and Wales	Higher rates:	lung disease
Scotland	Higher rates:	tuberculosis

(2) Ethnicity and blood disorders

North European:	Higher rates of haemophilia
Afro-Caribbean:	Higher rates of sickle cell anaemia
Middle Eastern:	Higher rates of thalassaemia
Asian:	Higher rates of thalassaemia

(Sources: (1) Adapted from M. Whitehead, The Health Divide, London, Penguin, 1992; (2) adapted from Culley and Dyson, 'Race, Inequality and Health', Sociology Review, September 1993.)

In short there are different patterns of blood disorders between ethnic groups: Afro-Caribbeans suffer higher rates of sick cell anaemia and north Europeans suffer higher rates of haemophilia. In addition blacks appear to suffer higher rates of accidents and violence than many other ethnic groups, whilst some Asians suffer higher rates of heart disease than whites in England and Wales. One problem with the data in Item B is the issue of extraneous variables. There are likely to be large variations within each ethnic group depending on age, gender, location and social class.

ITEM B   *Exercise 7.6   Ethnicity and patterns of ill health*

Examine Item B and answer the following:

[i]   1. Summarise the patterns of morbidity and mortality for the various ethnic groups.

[e]   2. Do you find it easy or difficult to compare the results of the different studies? Why?

What are the explanations of ethnic morbidity and mortality patterns?

Evidence of patterns of ill-health among ethnic groups is very sparse but this does not necessarily mean that illness is usually distributed evenly between ethnic groups. It might mean that we need to ask *why* so little evidence is available.

How might we explain those patterns we have examined? The explanations focus on the following factors:

- Genetic/biological factors.
- Individual behaviour/cultural factors.
- Material/structural factors.
- Migration and racism.
- Unequal treatment by the health service.
- Artefact.

Rather than attempting to choose which is the most convincing explanation overall, why not ask yourself: for what particular *type of illness* does an explanation seem useful?

The genetic or biological explanation of ill-health

Evidence suggests that some disorders have genetic causes (a 'faulty' gene). For example the genetic explanation examines the problem of sickle cell anaemia among Afro-Caribbeans and Tay–Sachs disease among the Jewish population. About one person in 250 of the general population carries one copy of the Tay–Sachs gene; among the Jewish community up to one person in 25 is a carrier. Carriers themselves are perfectly healthy, but if two carriers have a child there is a one in four chance that their child will receive two copies of the Tay-Sachs gene. A child with two copies of the gene will be unable to produce a vital enzyme, hexosaminidase A, and will have a life expectancy of only three or four years. Of the 10–12 children born in Britain each year with the disease, 3–4 are likely to come from the Jewish community. Although there is no cure for Tay–Sachs, screening can identify carriers.

The explanation for Tay–Sachs disease is clearly genetic, and genetic explanations have been offered to explain some patterns of illness. However this explanation is probably only of value for a limited range of disorders. Zubin and Spring (1977) argue that although people may be genetically *vulnerable* to a disorder (such as schizophrenia), it is the quality of their lifestyle (housing, state of mind, money, diet) that decides whether the schizophrenic symptoms are drawn out. Thus the genetic explanation may be useful for some illnesses but we cannot study it in isolation from the lifestyle people lead or are subjected to.

We now examine an explanation that suggests the choices people make about lifestyle have a large effect on their health.

Individual behaviour/culture as a cause of ill-health

Individual behaviour

We all have a degree of choice over our behaviour. We can choose whether to do more exercise or eat more healthy foods, although factors such as income, opportunity and knowledge might limit the choices open to us. Individuals have been blamed for making the wrong decisions regarding their health. For instance in 1986 Conservative politician Edwina Currie notoriously argued that the real cause of the poorer health of 'northerners' was their choice of diet. People should 'look after themselves better', Currie stated. In the same way it might be argued that certain ethnic groups tend to make more or less healthy choices. However the degree to which individual choices can be viewed as distinct from cultural beliefs and structural factors (income, housing, work) is problematic.

People do make decisions that may help to keep them healthy, or conversely increase their risk of illness. However this explanation of ill-health does raise important questions. Do people *know* what is the 'healthy choice'? How free are people to choose their lifestyle? When people do have choice, why might they choose a less healthy lifestyle?

Exercise 7.7 Individuals and healthy behaviour (a)

[a] 1. List the activities you do that you believe could lead to ill-health. (Hint: diet, smoking, drinking too much alcohol.)

[a] 2. List four activities you avoid because you consider them a risk to health.

[a] 3. Compare the activities on your two lists by copying and filling in the table below:

Activity	High or low risk of illness?	Serious or minor illness?	In the near or distant future?	Reasons for doing/avoiding the activity?

How closely is your choice of activities linked to your ideas about health risks? Are your choices of activities and ideas on health risks similar to or different from other people's?

 4. Identify activities that may lead to a healthier lifestyle. (Hint: exercise, eating 'healthy' foods.)

The items you have listed in 1–4 above relate to a behavioural explanation of health/ill-health, that is, it is what you do in life, the lifestyle you choose to adopt, that affects your health. Item C is about a survey in Manchester that, among other things, examined the respondents' understanding of what would cause them to become ill.

ITEM C

The Manchester Health Needs Survey, 1992

Postal questionnaires were sent to 10 000 Manchester households. There was a 55 per cent response rate. Although the questionnaires were produced in Bengali, Gujarati, Urdu, Cantonese and English, the sample slightly under-represented Pakistani, Bangladeshi, Indian and black Caribbean households. Of the addresses used (obtained from the Family Health Services Authority which keeps lists of GPs' patients) 23 per cent were found to be incorrect.

The results

Questions on lifestyle revealed high levels of smoking and low levels of exercise. A question asking 'what do you think influences your health?' revealed the following:

- Most important: stress, smoking, relationships.
- Quite important: unemployment, pollution, housing.
- Not important: exercise, weight, check-ups.

(Source: Manchester Health Needs Survey, Manchester Public Health Resource Centre, 1993.)

ITEM C   *Exercise 7.8   Individuals and Healthy Behaviour (b)*

Refer to Item C and answer the following:

1. How close was the link between people's behaviour and their ideas on health?

2. How closely does the Manchester list of factors influencing health match your own list?

3. How much control do people have over the factors listed in the Manchester study?

4. What are the advantages and disadvantages of using postal questionnaires for this type of study?

Cultural explanations of ill-health

Identifying the dividing line between individual choice and cultural patterns of behaviour is problematic. It must be stated that individual choices may be affected by upbringing as well as structural factors such as income.

Explanations of patterns of ill-health among ethnic groups can focus on how the way of life of different ethnic groups affects their chances of becoming ill. For example the use of fats such as ghee in cooking has been linked to higher rates of heart disease among Asians. However it has also been noted that many Asians, particularly those from Southern India, have very healthy vegetarian diets, so regarding all Asians as similar is problematic. Greehalgh (*The Times*, 9 February 1995, quoting 1995 Health Education Authority research) points out that 'Asian women rarely smoked [but] Indians and Bangladeshis of both sexes consumed beetle nut and chewed tobacco, an important cause of mouth and throat cancer'. The cultural explanation can appear similar to the 'blame the victim' explanation directed at those in lower social classes (where higher rates of illness are blamed on too much smoking and an inadequate diet with 'too many chips'). Few studies have examined the impact of lifestyle on the health of ethnic minorities. There is also the problem of other variables (factors) that could equally explain health patterns.

Exercise 7.9   Cultural behaviour and health

 1. Identify the cultural group(s) to which you feel you belong by completing the table below. (Hint: would you say that you identify with any particular groups of people who share a similar lifestyle and set of beliefs?)

Cultural group	My membership
Religious Ethnic Social class Age Region Other?	

 2. Do you believe any of these 'cultures' exist? Give reasons for your answer.

 3. In the table below, identify any patterns of behaviour that may lead different cultural groups to adopt a healthier or less healthy lifestyle (Hint: foods eaten often that are healthy/unhealthy, alcohol allowed/not allowed, contraceptives such as the condom allowed/not allowed). In the first column, show which section of each group the patterns refer to, for example 'social class (working)'.

Cultural group	Healthy pattern	Unhealthy pattern
Religious Ethnic Social class Age Region Other?		

How do some people respond to cultural needs?

The employment of many Chinese in the catering and clothing trades (why these trades?) makes it very difficult for Chinese workers to visit their doctors during the week. The restaurant trade is extremely busy throughout the day and evening, and it is not unusual for a waiter to work from 11 a.m. to 1 a.m. with a break some days from 3–5 p.m. (Pui-Ling Li, 1992). As a response to these antisocial hours and language difficulties, in 1988 the London Chinese Health Resource Centre was set up to cater for Chinese health needs. The centre calls on the services of a number of interpreters to cater for the diversity of Chinese languages, and also opens on Sundays. This is an example of people tailoring their health care to suit their own cultural needs. Other issues concerning health services and ethnicity may focus on whether minorities live in areas with poorer health facilities.

Exercise 7.10   Catering for cultural health care needs

Having read about the London Chinese Health Resource Centre, try to answer the following:

[i][a] 1. Can you identify other groups who might find it difficult to visit their doctors?

[a] 2. (a) In what ways might language differences cause obstacles to medical care?
(b) How can these obstacles be overcome?

Exercise 7.11   Evaluating the behavioural/cultural explanation

[i][a] Complete the gaps in the following using the key words provided below:

The issue of . . . . . . is an important one because people do have a degree of choice over their lifestyle. There is limited . . . . . . on the behaviour adopted by different cultural groups, however the issue of culture and its impact on health should not be ignored. A criticism of the cultural explanation is that it appears to '. . . . . .' in the way it examines how individual lifestyles or cultural values affect healthy/unhealthy behaviour. A further criticism is that the cultural explanation distracts attention from the . . . . . . basis of ill-health, for example the effect of . . . . . . on health. To gain a more sophisticated understanding, perhaps both the role of . . . . . . and behaviour as well as the . . . . . .

circumstances in which people find themselves should be studied to account for some of the patterns of ill-health among . . . . . . groups.

Key words: culture, evidence, ethnic, material, behaviour, poverty, blame the victim, material.

The material/structural explanation of ill-health

This explanation examines the quality of people's material surroundings/living conditions as an explanation of ill-health. We are speaking here not of the effect of people's culture on illness but the effect of their position in a social structure in which resources (for example income, wealth) are distributed unequally. Occupation has been a common focus for measuring the quality of a person's lifestyle (income, quality of housing, diet, working conditions, stress). When examining ethnicity and health we might need to ask whether some ethnic groups are materially better off than others.

Is there a relationship between ethnicity, unemployment and ill-health?

Unemployment has been linked to increased rates of ill-health. If unemployment affects ethnic groups to different degrees then the issue of those lacking paid employment should be a sociological consideration. The table below shows that blacks and Pakistanis experience far higher rates of unemployment than whites and Bangladeshis. Would the table be more helpful if it showed the relationship between gender, ethnicity and unemployment?

Unemployment rates by ethnic group, 1993 (per cent)

Ethnic group	Unemployed	Long term (1 year+)
White	9	4
Black (Afro-Caribbean and other black)	28	15
Pakistani	30	15
Bangladeshi	13	6

(*Source*: Adapted from *Social Trends*, London: HMSO, 1994.)

How might type of work affect ill-health?

The type of work people engage in is also an issue. Amin (1992), claims that some ethnic minorities are concentrated in more hazardous work and thus are exposed to more accidents at work and work-related illness.

The NHS is a major employer of ethnic minorities (particularly women) in the lowest strata of the health service; this involvement of ethnic minorities in low-paid health care work is coupled with antisocial working hours and unpleasant working conditions.

ITEM D

Islington Local Poverty Survey

Islington Council's 'Poverty in the 1980s' found that 40 per cent of ethnic minorities were suffering from poverty (defined as 140 per cent of supplementary benefit or less). People suffered from material deprivation (low income, poor working conditions, diet, clothing, housing, home facilities and local facilities) as well as social deprivation (lack of rights in employment, politics and education). The survey therefore tried to investigate more than just low income. It also found that members of the Irish community were the most materially disadvantaged and socially deprived.

Birmingham Local Poverty Survey

Birmingham City Council's 'Poverty in Birmingham' (1989) used data from the 1981 census and found that the recession in the 1980s had affected ethnic minorities more than whites. This could be due to some areas of industry employing proportionately more ethnic minorities (for example textiles). These industries may have been affected more than others by the recession.

Employees in managerial and professional occupational groups by ethnic origin and sex, 1987–9 (per cent)

	Men	Women
White	35	27
West Indian/Guyanese	34	29
Pakistani/Bangladeshi	27	23
Indian	41	Not available
All other origins	43	30

(*Sources*: K. Amin with C. Oppenheim, Poverty in Black and White: deprivation and ethnic minorities, CPAG/Runnymede Trust, 1992; Department of Employment.)

ITEM D   *Exercise 7.12   Different ethnic groups, different living conditions?*

[i]   1. According to Islington Council (Item D), what is the difference between social deprivation and material deprivation?

[i]   2. According to Birmingham City Council, why did some ethnic minorities experience greater deprivation and unemployment during the 1980s recession?

[e]   3. Why is unemployment an important issue for the study of ethnicity and ill-health?

[i][a]   4. In what way does the table contrast with the two items preceding it?

Ethnicity, housing and homelessness

Investigations into ethnicity and housing have revealed that some ethnic minorities live in poorer accommodation and in poorer inner city areas. The 1980s boom in home ownership may well have polarised housing, with the more desirable local authority houses being bought by tenants and the worst remaining in the hands of the authorities. Hence those remaining in the local authority rented sector may well have inferior houses. Given the concentration of ethnic minorities in some inner city areas, along with higher rates of unemployment for some ethnic minorities, quality of housing may well be a worsening problem for these groups.

A survey of homeless households placed by the local authority in bed and breakfast (B&B) hotels around Paddington in central London showed that most of the adults were young (that is, between 16 and 34 years) and most of the people were from ethnic minority groups (35 per cent of whom were black; 30 per cent were white and from the UK; only 56 per cent spoke English as their first language). Lissauer *et al.* (1994) examined the complaints made by people living in B&B accommodation:

- Lack of space (70 per cent).
- Nowhere for the children to play (68 per cent).
- Isolation (58 per cent).
- Noise (38 per cent).
- Lack of privacy (32 per cent).

The mothers interviewed in B&B accommodation complained of depression and the children were diagnosed as experiencing a greater number of mild illnesses than their counterparts in private households. Other research has revealed that B&B users are more likely to use hospital services (Victor *et al.*, 1989). An example of how B&B life can affect health is provided by one B&B respondent: 'I was pregnant, I couldn't stay in bed and breakfast, because I wasn't eating properly, because I was getting very ill living off fish and chips all the time' (Connelly and Crown, 1994).

Further health problems for people in temporary accommodation have been reported. Families are often moved many times before more suitable, if any, housing is found. This movement makes it difficult for them to stay with a regular GP. A pregnant woman's relationship with her midwife is important and this is complicated if the woman has to move. Since a large proportion of B&B users are from ethnic minorities and English may not be their first language, access to health care is made even more difficult. Health authorities also find it difficult to tailor health care to the needs of the homeless people in their area if the homeless population keeps moving.

Finally, every person has a statutory right to register with a GP, but to date GPs have not been obliged to accept patients that have not been assigned by the local family health service authority (FHSA). Whether this right will remain under the new 'health areas' now that the FHSAs have been abolished (April 1996) is yet to be determined. The FHSAs had the right to refuse to register those without a permanent address. It might be made even more difficult for people to register if they do not have a permanent address, for example GPs may not receive payment for patients who are only on their list for a few weeks. This is an example of being caught in the 'poverty trap', where being poor and homeless causes even greater problems that increase the difficulty of finding a way out of the situation.

Exercise 7.13   Housing and ill-health

 Write down as many examples as possible of factors that might affect the health of a person living in bed and breakfast accommodation. (Hint: for example access to cooking facilities.)

Exercise 7.14   Evaluating the material/structural explanation

 Sort the following into strengths and weaknesses:

- The material explanation is supported by a variety of evidence showing that ethnic groups may suffer higher rates of unemployment and material deprivation.
- The material explanation tends treat ethnic minorities as one homogeneous group rather than attempting to explore the differences between ethnic groups.
- The material explanation needs to consider the relationship between lifestyle and material circumstances rather than simply view poverty as the main cause of illness.
- The material explanation should consider relationship between gender, age and region along with material circumstances.
- The material explanation does not 'blame the victims' for their illness but examines the way society is organised, which causes some ethnic groups to suffer material deprivation and poor housing.
- It is difficult to establish a causal relationship between poverty and ill-health as lifestyle factors may well play a role.
- Material factors may be useful to explain some illnesses but not all illnesses.

Strength	Weaknesses

Migration and racism as causes of ill-health

Migration is the movement of people from one place to another. Britain's history is one of immigration (for example Romans, Danes, Jews, Irish, Caribbeans, Africans, Indians, Pakistanis, Chinese). Would we expect the experience of immigration to this country to affect patterns of health and illness? Several factors might be relevant here. For example do cultural patterns change as a result of migration? Do material circumstances improve or deteriorate? Do ethnic minorities experience racism? Does access to health care change?

Racial discrimination

Brown (1994) states that racial discrimination (for example in employment and housing) and harassment (for example racial attacks) may have an adverse effect on health (for example stress, personal injury). Home Office figures suggest that Asians are 50 times more likely to suffer racial victimisation and Afro-Caribbeans are 36 times more likely to suffer racial victimisation than whites.

Irish migration

Raftery et al. (1990) state that those born of Irish parents in Britain on average suffer higher rates of death than those born in Ireland. Williams (1992) considers this may be due to the fact that many Irish occupy poorer housing, suffer higher rates of unemployment and are overrepresented in manual occupations. However we have additional problems here: are we measuring the effects of social class or ethnicity, and has their treatment in Britain meant that many Irish have not been able to diversify into other occupations? Another factor is that of gender. Williams (ibid.) claims that women's health has improved since migration whereas that of males has worsened. Thus the experience is not the same for men and women. Women seem to have experienced more rapid social mobility. Why might this be? Are Irish females performing better in school? Could marriage have made a difference (that is, have Irish women married into a higher class?) Once again health issues may vary between men and women from the same ethnic group.

The health service as an explanation of ill-health

Access to health services

We may wish to examine the way different ethnic groups make use of the health services. Are the health services taking account of their widely varying cultural needs? For example many Chinese do not speak English but a variety of Chinese languages, which makes dealing with the traditional health service very difficult (Pui-Ling Li, 1992). The type and nature of their work (long hours with speakers of the same language) limits their opportunity to learn English.

ITEM E

'The concept of access to health care for black people still requires analysis. Access to health care for black people in comparison with whites may be classified in three ways: comparatively high access rates, comparatively low access rates, and similar access rates. Generally, access to health care is viewed as a desirable goal, but when black people's access rates are higher than white people's this might not always be the case. High access rates for Afro-Caribbeans in the speciality of mental health might not be viewed by the Afro-Caribbean community as serving its interests and might be deemed discriminatory in effect; it has often been suggested that the diagnosis of mental illness and treatment is based upon dominant white cultural values.

The small recorded number of elderly Asian and Afro-Caribbean people in hospital wards and nursing homes might indicate these two groups are discriminated against. Professionals usually explain the low numbers by asserting that care is provided by and within the family. This assertion, however, ignores the evidence. In a study in Birmingham in 1981, 26 per cent of elderly Asians had no family in Britain and 36 per cent had no family in the neighbourhood, as compared to 9 per cent of Afro-Caribbeans who had no family here and 46 per cent who had no family in the neighbourhood.

Screening for Sickle Cell disease provides a further example of low access rates for Afro-Caribbeans. While the incidence of sickle cell anaemia is approximately one in 400 births among Afro-Caribbeans and sickle cell traits are present in one in ten Afro-Caribbeans in Britain, screening for the disease is not offered to all Afro-Caribbeans. On the other hand, screening for phenylketonuria, with an incidence of one in 1400 among the British population, is on offer to all new-born babies.

Where access to health care is the same for black people as it is for the white population, racial discrimination may still occur. Access to the treatment of diabetes provides a useful example. Mortality rates produced in the 1984 Office of Population Censuses and Surveys report showed that diabetes is more common among Afro-Caribbeans than among other racial minorities and the white population. On the evidence of a higher incidence of diabetes Afro-Caribbeans might expect qualitatively better investigation and treatment than other groups.'

(Source: Mel Chevannes, 'Access to health care for black people', Health Visitor, vol. 64, no. 1, January 1991.)

ITEM E   *Exercise 7.15   Access to health care for black people*

[i] 1. Outline the three pieces of evidence in Item E that suggest unequal treatment in the health service for ethnic minorities such as Afro-Caribbeans.

[e] 2. Can you generalise that unequal access occurs throughout the NHS? Explain your answer. (Hint: might some areas be delivering better care for ethnic minorities than other areas?)

[i][a] 3. Write to a local hospital and ask in what languages their health-related material is published, or visit a doctor's surgery and examine their health-information leaflets. Are the leaflets in many languages? Which ones?

Health officials and racial stereotypes

Stereotypes are oversimplified images or views of groups of people. The stereotypes held by health service officials (doctors, nurses, midwives) might affect the care and treatment of some ethnic groups. Littlewood and Lipsedge (1982) claim that black patients are twice as likely to be detained involuntarily for mental illness, arc likely to receive heavier doses of drugs and are more likely to see a junior doctor. However we cannot explain rates of mental illness simply in terms of racist doctors. It is interesting to note that Littlewood and Lipsedge point out that black patients are more likely to be seen by black doctors. How does this relate to the suggestion of racist treatment by doctors? Perhaps it shows unwillingness on the part of white doctors to treat black patients, or is it recognition of cultural differences (if any)?

ITEM F

Isobel Bowler (1993) conducted small-scale observations in maternity wards and interviewed 25 midwives over three months in the summer of 1988. The majority of patients observed were Moslem of either Pakistani or Bangladeshi descent and were often assessed to be working class. Bowler found that the midwives held a number of stereotypes, which she claims may have affected the quality of care these patients received.

'They're not able to communicate'

The patients' command of English was reported to be very poor, and consequently they were assumed to be rude and unintelligent. One consultant said, 'If you ask me they shouldn't be allowed into the country until they can pass an English exam'. The midwives' use of colloquial terms and euphemisms was also a problem: the patients found it difficult to understand terms such as 'waterworks', 'down there', 'the other end' and 'tummy'.

'They're abusing the system'

The patients were often considered to be 'abusing' the system by having too many children. Some of the midwives thought the Asian mothers needed to use contraceptives. However when Currer (1983) carried out a survey of Asian women in Bradford it was found that of 17 Asian women questioned, nine were using a method of contraception. The idea that Asians do not use contraception is therefore questionable. We might also ask who is to decide how many is 'too many' children? Stereotypes of large Asian families may affect the treatment and care received by Asian women. For instance one Asian woman reported to Bowler that she wanted to discuss an unwanted pregnancy with the senior house officer (SHO), who replied, 'It's only her second baby. I thought these people liked large families'. The possibility of a termination was not discussed as an option.

'They're making a fuss about nothing'

Asian women are also believed to make a fuss about nothing: 'Well, these Asian women you're interested in have very low pain thresholds. It can make it very difficult to care for them'. One patient who suffered vomiting during a long childbirth later complained of a sore throat. The midwife replied, 'Oh, I expect you were shouting a lot during labour. That's why your throat hurts'.

Bowler claims that the stereotypes held by midwives and hospital officials can lead to differences in the quality of health care received on the ward and throughout childbirth. One Asian woman suffered a long and painful labour but did not receive the pain-relief drug pethidine, unlike many white women in a similar situation. The treatment of Asians as an homogeneous group – 'they're all the same' according to one midwife – may lead to the absence of a relationship between midwife and patient, and consequently inequality of care.

(Source: Adapted from I. Bowler 'They're not like us: midwives' stereotypes of South Asian descent maternity patients', Sociology of Health & Illness, vol. 15, no. 2, 1993.)

ITEM F   *Exercise 7.16   Racial stereotyping and the health service*

Answer the following questions, which relate to Item F:

a 1. What is a stereotype?

i a 2. How do stereotypes such as the ones described by Bowler develop?

a 3. What effects do you think such stereotypes have on the medical care of ethnic minorities?

e 4. Can stereotyping be avoided?

e 5. Can we generalise from Bowler's evidence to make statements about how all ethnic minorities are treated by the health services? Why/why not?

The artefact explanation of ill-health

Claiming that patterns in the data show a link between ethnicity and illness or death could be misleading. It could be that social class is a far more important cause of ill-health, and since many members of ethnic minorities are within the poorer sections of society (with higher unemployment or more hazardous working conditions) it just appears that ethnicity is the cause. We therefore have the problem of separating a number of different variables, including ethnicity, social class, region, age and gender. The idea that patterns are produced because of the way a researcher has gathered the data has been labelled an artefact: a phenomenon that isn't necessarily true can appear to exist because of the way data is gathered and organised.

Rather than attempting to determine which variable is the most important, perhaps we should be focusing much more on the relationship between variables.

Which explanation is most useful?

Postmodernists argue that the search for a single explanation (a metatheory) of social phenomena (for example patterns of health) is likely to be fruitless. Different explanations might be useful in different circumstances.

Examining patterns of infant death is sociologically useful here because there may be different reasons why infants die at different stages of their early life. One explanation may not be adequate to cover all infant illness and death.

ITEM G

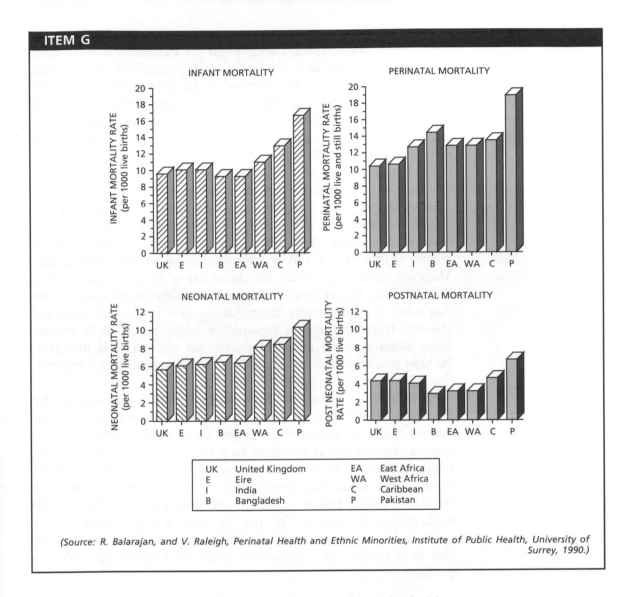

(Source: R. Balarajan, and V. Raleigh, Perinatal Health and Ethnic Minorities, Institute of Public Health, University of Surrey, 1990.)

ITEM G **Exercise 7.17   Infant deaths and ethnicity**

[i] 1. According to Item G, which ethnic group appears to have the highest rate of infant mortality?

[a] 2. How might the material/structural explanation account for higher rates of infant mortality?

[i] 3. Outline the pattern shown among Bangladeshis in the different measures of mortality.

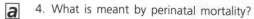

[a] 4. What is meant by perinatal mortality?

[a] 5. Why might antenatal clinics have a low take-up by Bangladeshis?

[e] 6. How does the research illustrate the limitations of metatheory?

According to Andrews and Jewson (1993), Pakistanis and Bangladeshis share similar social backgrounds yet Pakistanis seem to have a consistently higher rate of infant mortality (deaths under one year old) than Bangladeshis. The material explanation would claim similar levels of occupational class would produce similar patterns of infant mortality. Yet there are quite wide differences in the rates of infant mortality for Pakistanis and Bangladeshis of the same social class. Therefore even if we find material factors that are contributing to the high Pakistani infant mortality, we will need to identify some other factor to explain the difference between the two groups.

Bangladeshis suffer a higher rate of perinatal mortality (death of infants between four weeks prior to birth and three months after birth) than all other ethnic groups (except Pakistani). Perhaps this is related to the use of and treatment received in antenatal clinics. MacVicar (1990) claims that low Asian use of antenatal clinics is to blame for the higher rate of perinatal mortality (as sociologists we may wish to examine why some Asians seem not to use antenatal classes). Thus the material explanation might be useful to explain some mortality, such as infant death, but not perinatal mortality. Perhaps treatment and use of medical care is a more useful explanation of this type of infant death.

An issue when trying to select a single explanation to account for a particular health pattern is the question of whether different explanations *can* be separated (for example it cannot be assumed that the material explanation is unrelated to behavioural and cultural explanations). Material factors such as income might influence the decisions people make about how to behave (for example whether they decide to visit a leisure centre to do more exercise). Clearly the explanations are separated for the purposes of understanding them, yet sociologists must view explanations as sometimes interrelated, that is, a number of explanations might be required to explain a problem.

Structured exam questions

The following exercises will help you to apply the issues and practise skills you have learned in Chapter 7.

Question

1. Describe and explain the relationship between health and either gender or ethnicity. (*25 marks*) (London, now InterBoard, June 1993)

(a) Using the following key words to fill in the gaps in the student essay below: evidence, defining, victimisation, use, limited, victim, morbidity, class, local, biological, sickle, variations, stereotypes, artefact, poisonings, environment, choice, relationship, cultural, similar, living, position, housing.

Student answer

(a) Theory and research conducted by sociologists show that there are some differences in mortality and . . . . . . associated with ethnic group membership. The Office of Population, Census and Surveys found that nearly 6 per cent of the UK population is made up of ethnic minorities. We must ask why ethnicity and health are such important issues for sociologists, particularly considering that these figures seem quite small. However, by examining . . . . . . figures, for example of those in the London Borough of Brent, the percentage of ethnic minorities is much greater than the national figures would suggest. In addition, should sociological interest be governed by the number within a population who to appear to be affected by a problem?

(b) Morbidity patterns suggest there are differences in the nature and extent of illness between ethnic groups. Afro-Caribbeans seem to suffer from higher rates of . . . . . . cell anaemia, and white Europeans seem to suffer from higher rates of haemophilia. Mares *et al.* (1987) identified another pattern where black communities suffer disproportionally from deaths due to accidents, ... and violence.

(c) Sociologists face many problems when studying the issue of health and ethnicity. There are problems in . . . . . . ethnicity. Ethnicity refers to a person's culture and sense of cultural identity. Members of an ethnic group may share a common culture, for instance language, religion, customs and traditions. However, there may be large . . . . . . within each ethnic group, for example between men and women within the ethnic group, social class and age as well as location: all these identities may contribute to health chances more than ethnicity.

(d) The next problem for sociologists is the lack of . . . . . . There are few studies on ethnicity and health therefore we have little access to up-to-date data. It was not until 1991 that the census included a question on ethnicity, thus we have little access to comparative large-scale data on ethnicity and illness (the census asks a question about long-standing illness). However studies by the Health Education Authority and the Kings Fund Institute are starting to fill the gap.

(e) Having discussed the problems sociologists face, we can look at their actual explanations of the relationship between ethnicity and ill-health. One explanation examines . . . . . . causes of ill-health. Evidence suggests that some people suffer genetic disorders, such as sickle cell anaemia among Afro-Caribbeans and Tay Sachs disease among the Jewish population. Whilst these disorders clearly appear to be inherited genetic disorders, this explanation is only of limited value as it only deals with a . . . . . . range of disorders. However the genetic explanation has been applied to explain the incidence of schizophrenia. Zubin and Spring (1977) claim that both genetics and . . . . . . are important factors to consider as people, including different ethnic groups, may have a genetic predisposition for schizophrenia but it is the nature of the environment (for example stressful) which draws out these symptoms.

(f) We all have a degree of . . . . . . over our behaviour, though some people have more choice than others. We choose whether to do more exercise or eat more healthy foods. The focus on people's lifestyle choices may lead to 'blaming the . . . . . .' for their ill health. Some individuals have been blamed for their behaviour, even though unhealthy lifestyles may be caused by cultural ways of life or material/structural factors such as poverty and poor housing.

(g) . . . . . . explanations focus on how the 'way of life' of different ethnic groups affects their chance of becoming ill. For example the use of fats such as ghee in cooking has been linked to higher rates of heart disease amongst Asians. However it has also been argued that many Southern Indian Asians have very healthy vegetarian diets, so regarding all Asians as similar is problematic. The cultural explanation can be viewed as . . . . . . to the 'blame the victim' explanation, which is directed at individuals (and in this case an ethnic group) whose unhealthy behaviour is blamed for their ill health.

(h) The material and structural explanation examines the quality of people's material surroundings or . . . . . . conditions as an explanation of ill-health. People's . . . . . . in the social structure in which resources such as income or wealth are distributed unequally may cause some people and some ethnic groups to suffer higher rates of illness. Thus unemployment may cause certain ethnic groups to suffer higher rates of poverty than others and therefore they may suffer more illness than other, more prosperous ethnic groups.

(i) Racism may be the cause of the unemployment rates as well as directly causing ill-health through racial . . . . . .: however victimisation is not likely to account for widespread differences in ill-health.

Raftery *et al.* (1990) claim that Irish people born in Britain on average suffer higher rates of mortality than those born in Ireland. Williams (1992) claims that this is due to living in poorer . . . . . . and higher rates of unemployment, which may be due to discriminatory employment practice. We do have the problem with additional variables: are measures of social class being accounted for along with ethnicity; which of these two variables is more important and is the search for one main variable failing to see that there may be a . . . . . . between ethnicity and social class which, taken together, may be important in explaining health chances?

(j) Sociologists may like to research whether ethnic groups make equal . . . . . . of the health service. Of course if the notion of doctor-caused diseased (iatrogenesis) developed by Illich (1990) is to be believed, then use of the health care system may be viewed as a problem. However are the health services taking account of varying cultural needs, for example the languages spoken by patients, health needs such as sickle cell awareness? Pui Ling Li (1992) states that many Chinese do not speak English but a variety of Chinese languages. This may make dealing with this group very difficult. The type and nature of work (for example shift work, late hours) may restrict the hours at which the members of some ethnic groups can visit their doctors. Bowler (1993) claims that from observations of midwives on a multicultural maternity ward, nurses held . . . . . . of the Asian mothers, which may have affected their care in the hospital. The evidence that such stereotypes are held by medical staff may be used to explain why some ethnic groups may underutilise the health service.

(k) For sociologists it is vital to establish whether explanations linking ethnicity to ill-health are really genuine. It could be that social class is a major contributor to ill-health, as the Black Report (Townsend and Davidson, 1980) and Whitehead (1992) claim. Some ethnic groups may tend to occupy a particular social . . . . . ., thus it may be social class that is the main factor, not ethnicity; and the way research is gathered can create an impression of ill-health differences which are not really present. This is known as the . . . . . . explanation. However, instead of trying to establish which explanation explains *all* patterns of ill-health between ethnic groups (which postmodernists call a 'metatheory') perhaps sociologists should be examining the relationship between ethnicity and social class as well as gender and age. Only then might sociologists gain more sophisticated data which reflects a range of identities.

(b) Now match the following comments on skills to the appropriate essay paragraphs:

Comment

(1) *Evaluation: the conclusion attempts to add further evaluation points by offering the artefact criticism of ethnicity and ill-health figures as well as by offering the view that relationships between variables need to be examined rather than simply examining the issue of ethnicity. The point of metatheories is applied to draw attention the postmodernist position that no single explanation can explain all social phenomena. This is a strong conclusion as it deals with a number of evaluation points that are clearly related to the essay question. Knowledge and understanding: the candidate provides some relevant points (for example metatheories) that draw on sociological theory. Clearly the candidate understands the essay question and is also able to provide appropriate sociological knowledge. Interpretation and application: the conclusion shows that the candidate has accurately interpreted the essay question by applying relevant points that contribute to a further critique.*

(2) *Interpretation and application: the answer very clearly shows that the student has interpreted the question accurately by discussing both ethnicity and two aspects of ill-health (morbidity and mortality). Evidence has been applied to deal with the importance of the ethnicity issue. Evaluation: a criticism of the national ethnicity figures has been offered as well as showing awareness of whether the number of people being affected by an issue should govern sociological concern. Knowledge and understanding: by drawing on OPCS data on the proportion of ethnic minorities in the population the candidate exhibits sociological knowledge of ethnicity.*

(3) *Interpretation and application: the question is being addressed because the answer deals with an explanation of ethnicity and ill-health. The genetic/biological explanation is applied accurately to the question. Evaluation: a criticism is offered of the genetic explanation. Knowledge and understanding: the paragraph suggests the candidate does know about the genetic basis of some illnesses. The answer also draws on the work of Zubin and Spring (1977) to provide an Evaluation point.*

(4) *Interpretation and application: evidence of morbidity patterns among ethnic groups has been applied, for example Afro-Caribbeans suffering from higher rates of sickle cell anaemia. The evidence has been selected to address the issue being examined, that is, ethnicity and ill-health. Knowledge and understanding: mention of the work of Mares et al. (1987) and genetic diseases suggests the candidate has learned some actual sociological information. Evaluation: no evaluation is offered.*

(5) *Evaluation: the problems faced by sociologists (for example the problem of defining ethnicity) when studying ethnicity provides useful evaluation. A number of problems are outlined that relate to the essay question.*

Knowledge and understanding: the problems discussed (for example the wide diversity among people of the same ethnic group) suggest the candidate understands the issues related to studying health and ethnicity. Interpretation and application: the candidate has applied some useful points to the question and appears to have interpreted the question clearly.

(6) *Evaluation: presenting other problems faced by sociologists, such as lack of evidence, provides more evaluation. Knowledge and understanding: the problems presented (for example the lack of available evidence) suggest the candidate understands the issues surrounding the study of health and ethnicity. Interpretation and application: the candidate has applied some useful points to the question and appears to have interpreted the question clearly.*

(7) *Interpretation and application: the student applied the cultural explanation to the question by giving as an example an Asian diet. Evaluation: the student shows that care must be taken not to assume that all members of an ethnic group share the same lifestyle. There is also a comparison of this explanation to the individual explanation by focusing on the 'blame the victim' issue. Knowledge and understanding: no studies of the cultural causes of ill-health, are cited, however a limited number of examples are supplied, for example diet and its effect on health.*

(8) *Interpretation and application: the issue of racism deals with the question in a way that shows the student is still dealing with the essay question appropriately. Evaluation is offered by discussing extraneous variables such as social class and gender. Although this point has been made before, here it is being used to evaluate a different explanation. Knowledge and understanding: appropriate knowledge is drawn on, for example the work of Raftery et al. (1990) on the health of the Irish in Britain. The issue of discrimination within the health service may have been a useful point to include.*

(9) *Interpretation and application: an additional explanation is offered that deals with individual behaviour, although limited information is applied to the issue. Evaluation: a note of caution is offered because of the implication that accepting the behaviour explanation is to blame victims for their ill-health – perhaps the student could have dealt with the problem of blaming the victim, for example people may be treated differently if workers in the health services believe patients such as smokers are responsible for their illness. Knowledge and understanding: limited information is provided, however the issue of individual behaviour is outlined, albeit briefly.*

(10) *Interpretation and application: further evidence that the student has interpreted the question accurately is shown by the inclusion of another relevant explanation: the use of the health service. Chinese health care issues are raised and an author (Pui Ling Li, 1992) cited clearly and succinctly. Knowledge and understanding: evidence of this is shown by the student drawing on the work of Pui Ling Li (1992), Illich (1990) and Bowler (1993). Evaluation: no explicit evaluation is provided. Perhaps the* *point that the health service alone is not likely to explain all patterns in morbidity among ethnic groups could be included.*

(11) Interpretation and application: the material explanation is clearly outlined with further application of examples of relevant issues, for example unemployment. Knowledge and understanding: very little evidence is provided to support the material explanation. Knowledge of any relevant work on poverty among ethnic groups could be usefully applied, which might then be related to different patterns of ill-health between ethnic groups. Evaluation: no evaluation is provided. It might be useful to point out that limited evidence on ill-health, ethnicity and social class is available.

Question

2. A further essay to practise: Assess the extent to which the cultural explanation adequately accounts for differences in ill-health between ethnic groups. (*25 marks*)

Summary

Defining both race and ethnicity is problematic. There is limited evidence on the patterns of morbidity and mortality among different ethnic groups. However there are a number of explanations for these patterns, some of which may be more useful than others, depending on the type of illness being examined.

Sociologists must be aware of the importance of variables such as age, social class, region and gender, which may have an impact on the patterns of morbidity and mortality among different ethnic groups. Sociological research into patterns of ethnicity and ill-health should examine the relationship between age, social class, region, gender and ethnicity, for example what is the effect on health of being Chinese, working class, female, disabled or living in an urban area with little access to health services? Examining a number of variables is more likely to uncover the diversity of experiences people face as they attempt to maintain their health.

8 The relationship between age, dependency and health

By the end of this chapter you should be able to:

- define 'age' and 'generation';
- apply the notion of 'age' as a social construction;
- identify the changing age structure of the population;
- evaluate health issues concerning childhood;
- evaluate health issues concerning old age;
- understand abuse as an issue in childhood and old age;
- understand the issue of death, dying and bereavement;
- appreciate the issue of disability.

Introduction

This chapter examines the social construction of 'age' and 'generation', words that identify particular age groups as relatively distinct entities. 'Ageing population' refers to a decreasing proportion of young people and a growing proportion of elderly people, resulting in the need for increased health care resources for the elderly.

Health issues of the young and the elderly are then examined and the theme of abuse (that is, child abuse and abuse of the elderly) explored. Additional issues, such as illnesses experienced by young people or elderly people, are outlined and explained. There is a discussion of death, dying and bereavement: this is an area that has recently attracted greater sociological interest, after all ill-health cannot be explored without consideration of one of its extremes – death.

Finally, a discussion of the nature of disability is provided, in which aspects of disability such as 'impairment' and 'handicap' are defined. There is an outline of some of the problems of examining health issues that relate to the disabled.

What is meant by 'age' and 'generation'?

Age refers to chronological age: being sixteen years old or sixty years old. How people identify distinctive groups based on age (for example children, young people, adults, the elderly) is problematic: what distinguishes a child from an adult or an adult from an elderly person? The notion that we can distinguish groups by age is not 'natural' but socially created by people. For example women have been able retire at sixty years old and might therefore be regarded as elderly at that age; men, on the other hand, have had to wait an additional five years to be placed in the same category because their official retirement age has been sixty five. This example shows that to be regarded as elderly may depend on society's laws about retirement. Thus categories such as childhood, adulthood and old age are 'socially constructed'.

Generation refers to the shared experiences of groups of people, for example the more liberal times in the post Second World War years are claimed to have produced a distinctive '1960s generation'. The generations with which people identify are again socially constructed. Who decides which 'shared experiences' (will all those in the 1960s have shared the same experiences?) bind a group of people together to form a generation? The attitudes towards health among a generation of young people might be explored. However people themselves determine the cut-off point separating those considered to be part of and those outside the 'youth' generation: thus even a youth group or youth culture is socially invented. It might be argued that age groups do share a common set of experiences (a possible change in attitude towards the use of private health care; taking more exercise) that might shape a similar pattern of behaviour (for example more people of a particular generation taking out private health care insurance).

Exercise 8.1   The social construction of 'age' and 'ageing'

[a] 1. With a colleague decide what age you believe should be the 'cut off' point for being regarded as:

- An infant
- A child
- An adolescent
- A young man/woman
- Adult
- Middle aged
- Old
- Very old

[e] 2. Would people from non-Western cultures agree with your answers? Give reasons for this.

[a] 3. What factors/issues did you consider when deciding the cut-off point between the age categories?

[e] 4. How does this activity illustrate that age groups are socially constructed?

Why is 'age' an issue for the sociology of health and illness?

People in society have divided peoples' ages and classified them (for example) into infants, children, adults, the elderly and even the very old. These socially constructed categories appear to have distinctive patterns of ill-health and mortality that are of sociological interest, as were the patterns of ill-health associated with gender and ethnicity.

Sociologists are interested in age and health because of the effect recent changes in population structure could have on health and welfare resources. In many countries around the world, both non-Western (for example India, Sri Lanka, Ghana) and Western (for example Britain, France, Germany, the USA), there is a growing proportion of elderly, necessitating serious consideration of their health needs and how to cater for them.

A sociological study of health and illness must attempt a full examination of health in society. To treat social class, gender and race as the only processes that can affect health is to place a narrow restriction on the study of health.

ITEM A   *Exercise 8.2   Main changes in the age structure of the population*

a   1. Identify the following groups in the population pyramids
     (a) Young (aged 0–15).
     (b) Main working population (16–65).
     (c) Elderly (66+).

i   2. What general trend is shown between 1901 and 2021 in the:
     (a) young dependent population;
     (b) working population;
     (c) elderly dependent population?

i   3. Which sex makes up the larger proportion of the 80+ age group in 1931, 1981 and 2021?

Refer to a suitable geography textbook or the population chapter in the GCSE sociology textbook by Ken Browne (1992) to help you answer the following questions:

i   4. What is meant by 'ageing population'?

i   5. Why might countries be experiencing an ageing population?

i **a**   6. What is meant by the 'burden of dependency' and how might this concept apply to the trends identified in question 2?

e   7. What effect might the word 'burden' have on the way some people view the young, the unemployed, the sick and the elderly?

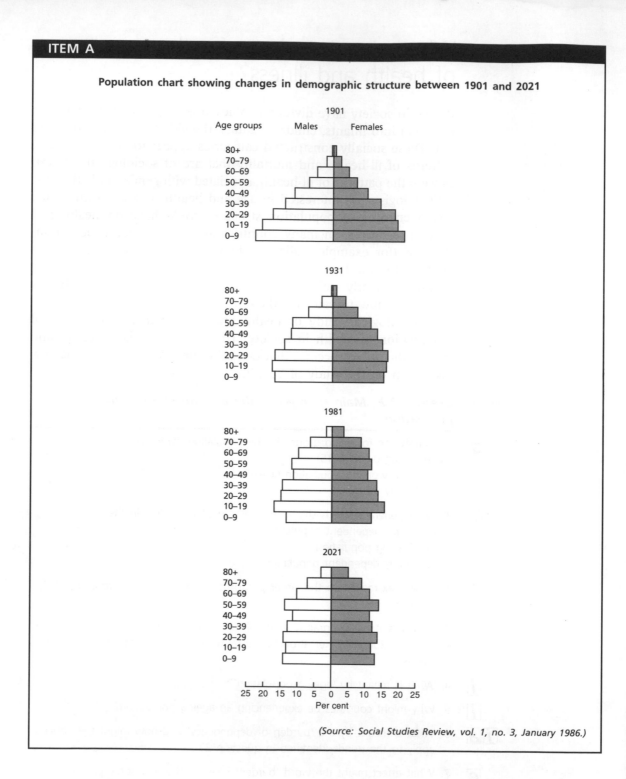

Population chart showing changes in demographic structure between 1901 and 2021

(Source: Social Studies Review, vol. 1, no. 3, January 1986.)

Do different age groups suffer from different illnesses?

Patterns of ill-health and mortality may well vary according to age, for example the amount of chronic sickness reported increases with age. But age cannot be considered in isolation; it must be considered alongside other variables such as social class and gender, ethnicity and location. Sociologists might ask questions such as 'what *relationship* exists between age and social class, age and gender, and age and ethnicity?' The following table illustrates the way social class and gender are additional variables to consider when examining health and age.

Chronic sickness: percentage reporting limiting longstanding* illness, by age, sex and socioeconomic group (SEG), 1992

Age	SEG	Males (%)	Females (%)
0–15	Non manual	6	5
	Manual	8	7
16–44	Non manual	8	12
	Manual	12	13
45–64	Non manual	19	23
	Manual	31	28
65+	Non manual	38	41
	Manual	47	47

* The General Household Survey defines a longstanding illness as any illness, disability or infirmity that has affected the respondent in the past and is likely to continue in the future. To an extent 'longstanding' is defined by the respondent.
(*Source*: adapted from General Household Survey, London: HMSO, 1992.)

The table shows that the pattern of longstanding illness varies with age, but within each age group there are variations based on social class and gender. Such variations must not be overlooked.

Item B clearly shows that different age groups have different patterns of mortality. Young people are far less likely to die, but when they do the cause often tends to be an accident or act of violence. For those over 60 the most common causes of death appear to be cardiovascular problems (for example heart attacks) or cancer. Once again there are variations between men and women.

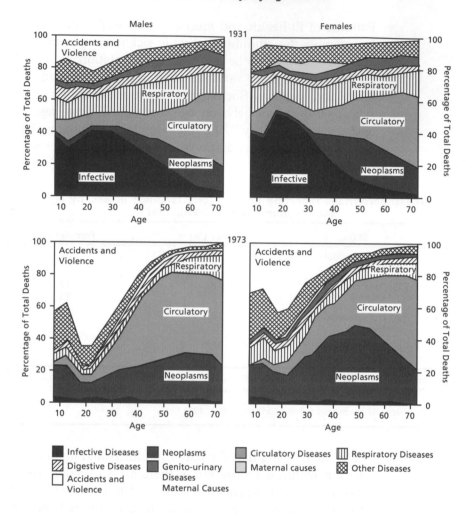

Causes of mortality, by age and sex

(Source: OPCS, Trends in Mortality, London: HMSO, 1978.)

Does visiting the doctor vary with age?

According to the General Household Survey (1992), consultations with GPs do seem to vary with age. The survey data suggests that the young and the old tend to visit their doctors more often than those in the working population, and it might prove useful to know if the reasons for the visits are significantly different by age. It should also be remembered that visiting a doctor is the result of a decision to do so – are some age groups more inclined to visit their doctors than others? For instance do those people in the working population (16–65 years) have less time and opportunity to visit their doctors than those in the younger and older sections of the population?

Exercise 8.3   Trends in consultation with an NHS GP, (1992)

Percentage reporting they had consulted a GP 14 days before interview

Age	Males	Females
0–4	22	22
5–15	10	11
16–44	9	18
45–64	13	18
65–74	18	21
75 +	22	21

(*Source*: Adapted from General Household Survey, London: HMSO, 1992, Table 3.9, p. 37.)

Study the table above.

1. Which age groups are likely to visit a GP more frequently?

2. (a) What similarities and differences do you notice in male and female consultation rates?
   (b) How might sociologists explain these gender differences?

3. What other information would you wish to be included in the table to help us gain a more valid picture of the relationship between age and visits to a GP?

What is the relationship between childhood and health?

According to Aries (1973) the notion of childhood began to develop in the late nineteenth century. Before that time childhood did not exist: 'in mediaeval society the idea of childhood did not exist ... as soon as the child could live without the constant [care] of his mother ... he belonged to adult society'.

Children, or perhaps we should use the term 'very young people' given that childhood might not have existed in the past, were put to work at an early age. Thus childhood today might be a period in young people's lives that has been invented and in which young people receive special legal treatment (for example minors cannot be prosecuted for their actions), special educational status (for example free compulsory education) and special health treatment (for example free dental treatment).

What was children's health experience in the past?

The workplace

The notion of childhood was no doubt different in Britain during the industrial revolution. Poor children often worked long hours, sometimes in very unsafe and unhealthy conditions in factories with potentially harmful machinery. Thus for children 'childhood' may well have been a period where ill-health was commonplace and death could be expected quite early. Indeed the average life expectancy **for** a labourer in Manchester in 1842 was 17 years, and in Liverpool it was a mere 15 years. These figures contrast with those for members of the gentry in Bath, who in 1842 could enjoy the prospect of an average life expectancy of 55 years (Hopkins, 1979, p. 24).

Hopkins (ibid.) describes how nineteenth-century factory life could affect the health of many very young people. From local historical data he discovered that boys of eight worked 12 hours a day in an ironworks, where they were in considerable danger of suffering severe burns from the furnace and from transporting buckets of molten metal from the furnace to the casting areas. In a brick yard six-year-old girls carried heavy loads of six or more bricks at a time. Wet clay had saturated their clothing by the end of the day. A Chesterfield doctor who visited those working in the brick yards and the potteries noted that rheumatism was common among those working in the wet while the health of kiln boys was damaged by loss of sleep and the constant pollution in the factory air. Before 1850 there were no restrictions on the age of young people being employed, except in the coal mines and textile factories (ibid.).

Cruelty in the workplace

Not only did working conditions damage children's health, they were constantly exposed to cruelty by both employers and workers. Hopkins (ibid.) reports the cruelty at work experienced by one boy:

> I have seen the time when two hand-vices of a pound weight each, more or less, have been screwed to my ears at Lytton Mill, in Derbyshire. There are scars remaining behind my ears ... three or four of us at once have been hung on a cross beam above the machinery, hanging by our hands, without shirts or stockings.

Whether these experiences were typical of all mills is not clear. Some have said that the very worst experiences were publicised to support the reformers' quest for government legislation to restrict the use of children in the workplace.

Exercise 8.4 Childhood and health

[i] 1. What does the preceding text illustrate about the the way childhood was viewed in the past?

[i] [a] 2. What do the examples suggest about the health chances of some children during the early period of the industrial revolution in Britain?

Has the quality of children's health improved?

The infant mortality rate records the number of deaths in the first 12 months of life per 1000 live births. Examining the infant mortality rate (IMR) it would seem young children are far more likely to survive today than in the past. In 1902 the IMR was around 142 per 1000 live births but by 1990 it had fallen to 9.3 per 1000 live births (OPCS, 1991). Not only has the death rate decreased for children but the causes of death have changed dramatically, for example far fewer children die of infectious diseases such as smallpox and tuberculosis.

There is a debate over the cause of the improvement in the IMR. Some claim the introduction of immunisation and an improvement in medical care are the main factors, whereas McKeown (1976) claims that improvements in sanitation and living standards prevented people from developing infectious diseases. The main causes of death for children today tend to be accidents, particularly roadside accidents, respiratory problems such as asthma, and various types of cancer (OPCS, 1978). Infant and childhood mortality in Britain are now rare events rather than the relatively normal feature they were in nineteenth-century family life.

A case study in children's health: child abuse

One of the most recent concerns with regard to children's welfare is the quality of emotional and physical care children receive and the consequences of their not receiving this care. Terms such as emotional, physical and sexual abuse have been used to describe the traumatic treatment some children are subjected to by their carers. Defining what amounts to abuse and neglect is problematic. In 'extreme' cases (who decides what is extreme?) perhaps there would be widespread agreement within a culture and perhaps cross-culturally; however Stainton Rogers (1993) states that one needs to reflect on what constitutes inappropriate childrearing practice before judgments are passed.

The problems involved in collecting data on child abuse are similar to those on suicide or crime. For officials to know about the extent of abuse the victim (or someone else) must report their unpleasant experience. Not every child will approach an official; indeed, not every child will know they are suffering from 'abuse', and some children will be too young to report the incident. Thus a social process is involved in the collection of figures on child abuse. A change in the willingness of people to report child abuse or the willingness of officials to define cases as genuine will affect the statistics that are produced.

The following adaptation from Taylor (1992) illustrates the process by which some cases of abuse become reported cases of abuse:

1. Child abuse: known to perpetrator and (probably) victim. This may/may not be:
2. known to others in the family/community. May/may not be:
3. reported to or suspected by professionals. May/may not be:
4. investigated. May/may not be:
5. recognised and reported as abuse.

Exercise 8.5   Examining child abuse figures

Examine the following table, which shows the estimated child abuse figures for 1985 and 1989.

Estimated number of abused children aged 0–16 years, in England and Wales

	1985	1989
Physically injured	9 800	10 500
Sexually abused	3 000	6 600
Total on register*	17 100	36 200

* Abused or giving rise to grave concern over their safety.
(*Source*: Creighton (1990)).

 1. What do the figures indicate?

 2. What might account for the change in the figures? (Hint: in your answer you will need to refer to the adaptation from Taylor, 1992, above).

Baker and Duncan (1986) conducted a study into child sexual abuse using a representative sample of 1029 adults interviewed in 1984. Baker and Duncan (ibid.) define sexual abuse as follows: when 'another person who is sexually mature, involves the child in any activity which the other person expects to lead to their own sexual arousal. This might involve intercourse, touching, exposure to sexual organs, showing pornographic material or talking about things in an erotic way.' The 10 per cent who claimed to have experienced abuse were asked which of a selection of prepared statements best described the effects the experience had had on them. The results were as follows:

	Total from a sample of 206(%)
Permanently damaging and long-term effects	9
Unpleasant and harmful at the time, no long-lasting effects	42
No effects at all	41
Has improved the quality of my life	3

(*Source*: A. Baker and S. Duncan, 'Prevalence of child sexual abuse in Great Britain', *Child Abuse and Neglect*, vol. 9, 1996.)

Whether a sample of 206 is representative enough to make generalisations about all those who have experienced sexual abuse needs to be seriously considered. Kenward and Hevey (1992) describe quite severe physical, emotional and behavioural responses to child abuse.

Any study of child abuse must acknowledge the problem of defining a child rearing practice as 'abuse'. Stainton Rogers (1993) points out that what is deemed acceptable as child rearing in one culture, one social group, or one family may be deemed as abuse in another social setting.

Abuse and neglect during childhood can affect the psychological, social and physical development of children. Such issues are therefore worth considering as as a part of a sociology of health and illness. Patterns of abuse may well be publicised (for example more/fewer middle-class families are abusing their children; more/fewer men are abusing their children) and explanations may be produced. However, as with crime statistics and health statistics generally, there are social processes involved in gathering the data: people need to report the incident, but how much abuse and neglect is reported? The incident needs to be defined as abuse or neglect, but who defines the case as abuse? Thus a study of abuse and neglect is one that is problematic but nevertheless important.

Abuse and neglect are not exclusive to childhood; they can be inflicted on people throughout their lives, particularly, perhaps, in old age.

Society, ageing and ill-health

Is dependency socially created?

Growing recognition that the population is ageing has brought with it a language or discourse (language plus a way of thinking) that has referred to the increase in the elderly as a growing 'burden' of 'dependency', a social 'problem' and a future welfare 'crisis'. The notion of 'burden' is a negative one in which resources are 'unproductively drained away' as more taxes are required to care for the needs of an increasingly elderly population.

The Griffiths Report (1988) reported to the government that elderly people consume the lion's share of hospital and community care and that the costs would increase in the future as the proportion of elderly grew. In particular it said that growth in the number of 'old' elderly (75 and over) was about to occur. Thus ageing in society has been viewed as a 'problem'.

Townsend (1981) argues that 'dependency' in old age (on the state pension, free health care) has been socially created by setting a statutory retirement age at which most people must stop paid work and are forced to rely on benefits. The state pension is so low that it causes poverty for many retired people. Townsend therefore claims that dependency is forced on older people. Interestingly, despite the longer life expectancy today, the increase in redundancy or early retirement can result in adults leaving the labour market well before the normal retirement age: some people can therefore anticipate a period of 'retirement' that lasts longer than their full-time employment.

However, should people have to carry on working to be able to survive? Some Marxists might argue that to raise the retirement age would increase the supply of available labour (the 'reserve army of labour'), causing a decrease in wage levels and even more poverty in society. For some Marxists the state pension and other old age 'benefits' or 'entitlements' are the product of a working-class struggle to secure a better 'social' wage: more resources directed at the working class in forms other than a paid wage. Why should poor people be forced to work even longer than their wealthier counterparts in order to stay out of poverty?

Ageing and prejudice

Ageing has often been thought of as a negative process whereby people become increasingly helpless and dependent on others. The following article by van der Gaag (1995) illustrates the way ageing and ill-health are socially constructed processes: the way elderly groups are identified and treated may lead to particular concerns for the health and health care of the elderly.

Ageing with attitude

"'Will you still need me/Will you still feed me/When I'm 64?" The Beatles' song may be old itself, but it lies at the heart of what most of us fear about ageing: not death, but neglect; not the added years, but lack of love, lack of respect. "Ageing", says Alex Kalache, Head of the programme on Ageing at the London School of Hygiene and Tropical Medicine, "is the number one problem in the world. And if it is not addressed *now*, there will be serious consequences".

It is the "number one problem" because the numbers of people over 60, and particularly those over 80, are growing fast. In 1959 there were 200 million people over 60 in the world, accounting for eight per cent of the total population. By 2025 there will be 1.2 billion, 14 per cent of the total. Contrary to popular myth, by early in the next century three-quarters of these will live in the Third World.

And it is in developing countries that the growth is greatest and the problems are most acute. Their elderly populations are growing at many times the rate of those in the West. For example, over the next 50 years the numbers of those over 60 in Britain will increase by 23 per cent and by 100 per cent in the US – but by 201 per cent in Bangladesh and by 300 per cent in Brazil. Even countries which have had an older population for longer are struggling for positive ways of responding.

They are not helped by the fact that "age" is a relative concept. Each one of us will know people in their sixties who regard themselves as "old" and are therefore seen as "old" by everyone else. We will also know people in their seventies, eighties or even nineties who remain very much part of society and who are mentally if not physically agile.

In Vilcabamba, you may not be considered "old" until you are 90. In Potosia, you might be "old" at 30.

The Vilcabamba Valley in Ecuador . . . is one of three places in the world where many people live to be over 100. Further down in South America, in Potosia in Bolivia, life expectancy is at the other extreme: people don't expect to live beyond their 40th birthday. Mining is the main occupation. The miners and their families suffer from harsh conditions, poverty, overwork, accidents, silicosis and other forms of lung poisoning.

People's need for health care increases as they grow older, and the seriously disabled minority need special care and attention. But many people who do not have serious physical or mental disabilities have nonetheless been shut away in unsuitable homes, cut off from the rest of the world.

Today a growing number of governments are promoting another model which ostensibly helps people to live more independently: "care in the community", as it is often known. What it usually means is care in the family.

This is all very well, but it puts the burden of caring very much back into the family, usually the women. While families can in some cases provide the support needed, the breakdown of the extended family and the squeezing of household resources have often led to neglect of, rather than succour for, the elderly. When resources are stretched, the old are likely to be the ones who go without.

Katuri Sen, a specialist on ageing and policy issues, [claims] the circumstances that people find themselves in when they are older . . . are simply a continuation of the situation that they have been in throughout their lives. If you are poor, overworked and in ill-health when you are young, these conditions are likely to be the same or worse when you are old. She argues that in order to improve the quality of people's lives – and especially the lives of women, who in most societies live longer – policies should aim at improving education in earlier life, helping people to move in and out of the labour market and enabling women to take out financial credit and buy land. These things, she says, would do more than anything else to "reduce the possibilities of acute vulnerability in later stages of life". In other words, the "problem" of the elderly is something which concerns us not only in old age but in youth and middle age as well.

1999 will be the International Year of Ageing. Let

us use the four years between now and then to take up the challenge of David Pitt, a non-retired "retired person" who volunteers here at the New Internationalist:

"Let us direct our energies against those responsible for the poverty . . . and for declining health services. Let us also do what we can to support those living in other countries where care for the aged is a matter of gross neglect. Let us band together and be wilful and cantankerous and obstreperous. Above all, let us never apologise for growing old."'

(Source: Nikki van der Gaag, 'Ageing with attitude', New Internationalist, February 1995.)

Exercise 8.6   The social construction of age and dependency

Read Item C, then answer the following:

[i] 1. According to Kalache, why are the elderly a 'number one problem'?

[e] 2. What criticism might you make of the claim that the elderly are a problem? (Hint: a problem for whom?)

[i] 3. In which part of the world will the greatest number of elderly be living?

[i] 4. Outline an example from the extract that clearly shows that being 'elderly' is a socially created (invented) notion.

[a] 5. What impact might community care have on some families?

What is the relationship between ethnicity and old age?

Studying ethnic minorities and old age is rather like studying a minority within a minority. But as Blakemore and Boneham (1993) state, the size of a group may not reflect the needs of that group, nor the sociological significance of that group. In terms of numbers and as a proportion of all ethnic groups there are more white elderly than black elderly. Recent immigration patterns show it has largely been young people who have migrated to Britain from the New Commonwealth (for example the West Indies, India, Kenya, Uganda), and this is why many ethnic minority groups, tend to have a smaller proportion of elderly in comparison with whites:

Percentage of people of pensionable age, by ethnic group, 1986–88

White	19
West Indian	5
Indian	4
Chinese	4
African	2
Pakistani	2
Bangladeshi	1

(Source: Bond et al., Ageing in Society, London: Sage, 1993.)

It has therefore often been assumed that old age is largely a white concern. In number and percentage terms there is some merit in the assumption, but as Blakemore and Boneham (1993) point out, why should numbers determine the amount of sociological concern?

Blakemore and Boneham highlight the fact that in the next twenty years Britain will experience a rapid increase in the ageing of minority groups because those who migrated in the 1950s and 1960s will reach old age. Perhaps due to the low proportion of elderly within ethnic minorities there have been relatively few studies of ethnicity and old age (Barker, 1984), but this may change when it is recognised that the number of elderly ethnic minority people is growing.

Exercise 8.7 Poverty, age and ethnicity

Percentage in receipt of benefit, by ethnic origin

Benefit	White	West Indian	Asian
All households:			
Child benefit	34	60	75
Unemployment benefit	7	17	16
Retirement/widows pensions	35	6	6
Pensioner only households:			
Retirement pension	95	80	74
Supplementary pension	25	31	26

(*Source*: K. Amin with C. Oppenheim, *Poverty in Black and White*, Child Poverty Action Group Runnymede Trust, 1992.)

Study the table above, then answer the following questions:

1. Which ethnic group has the highest proportion on retirement pension?

2. Which ethnic group has the lowest proportion on retirement pension?

3. Which ethnic group has the highest proportion on supplementary pensions?

4. How might the figures show that poverty in old age may not be distributed evenly between ethnic groups?

5. In what ways might living off a low pension affect health status? (Hint: diet, housing.)

What is women's experience of old age?

The traditional caring role 'allocated' to many women is a major factor influencing their experiences of employment and old age. Many women engage in low-paid, low-status work, often carried out on a part-time basis. Women's poorer pay limits their chance of contributing adequately to an occupational pension. This is compounded by possible 'career breaks' for childbearing and childrearing. The net effect is that women, who on average survive longer than men, have a greater chance of experiencing poverty in old age.

Hunt's (1978) survey supports the view that more women than men are likely to suffer poverty throughout old age. Of the non-institutionalised elderly, Hunt found that 45.5 per cent of men compared with 20.3 per cent of women were receiving a pension from their own or their spouse's former employer. In addition 34 per cent of women had sought state financial assistance, compared with 20 per cent of men.

Link Exercise 8.1   Gender and Caring

Turn to Chapter 10 and read through the section on informal care, starting on page 294, then complete the following exercises.

[i][a] 1. In no more than a paragraph, outline the reasons why gender is an issue when examining caring.

[a] 2. How might a caring role affect health chances? (Hint: for example giving up paid work to care.)

[e] 3. Why is informal care an issue to consider when examining gender and ageing?

Among the 75+ age group, the so-called 'old elderly', women outnumber men by more than two to one. Not surprisingly the experience of living alone (usually as a consequence of widowhood) is increasingly common for older women. Hunt's (1978) survey found that 29 per cent of women aged 75–84 lived alone. Of these 44 per cent had done so for more than twenty years. In addition, because the imbalance between men and women rises rapidly among the 'very old', (there are 289 women to every 100 men for those over 85) there are likely to be more women than men in institutional care (Arber and Ginn, 1991).

It has been found that the health of other family members was an important factor influencing women's retirement. Arber and Ginn (1991) stated that manual workers' wives were more likely than the wives of non-manual workers to give up their jobs upon their husbands' retirement, thus limiting the pension contribution of the wife which could lead to poverty in later life which, in turn, could lead to ill health.

Exercise 8.8   Women, health and old age

[a] Copy the table below and list the factors affecting the health chances of elderly women. For each factor add a brief explanation of how the factor might affect health chances.

Factors affecting the health chances of elderly women	Explanation
1. Survive longer than a man 2. Lower occupational pension 3. Socialised into caring for others 4. 5. 6.	

What are the main theories of old age?

Functionalist theories

Parsons (quoted in Fennell *et al.*, 1988) focused on role changes from a 'useful' working role to a retired and isolated role. The loss of work left the retired individuals 'in a peculiar functionless situation, cut off from participation in the most important interests and activities of the society'. The focus on loss of role is supported by Cumming and Henry's psychologically orientated 'disengagement theory'. Cumming and Henry (1961) based their theory on 275 50–90 year-olds in Kansas City. Social disengagement describes the way people withdraw from society (retire from employment and withdraw from social activities and posts of responsibility, for example as a trade union representative), thus psychologically adapting their attitudes and social lives for eventual death. But some researchers have questioned whether such withdrawal is natural or even necessary.

Havinghurst *et al.* (1968) followed up the 275 people in the Kansas City sample and found that many of them had created new relationships, roles and responsibilities. On the whole, the most active were the happiest. Havinghurst *et al.* proposed a 're-engagement' or 'activity theory'. Healthy ageing involves staying active and maintaining a 'role count', so that as one role is lost another is gained. We might question whether every individual needs to maintain a 'role count' to be happy: does some reward come from doing less?

Exercise 8.9 *The functionalist perspective and old age*

a 1. In what ways might elderly people be forced to 'disengage from various social roles'? (Hint: for example age restrictions.)

a 2. How might withdrawal from various social roles (for example unions, clubs, job) affect health?

Material theories of old age

In 1892 Charles Booth's poverty surveys found that the elderly were the largest group in poverty. In 1993 a special House of Commons Social Security Committee reported that three out of five older people (5.5 million) were living in or on the margins of poverty (incomes within 140 per cent of the income support rate), compared with less than one in four of those under pensionable age; in other words 60 per cent of pensioners were in poverty as opposed to 25 per cent of non-pensioners. For many people poverty in old age is likely to be a prolonged experience, particularly for women, who have a longer life expectancy.

The 'labour-continuity theory' argues that poverty in old age is merely a continuation of poverty during one's working life: low wages mean low occupational pension contributions, resulting in a low pension in retirement; while those who were on higher wages will have been able to afford larger pension contributions and even to 'top-up' contributions to increase the size of their retirement pension.

Traditional Marxists may well agree with the labour-continuity theory, but would go further and ask why there are wage differences between social classes in the first place. The traditional Marxist theory argues that capitalism creates two opposing social classes in which the bourgeoisie pay the proletariat (the workers) as little as possible, thus creating poverty. To focus attention on appropriate wage rates, pension contributions and state benefits is to deal with the *distribution* of available resources not the *economic system*, which causes the inequality in the first place. In other words traditional Marxists are interested in the way an economic system (capitalism) creates inequality rather than concentrating on how to allow the working class to earn more wages and to be awarded a larger pension. Capitalism is the cause of the inequality, so there needs to be a change in the way resources are *produced* rather than just a change in the distribution of the resources.

Neo-Marxists might point out that any additional working-class benefits, such as higher wages and increases in state benefits, redirect resources from the bourgeoisie to the proletariat and increase the worker's social wage. In the class struggle this redirection of resources can be viewed as a partial victory for the working classes. However redirecting resources does not alter the system that created the inequality in the first place.

Postmodernism and old age

Some of the key themes of postmodernism are 'fabrication', 'discourse' and 'power'.

'Fabrication' is a term used by Foucault in *The Order of Things* (1973), in which he claims that much of our knowledge about the world and the way we see ourselves and others (for example perceive others as 'old' or 'young') is not natural but socially constructed, that is, it is created by people. Thus 'fabrication' of the elderly would suggest we need to question the use of the term 'old age'. What might be considered old by one person might not be considered old by another.

'Discourse' largely refers to language. The words used to communicate with others may be quite powerful in influencing the way we think. Thus language plus power equals discourse and discourse reflects the way we communicate and think. The very use of words such as 'old', 'elderly' and 'aged' show we distinguish between different groups of people. Describing a group as 'the elderly' reflects the fact that we think in terms of a separate stratum of people. Predominantly negative connotations are associated with old age and these might unconsciously influence the way we think of elderly people. Influencing the way people think about the elderly is a form of power. For Foucault knowledge is power. This notion of power contrasts with the traditional Marxist notion that power is largely economic: those who own the means of production possess economic power, which in itself provides political power.

ITEM D

'[T]he "problem" of the elderly is something which concerns us not only in old age but in youth and middle age as well. This is also one of the key messages of activist groups on ageing issues like the Grey Panthers. Started in the US in 1970 to oppose the war in Vietnam, they have become a worldwide network active on health care, housing, discrimination and work. Maggie Kuhn, one of the founders . . . [said] "I think we've established the fact old age is a triumph. What we've done is establish the intergenerational bond necessary for real social change, the continuity of life. The old and the young need each other. We're opposed to the segregation of old people"'.

(Source: Nikki van der Gaag, 'Ageing with attitude', New Internationalist , February 1995.)

ITEM D   *Exercise 8.10   Applying the notion of fabrication: changing the discourse of the elderly*

[a] 1. Why is the word 'problem' placed in inverted commas?

[a] 2. Why might the Grey Panthers be opposed to the segregation of old people?

[a] 3. How are old people segregated from others?

[a] 4. How might forming an activist group of elderly people change the negative 'discourse' of the elderly?

[i] 5. How does the extract illustrate the way knowledge or ways of thinking about the elderly are 'fabricated'?

Abuse and neglect of the elderly

As with child abuse and neglect, there are difficulties in defining abuse and neglect of the elderly. Greater attention is now being paid to the issue and the British Geriatrics Society and the British Association of Social Workers have run conferences on the matter . A national pressure group, Action for Elder Abuse, has been formed and increasing numbers of articles are being produced; see, for example, Kingston and Phillipson (1994), who summarise research into possible locations where abuse might most often be found:

- Elderly care wards in general and psychiatric hospitals.
- Accident and emergency departments.
- Outpatient departments.
- Community settings.

The very fact that potential settings have been identified might mean that people are more likely to attempt to investigate mistreatment in these rather than other areas. This may be similar to the way in which identification of 'problem crime areas' raises awareness of crime there and results in more crime being reported.

George Castledine in 'Elder abuse by nurses is on the increase' (1994) claims that the NHS is focusing more on high technology surgery than on the care of older people. Castledine points out that geriatric nursing is seen as being of lower status than acute care. Improvements need to be made in nursing care practice and nursing training to educate geriatric carers to regard care for the elderly as important and the emotional, spatial, physical and psychological needs of the elderly as legitimate. Lee-Treweek (1994) states that daily mistreatment becomes acceptable to carers:

> Workers felt resistance to the individual's emotional needs was central to timesaving. Emotional work had to be repressed and physical labour prioritised as more important. Patients who demanded too much emotional time who refused the role as 'object' were negatively labelled as 'whiners' and were avoided . . .

Lee-Treweek (1991) conducted field research at two Swedish medical institutions specialising in the long-term care of the elderly. She found that the patients' behaviour was constrained by the set daily routines created by the institution: the patients ate at a fixed time and had coffee breaks at fixed times – extra coffee was deemed an administrative problem. Minimal communication took place between staff and patients. From the staff's perspective all activity had to be strictly regulated. As one nurse said: 'If things get delayed here, then we finish late.' The staff were under pressure to get a lot of work completed within a short space of time (ibid.)

Goffman (1968) claimed that 'total institutions' stripped people of their personal identity (mortification of self), a process that appears evident in the research by Lee-Treweek (1991). The patients were forced to comply with the time schedule created by the institution. This schedule meant that patients' individual requirements (for example an extra cup of coffee) were secondary to the daily routines. Sociologists may therefore need to continue to research the quality of care received in 'caring' institutions.

It might be important to ask why abuse and neglect of the elderly are on the increase, if that really is the case. After all, it could be that awareness is growing of the forms mistreatment takes. Castledine (1994) claims that reported mistreatment is increasing due to the increasing number of elderly in institutional care settings. Perhaps changes in the staffing of geriatric wards and nursing homes means that nurses are being forced to ignore the full needs of their elderly patients to allow time to complete their routine tasks. Thus it may be staffing levels that are leading to mistreatment, rather than carers' attitude towards the elderly.

Formal care settings are not the only places where mistreatment occurs. Conflict within the family over property and relatives caring for the parents have also been documented.

The question of mistreatment of the elderly is of sociological concern as it raises issues relating to the quality of care throughout ill-health and dependency, as well as concern about people's physical, social and psychological well-being. It is not enough simply to examine *access* to services without investigating the *interaction* that takes place within the formal and informal care setting.

Exercise 8.11   Elderly abuse

[a] 1. Which social groups other than the elderly might be abused and neglected within (a) a formal health setting and (b) an informal health setting?

[a] 2. Why might the people you have identified be prone to abuse and neglect?

[a] 3. What strategies might be adopted to limit mistreatment of the elderly within (a) a formal and (b) an informal health setting?

[e] 4. What are the problems of enforcing such strategies?

Death, dying and bereavement

Because the infant and child mortality rates are very low in Britain, as in many rich industrialised countries, the subject of death and dying is more commonly applied to old age rather than the young. The young may be more likely to experience bereavement, although more often due to the loss of elderly relatives rather than parents. Sociologists have long studied atypical deaths such as suicide (Durkheim, 1970) but few have studied more typical deaths.

Where do people die?

In 1990 23 per cent of deaths occurred at home whereas 72 per cent happened in formal institutions such as hospitals (54 per cent), nursing or residential homes (14 per cent) and hospices (4 per cent) (OPCS, 1992). People may have preferences about where they would 'like' to die: some may want medical attention at hand and prefer a hospital; others may want familiar settings and family around them.

The way in which people cope with the death of someone else may depend on a number of factors, such as their relationship with the deceased, the age of the deceased, the context in which they died and the predictability of the death.

Ethical issues and dying

Sociologically typical deaths may be of importance: the issue certainly affects us all and our relatives and friends. The way formal carers and (increasingly important, with the onset of the government's community care programme) informal carers deal and cope with death and subsequent bereavement is of concern. Death has a particular meaning in our society as it raises the question of the importance of life. The rights and wrongs of euthanasia are increasingly debated, for example whether people should have the right to take their own or another's life if that life is deemed to be permanently devoid of meaning and enjoyment. The 'cut-off' between those that would be allowed by the courts to live and those allowed to die is a controversial moral issue. With the rising cost of keeping people alive in an increasingly cost-conscious health service, death and euthanasia are likely to become even more frequently debated.

Care and dying

For nurses and lay carers the issue of disclosure and communication is important: should news of terminal illness be conveyed and, if so, how and when? Whilst some consultants have forbidden nurses to disclose news of a terminal illness to the patient, hospitals are becoming increasingly open about information about dying. Access to news about possible death is surely as important to some patients and relatives as access to health services.

Recent articles in nursing journals suggest that death is not an event that nurses are adequately trained to deal with, and not all hospitals have policies and practices to deal with death and dying, for example having a quiet room in which to inform relatives of bad news. Although only a small percentage of patients end their lives in hospices, the hospice movement has made an important contribution to dealing positively with the last stages of a patient's life, rather than perceiving death as an embarrassing indicator of the limitations of medicine.

Link Exercise 8.2   Death and dying

1. Using the text on dying, identify the issues that nurses may need to be aware of when dealing with a patient who has died.

2. Turn to Chapter 2 and look up the term 'cultural iatrogenesis'. In what ways might the notions of death and dying support the view that the medical profession has robbed people of their ability to cope with dying.

The social construction of dependency and disability

How extensive is disability?

Disability is an issue that has long been ignored in many sociology text books, but then again so are issues of gender and ethnicity. It may be that disability has attracted little attention because so few sociologists are 'disabled'. Only 12 per cent of the disabled paid workforce occupy managerial or professional posts compared with 21 per cent of the non-disabled workforce (RADAR, 1994). Similarly many sociologists were (are?) male and white, which might explain why issues of gender and ethnicity have not been treated as problematic until relatively recently. According to the Office and Population Censuses and Surveys (OPCS, 1991) 14 per cent of the people in Britain are registered as disabled. The ethnic minority population of Britain is far smaller than 14 per cent: closer to 5 per cent, depending on the measure of ethnicity used, yet ethnicity is a more central issue in sociology than is disability.

What is meant by 'impairment'?

Impairment refers to any disturbance or interference with normal psychological, physiological or anatomical structure or functioning. Impairment can range from an ingrowing toenail to severe eczema. Impairment may or may not lead to disability or handicap.

What is meant by 'disability'?

There is a debate about the meaning of such a label. Disability tends to refer to a loss or reduction in the performance of 'normal' activities. Because this definition could include so many types of restriction, there are scales of severity.

What is meant by 'handicap'?

Handicap now refers to the way people in society create difficulties for people with disabilities. For example a hearing impairment might make it difficult to listen to a conversation (disability), which can then lead to a *disadvantage* (handicap) when dealing with others who are unable to communicate with someone with this impairment.

Critique of impairment as a basis of disability and handicap

Laqueur (1990) points out that throughout history people have been inclined to identify differences between people, for example men and women, old and young. It might be useful to use Laqueur's notion of 'difference' to examine the way people in society treat some things as impairment and some not. For instance I have a very low concentration span during meetings at work. I constantly switch off from discussions only to find that I have missed vital pieces of information. What is the difference between a low concentration span and a hearing impairment? Both may result in missing information in meetings. Just because I might have more control over concentration than over hearing doesn't necessarily mean that one is more legitimate than the other. Yet society creates social divisions: differences between the able and the disabled, between the hearing and the deaf, and between the sighted and the blind. These distinctions might be socially invented or fabricated ways of creating differences.

How many disabled people are there in the workforce?

The Labour Force Survey, estimates that 14 per cent of the working population have a health problem or disability which limits the type of work that they can do. This is a broad definition, and includes a wide range of people who do not fit into the common stereotype of disability, for example, people with heart conditions, epilepsy, mental health problems or learning disabilities. This survey found wide variations between regions, from under 12 per cent in the South East (excluding London) to over 16 per cent in Wales and Northern England.

How many are unemployed?

- The Labour Force Survey for 1992 showed an unemployment rate for disabled people of 20 per cent, and a 'non-employment' rate of 60 per cent.

- The real unemployment rate of disabled people is much higher. Many disabled people are not included in the unemployment statistics because they are not counted as part of the active labour force. It is not clear how many 'economically inactive' disabled people would want to work in appropriate circumstances (i.e. an accessible transport system, flexible work arrangements, appropriate state benefits). The OPCS survey found that over half such people wanted to work. This suggests a true unemployment rate of about 40 per cent. The comparable rate for non-disabled people in 1992 was 9 per cent.

Under-employment of disabled people

- Disabled workers in full-time employment earn approximately 20 per cent less than their able-bodied counterparts.

- Disabled people are more likely to be in low-status, unskilled jobs. 12 per cent of disabled workers are in professional or managerial positions compared to 21 per cent of non-disabled workers, whilst 31 per cent of disabled workers were in low skilled manual occupations, compared to 21 per cent of non-disabled workers.

- The situation is particularly bad for people who are born with a disability. They are likely to receive poorer education, and also find that many further and higher education establishments are inaccessible. Nevertheless, 7 per cent of graduates are disabled, and companies should seek to reflect this figure in their recruitment process. Advancement in many organisations depends on entering as a graduate.

(Source: Royal Association for Disability and Rehabilitation © RADAR, June 1994.)

Exercise 8.12 Disability, employment and health

Use Item E to answer the following questions:

☐i 1. What proportion of the population are estimated to have a health problem or disability that limits the type of work they do?

☐i☐a 2. Is disability viewed as evenly distributed throughout Britain? Explain your answer.

☐i 3. Why are many disabled people excluded from the unemployment statistics?

☐i 4. What evidence suggests that disabled people appear to earn less and do jobs with less status than non-disabled people?

☐i☐a 5. By reviewing the evidence on employment and unemployment in Chapter 5, write one short paragraph to show how (un)employment may affect the health of disabled people.

Models of disability

The medical model of disability

The medical model tends to focus on the physical impairment that leads to the disability. Thus the physical loss of hearing leads to problems with hearing.

The social model of disability

Being unable to walk unaided may be an important issue, but the creation of a difference can create more of a problem: the stigma associated with being different may restrict opportunities for relationships, education and employment. Some argue that social arrangements with people such as family, friends, employers and teachers determine the degree to which an impairment will be disabling.

Link Exercise 8.3 Disability and health chances

Turn back to Chapter 4 and examine the sections on changes in material circumstances (page 59) and life disruption (page 60) as a result of illness.

☐i☐a 1. In what ways might severe disability result in material problems and disruption of life?

☐a 2. In what ways might society create problems for people with severe disabilities?

What are the problems of researching disability?

Oliver (1992) recalls the question asked by Howard Becker over 30 years ago: whose side are you on? Oliver claims that researchers tend to assume that all the technical, conceptual and 'important' knowledge is possessed by the researcher. Such research is assumed to be dispassionate and relatively objective: after all, traditional notions of scientific research aim to be as objective as possible. However Oliver considers that much research into disability fails to alleviate the oppressed position of the 'objects' (they are treated as such) of the study. Women have been warned against being studied (Finch, 1986) and black people have been advised to tell researchers to 'fuck off' (Jenkins, 1971). Both women and ethnic minorities may claim to be oppressed, and as such why should they cooperate in order to enhance the career position of academic researchers? The same point applies to research into disability.

Disability research tends to individualise the problem (how difficult is it to get about your neighbourhood?) instead of locating the problem outside the individual (what are the environmental constraints that make it difficult for you to get about your neighbourhood?) Oliver (1992) suggests that research into oppressed groups should be emancipatory research: it should be based mainly on 'empowerment', which aims not to change people's lives for them, but to provide information that shows people what they can do to facilitate change.

Critics might argue that in the long term academic research may well help to bring about change, even if it has no direct link to the official decision-making groups in society. However it might be difficult to obtain funding for research if the object appears to be to facilitate change: perhaps such research is not worth carrying out anyway, according to Oliver.

Oliver's main point – 'who does research benefit?' – is an important one that can be applied to other areas of research in sociology. To be neutral is to maintain the status quo, whereas to be emancipatory is to change society. Both are political decisions, so for some academics, such as Oliver, any research is a political activity. The question must still be asked, 'whose side are you on?'

The effects of disability

The disabled may well experience the level of discrimination usually associated with other oppressed groups, such as women and ethnic minorities. Employment problems may cause poverty, which in turn may lead to ill-health. The psychological effects of stigmatisation could increase disabled people's chance of ill-health through factors such as stress. Chapter 1 examined chronic sickness and disability through examples such as repetitive strain injury and ankolising spondilitis, and it might be useful to re-examine this. To use Oliver's (1992) point about the value of research into the disabled, you might ask why it is important to explore the effects of discrimination: why might an examination syllabus be a justification? Would sociologists learn enough if they followed Oliver's request to restrict research to emancipatory ends?

Structured exam questions

Complete the following exercises in order to apply the issues and practise skills you have learned in Chapter 8.

Question

1. Evaluate sociological accounts of the relationship between age and health. (*25 marks*)

(a) Read through the following essay introduction about the relationship between age and health. Each paragraph deals with a separate issue. Write out the introduction, rearranging the sentences into a logical order. Try to organise the paragraphs so that each criticises or supports a previous point. The suggested order appears at the end of the introductory sentences. Once you have written the introduction find the appropriate supporting points in Chapter 8.

Answer guidelines

(1) There are also health issues that appear to affect young people more than many other age groups. Child abuse is an issue that has been increasingly examined by sociologists. There are problems with defining child abuse, which make the study of child abuse problematic.

(2) Not only does there appear to be abuse of children within society but also 'elder abuse', particularly abuse of the elderly in caring institutions. Health problems in old age may be socially produced rather than part of a natural period of biological decline. Society's attitude towards the elderly may seriously affect the rate of decline among the elderly.

(3) As an issue, age has tended to be ignored by much sociological work in health and illness. However with an ageing population, whereby a growing proportion of the population are elderly, the issue of age and health care has become an increasingly important topic.

(4) The issue of age cannot by isolated from other key factors such as ethnicity, gender and social class.

(5) There does appear to be some relationship between age and number of visits to a doctor.

(6) The mortality figures also show patterns between the age groups: death through accidents and violence tends to be experienced more by the younger age group.

(7) Health issues that relate to the elderly have often been assumed to be problems mainly faced by white people, but increasingly ethnic minorities are experiencing an ageing population, and therefore health issues of elderly ethnic minorities may became of increasing concern.

(Suggested order: 3, 7, 4, 5, 6, 1, 2.)

(b) Match each of the following evaluation points to one of the previous sentences from the essay introduction:

Comment

- *Morbidity figures might not be a valid measure of the extent of illness among different age groups but merely a measure of the number of people from different age groups who decide to visit the doctor.*

- *There are problems with studying child abuse because it is a sensitive issue and detecting abuse is difficult. Thus current awareness the extent of child abuse must be seriously questioned.*

- *Even though age has become an increasingly important topic it must be viewed alongside other variables such as gender, social class and ethnicity.*

- *There is evidence to suggest that ethnic minorities are facing an ageing population in Britain. However a thorough analysis should examine gender and social class along with ethnicity and ageing.*

- *There are problems with defining abuse of the elderly: for examples caring staff are unlikely to reveal the true extent of abuse and elderly people in care may have a number of different definitions of abuse.*

- *There are problems with examining age. Other variables such as gender and social class tend to dominate the research: much secondary information is limited to just one or two variables, which usually do not include age.*

- *On the whole mortality figures tend to be more objective than morbidity figures: the mortality figures usually represent all recorded deaths, thus generalisations can more easily be made.*

Question

2. Answer the following specimen exam question: Discuss the view that health and ill-health of young and older people are socially, not biologically, determined. (*25 marks*)

Summary

Sociologists have extended their analysis of inequality and health to include not only social class but ethnicity and gender. A person isn't just working class or middle class, but also a man or a woman as well as a member of an ethnic group.

The issue of age is an important consideration. A person may be 'young' or 'old' or an 'adult'. To examine 'health chances' fully a sociologist should consider age as problematic. In addition the issue of dependency is one that may be relevant to age: young people especially are often dependent on parents or guardians, and some elderly people may find themselves dependent on others. All of us have to depend on others at some point in our lives, it is the extent and nature of dependency that changes. Therefore disability is not an issue that is confined to a small minority of people, it is a position in which many of us can at times find ourselves because of dependency.

When examining dependency it might be important to consider the points at which people require more or less assistance. Not only is age relevant to the issue of dependency, disability too should be examined. Depending on the extent of disability, social relationships may need to change and more assistance may be required. There is a problem with 'lumping' all disabled people together and stating that they all require assistance. Severely immobile people may well have to depend on the provision of adequate facilities to enable them to take control of their own lives. However just as age is a social construct, so too is disability: the reason why some people with an impairment are viewed as disabled and dependent on others may be due to the way society is organised. Society is organised for able-bodied people, thus it is not surprising that some people with impairments are rendered disabled.

9 The sociology of 'mental illness'

By the end of this chapter you should be able to:

- assess measures of abnormality;
- apply problems of defining mental illness;
- apply the issue of labelling and mental illness;
- assess the impact of community care on mental illness;
- evaluate the causes of mental illness;
- identify the problems of treating mental illness;
- evaluate treatments for mental illness.

Introduction

This chapter uses the term 'mental illness' but treats both the term and the notion of mental illness as problematic. The problem with the term rests on the notion of discourse (language that influences thought). Some 'abnormal' behaviour that is labelled as a mental illness might not relate to any problem with mental processing nor be a symptom of an illness. The use of the term mental illness might provoke particular ways of understanding 'abnormal' behaviour.

The chapter goes on to examine the way in which mental illness is defined. Some sociologists, for example Szasz (1972), are very critical of the way in which mental illness is defined. Mental illness might not be an objective state that can be taken for granted but a negative label conferred on people by powerful members of the medical profession (particularly psychiatrists). Critics of the labelling approach point out that some people's behaviour is so severely abnormal that labelling is not an important factor in determining that behaviour, indeed people exhibiting such extreme behaviour might benefit from being labelled mentally ill so they can receive genuine care.

Care of the mentally ill is examined. Goffman (1968) is deeply critical of care for the mentally ill. He claims that institutions such as psychiatric hospitals might not aid the recovery of a patient. With the decline in psychiatric hospitals following the 1990 NHS and Community Care Act, the chapter examines the care in the community programme, which encourages people to be cared for in (and by) the community. The chapter also uses the case of schizophrenia to explore the various competing explanations of this severe mental illness. The cause might be biological or environmental, or both. Finally the common medical treatments for mental illnesses are explored critically, and the access of different social groups – for example according to social class, gender, age or ethnic group – to treatment is evaluated.

What is meant by 'mental illness'?

There is no commonly accepted definition of mental illness. The term is used in a variety of ways because it means different things to different people.

Exercise 9.1   Defining mental illness

 With a colleague define what you consider to be mental illness. You might add some examples of what you consider to be mental illnesses (for example schizophrenia).

There are commonsense notions of mental illness that often involve the use of derogatory language: 'nutter', 'mad', 'weird' or 'strange', for example. These are often applied to behaviour that does not conform to social norms. Some health officials, such as doctors and psychiatrists, believe they can define mental illness more rigorously than any commonsense notions. However medical definitions are still problematic: for instance whose values are being used to define mental illness?

Sociologists have examined a variety of behaviours that have been defined as deviant, including crime and suicide. Interest in deviance has been extended to include mental illness: a type of behaviour that some consider to be deviant from 'normal' behaviour.

Exercise 9.2   How was mental illness viewed in the past?

This exercise focuses on the range of ideas held on the cause of abnormal behaviour over nearly 2500 years:

400 BC: A complaint usually found in women was labelled 'hysteria'. The symptoms included headaches, dizziness, paralysis, blindness and lameness. 'Hysteria' derives from the Greek word *hysterikos*, meaning 'uterus', and the supposed cause of the symptoms was a 'roaming uterus' – the uterus wandered around the body and caused various types of abnormal behaviour depending on where it ended up (for example in the liver or the kidneys). Aromas were used to 'draw' the uterus back to its proper position.

400 AD: Galen argued that physical and psychological problems were a result of an imbalance between the four bodily 'humours' or

fluids (blood, phlegm, yellow bile and black bile). For normal functioning a correct balance had to be restored. This view remained influential for many years.

10th century: The 'wandering uterus' notion had continued for centuries: the tenth century saw prayers to draw the uterus back to its proper position. 'I conjure thee, O womb . . . to lie down quietly in the place which God chose for thee, so that this maid of God . . . be restored to health' (quoted in Rosenhan and Seligman, 1989).

15th century: Strange or abnormal behaviour was deemed to be caused by witchcraft, which was overwhelmingly ascribed to women. 'All witchcraft comes from carnal lust', claimed two Dominican monks. There was no cure for witchcraft except physical destruction of the witch: hence the burning of 'witches' was common. Deutsch (1949) estimated that nearly 100 000 people (mainly women) died in Europe and the American colonies as a result of witch-hunts.

19th century: Debate took place between those who believed abnormal behaviour had biological causes and those who supported a psychological explanation. Sigmund Freud placed himself in the psychological camp and was shunned by the dominant medical establishment, which supported biological causes such as hormone imbalances or brain abnormalities. Freud and others pursued hypnosis as a means of discovering the psychological cause of abnormal behaviour.

20th century: The notion of physical causes gained prominence within the medical establishment, where schizophrenia is now explained by genetic inheritance, chemical imbalances such as excessive dopamine levels, and brain abnormalities. Nonetheless proponents of psychological causes continue to prevail. Both attempt to reduce the behaviour to a single cause that can then be treated. In this way the medical model is dominant in the explanation of both physical illness and psychological disorders.

(Adapted from Rosenhan and Seligman, 1989.)

 1. Select the key words from each paragraph that suggest a cause of abnormal behaviour.

 2. According to the information provided, how have explanations of the causes of mental illness changed over time?

How is abnormality measured?

The measurement of abnormality is problematic. This section examines a number of criteria used to identify abnormality or deviant behaviour and presents a critique of each criterion. From using any of these competing criteria to measure abnormality some people claim that the cause of 'abnormal' behaviour is 'mental illness'. The label 'mental illness' is also problematic, and a later section examines the use of this term.

The statistical criterion

Method

This method classifies any behaviour that is infrequent or untypical as abnormal behaviour. In other words, if the majority of the population do not shout at themselves in the street then anybody who does is deviating from the statistical majority and is therefore exhibiting abnormal behaviour (which might then be called a mental illness).

ITEM A

One in seven adults hit by mental disorder

'More than six million people are suffering from neurotic disorders, according to official figures released yesterday. One in seven adults is blighted by depression, anxiety or some other kind of psychological disorder, the figures showed.

Sufferers were often plagued by fatigue, sleep problems, irritability and worry. Women were more likely to be victims. This snapshot of the nation's mental health was revealed in one of the largest surveys on mental illness.

The study by the Office of Population, Censuses and Surveys was jointly commissioned by the Department of Health, the Scottish Home and Health Office and the Welsh Office.

Interviews were carried out with 10 000 adults plus 350 people suffering from psychosis, 1200 in psychiatric hospitals and 1100 living in hostels or sleeping rough.

People were asked if they suffered any of 14 symptoms over the past month and to give details of their frequency and severity. The symptoms – all indicators of varying degrees of mental illness – were fatigue, sleep problems, irritability, worry, anxiety, obsessions, depression and depressive ideas, including thoughts of suicide.

Lack of concentration and forgetfulness, unexplained aches or pains brought on by stress, compulsions, phobias, worries about physical health

and panic or fear of losing control were also measured.

Preliminary findings showed the most common neurotic problem was a mixed anxiety and depressive disorder, affecting 7.1 per cent. Next, at 3 per cent, was a generalised anxiety disorder.

Severe disorders such as schizophrenia and manic depression, affect four people in 1000 every year, researchers estimated.

The number of people found to be dependent on alcohol and drugs was 4.7 per cent and 2.2 per cent respectively, with men three times as likely to be alcoholics as women and twice as likely to have a drug problem.'

(Source: © Mental Health, Independence Publishers, 1995.)

Exercise 9.3 prevalence of mental illness

i 1. In Item A, how was the OPCS study carried out?

i 2. What types of 'disorder' were reported by the respondents?

i a 3. Were the 'mental disorders' reported in Item A experienced by a majority or minority of the population?

a 4. If one in seven of the population experience some type of mental disorder, should mental disorders be viewed as statistically infrequent? (Hint: is one in seven quite a high frequency?)

a e 5. Do you agree with all the examples of mental illness listed in Item A? Justify your answer.

Critique

Does all statistically infrequent behaviour imply abnormal behaviour? For example a very high intelligence quotient (IQ) would be classified as atypical, yet would somebody with a high score in an IQ test be regarded as abnormal? Whose values will be used to determine which unusual behaviours indicate abnormal behaviour? A second problem with this criterion is the nature of the 'population' being measured. Different groups or populations might well have different patterns of behaviour: thus the behaviour might be statistically frequent in one population but not in another. Take the case of a young girl or boy shouting at themselves in the street: they might be considered to be showing imagination or playing a game. Thus for a population of young children the behaviour might be frequent, whilst for adults it is infrequent – which population should be used to measure the behaviour? Who decides whether to separate populations by age, gender, region, country, nation state, social class, ethnicity or religion?

Deviation from the norm criterion

Method

If statistically infrequent behaviour cannot distinguish between the unusual and the abnormal then one could simply examine behaviour that deviates from the expected patterns of behaviour, that is, social norms. Thus it might be expected that young children who shout at themselves in the street are behaving normally but similar behaviour would not be expected from adults.

Critique

The main problem with this method is whose values are being used to judge normal behaviour: male values, middle-class values, white values? One example of this is the use of different words to describe sexual activity by males or females. A number of words are used to describe females with a 'low' sexual appetite, including 'frigid'. Conversely women who engage in frequent sexual activity may be subjected to the words 'slut', 'slag' or 'nymphomaniac'. Yet an examination of the language of male sexual behaviour suggests there are few words to describe variations in sexual activity; and indeed those used to describe males who have frequent sexual intercourse (for example 'stud') have a positive connotation. Thus the boundaries of 'normal' female sexual activity are narrower than those for men. Who set these boundaries: men perhaps? Likewise homosexuality as a mental illness was only removed from the American Psychiatric Association's diagnostic manual in 1974. It is important to question the values used to determine whether sexual preference is 'normal' or 'abnormal'.

Rosenhan and Seligman's 'Seven elements of abnormality'

Method

Rosenhan and Seligman (1989) propose seven main elements or guidelines that help decide whether behaviour is abnormal.

- *Suffering*: a person, if aware of their behaviour, might be suffering with their condition, for example feeling depressed or miserable.
- *Maladaptiveness*: a person's behaviour might be self-damaging or make them incapable of taking good care of themselves.
- *Irrationality*: the person might not communicate rational or logical thoughts.
- *Loss of control*: the person might be unable to control their own behaviour and be consistently unpredictable.
- *Unconventionality*: unusual behaviour might cause the person to be described as abnormal.
- *Observer discomfort*: if a person's behaviour produces discomfort in observers, then that behaviour is more likely to be defined as abnormal.
- *Violation of moral standards*: if a person's behaviour breaks many of society's moral codes, such as defecating in the street rather than using the toilet, then a decision of abnormality might be more likely.

Critique

The elements of abnormality approach appears more flexible and sophisticated that simply examining statistically infrequent behaviour or behaviour that deviates from society's accepted standards of behaviour (whose standards?) No single element is sufficient for a decision of abnormality to be made. However the more elements shown and the more extreme the behaviour within each element, the more likely a decision of abnormality. However this method still relies on value judgments.

This examination of three methods of defining abnormality should indicate that there is no commonly agreed notion of abnormality.

Exercise 9.4 Defining mental illness

Examine the examples of different behaviours listed below. Decide to what extent you consider each example to be normal or abnormal. Indicate your answer by placing a circle around the appropriate value (1–4). If you believe the behaviour to be abnormal, decide whether the abnormal behaviour could be a result of mental illness by placing a tick under the heading 'Mentally ill'.

	Very abnormal		Not abnormal		Mentally ill
A man shouting at himself in the street	1	2	3	4	
A man shouting at himself in his own home	1	2	3	4	
A crowd shouting at a football match	1	2	3	4	
A cleaner who believes she is the Queen	1	2	3	4	
A young boy who claims to have an imaginary friend	1	2	3	4	
An adult who claims to have an imaginary friend	1	2	3	4	
A woman who hears voices in her head telling her to be quiet	1	2	3	4	
A woman who hears voices in her head telling her to kill men	1	2	3	4	
Someone who claims to be heterosexual	1	2	3	4	
Someone who claims to be homosexual	1	2	3	4	
A man who claims to be a messenger from God	1	2	3	4	
A man who feels constantly depressed	1	2	3	4	
A woman who feels that she cannot face housework anymore	1	2	3	4	

| i | 1. Which cases did you believe to be very abnormal, that is, scored a value of 4?

| a | 2. Explain why each of those cases might be viewed as abnormal; then find a reason why, in each case, the behaviour might *not* be viewed as abnormal.

| i | 3. (a) Which abnormal behaviours did you decide were due to mental illness?
(b) How did you decide whether the behaviour was due to mental illness?

[a] 4. Homosexuality was defined as a mental illness in the USA until it was removed from the American Psychiatric Association's diagnostic manual in 1974. What might this suggest about the ability of the medical profession to define mental illness?

[a] 5. Do your colleagues agree with your rating scores of mental illness? If not, what might the lack of consensus suggest about the notions of abnormality and mental illness?

What are the problems of defining 'mental illness'?

Not only are there problems with measuring abnormality, but the term 'mental illness' also raises issues of concern.

How does language affect our thoughts about mental illness?

Foucault, a post-structuralist, claims language influences the way people think (Foucault, 1963). For example if people use sexist words such as police*man* to describe all police officers then it might reflect the point that all officers of the law are perceived as men. Terminology is important. Language isn't just a series of words, it is a discourse: a way of thinking expressed through language. Language trains people's minds to think in a particular way, which is why efforts are made to stop the use of racist, sexist and ageist language and language considered derogatory towards the disabled. Some might claim that the debate on 'politically correct' language is a more serious battle about discourse.

To use the term 'mental illness' reflects a way of thinking. Foucault (1963) argues that doctors and other health officials deliberately formed themselves into a 'profession' with status in society. Technical jargon, unfamiliar to lay people, was then invented to describe the body and its conditions, for example 'symptoms' and 'disease'. The dominant medical institutions' adoption of the word illness to describe 'strange' behaviour suggests the problem is similar to physical disorders such as flu or measles. Some illnesses can be caught through contact with the carrier. Can mental illnesses be caught? Do people 'catch' a dose of schizophrenia? Few assume mental illnesses can be 'caught', so why is the comparison with physical illness necessary? To use the word 'illness' is to shape the way people think about the behaviour.

Exercise 9.5 Language and mental illness

 1. Write out a carefully worded question to ask a cross-section of the public (for example various age groups of both sexes) about their definition of mental illness.

 2. Search what you have written for negative and derogatory language. How do your findings relate to the notion that mental illness is part of a discourse, that is, that language affects the way we think?

Is mental illness really 'mental'?

The use of the word 'mental' assumes there is a problem with the mind. Szasz (1961) asks whether abnormal behaviour really stems from problems with the mind. By using the words 'mental' and 'illness' our thoughts are already being shaped about the nature of the problem. In other words abnormal behaviour is a form of discourse. Within this discourse the words chosen to express ideas shape the way the problem is understood: the common discourse assumes mental illness is like many other physical disorders with identifiable causes (such as bacteria, a virus, stress) that can be treated by health officials much as doctors deal with physical symptoms. It is assumed that problem behaviour stems from the mind, and therefore treatment must deal with the mind, for example through the use of drugs that alter the functioning of the nervous system, or shock therapy, which alters nerve functions in the brain.

Szasz claims that some abnormal behaviour that is labelled mental illness is in fact a 'problem of living' (for example behaviour induced by a stressful lifestyle).

Is mental illness really an illness?

Foucault (1976) used the term 'gaze' to describe the way powerful groups such as doctors created a way of 'gazing' at (viewing and understanding) an issue such as mental illnesses in such a way that other people think about the issue in the same way. In other words, doctors treat abnormal behaviour as if it has a cause that can be identified and then treated. Perhaps mental illness is just an unusual way of behaving that has nothing to do with being ill or having a 'problem with the mind'? According to Foucault, the way people 'gaze' at mental illness is not natural nor is it the 'truth'; it is merely a dominant or powerful way of thinking about an issue, in this case the issue of 'abnormal' behaviour.

Doctors impose their own values on deciding who is mentally ill

Theorists such as Becker (1963) claim that deviance is in the eye of the beholder. By this he means that views of deviance or abnormality are simply an individual's own interpretation of behaviour. What one person considers abnormal another might consider quite normal. Take the example of homosexuality, once classified as a mental illness: would homosexuals see their own sexual orientation as abnormal or the product of a mental illness?

Heather (1976) supports Becker's claim that abnormality is problematic. Heather suggests that decisions about mental illness are not medical ones, but moral ones. Psychiatrists draw on their own experience to determine abnormality. These experiences are likely to lead to male, middle-class, white, Western values being imposed on many people, including women, ethnic minorities, non-Westerners and the working class. Littlewood and Lipsedge (1982) found that blacks are overrepresented in psychiatric hospitals, and consider the main reason for this is the way white psychiatrists impose their own ideas of normality on black behaviour. Critics might argue that institutional racism in the wider society causes blacks to experience higher unemployment and poorer housing, which leads to increased levels of stress, which in turn causes more mental illness.

A study of doctor diagnosis: 'Being sane in insane places'

Rosenhan (1973) conducted an experiment titled 'On being sane in insane places,' which involved eight 'sane' people entering 12 different psychiatric hospitals in the USA and undergoing a diagnosis by psychiatrists. Would these 'stooges' or actors be defined as 'insane' by staff and doctors? What care would they receive in a psychiatric hospital? After calling a hospital for an appointment, each pseudo-patient arrived complaining he had been hearing voices that were 'empty', 'hollow' and 'unclear', symptoms that are ambiguous to interpret. All information, apart from the above and the pseudo-patient's occupation, was kept as close to the truth as possible: family, relationships and feelings were described accurately. All eight pseudo patients were admitted (seven with a diagnosis of schizophrenia) and were able to study life on the ward. Only their fellow patients detected the pseudo-patients, often accusing them of being journalists. Rosenhan pointed out that on the basis of a single symptom of hearing empty, shallow voices people were being admitted to psychiatric wards. The study illustrates the way diagnosis of mental illness is problematic. After all, who says there is something wrong with hearing voices?

Critics of Rosenhan's study considered that the psychiatrists were simply being very cautious. Doctors were wary of allowing a 'real' problem to pass undiagnosed, so they tended to be more willing to define the stooges as mentally ill. This could result in a type-two error (a false positive), calling a healthy person sick, rather than a type-one error (a false negative), calling a sick person healthy. It is clearly more dangerous to define a mentally ill person as 'sane' and let them walk free than to call a healthy person 'sick'.

A further study took place. Rosenhan told newly inducted hospital staff about the initial study. They were told they would, in due course, encounter a 'stooge' who would be trying to gain entry to the ward. They had to rate each new patient on a ten-point scale to indicate their likelihood of being a stooge. Forty-one patients were judged to be a stooge by at least one member of staff. In fact all the patients were genuine: no stooges were ever sent. It seems, therefore, that staff can also make type-one errors (a false negative), that is, 'real' patients were diagnosed as having no psychiatric problems. But were the staff overcompensating by being more careful not to make type-two errors?

Sarbin and Mancuso (1980) claim that the newer classification systems employed by psychiatrists today (for example the Diagnostic and Statistical Manual IV) are more valid because they require more rigorous inspection of the person's problems (for example physical problems, social difficulties, personality problems, problems with relationships) and the symptoms have to be persistent (for example the US diagnosis system requires schizophrenic symptoms to exist for at least three months).

How powerful is labelling on decisions about abnormality?

Rosenhan (1973) argues that once a label of 'mentally ill' is applied by those in the medical profession then all subsequent behaviour supports the label. Just how powerful is a label when interpreting behaviour? Lindsay (1982) showed video tapes of 'normal' and 'schizophrenic' patients to two different groups of participants. One group was given no information about the people featured in the video. The other group was told the difference. All participants were asked to rate the observed behaviours of those on the video as abnormal or normal. Rosenhan had predicted that those informed of the difference would be more likely to define the schizophrenics' behaviour as abnormal. This was not the case. Both groups defined the schizophrenics as exhibiting abnormal behaviour.

Lindsay concludes that viewing mental illness as the result of

labelling is too simplistic. However labelling is a very important issue
to consider when defining which behaviour counts as 'mental illness'.

What effect might labelling have on the individual?

Goffman (1968) believed that labels stigmatise people. For some people
mental illness is not just an illness: all sorts of other negative characteristics are conferred on the individual, for example 'evil', 'harmful', 'unpredictable'. As Sontag (1983, 1990) argues, 'why cannot illness
just be an illness?' Instead some people 'demonise' the mentally ill.
With the onset of community care, with large, remote psychiatric
hospitals giving way to smaller care homes in the community, some
residents may attempt to prevent psychiatric care homes from being
set up in 'their' neighbourhood.

Just as physical illness can change self-identity (for example Kelly
(1992) describes the change in identity of people with colostomy
bags) so a similar change can take place in those labelled mentally
ill. Sontag (1983, 1990) shows how in the past society created negative beliefs about those with tuberculosis as it does today about AIDS
sufferers. Attempts have been made by organised pressure groups such
as SANE to change people's perceptions of the mentally ill and reduce negative labelling.

Blaney (1975) believes labelling is necessary and positive in attempting to support some of the mentally ill. By labelling patients
'mentally ill' Blaney believes society can then attempt to care for or
treat them. In addition the patients might be relieved of responsibility for their actions.

Exercise 9.6 Problems of defining mental illness

 Copy and complete the following table with appropriate information obtained
from the earlier section on the problems of defining mental illness? (pages
223–7)

Issue	Key names	Application to defining mental illness
Discourse	Foucault Szasz Becker Heather Rosenhan	The term mental illness shapes thinking
Labelling	Lindsay Blaney	
Stigma	Goffman	

Do the 'mentally ill' receive adequate care?

Exercise 9.7 Care of the mentally ill

Watch the film 'One Flew Over the Cuckoo's Nest' starring Jack Nicholson. Most video rental stores will have this in stock. The film provides an insight into life in a secure psychiatric ward in the USA during the 1960s.

 1. In no more than a paragraph explain which of the patients you feel were not 'mentally ill'.

 2. Do you believe the care of the patients was adequate? Explain your answer (Hint: civil rights, labelling.)

Having been admitted to psychiatric hospitals the stooges in Rosenhan's (1973) study documented life on the ward. Their summary makes rather depressing reading:

- Staff and patients were strictly segregated, with separate washing and toilet facilities, as if they were two classes of people.
- Staff were often unavailable. (It was noted that the hierarchy in hospitals is very interesting: those with most power have the least to do with patients; it is the attendants who are often closest to patients.)
- In four of the hospitals housing the pseudo-patients, when the pseudo-patients asked when their case would be heard by the doctor they were not answered; instead one reply was 'How are you today?' (Note: the nurse spoke without eye contact and was still on the move, walking past the pseudo-patient.)
- Patients were often powerless, deprived of many civil rights and personal freedom. Any staff member could read the patients' personal medical files. Physical and verbal abuse was also used when dealing with patients; patients were depersonalised.

Goffman (1968) claimed that people who enter 'total institutions' such as psychiatric hospitals change their behaviour and their self-identity to survive their new 'prison-like life'. The attempt to strip away the person's previous identity is called 'the mortification of self'. Goffman was also critical of the amount of help and treatment received in psychiatric hospitals, feeling that often they are little more than 'storage dumps' for patients.

Descriptions of care in psychiatric hospitals (such as those in Rosenhan's study) along with images produced by the media and the film industry (such as those in 'One Flew Over the Cuckoo's Nest') preceded a very significant change in social policy on the care of the mentally ill, and by 1989 the care in the community programme had become prominent in Britain. The closure of large psychiatric hospitals means that more people are now being 'cared for' in the 'community'.

Exercise 9.8   Care in the community

[i] Examine the sentence preceding this exercise. Write no more than a paragraph to explain why the words 'cared for' and 'community' are in inverted commas.

What is 'care in the community'?

Caring for People (DoH, 1989a) is a government white paper that incorporates many recommendations of *Community Care: Agenda For Action*, also known as the The Griffiths Report after its author, Roy Griffiths (1988), who had formerly been employed in the retail trade. The National Health Service and Community Care Act 1990 made some of the recommendations in the report statutory.

The key themes of community care are:

- Assessment of need: each individual case that might prove expensive should have a thorough assessment of the care needed. A debate exists here about who should decide the patient's needs: the client or the assessor?
- Care management: a 'key worker' tailors services to individual needs (DoH, 1991a). However a debate exists as to how a 'key worker' or 'key system' manages and meets needs.
- Quality assurance schemes have to operate in social services departments and a formal complaints procedure has to be set up.
- Better planning and coordination should take place between local authorities and district health authorities or 'health areas'.
- More choice of services should be available to the consumer or user.
- A greater variety of providers of caring services: not just local authority schemes but a greater role for charities, the voluntary sector and the private sector.

Community care

'What is community care?

Community care is intended to provide help and support for people who could not otherwise manage on their own. The sort of people who may be eligible for community care include frail older, people, those with physical disabilities, drug or alcohol problems, learning disabilities or mental health problems.

Community care for people with mental health problems has been talked about ever since the early 1960s when it became widely accepted that the large, Victorian asylums were no longer appropriate and that care should be provided in the community where possible. There is now increasing concern that resources allocated for community care services do not match needs and that patients are sometimes being discharged from hospital without the necessary support being in place. The Mental Health Foundation has conducted a major Inquiry into Community Care of Severely Mentally Ill People to address some of the problems which have emerged. *"Creating Community Care"*, the report of the Inquiry, was published in September 1994.

Community care means that, where appropriate, services and support are provided in people's own homes or in a residential or care home rather than in hospitals. This is a Government initiative which began as a response to the many reports of inadequate treatment received by people. The policy is aimed at giving people as much independence as possible whilst continuing to care for and support them. It will prevent people becoming "institutionalised" and enable them to develop relationships with friends and family.

Community care also considers the needs of carers, and aims to provide them with practical support and information.

Where does the money come from?

Funds for social and residential care in the community are transferred from Central Government and distributed to local authority social service departments. Each authority is then responsible for purchasing services from a wide range of providers.

Funds for health care in the community come from health authorities and Family Health Services Authorities who purchase services from hospitals, community mental health teams and GPs. There is not a direct connection between money saved from the closure of psychiatric hospitals and that allocated to community care.

Who is responsible for community care?

At present there are two routes to community care for people with mental health problems.

The local Social Services department has overall responsibility for co-ordinating social and residential care. This might mean making available such services as: home helps, district nurses, meals on wheels and day-care facilities.

Some services such as meals on wheels may not be provided free, but this varies according to individual local authority policies. Anyone can apply for help and the local authority should carry out an assessment of their needs but that does not necessarily imply an entitlement to services. It is the local authority's responsibility to decide who will receive services.

Each assessment should involve representatives from a number of the caring professions such as social workers, psychiatric nurses and doctors so that all medial and social needs can be considered. A carer or other friend or relative can attend the assessment and all findings must be put, in writing, to the user. An appeal is then possible if the user feels that a fair assessment has not been given.

If someone is assessed as needing social or residential care, a "Care Manager" will be appointed to ensure that they get all the services they need.

If someone has been in hospital, even for a relatively short period of time, the most likely route to community care is via a process called the "Care Programme Approach". This is the responsibility of the local health authority. An individual aftercare plan will be drawn up and the relevant service providers contacted before someone is discharged to ensure that full support is in place before they go home. A "key worker" will be assigned to oversee the transition into living in the community and to liaise with service providers. It is a legal requirement for all patients admitted to hospital under the Mental Health Act 1983 to have a formal after-care programme prepared when they are discharged from hospital.

The two alternative routes to community care can cause confusion and uncertainty as to which agency has responsibility. This is an area to which our Inquiry paid particular attention.

What services are provided for carers?

If it has been mutually agreed that a friend or relative should act as a carer then assessments should consider the needs of the carer as well as the user. A carer has the right to receive all the practical support and information they need to continue to provide care. All social services departments are obliged to appoint an officer specifically to deal with complaints and carers have the right to demand additional services if they feel they need them.

Is there still a need for psychiatric hospitals?

Community care does not mean that everyone will be able to cope in the community all the time. For a minority of severely mentally ill people who may be at risk to themselves or others, some form of hospital accommodation or sanctuary may be necessary from time to time in a crisis or for respite care. However, their base will remain in the community.

What about the particular needs of people who are seriously ill?

The Government has recently introduced some new measures in an attempt to ensure that people who may be at risk to themselves or others continue to receive support and supervision in the community. Health authorities are required to ensure that all hospitals and trusts providing mental health care set up "supervision registers" which identify and provide information on those considered to be 'at risk'. Patients should normally be informed of this.

The Department of Health is also introducing a system of 'supervised discharge' under a new Mental Health Bill. This will mean that psychiatric patients who are discharged from hospital but considered at risk must comply with their treatment plan. If they do not, their case will be reviewed and they may be recalled into hospital.'

(Source: Mental Illness: The Fundamental Facts, The Mental Health Foundation, 1994.)

ITEM B   *Exercise 9.9   Community care*

Using Item B, answer the following:

[a]   1. What is community care?

[i]
[i]   2. (a) Where do the funds for community care come from?
      (b) With the closure of many psychiatric hospitals are the funds being switched to fund the expansion of community care?

[i]
[i]   3. (a) Who appears to care for the mentally ill?
      (b) Outline one criticism of the use of relatives as the main carers of the mentally ill?

[i]   4. What care is offered for the 'seriously' mentally ill?

What are some of the criticisms of community care?

The community care programme has failed to be sensitive to the range of needs of ethnic minorities: it has failed to examine whether there are particular needs to be met in the community to cater for ethnic minorities. In addition there has been no mention of the role of clients/patients/customers in shaping the care they receive. This is an issue of advocacy, which means enabling people to have their views heard and represented.

The quality of care received by people in privately run institutions for the mentally ill is an important issue. The level of expertise being employed to care for the mentally ill in these new privately run, profit-making businesses might not be adequate to care properly for the patients/clients. The main interests of the people who set up such homes might therefore be questioned: there might be a conflict of interest between the profit motive and spending more to offer better quality care to the clients.

Local authorities have an increased role in assessing and providing care for the mentally ill but this role may be limited because some local authorities may not be equipped financially to deal with all those requiring care. Because local authorities pay the bill for care of the mentally ill they might have a vested interest in slowing down the assessment of patients/clients to cut the costs of caring for them.

The way the government perceived the role of the care manager was on the purchaser side of the purchaser/provider relationship. The care manager was to make decisions about the cost of care as well as the need for care. Alternative models may develop whereby the care worker makes decisions that are primarily based on need.

Some claim that the changes contained in the care in the community programme are intended to offer better quality care than that provided in psychiatric hospitals. Others argue that the programme is simply a way of closing down expensive psychiatric hospitals to reduce the expenditure of an ever cost-conscious government. Connelly and Crown (1994) highlighted the overrepresentation of schizophrenics among the single homeless, and there have been media reports of patients being released from psychiatric hospitals into the community. One former patient killed a man within twenty days of being discharged from hospital, and there have been other cases where people have been released from institutions but were not mentally fit to be discharged. On one occasion the lack of beds in the few remaining psychiatric institutions has resulted in new patients not receiving treatment. A case in point happened in June 1994, when a man was jailed for life at the Old Bailey after the court was informed there were no hospital beds for him, even though he was diagnosed as schizophrenic and had attacked a housewife with a baseball bat. A psychiatrist who had treated the man commented that the, 'experts should have listened to his parents, who had campaigned to have him treated properly.' (*Guardian*, 10 June 1994). There is no doubt that some people will benefit from being cared for in the community, where they can learn to be more independent rather than being institutionalised. However the quality of care received by those in the community remains an issue. In addition concern has been expressed that those released from psychiatric care institutions may well be the 'least unwell' rather than those more suitable for discharge.

Some patients released from psychiatric hospitals into the community do not receive adequate care or coordinated support, and may also face stigmatisation. A recent government report (House of Commons Health Committee, 1994) states that one patient 'writes of the importance she attached to the institution as a place where she could roam in open spaces without fear of stigma'.

ITEM C

(Source: Mental Health, vol. 21, 1995.)

ITEM C **Exercise 9.10 Labelling and stigmatisation**

1. Media reports have highlighted the harm some discharged mentally ill people have caused in the community. What criticism of this view does the cartoon put forward?

2. In what ways do you think that the label 'mentally ill' can affect a person's life chances? (Hint: job, housing, relationships.)

Schizophrenia: definitions, causes and treatments

Schizophrenia is a useful example of a mental illness to examine sociologically. Defining and classifying schizophrenia is problematic, and establishing its causes and providing suitable treatment are also problem areas.

What is schizophrenia?

Schizophrenia was originally called dementia praecox ('senility of youth'), which embraced a mixture of symptoms including delusions and hallucinations. Bleuler (1911) renamed the condition schizophrenia (literally meaning 'split mind'). Diagnosis of the condition relies on a list of symptoms, of which clients may show some or all.

What are the problems of diagnosing schizophrenia?

Diagnosing of schizophrenia is problematic because there is a great deal of disagreement about which symptoms are the key features of the disorder. Schneider (1959) regards hallucinations as the main or 'first rank' symptom whereas as Slater and Roth (1977) claim hallucinations are the least important feature of schizophrenia because they are not exclusive to the disorder.

Another problem with diagnosing schizophrenia is how long the symptoms should persist before a final diagnosis can be made. The British classification system, known as the International Classification of Diseases (ICD-10), requires only one month's duration of the symptom, whereas the US classification system, the Diagnostic and Statistical Manual IV, requires symptoms of six months' duration. It is therefore easier to be diagnosed as schizophrenic in Britain than in the USA: so how valid (accurate) and reliable (consistent) is the diagnosing of schizophrenia?

Is there a genetic basis to schizophrenia?

The cause of human behaviour has social, economic and political implications. If human behaviour is viewed as genetic then people have no control over what they do. Taking criminal behaviour as an example, people might not be prosecuted for their crimes if their genetic make-up meant they were not responsible for their actions. If criminal behaviour is viewed as genetic then the implication might be to abandon any costly schemes to reduce poverty (for example welfare schemes, urban regeneration projects) because poverty is not the cause of the problem. Also, if crime is genetic, people's attitudes might change towards criminals: if a person cannot help being a criminal how might people change their perceptions of a burglar?

Thus the cause of a problem will have social, political and economic implications. Some people, for example the members of a government, may favour a particular cause because it suits their political and economic motives. The case of mental illness is similar to that of criminal behaviour. If the 'problem' is deemed to have a genetic basis then the 'treatment' is likely to be very different from the solutions provided for a socially caused mental illness (for example due to poverty or stress) such as schizophrenia. The following subsections discuss the key issues regarding the causes, implications and treatment of schizophrenia.

Is there evidence to support a genetic basis?

Studies of twins have been conducted that suggest there may be a genetic basis to schizophrenia. If one twin of a genetically identical pair that arose from the division of a single fertilised egg (monozygotic twins, as opposed to twins that develop from two separate eggs) develops schizophrenia then, if the disorder is genetic, the other twin should develop similar symptoms. According to Harrison (1995) the concordance rate (similarity rate) in identical twins developing schizophrenia is no more than 50 per cent. A person's risk of getting does appear to increase if one or more member of the family has it. But the increased chance might be due to shared genes or a shared environment. The genetic explanation is reinforced by studies of children born to schizophrenic parents but then adopted and therefore brought up in a different environment: the evidence suggests these children have just the same chance of developing schizophrenia as those brought up by their natural parents. However, as the most commonly found concordance rate for monozygotic twins is around 50 per cent this indicates that schizophrenia cannot be totally genetic: if schizophrenia was purely genetic the concordance rate for such twins would be 100 per cent (in other words if one twin develops schizophrenia, so will the other twin).

In what other ways can the genetic explanation be criticised?

Firstly, twin studies have used very small samples, so generalisations are difficult. Secondly, the diagnosis of schizophrenia might not have been valid; after all diagnosing schizophrenia is problematic, and there might have been some pressure to define some 'problem' behaviours as schizophrenic in order to support the studies. Finally, twins might experience very different environments despite being from the same family. Therefore schizophrenic symptoms might be brought out in one twin and not the other.

Zubin and Spring (1977) offer a conclusion. They argue that schizophrenia could have a genetic basis, but something environmental (for example stress) draws out the symptoms in some cases but not in others. Thus both genes and the environment are important, but the question still remains: which one is *more* important?

What are the implications of supporting the genetic explanation of schizophrenia?

The idea that behaviour has a genetic basis is one that merits consideration, not only because it might or might not be true but also because it implies our behaviour might be outside our control. If people's genes govern their behaviour, can they be held legally responsible for their actions? If schizophrenia is viewed as genetic then the way society treats the disorder needs consideration. In the future genetic screening of a foetus could indicate possible schizophrenia, and the pregnant woman might well decide to terminate the pregnancy. Some people view the possibility of such genetic selection as a step towards eugenics: selecting the 'best' and terminating the 'unhealthy' or the 'genetically undesirable'. Nazi Germany provided an extreme example of eugenics, where millions of supposedly 'sub-standard' people (not only Jews but also homosexuals, gypsies, the disabled and others) were killed or sterilised. To what extent might genetic explanations lead to the creation of a new list of undesirables? Should such a list exist and should schizophrenics be on it? This question is even more significant in view of RD Laing's claim that schizophrenia can be a very positive experience.

Is there a biochemical basis to schizophrenia?

Iverson (1979) carried out postmortems on schizophrenics and found high levels of a biochemical called dopamine (a neurotransmitter) compared with the levels normally found in non-schizophrenics. The high degree of nerve cell activity stimulated by dopamine was assumed to produce schizophrenic symptoms. Others argue that the high levels of dopamine could have been the *result* of schizophrenia rather than the *cause* (for example Lloyd *et al.*, 1984).

The main implications of acceptance of the biochemical theory stem from the drug treatments it recommends. The side effects of such drugs have been criticised and complaints of becoming a 'chemical cocktail' have been lodged by schizophrenic patients. Often drugs are the only therapy and although some drugs might well be useful in treating the symptoms, some people claim additional therapies are needed to help people overcome their problem. Focusing on organic (biological) causes of schizophrenia distracts attention from its social catalysts such as poverty, stress and family conflict.

Is there a neurological basis to schizophrenia?

The search for brain disorders began as early as the identification of schizophrenia. Postmortems of schizophrenics have revealed some brain abnormalities. One major piece of research examined the connection between neurological causes of schizophrenia and the flu virus. High peaks in schizophrenia diagnosis have been shown to to correspond with major flu epidemics. In cases where pregnant women have contracted flu, particularly at the 25–30 week stage, researchers have found higher incidence of schizophrenia later in the child's life (for example Torrey *et al.*, 1988). A high proportion of those diagnosed as schizophrenic were born during the winter or early spring, so were developing in the womb at the time when seasonal flu epidemics were most widespread (ibid.)

One problem that can be applied to most studies of the causes of schizophrenia: the way in which schizophrenia is diagnosed has changed over time because the medical criteria have changed. For example the main criteria used by psychiatrists to diagnose schizophrenia are laid down in the Diagnostic and Statistical Manual, which has been revised four times. Changes to the system used to diagnose schizophrenia might change the number of cases of schizophrenia. Thus trusting the diagnosis in studies of mental illness is problematic; the neurological examinations may not have been carried out on genuine schizophrenic patients.

One main implication of the neurological theory is that the principal treatment appears to be surgery, which might cause patients to suffer side effects such as memory loss and emotional dulling. Again, focusing on organic (biological) causes of schizophrenia distracts attention from social factors such as poverty, stress and family conflict.

Is there a social basis to schizophrenia?

Is social class a cause of schizophrenia?

Studies have shown an association between social class and the frequency of schizophrenia. Hollingshead and Redlich (1958) analysed the incidence of schizophrenia by social class and found a much higher rate in Class V than in Class I. Kohn (1973) found a similar marked difference between Class V and Class I in Denmark, Norway and England. However the differences seem to be marked in urban rather than rural areas (Clausen and Kohn, 1959).

As studies of schizophrenia still rest upon diagnosis of the condition, whether more cases of schizophrenia among the lower social classes are reported to psychiatrists is a consideration, as is the possibility that diagnoses by middle-class doctors might well be biased against the working classes. Support for the social class explanation comes from the sociogenic hypothesis: this argues that the stressful experience of being in Class V produces schizophrenia. However some critics believe that schizophrenia occurs equally in all social classes but because the symptoms may lead to family disruption, hopelessness, loss of a job and poverty the schizophrenic may drop down the social class scale, finally reaching Class V. This is known as the social drift (or social selection) hypothesis. Evaluation of the sociogenic hypothesis versus the social drift hypothesis is inconclusive: evidence has been found in support of both.

If schizophrenia is caused through stressful lives or overexposure to family conflict then the implication is that people need to change their environment. If too much stress stems from poverty then a radical option would be to change the structure of society: changing the nature of society to create greater equality could reduce poverty and therefore possibly reduce stress.

Is the family a cause of schizophrenia?

Some researchers believe family relationships are the cause of schizophrenia. Somewhat sexist attention has been paid to the schizogenic mother who develops a 'faulty' relationship with her siblings, resulting in schizophrenia (Fromm-Reichmann, 1952). Laing and Esterson (1970) used 12 case studies of schizophrenics to establish whether family conflict could be the cause of schizophrenia in sons and daughters. Family conflict caused people to focus in on themselves rather than the world around them. The authors went as far to claim that the new 'inner world' could be a positive experience. For them, schizophrenia is not a medical condition but simply a label applied to a relationship between people; a relationship in which people have developed their own inner world. Bateson *et al.* (1956) call this process of introspection, 'a voyage of discovery . . . returning to a normal world with new insights'. According to Laing and Esterson (1970) the view of the schizophrenic patient should be regarded as valid rather than corrected to a more rational view.

A criticism of Laing and Esterson's (1970) work is that it is based on very small samples, so it is very difficult to view it as a generalisable study or a comprehensive examination of schizophrenia. The idea that schizophrenia is positive (Bateson *et al.*, 1956) might also be questioned.

If family conflict causes schizophrenia, this might lead some to question whether the conventional view of the nuclear family is a healthy one. Perhaps different child rearing practices need to be developed? Accordingly, the health and social care services might need to be adapted to train parents to create a stable environment in which to rear children. Leff (1992) might agree with such training for parents. He claims that training family members (for example to reduce hostility, increase positive feedback and increase emotional warmth) should lower stress within the household and might even result in decreased incidence of schizophrenia.

Is labelling a cause of schizophrenia?

Labelling theories claim that mental illness is not an objective state but rather a social status or label conferred on a person by powerful agents of social control (that is, doctors and psychiatrists). Labelling theorists such as Becker (1963) view abnormality as simply an individual's own interpretation of behaviour. What one person considers abnormal another might consider quite normal. Heather (1976) supports Becker's claim that abnormality is problematic. Heather considers that decisions about mental illness are not medical ones, but moral ones. Psychiatrists draw on their own experience to determine abnormality. These experiences are likely to lead to male, middle-class, white Western values being imposed on many people including women, ethnic minorities, non-westerners and the working class. Scheff (1966) argues that the cause of mental illness is less important than the way society reacts to unusual behaviour: once a label is applied the behaviour will continue and people will live up to the role of being mentally ill. Thus schizophrenia is not a medical condition, simply a 'social role'.

Becker (1963) claims that once a deviant label is applied to a person such as a criminal or a schizophrenic then the bearer of the label might be treated differently: they might find it difficult to get a job or, in the case of schizophrenia, be placed in a psychiatric hospital. The circumstances in which people are placed because of their label might well make them act even more deviantly in order to survive. Thus the label causes even more extreme behaviour.

An example is given by Goffman (1968): he points out that patients in mental hospitals often hoard things (for example in their pockets), and that the staff may interpret this as another sign of their mental illness. Goffman himself, however, explains hoarding as a very reasonable response to living in an institution with nowhere to keep personal possessions. Goffman considers the treatment in psychiatric hospitals to be so degrading that patients are stripped of their original self-identity and develop a new self-identity that suits the negative label. This process is known as 'mortification of the self' and hinders any progress made in the so-called 'treatment'. Goffman does recognise, though, that inmates can respond in a variety of ways to the experience of living in a total institution: some become 'institutionalised' and have no wish to return to 'normal' life outside; however most patients 'play it cool' while inside and do not experience any dramatic change to their 'self'.

The following experience was recounted by a psychiatrist, Paul Meehl, a famous schizophrenia theorist, who was giving a lecture on the genetic basis of schizophrenia. Someone in the audience claimed schizophrenia was simply a label confirmed on individuals. Meehl had the following reaction:

> I just stood there and didn't know what to say. I was thinking of a patient I had seen on a ward who kept his finger up his ass 'to keep his thoughts from running out', while with his other hand he tried to tear out his hair because it really 'belonged to his father'. And here was this man telling me that he was doing these things because someone had called him a schizophrenic. What could I say to him? (Kimble *et al.*, 1980).

This suggests that some extreme forms of behaviour might not be the result of a simple label.

A contrast to the negative view of labelling is provided by those who believe labelling is necessary and positive in attempting to support some of the mentally ill. By labelling a patient as mentally ill, it is believed that society can then attempt to care for or treat them. In addition patients might be relieved of responsibility for their actions.

All in all, if it is believed that schizophrenia is simply a label conferred by doctors on people who are viewed to have slightly unusual behaviour, then this throws considerable doubt on the ability of the psychiatric profession adequately to define mental illness. It is therefore important to consider the values doctors hold when defining schizophrenia rather than the nature of the 'symptoms' shown by 'patients'.

Exercise 9.11 The causes of schizophrenia

Having read about the theoretical causes of schizophrenia:

e 1. (a) Rank the following causes you have examined in the order you find them to be convincing: genetic, biochemical, neurological, social class, family, labelling.

e (b) Justify the reasons for your choice.

a 2. State which causes you believe focus on the individual as the problem.

a 3. State which causes blame society for schizophrenia.

a 4. What are the implications of accepting that schizophrenia is due to (a) biological problems, (b) social problems?

Evaluating treatment for mental illness

Appropriate treatment partly depends on the prevailing views of the cause of mental illness. Sociologically it might be important to examine two main issues:

- What treatment do people have access to?
- How effective is this treatment?

Access to treatment

Social class

Evidence suggests that some people have better access to treatment than others. Although a dated piece of research, Brown *et al.* (1975) found that, of a sample of working-class women living in Camberwell, 25 per cent of those suffering from depression were not receiving psychiatric treatment. Some researchers criticise Brown's study by claiming that depression is not a condition that requires medical response (what was a feeling of being 'sad' in the past is now diagnosed as 'depression': another example of the medicalisation of the human condition).

The problem with most studies of the incidence of psychological illness is that they rest on labels conferred on the patients. These labels might not all be valid because some psychiatrists might be willing to diagnose psychological disorders (for example clinical depression) as mental illness more readily than other psychiatrists. Thus the reported incidence of mental illness in an area may tell us more about the willingness of psychiatrists to diagnose mental illness than the real rate of psychological disorders.

Starr (1985) considered a variety of research findings and claimed that depression and other 'mental illnesses' in working-class women did not require psychiatric treatment but a change in living conditions, that is away from stress, poor housing, poverty, the strain of child care and violence within the family (*Social Work Today*, 26 August 1985).

Some people might only be able to access services that are within easy reach of their home. Poverty might well restrict the distances some people are able to travel to gain access to preferred services. People are also subject to the planning of their health authority. Some health authorities provide a range of treatments whereas others restrict the choice available. The introduction of community care might mean the closure of psychiatric hospitals for cheaper care homes that may or may not offer improved care.

Mental health on the streets

- Approximately one-third of homeless people have mental health problems. Confounding popular myth, very few of them have, in fact, been released from psychiatric hospitals (follow-up reports show that most of these people were found some sort of secure accommodations).
- 50 per cent of the clients seen by the initiative have very severe mental health problems.
- There have been 34 homicides by mentally ill people in the past three years but they are much more likely to hurt themselves. One hundred and seven former psychiatric patients discharged from hospital killed themselves between September 1992 and September 1993. Statistically, you are far more likely to be killed by your partner than by someone who is homeless with mentally ill problems.
- In the next couple of weeks, the Zito Trust will get full charity status. Set up last July by Michael Howlett and Jayne Zito, whose husband was stabbed to death by Christopher Clunis, a schizophrenic who had seen 33 different agencies in the community, the Trust aims to provide support for victims of the failures of Care in the Community.
- Hospitals and medication account for 77 per cent of the NHS mental health budget.
- Last month a report by a team led by Sir Louis Blom-Cooper QC, into the death of occupational therapist Georgina Robinson at the hands of a patient at the Torbay General Hospital made the case for introducing compulsory treatment as part of comprehensive care plans for patients.
- On January 24 1995 Dulwich MP Tessa Jowell presented the Community Care (Rights) Bill in Parliament. Drafted by mental health charity MIND, the Bill proposes to provide 24-hour crisis care for people diagnosed as mentally ill, giving them the level of support they need to live in the community.

(Source: © The Big Issue February, 1995.)

ITEM D *Exercise 9.12 Homelessness and access to medical services*

1. Read Item D, then write one paragraph that explains the relationship between homelessness and mental illness.

2. Why might the extent of homelessness and mental illness be underestimated? (Hint: The problems of measuring homelessness.)

3. Turn to the section on homelessness in Chapter 5 (page 123–4). What information can you apply to the issue of mental illness and homelessness?

Ethnicity

The relationship between mental illness and ethnicity has not been a significant focus of research funding. Littlewood and Lipsedge (1982) claim that the psychiatric profession is more likely to impose its own cultural values on patients' behaviour, resulting in ethnic minorities receiving unequal treatment in psychiatric institutions – greater use is likely to be made of sedatives because no productive relationship has built up between the white doctor and the black patient. Sedatives reduce the need to negotiate with patients.

In 1988 a report by the National Association of Health Authorities (now NAHAT) claimed direct and indirect racism was occurring in the NHS. One example was of a devout Muslim patient who was diagnosed abnormal because he wished to continue his religious custom of praying five times a day while facing Mecca. Whether this case represents a common experience is an issue to be considered. There is a tendency to 'doctor-bash' with such evidence, much as some sociological research suggests that all teachers and police officers are racist. However the issue of cultural awareness in diagnosing and treating patients within the mental health service does need more up-to-date research that uses large samples and is both rigorous and representative. Unfortunately such research is costly and requires funding bodies to treat the issue as problematic.

The rates for depressive illnesses in Britain appear to be lower for ethnic minorities than whites. But the rate of schizophrenia appears much higher among people of West Indian origin (Donovan, 1986). To what extent the figures of mental illness reflect overwillingness or underwillingness to diagnose mental illness in ethnic minorities is much debated. Littlewood and Lipsedge (1982) claim that schizophrenia among black immigrants is simply misdiagnosed paranoia caused by the institutional racism they have experienced in British society.

The problem of language might restrict the use of services among some ethnic minorities. Certainly there appears to be very low use of antenatal clinics by some Bangladeshi women. This highlights the fact that other services might be underutilised by some ethnic minorities.

Ethnic minorities are not classless, so some consideration must be given to the relationship between mental illness in ethnic minority groups and social class. Services may well be limited in the local area, and poverty may well reduce access to appropriate (or private) services some distance away.

Finally, the stereotypical view that some ethnic groups prefer to take care of family members rather than put them in residential care has been examined by Fennell *et al.* (1988).

Link Exercise 9.1   Defining Ethnicity

 Look back at Exercise 7.4 (page 163). From what you have learned about the problems of measuring ethnicity, suggest reasons why the study of ethnicity and mental illness is problematic (for example will you be able to gain an accurate measure of ethnicity?)

Gender

The overall mental illness admission rates show that more women than men are treated each year. Blaxter (1990a) conducted a survey and found that more women than men claimed to being prone to psychological distress. However it has to be considered whether admission rates are a reflection of the incidence of mental illness or of a greater tendency for the male-dominated psychiatric profession (at doctor and consultancy levels) to diagnose women's problems as mental illness.

The socially created traditional role for women might well mean that the stresses and strains of childrearing, spending longer at home in poor housing than their working partners and in greater isolation might result in a higher incidence of particular psychological problems. However such problems might have become 'medicalised'. Why treat depression caused by stress as a medical problem or mental illness? Illich (1990) calls the process of creating a medical term such as depression 'social iatrogenesis'. This term describes the way the medical profession creates work for itself by claiming that bodily and psychological states are medical problems with medical solutions rather than social problems with social solutions. Surely one response to the problem of depression among some women would be to change their stress-inducing situation. In other words rather than a medical response (for example drugs), domestic gender relations need to change along with the gender relations of production, so that men and women share the childrearing role.

Liz Sayce, policy director of MIND, on MIND's campaign to improve health services for women

'One in four people suffer some form of mental/emotional distress . . . . In fact one in ten of the population is diagnosed by their GP as 'mentally ill' which in any given year will amount to six million of us . . . . Women are particularly prone to being diagnosed as having a "mental illness". On average, every women in the UK receives more than one prescription for a psychotropic drug each year. A total of 45 million prescriptions for psychotropic drugs are dispensed – and over 30 million go to women. Women are also more likely than men to be admitted to a psychiatric hospital and black and older women are more likely to be offered only physical treatments such as drugs.

The government has finally recognised the scale of the problem by making mental health one of the five target areas for inclusion in "The Health of the Nation" white paper . . . . A [target] outlined for mental health [is] making improvements in health and social functioning . . . possible action would include improving the education of primary care teams about non-prescrib-ing interventions in the management of anxiety disorders and in graded withdrawal of benzodiazapines' [addictive and possibly harmful drugs]. These sound fine words but how do you put them into practice? Firstly you need to recognise that a problem exists, then try to find out some of the causes before offering practical assistance. The forms assistance can take are promoted in part by MIND's year long campaign 'Stress on women'. [The campaign aims to] improve services for mothers with young children, and win the right for women to have a choice of a women key worker. Women with young children are often afraid to seek help with postnatal problems because of fears that their children will be taken from them and into care.

Black women often have a particular fear of seeking help since black children are more likely to end up in local authority care than white children. Black women are particularly likely to have their children taken into care following a diagnosis of 'mental illness'. One study found that 80 per cent of black mothers with children in care were referred for mental health reasons, as compared with 20 per cent of white mothers.

Although it has been known since 1978 that looking after young children at home increases vulnerability to depression, almost no day centres and other community facilities provide creches or priority nursery places. A survey of community mental health centres found only seven per cent had creches. Of new mothers, 10 to 15 per cent are known to experience postnatal depression. All too often the choice for a women with mental health problems is either to cope with no support or have the child cared for elsewhere. There is no middle ground.

MIND . . . want to see child care needs explicitly included in all mental health assessments and specific training on mental health provided in child care decisions. But in particular, MIND backs calls made by many other agencies for accessible, affordable day care for all children who need it.

Other pressures on women

can include caring for older relatives or the isolation of rural living.

Drug treatments rarely, if ever, cure problems with social and economic roots although they may temporarily lift depression or anxiety to enable a woman to have a different view of her circumstances. If asked, most women would prefer to have some sort of counselling or merely a listening ear. MIND has 230 local groups in England and Wales. Although each group offers very different services tailored to meet local needs, some offer counselling and self-help groups. These include benzodiazapine withdrawal groups.

Debt counselling for women with money problems can be more helpful than the queue at the local surgery, by helping clients to represent themselves to the many headed hydra of bureaucracy, for example the housing department, ensuring clients have their full entitlements to benefits, getting access to child care as a preventative measure. This is often offered only after a crisis has arisen.

Health visitors are key players in the campaign to improve women's mental health – recognising distress, supporting individual women with young children, setting up groups for women with postnatal depression and linking women in to the full range of supports they may need.'

(Source: Liz Sayce, 'Preventing breakdown in women's mental health', Health Visitor, vol. 66, no. 2, February 1993.)

ITEM E *Exercise 9.13 Preventing breakdown in women's mental health*

i 1. In no more than one or two paragraphs explain how non-medical support might be useful in promoting mental health for mothers with young children.

a 2. How might medical responses to postnatal depression rob mothers of their ability to cope with the demands of child care (Illich would call the process 'cultural iatrogenesis')?

i 3. According to MIND, what services would be more useful to enable mothers with young children to cope with the demands of the caring role?

Age

Examining age and mental illness is difficult because very few works deal with the issue. However access to services might well vary with age. It must be borne in mind that age is a socially defining feature of people that has a relationship with social class, ethnicity and gender. A person might be considered 'old' or 'young' as well as being, for example, a working-class, Chinese woman.

Whether people have more or less access to mental health services because of their age is important. Does society expect more mental illness among older people than adolescents? Is mental illness 'normalised' in the elderly but 'problematised' in the young? Perhaps these are issues that could be researched as a piece of sociological coursework.

Any reader should ask why no research is quoted in this particular section. Postmodernists would certainly view sociology as presenting not a neutral or critical view, but a very particular way of looking at the world. The fact that some issues have been researched whilst others have not may shape the reader's understanding of the issues presented. What other variables might be considered to affect people's access to services? Why have they been omitted from this publication?

Link Exercise 9.2 Labelling, age and mental illness

 Examine the section on labelling in this chapter (page 226). Why might similarly unusual behaviour be labelled differently when exhibited by a child and by an elderly person.

How effective are therapies for mental illness?

Can treatment cause harm? Iatrogenesis

Can treatment actually cause harm to an individual? The term 'clinical iatrogenesis' describes the way medical treatment can do physical harm to a patient. Drake and Sederer (1986) sound a note of caution about some treatments for schizophrenia:

- Intrusive and very intensive therapies such as psychoanalysis can worsen symptoms, making them more intense than before treatment.
- Medical treatments such as 'stabilising' drugs (phenothiazines) can cause discomforting symptoms such as dryness of the mouth, blurred vision, grogginess and constipation. Irreversible conditions can occur, for example Tardiv dyskinesia, which results in abnormal voluntary and involuntary muscular activity, leading to arching of the back and a twisted positioning of the neck and body (Davison and Neale, 1987).
- Group therapies where patients discuss their problems can involve psychologically damaging discussions among members of the group, affecting the patient's self-image. For an example of intrusive and badly handled discussion work you could watch 'One Flew over the Cuckoo's Nest', starring Jack Nicholson.

Does treatment stigmatise individuals?

The effects of being stigmatised with the label 'mentally ill' can produce even more problem behaviour. The reactions of members of society can alter patients' self-identity in such a way as to hinder any progress; sometimes the label can propel patients into a 'deviant career', in which they progressively live up to their label by adopting even more extreme behaviour. Blaney (1975) argues that labelling is positive, as it allows people to receive care rather than chastisement from members of society.

What are the problems of measuring the effectiveness of therapies?

Assuming that the medical profession does offer some therapies that appear useful in treating some psychological conditions, how can the therapies be judged to have been effective? Bergin (1971) proposes that any measure of a therapy must not ask 'is the therapy effective?' but rather 'is a particular treatment, given by a particular therapist, to a particular client effective?' The following points illustrate just how complicated an evaluation of therapies can become.

The problem with time Some people might simply get better with time – recovery might have everything to do with allowing time for progress to be made. Spontaneous recovery among some clients can complicate any study of treatment.

The problem with the sample Setting up a study to test the most effective therapy would prove problematic for a number of reasons. Firstly, one therapy may well have a sample of clients with very severe psychological problems whilst another therapy could have clients with very mild symptoms. Given that even diagnosing mental illness is problematic, gauging the severity of symptoms is very complicated. To treat all mental illnesses as though they are the same would be to 'totalise' the group: to regard the group as 'all the same'. We do not assume that all women, men, Asians, whites, young, old and disabled are the same, so why should people carrying the label 'mentally ill' be regarded as an homogeneous group?

The problem with the therapy Some therapies might suit some disorders whilst others might be effective with very different problems. For instance electroconvulsive shock therapy (ECT) appears to have no positive effect on schizophrenia yet it is reported to have made some contribution to treating depression (whether such treatment is necessary is another issue). Therefore, just because a therapy is effective (or ineffective) with one disorder it cannot be assumed it will be equally effective (or ineffective) with a different disorder. Some disorders might be intrinsically easier to treat than others.

The problem with the therapist Rather than the therapy being at fault it could well be a failing on the part of the person applying the therapy. One therapist might be highly effective whilst another is extremely ineffective. An additional problem with therapists is their vested interest in claiming success rates with their patients.

Problems with measuring a successful treatment

Just as there exists a problem in judging when a person is to be labelled 'mentally ill', so too is there a problem with removing this label. At what point can somebody be judged to be mentally healthy?

Recovery is the ability to return to work Perhaps patients themselves can define when they are ready to remove their label. Some claim that patients can be considered mentally healthy when they consider themselves fit to return to work. Denker (1946) advocates caution to this approach. Denker believes some patients wish to retain their label so as to claim disability allowance whilst medically diagnosed as mentally ill. Today, disability/sickness allowance is paid at a higher rate than income support. Denker claims success has to be measured over a long period to account for those who wish to delay their return to work. In some ways Denker might be pessimistic in assuming people will wish to retain a stigmatising label for financial gain, but he could be recognising the fact that a return to employment might prove difficult after having been labelled mentally ill; hence some patients may not wish to have their income cut upon declaring recovery.

Recovery is more than a return to work Denker (1946) claims measurement of recovery needs to be over a long period of time and should be based on: (a) ability to return to work, (b) cessation of the symptoms and (c) forming successful social relationships. Although this measurement is broader than a simple return to work, it still has its problems. What sort of work do patients feel able to return to? A similarly demanding job? What about the stigma associated with mental illness in limiting job opportunities? Might patients deliberately fail to report symptoms to avoid being labelled once more? Might having been labelled mentally ill restrict opportunities for social relationships?

Exercise 9.14 *Measuring the effectiveness of therapies*

You have been given the job of advising a local authority about researching which therapies for mental illness should be funded. There is not enough money to allow all the therapies to continue to be publicly funded.

1. What advice would you give the local authority with regard to research into the most effective therapy?

2. What ethical implications might be applied to the use of drugs as a treatment for mental illness?

3. What causes of mental illness would you advise a local authority to consider and why?

Structured exam questions

Complete the following exercises to help you apply the issues and practise skills you have learned in Chapter 9.

Question

1. Evaluate the contribution of the medical model to an understanding of the causes and treatment of mental illness. (*25 marks*)

Use the following key points to help you organise your essay. The subject matter is more complicated than some because you are asked to discuss two issues: the causes of and the treatments for mental illness. The following guidelines are divided into three parts corresponding to the three sections of your essay:

(a) The medical model and the *causes* of mental illness.
(b) The medical model and the *treatments* for mental illness.
(c) *Alternatives* to the medical model for *both* causes and treatments.

Fill in the gaps with the words provided beneath each group of key points.

Answer guidelines

(a) The medical model and the *causes* of mental illness

- Outline what is meant by the . . . model: state it assumes mental illness is like . . . illness. Medical officials can . . . diagnose and classify mental illness. Cause of mental illness is biological (genes, biochemicals, ...).
- Evaluation points include: 'mental illness' is a term that cannot be taken for granted; it may have social causes such as . . . not biological roots.

Words to insert in the gaps: neurological, physical, medical, objectively, stress.

(b) The medical model and *treatment* for mental illness

- Outline examples of treatment discussed in the section on schizophrenia (pages 234–40), for example . . . and surgery.
- Evaluation points include issues such as . . . Iatrogenesis, for example the side effects of prescribed drugs. By adopting an individual approach to treating mental illness people may ignore the . . . basis of mental illness, for example poverty. Thus addressing poverty should reduce the rate of some mental illnesses. The labelling of the mentally ill may . . . patients and make them worse. Current care for the mentally ill is being encouraged to take place within the community: the care may not be. . . .

Words to insert in the gaps: drugs, structural, clinical, adequate, stigmatise.

(c) *Alternatives* to the medical model for *both* causes and treatments

- Outline the . . . basis for mental illness, for example social class, stress. Care in the . . . may allow people the opportunity to integrate with the rest of society rather than being excluded from society within psychiatric institutions.
- Outline the problem of using the words 'mental' and ' . . . ' because they shape our understanding of problem behaviour (discourse). Perhaps the term 'mental illness' is simply a label applied to unusual behaviour.
- Evaluation: some behaviour is clearly detrimental to the individuals concerned so it might be positive to label them mentally ill so that they can receive adequate care, not . . . for their behaviour. Labelling a person mentally ill may mean . . . ., but labelling itself may not be the cause of mental illness. There are problems with treating individuals as it is difficult to measure how successful a . . . programme has been.

Words to insert in the gaps: illness, social, community, treatment, punishment, stigmatisation.

Question

2. Write an essay on the following: Assess the view that mental illness is a socially created concept. (*25 marks*)

Summary

There is no agreement about 'unusual' behaviour, although some behaviour is so extreme that many view it as abnormal: whether the behaviour results from a 'mental illness' is another matter. Mental illness is an important area of sociological study. Mental illness cannot be explained into non-existence by sociologists as simply the product of labelling. However the very notion of mental illness must be examined critically, not least because some problems might have nothing to do with the mind and some problems might be mistakenly taken to be an illness.

The response of individuals who are labelled mentally ill and the reaction of the rest of society is of sociological concern. Issues of self-identity, civil liberty, social control, and access to quality care and attention are all relevant to those labelled as mentally ill. In addition, determining when people are no longer mentally ill appears to be as problematic as defining them ill in the first place.

10 The sociology of health care

By the end of this chapter you be able to:

- describe the gradual involvement of the state in health care;
- evaluate the NHS and its recent reforms;
- assess the rise in private health care;
- assess the role of informal health care.

Introduction

This chapter examines past and current health care. A brief history of health care is provided that outlines the way the state became increasingly involved in the health of its citizens (that is, through social policy such as the Poor Laws and the creation of the National Health Service). This is followed by a more detailed examination of health care today. Cross-cultural responses to health care are explored to provide a less 'UK-centric' sociology of health care. Formal care (involving paid workers whose main role is caring) is then treated in more depth by examining the creation of the National Health Service in 1948 as well as the recent changes to it (for example the role of purchasers and providers of health care and the role of GP fundholders) and their effect on access to care.

Contemporary health care issues are examined, including the increasing role of complementary/alternative medicine, voluntary care and private medicine. Private medicine is examined in more depth with an exploration of the recent growth of private medicine in Britain as well as the relationship between private health care and gender, ethnicity, social class and age. Finally, in contrast to the formal caring roles that are the usual focus of much sociological work on health care, the role of informal (unpaid) care (for example by family members) is explored, taking into account issues of gender, ethnicity, social class, sexuality and disability.

The history of health care

What approaches to health care existed in preindustrial societies?

It is possible to chart general trends in the way different societies have approached health care. There is evidence that the ancient Egyptians used drugs for health care treatment, the ancient Greeks studied the physiology of the body to explain illness, and the ancient Chinese practised acupuncture.

Throughout the Middle Ages illness was widely seen as a divine (religious) punishment. Before the Enlightenment research into anatomy was forbidden by religious authorities on the ground that it invaded the sanctity of the body (Foucault, 1973). However a consequence of the Reformation and Enlightenment (the demise of religious influence in Western Europe and the rise of 'scientific' thinking) was an increase in anatomical research to identify the causes of many illnesses, including 'abnormal' behaviour. The notion that ill-health is caused by biological factors remains a predominant belief today, and is usually referred to as the 'medical model' of illness.

Health care has therefore varied greatly between societies and over time; this might prompt us to question how the health care system, which many take for granted today, will be viewed in years to come.

How was health care organised in Britain before the NHS (pre-1948)?

Before answering this question it is worth examining the question itself. The use of the word 'organised' suggests that health care *should* be planned. The involvement of the state in health care provision was a gradual development that started before industrialisation.

In England in 1563 the Elizabethan state was concerned about the deteriorating condition of poor wage earners and so decided to intervene in the economy to give local justices power to regulate wage rates to prevent them from becoming 'too low'. This intervention marked a turning point towards greater state involvement in law making in order to shape the nature of society in general and health care in particular. In 1601 the Poor Law was passed. This legislation and later reforms of it might well have been for the self-preservation of the bourgeoisie (preventing living conditions from becoming so awful that people revolted), they might have been a victory for the proletariat in securing more resources or they might simply have been a charitable act.

It was during industrialisation, with factories becoming the main location of production and rapid urbanisation creating larger towns and cities, that health became an increasing concern of the state, which was now largely run by an 'elected' government. Item A lists the main legislation passed during this period.

A brief history of state involvement in health care

1800: Most care of the poor and destitute was provided by the church or in workhouses, where people worked for their living. Charles Dickens (born in 1812) was sent to a workhouse at 12 years of age when his father was imprisoned for debts. There was no formal local or central provision of health care.

1833: The Factory Act limited the working day for children aged 9–12 to a maximum of eight hours, with a 12 hour daily maximum for 13–18 year olds.

1834: Poor Law amendment marked the state's further involvement in health provision. Parish workhouses were expected to have wards for the sick. Health care was provided at the local level.

1848: Demand for sick wards increased and the central government passed the Public Health Act to create a General Board of Health, although it had very little power because it lacked links with the workhouses and voluntary hospitals.

1851: A growing number of voluntary hospitals were financed through charities and doctors who wish to further their medical careers through surgery and research. Chronic sickness was not often treated by these hospitals, rather it was left to the workhouses. However, people with chronic sickness naturally found it difficult to work.

1854–6: The Crimean War highlighted the inadequacy of organised health care. Florence Nightingale's nursing reforms stemmed from this period.

1860s: Sanitation was improved in some areas, but the policy was only enforced in areas with very high death rates (23 deaths per 1000 per annum). Some responsibility was taken for removing waste, mainly dung heaps (consider the main method of transport) and the contents of cesspools.

1867: The Metropolitan Poor Act gave more responsibilities to local authorities; local authorities in London were obliged to provide separate care for tuberculosis, smallpox, fevers and insanity. One year later an amendment to the Poor Law Act extended this provision to other areas.

1911: More responsibilities for central government. The British Medical Association put pressure on Prime Minister Lloyd George to pass the National Health Insurance Act; this allowed every low-paid worker (although not other family members) to have medical insurance. Doctors were paid a fixed fee for every person on their list.

1919: More responsibilities for local authorities. The Housing and Town Planning Act gave responsibilities to local authorities for building new homes: government subsidies were available. At the national level, the first minister of health was appointed.

1930: More responsibilities for local authorities. The availability of slum clearance subsidies further stimulated house building. By 1939 four million new homes had been built in Britain.

1939: More responsibilities for central government. Due to the outbreak of war the government set up an emergency medical service, making the minister of health responsible for organising health care. The state centrally organised and paid for the health care administered by the voluntary hospitals and local authorities. Rapid growth of services (for example X-rays) and beds, often in cheap prefabricated buildings.

1942: More responsibilities for central government. Sir William Beveridge published the Beveridge Report on National Insurance and Allied Services. This was never really intended to cover such a widespread welfare provision but the charismatic Beveridge promoted the report effectively (for example through radio broadcasts); this gave it popular appeal among the public (that is, the electorate) and therefore made it difficult for the government to ignore.
The Beveridge report aimed to eradicate the five evils of: idleness (unemployment), disease (poor health), ignorance (lack of education), want (poverty) and squalor (poor housing).

1948: 5 July marked the official beginning of the National Health Service; this continued largely in the same form until the Conservative government passed major new legislation in the 1980s and 1990s. When the NHS and other reforms were conceived it was believed the high initial cost of treating the sick would gradually reduce as the nation became healthier. In fact costs steadily increased largely due to the cost of labour, technology and capital and a growing demand for treatment.

(Sources: adapted from R. Levitt and A. Wall, The Reorganised National Health Service, Chapman & Hall, 1994; E. Hopkins, A Social History of the English Working Classes, Edward Arnold, 1979; and P. Deane, The State and the Economic System, Oxford University Press, 1989.)

Exercise 10.1 The increasing role of the state in the provision of health care

 1. Read Item A, which charts the history of health care provision, then copy and fill in the summary box below.

Summary of the Acts that increased the role of health care provision by:	
Local authorities	Central government

Link Exercise 10.1 An evaluation of the increasing role of the state in health care provision

Read the Marxist explanation of the NHS in the section on the Marxist perspective in Chapter 11 (page 314). What is the Marxist perspective on the growth in local and state involvement in health care (Hint: who benefits from the health service?)

How was the National Health Service organised in 1948?

The National Health Service Act 1946 established the four main principles of the NHS which was created in 1948:

- Equality (a free service).
- Universalism (available to all).
- Collectivism (the state is responsible for organising and planning the service).
- Professional autonomy (independence) for doctors.

The NHS Act 1946 was aimed at establishing 'a comprehensive health service designed to secure improvements in the physical and mental health of the people of England and Wales and the prevention, diagnosis and treatment of illness'. The minister for health was made personally responsible to parliament for the provision of all hospital and specialist services throughout the nation. The state had therefore accepted a collectivist principle of using its power to meet individual needs. The cost of the service was originally to be paid from national insurance contributions: a type of tax from income specially reserved or 'earmarked' for social security and health services and collected and distributed by central government.

Initially, fourteen regional hospital boards were created. They were attached to universities with a medical school. County councils were made responsible for community and environmental health services, for example child welfare, home nurses, vaccination and immunisation, care and after-care for mental illness, and health visiting. Some of these duties became problematic as they overlapped with the responsibilities of hospitals; and in times of cash shortages there was an element of 'passing the buck' in an effort to reduce costs.

Are rising costs a problem in the NHS?

Beveridge and other government officials such as Bevin assumed the NHS would mop up the 'pool of sickness' and eventually reduce state health expenditure. However the costs kept increasing (Item B). Whereas National Insurance was supposed to pay for the health service, by 1951 increasing amounts of income tax were needed to cover the shortfall. By the 1980s the NHS was largely paid for by central and local government tax revenues (81 per cent); a relatively small amount came from National Insurance contributions (16 per cent), and charges paid by users and income generation (3 per cent).

By 1989 the amount spent on health care in Britain had risen to 5.8 per cent of the gross domestic product (GDP: the gross amount of national 'wealth' generated in a year); this upward trend produced increasing concern about the financing of the NHS. However it is important to place these costs in context by looking at the level of health care spending in other Western countries. In comparison with the USA, France, Sweden and the Netherlands, in 1989 Britain spent the least on its health care provision (Item C).

ITEM B

The growth of social expenditure in the UK (percentage of GDP)

	1921	1931	1951	1971
Military	5.6	2.8	6.9	5.9
Housing	2.1	1.3	3.1	2.6
Education	2.2	2.8	3.2	6.5
Health	1.1	1.8	4.5	5.1
Social security	4.7	6.7	5.3	8.9

(*Source*: R. Levitt and A. Wall, The Reorganised National Health Service, Chapman & Hall, 1994.)

Health service expenditure by country, 1989

Country	Expenditure by person (£)	(%) GNP*
USA	1251	11.1
Sweden	1002	8.9
France	758	7.9
Netherlands	756	8.5
Britain	423	5.8

*Gross domestic product and gross national product (GNP) are similar concepts that attempt to create a measure of the total value of the goods and services generated in a year.

(*Source*: R. Levitt and A. Wall, 'The Reorganised National Health Service, Chapman & Hall, 1994.)

ITEMS B AND C **Exercise 10.2   Rising costs of the NHS – a critique**

$\boxed{i}$ 1. Examine Item B and identify the trend in government health spending between 1921 and 1971.

$\boxed{i}$ 2. Using Item B, compare health expenditure in 1971 with the other four main areas of spending.

$\boxed{i}$ 3. Examine Item C and identify which country spent (a) the most and (b) the least on health care per capita (per person) in 1989.

$\boxed{e}$ 4. How might you use Items B and C to evaluate the claim that Britain may be spending too much on health care? (Hint: write a short paragraph explaining whether health care spending really is a problem when compared with other areas of spending – Item B – or expenditure on health in other countries, as shown in Item C.)

What are the explanations of the rising costs of the NHS?

The competing (or perhaps complementary) explanations of Britain's increased state health expenditure largely centre on:

- Rising administrative costs.
- Patient demand.
- Technological change.
- Wages of health staff.
- Ageing population.

Is the NHS inefficient, with high administrative costs?

There has been much concern about the so-called inefficiency of the state-run National Health Service. As early as 1953 an investigation was set up to research any possible waste of government money within the NHS. This concern is still relevant today with the increasing number of managers needed to run the NHS trust hospitals, which now manage their own finances.

Exercise 10.3   Administration costs and inefficiency

In 1953, the 'Guillebaud Committee' was set up to investigate rising expenditure; it decided that the extra NHS costs were not due to waste or inefficiency. In 1985 less than 5 per cent of the NHS budget was spent on administration; this compares with 7 per cent in France and nearly 10 per cent in the USA. However the number of NHS administration and clerical staff increased from 128 180 in 1981 to 157 800 in 1991. The number of senior managers increased from 630 in 1986 to 12 760 in 1991. This increase in administration and management personnel coincided with a policy to create NHS trust hospitals, which would be responsible for managing their own budgets and organising health care provision.

[i] 1. In the paragraph above, is there any evidence to suggest that the NHS is not wasting money?

[i] 2. Is there evidence to suggest that the NHS is wasting money?

Do patients abuse the NHS because it is free?

Because health care is free it has been claimed that people abuse the service by using it when there is no real health need. However there is no professionally conducted research that provides valid evidence of patient abuse of the system; indeed there is considerable evidence to suggest that a great deal of illness is *not* reported to the health service (Last, 1963).

Link Exercise 10.2   Reporting illness

Examine Chapter 3, which explores the way in which people become defined as ill.

[i][a] 1. Write down some of the reasons why people might not report their symptoms to a doctor or hospital.

[e] 2. What does your list suggest about the extent to which people report their symptoms to the NHS?

Does the increasing use of technology increase costs?

It is suggested that increased use of technology has pushed up both the cost of treatment and the capital cost of building hospitals capable of housing expensive machinery. The early voluntary hospital service largely began by developing surgical techniques to deal mainly with acute rather than chronic cases of ill-health. This trend has continued and has required more (expensive) technological equipment. The health service is mainly curative (involving surgery and drugs) rather than preventative (involving screening and health promotion). Drugs are a major aspect of most treatments; the amount spent on drugs has been criticised along with that spent on surgery. Some believe that, by spending less on high-profile areas such as heart surgery, money could be switched to the prevention of heart disease through educating people to take more exercise, improve their diet and reduce smoking.

Exercise 10.4   Curative versus preventative medicine

 1. Both curative and preventative medicine have arguments for and against their use. Copy the following table and sort the evaluation points below according to whether they are for or against curative medicine or for or against preventative medicine.

Curative medicine		Preventative medicine	
For:	Against:	For:	Against:

Evaluation points:

- There are few studies that prove the effectiveness of health promotion campaigns.
- Equipment for surgeons is expensive.
- Surgery may be the most effective way of dealing with some medical problems.
- Drugs can cause serious side effects.
- There are few studies that prove the effectiveness of some drugs and surgery.
- If illnesses are prevented, fewer drugs and surgeons will be needed.
- If money is switched to preventing disease some surgical programmes might decline.
- Antibiotics have had a major impact on some medical problems.
- Drugs are expensive.
- Screening programmes, for example for breast cancer, are expensive.
- By preventing unhealthy behaviour (for example smoking, poor diet) there will be less demand for health care.
- Training for surgeons is expensive.
- Diseases can become resistant to treatment by antibiotics.

Do the wages of health staff increase costs in a labour-intensive health care system?

It is estimated that 60 per cent of the health service budget is spent on salaries (Taylor, 1986). This might mean that the salaries are 'too high'. However doctors in Britain tend to be paid less than doctors in the USA (Levitt and Wall, 1994). Although the health care system uses expensive technological equipment it is also very labour intensive (requires a lot of workers); machinery is unlikely to supersede humans as easily in the caring process as it has in the manufacturing process. However the introduction of local pay bargaining for nurses and ancillary staff might mean savings will be made by cutting or restricting the growth of salaries of health service staff. Redundancies might be more likely within financially accountable NHS trust hospitals. The issue of 'skills mixing' is one that is becoming more important. This is the notion that more highly paid, skilled ward staff can be mixed with cheaper, less-skilled staff. Overall spending on wages might decline as fewer highly trained carers will be needed to manage less-skilled caring staff.

Is the ageing population increasing NHS costs?

In many Western and non-Western societies the increasing proportion of elderly people is said to be resulting in a 'burden of dependency', as through taxes a shrinking working population is supporting a growing dependent population.

Although there are huge variations in the extent to which elderly people suffer ill-health and require social support from the state, health spending per head is greatest for the over 65s. However it must be remembered that it is the elderly who have paid taxes and National Insurance for the longest period of time!

The National Health Service reforms since 1980

Why was the NHS reformed?

The type of health care services provided free, and the cost of these services to the state (or taxpayer), has remained a political and economic concern of successive postwar British governments. In the 1980s a series of government reports recommended radical changes to the nature of the NHS. The New Right, typified by the then Conservative Prime Minister Margaret Thatcher, had prepared a new agenda for health care (in addition to educational reforms and widespread privatisation of the postwar nationalised industries). Some critics argued that the health reforms were not a thoroughly planned strategy but rather a series of ad hoc changes aimed at reducing the cost of the NHS. The plan was to reduce costs by introducing market forces into health care, expanding private and voluntary formal health care, and increasing the role of individuals and families in informal health care (for example caring for elderly or disabled relatives in the home).

The New Right Conservatives wanted to substitute market forces (letting individuals survive in the market place) for the previous guiding assumption of collectivism (using the power of the state to ensure particular individual needs are met). Hence it was widely held that the New Right wished to 'roll back the frontiers of the state' by providing fewer state services (gas, electricity, water) and more privately run services (privatised gas, electricity and water, more private hospitals, more personal health insurance) with a minimum or 'base line' of state services (for example defence, law and order).

Is it important to know about all the recent (or future) health reforms under the present (or future) government? Perhaps, depending on the questions you are trying to answer. Sociologically it is important to examine *access* to health care and the *type* of health care people have available to them.

How was the NHS reformed?

In the 1980s and into the 1990s the NHS was subject to significant review and reform. In the Griffiths Report (1983) Roy Griffiths (a managing director of the Sainsbury's supermarket chain) proposed that the NHS could be made more businesslike by:

- making health services manage their own finances and be held accountable for their own budget;
- making payments to the health service provisional on productivity, that is, the more patients treated the more money received (up to a maximum level);
- creating competition between state hospitals and private sector hospitals as well as between GPs.

It was hoped that by making the NHS into a market, costs would be driven down as the various health 'businesses' (hospitals and GPs) became more cost efficient.

With rising costs and a growing awareness of the consequences of the ageing population, the government recognised there was a shortfall of spending on the NHS and in 1987 responded by increasing the NHS budget. Subsequently, in July 1989 the government outlined its new proposals in a white paper called 'Working for Patients'. The NHS would continue to be centrally funded out of taxation rather than through private insurance; however health provision by the private sector was to be encouraged, particularly for the elderly. Money for treatment would now follow the patients – previously hospitals had been required to keep to a fixed budget regardless of the number of patients they treated.

The 'Working for Patients' proposals were built into the NHS and Community Care Bill (1989) to take effect from April 1991. Overseeing the changes was a new body called the NHS management executive, which worked on behalf of the health minister. Thus in some ways health planning had become more centralised, with the secretary of state directly influencing health policy through the management executive.

The main NHS reforms between 1983 and 1996

ITEM D

Summary of recent NHS reforms

1983: The Griffiths Report recommended that the NHS be more businesslike.

1989: In January the white paper 'Working for Patients' was published. The NHS was still to be funded from taxation, but there would be more competition, particularly from the private sector. A period of consultation with the medical profession followed.

In November the NHS and Community Care Bill implemented the proposals made in 'Working for Patients'. Hospitals were to be providers of health and would draw up contracts with GP fundholders and district health authorities, who would purchase health care on behalf of their patients (somewhat) in line with the targets set out in the 'Health of the Nation' document. Survival in the market place became a key concern.

1991: In April the first wave of GP fundholders and trust hospitals was established. In June the 'Health of the Nation' was published, outlining the targets the regional health authorities should use when setting aims for the district health authorities.

1993: In October 'Managing the New NHS' was published. This referred to abolition of the regional health authorities and the merger of the district health authorities with the family health services. More central control over health planning was instituted through a streamlined NHS management executive.

1996: On 1 April the regional health authorities, the district health authorities and the family health services authorities (FHSA) were disbanded. Since then there have been just eight regions, called outposts. These are managed directly by the NHS executive, which is answerable to the secretary of state for health.

Glossary

GP: general practitioner. GPs receive money for each patient on their patient register. The payments come from the relevant health authority.

GP fundholders: GPs who have chosen (and been allowed) to spend 20 per cent of their budget at any hospital they choose (trust or private) not just the local hospital.

Trust hospital: state hospitals that are now in charge of their own budgets. GPs buy or purchase health care from trust or private hospitals for their patients.

DHA: district health authorities purchased health care from providers of health care (mainly GPs and trust hospitals). They also had to ensure that suitable health promotion was taking place (for example anti-smoking campaigns, AIDS awareness). DHAs were accountable to their regional health authority, which set the targets for the DHAs (for example reducing coronary heart disease and HIV). Disbanded 1 April 1996.

FHSA: the family health services authorities managed the services offered by GPs and GP Fundholders. The FHSAs had to ensure that information was available about local medical services, transfer medical records when a patient changed doctor, and respond to patients complaints about GP services. FHSAs also managed registered opticians, dentists and family planning clinics. The FHSAs were accountable to their regional health authorities and were disbanded on 1 April 1996.

Health Authorities: previously known as DHAs. They combine the old DHA and FHSA.

NHS Executive Regions: previously known as RHAs, NHS Executive Regions are directly accountable to the NHS executive. They often cover a large area – there were 14 RHAs but now there are only eight regions.

RHA: regional health authorities were very large, serving up to three million people in some cases. They set targets for the DHAs (now health areas) in line with certain government targets, for example the targets set in the 'Health of the Nation'. They were accountable to the Department of Health and the Secretary of State for Health. Disbanded 1 April 1996. Now referred to as 'outposts'.

The main changes to the NHS have involved:

- Bringing health into the market place, establishing a *purchaser–provider* relationship.
- The introduction of *budgets* for GPs (GP fundholders) and for trust hospitals.
- The encouragement of a greater role for *private health care*.
- The *separation* (though still not total) of the roles of local authority social services, which cater for those needing long-term care, and the hospitals providing health treatment.

Exercise 10.5   Evaluating the 1990s NHS reforms

Using the information on the following pages, which review the changes outlined in Item D, complete the following table, which lists the main changes to the NHS. Copy the table, allowing enough room to add the appropriate information.

Main change	Brief explanation	Advantage	Criticisms	Inequality of access to the service
Purchaser–providers	Services now buy or sell medical care	May keep costs low	May increase administration costs	Not all patients are in a GP fundholding practice
GP fundholders				
Patient's charter				
More private health care				

The main NHS changes outlined and appraised

Health in the market place: the purchaser–provider relationship

The government white paper 'Working for Patients' concerned the delivery of health services. Regional and district health services, GPs and hospitals previously received an allocated budget every year. 'Working for Patients' proposed a division into purchasers and providers of health care. Britain was divided into areas known as regions (regional health authorities, RHAs), which provided funds to smaller district health authorities (DHAs) and family health services authorities (FHSAs). On 1 April 1996 the regional health authorities were replaced by regional offices, which may be referred to as NHS Executive Regions. Outposts are in charge of monitoring funds and health targets while the FHSAs and DHAs (now combined into smaller Health Authorities) draw up contracts with providers for the health care of patients within their geographical area.

In short, the reforms created purchasers of health care (for example outposts, Health Authorities and GP fundholders) and health providers (for example GPs and trust hospitals). Competition to secure contracts between purchasers and providers was then created. Because money followed patients' treatment, survival in the newly created health market rested on securing contracts to treat patients. Below is the structure of the NHS as it stood in April 1996:

Structure of the health service in April 1996 showing the purchaser–provider relationship

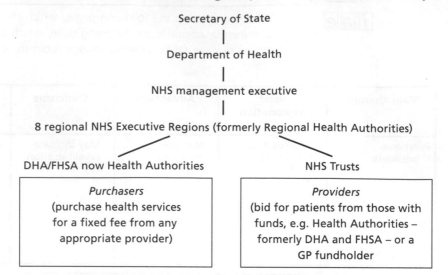

Secretary of State

Department of Health

NHS management executive

8 regional NHS Executive Regions (formerly Regional Health Authorities)

DHA/FHSA now Health Authorities

Purchasers
(purchase health services
for a fixed fee from any
appropriate provider)

NHS Trusts

Providers
(bid for patients from those with
funds, e.g. Health Authorities –
formerly DHA and FHSA – or a
GP fundholder)

The theory of purchasing and providing health care is similar to that for any other commodity (for example margarine) or service (for example banking). The health services that offer the best-quality care at the cheapest price are likely to compete most effectively for the money held by the smaller health areas (formerly DHAs and FHSAs) or any such body that pays for the health services used by the patients within its official area. NHS trust hospitals now compete with each other to provide health services for patients. Contracts are drawn up between the health areas and the hospital to provide a specified number of services for a particular number of patients: the hospital will go out of business if it fails to attract contracts from health areas or GP fundholders. Health areas are allowed to use the services of private hospitals, thus encouraging even more competition over health care. The purchasing authority must produce data for the management executive on such issues as treatment and waiting times.

Exercise 10.6 Purchasers and providers

 Copy the table below then, using the preceding information on purchasers and providers list the purchasers of health care and the providers of health in the relevant boxes.

Purchasers of health care	Providers of health care

Control over the type of contracts drawn up is maintained through the targets the health authorities have to meet. These targets were laid down in the government's 'Health of the Nation' (DoH, 1992a) report:

1. To reduce coronary *heart disease* and *strokes* by the year 2000, including:
   - reducing coronary heart disease by 40 per cent in the under 65s;
   - reducing coronary heart disease by 30 per cent in 65–74 year olds.
2. To reduce *cancer* by the year 2000, including:
   - reducing breast cancer by 25 per cent;
   - reducing cervical cancer by 20 per cent;
   - halting deaths from skin cancer by the year 2025.
3. To improve the health of the *mentally ill* by the year 2000, including:
   - reducing suicides by at least 15 per cent.
4. To improve *sexual health*, including:
   - reducing gonorrhoea by 20 per cent by 1995.
5. To reduce *accidents* by the year 2005, including:
   - reducing accidents among children under 15 by 33 per cent.

Exercise 10.7   The 'Health of the Nation' (1992) targets

 Having examined the 'Health of the Nation' targets, identify some health problems you believe the government should include in those targets (for example testicular cancer).

What is the critique of the purchaser–provider relationship?

Increased administration   One reason for the health reforms was to reduce wasteful administration costs within the NHS. With both NHS trust hospitals and GP fundholders in charge of their own budgets, waste and inefficiency might be reduced because managers would be accountable for their own finances. However, far from trust hospitals reducing their administration costs, the most identifiable growth in managerial staff has occurred in those hospitals:

Managerial staff trends in the NHS, 1981–91

	1981	1986	1991
Administration and clerical	128 180	137 770	157 800
General managers	–	610	740
Senior managers	–	630	12 760

Being accountable for finance means increased roles for finance managers, secretaries, contract managers and personnel managers. Thus a criticism of the latest health reforms might be that they are tending to divert money from direct patient care and into administration. However if increased administration leads to greater efficiency, better-quality patient care and reduced waiting times for treatment, then the growth in administration might well be viewed more positively.

Equity Whether the health service is more or less 'equitable' or 'fair' is essentially contested: fairness and equity mean different things to different people (Whitehead, 1993). Is it fair that more people are being offered private rooms in NHS hospitals? Fair to whom: to those who can afford to pay for private facilities? Fair to NHS trust hospitals, which require income to ensure their survival in the health market? Equity, then, is not a term that people can agree upon easily: it is essentially contested.

Competition by its nature leads to winners and losers. Where there are many losers, for example as a result of the closing down or 'retraction' of hospitals (why do some prefer to use the term 'retract' rather than 'closure'?), the quality of care and range of services offered might be adversely affected. Services for the chronically sick are expensive because they often require labour-intensive care; they might well be deemed less profitable than acute conditions (for example knee operations) which can be treated relatively quickly and cheaply. Research such as the Black Report (Townsend and Davidson, 1980), Townsend *et al.* (1987) and Phillimore and Beattie (1994) has shown that in socially and materially deprived areas there is a higher prevalence of illness, including 'expensive' chronic illness. Health service providers (for example trust hospitals) might then experience losses in these deprived areas, especially if the provider receives a fixed fee per patient that does not take into account the length and type of care each patient requires. Formal providers of health might well try to avoid disadvantaged areas in favour of the more prosperous regions. This will create inequality in the local provision of health services, with the poor having to travel further for treatment.

As early as 1971 Tudor-Hart claimed that an 'inverse care law' operated in the NHS, whereby health resources tended to be distributed in an inverse proportion to need: those in greatest need of health care received the least resources; deprived areas were claimed to have longer waiting lists, overcrowded facilities and shorter doctor–patient consultations. The inverse care law may well become more marked with the newly introduced competitive element of health care provision: deprived areas may well receive even fewer resources if health services fail to be financially viable in those areas. However one problem with the inverse care law is that of measurement: how do researchers measure quality of care and levels of service? This is a fundamental problem for health planners and health researchers.

Turn to Chapter 5 on social class and health and find the section on the role of the health services (page 109).

Turn to Chapter 5 on social class and health and find the section on the role of the health services (page 109).

$\boxed{i}$ 1. What evidence is there that there is unequal access to health services for different social classes?

$\boxed{a}$ 2. Explain the ways in which the new health service reforms have affected access to health care.

Health in the market place: GP fundholders

In April 1991, 306 general practitioners became fundholders; by 1994 this had increased to around 8000 GPs in 2000 practices serving 36 per cent of the population (Harrison, 1994). Only relatively large practices could apply to become fundholders. The qualifying patient-list size of the practice was reduced from 11 000 patients in 1991 to 9000 in 1993, and practices were encouraged to combine to enable them to qualify. The ability to combine suggests support for larger health centres serving a wider area rather than smaller health centres serving a very local clientele. GP fundholders pay for the health care of their patients at the hospital where they choose to send them; but it was considered important that GP fundholders did not balk at providing necessary but expensive treatment, and therefore the district health authorities (now health areas) rather than the GP fundholders pay the bill for any single hospital treatment costing over £5000.

What are the benefits of GP fundholding?

It was thought that GP fundholding would:

- Enable GPs to offer *better-quality care* by choosing hospitals that offer the best (but affordable) treatment.
- Allow greater *GP autonomy* in choosing more appropriate sources of health care.
- *Reduce inefficiency* and allow financial freedom from the local FHSA.
- Make GPs more *cost conscious*, particularly when prescribing drugs.
- Allow *computerisation* of GP practices: fundholders received extra funds for computerisation.
- Provide more *power to GPs* to determine patient care: that is, hospitals now have to take notice of GPs because the patients of fundholding GPs are worth money.

What are the criticisms of GP fundholding?

Geographical inequality   Fundholders were only serving around 36 per cent of the population by 1994, so if GP fundholders were offering a better-quality service then 64 per cent of the population were receiving inferior treatment. The geographical distribution of GP fundholders is uneven: some regions are served by more fundholders than others.

Exercise 10.8   Distribution of GP fundholders

Percentage of GP fundholding practices, by region, 1993

Region	Percentage of total
Mersey	35
Oxford	33
NW Thames	27
SW Thames	25
South West	19

(*Source*: Adapted from A. Harrison, *Health in the UK*, King's Fund Institute, London, 1994.)

1. Study the table and then identify the region with the largest proportion of GP fundholders and that with the lowest proportion.

2. How might you use the data in the table to evaluate people's access to GP fundholding care?

A two-tier system of care   If fundholders offer more choice of care to their patients, then inequality exists between the patients of fundholders and non-fundholders. One solution is to allow all GPs to become fundholders: but it might be that practices with smaller patient lists would not survive in the market place. It might also be said that non-fundholding GPs spend more time with patients, rather than working out budgets and creating contracts with hospitals. According to Peeke (1993), who analysed inpatient and outpatient waiting times in the Oxford region using 1992–3 data, fundholders were not offering a better service than non-fundholding GPs.

However Whitehead (1993) reviewed studies that monitored the impact of the NHS reforms and found that some fundholders offer a wider range of services, including health promotion, asthma and diabetes management and minor surgery. However does offering these services increase administration time and cost, and eventually detract from the time available for and the quality of doctor–patient consultation?

Whitehead (ibid.) considers there might well be many *perceived* benefits of fundholding that have not yet been borne out in reality. Indeed, Mahon *et al.* (1993), in a survey of 168 fundholding GPs, found that proximity and convenience were a major determinant when choosing hospitals for their patients; many contracts were renewed with existing hospitals rather than seeking other hospitals further afield. None of the fundholders in the sample reported a reduction in choice, whilst 17 per cent of non-fundholders argued that their choice would be reduced by the NHS reforms. However more GP fundholders were willing to exercise their choice about where to send patients.

It appears that a two-tier system might exist in some areas but not others, and between one practice and another. Improvements may have been made in some key areas, such as extending the number of GP services offered, but not in others, such as reducing waiting times for surgery. However more recent data is needed to give a valid reflection of the impact of GP fundholding on inequality in local health care provision.

Exercise 10.9 Evaluating hospital waiting lists

Hospital waiting time is sometimes used as a criterion for judging the quality of health care.

a 1. Find out what the stated maximum waiting time is at your local hospital and compare it with the stated waiting time two years previously (you can ask this question at your local hospital).

a e 2. How does any change in maximum waiting time affect the perceived quality of care at a hospital? (Hint: does it make the situation seem better or worse?)

a 3. What might a government do if it wanted to ensure that hospitals were staying within their maximum waiting time? (For example would it increase or decrease the waiting time?)

Inequality between fundholding GPs' budgets There has been some criticism of the amount of budget variation between GP fundholders. According to a study of GP fundholders in three regions, Glennerster *et al.* (1993) found that one fundholder received £100 per patient whilst another received £132 per patient. Considerable variation existed between the income received by the fundholders for drugs, hospital fees and outpatient fees. Thus to be a patient of one rather than another GP fundholding practice might be an advantage. This advantage conflicts with the principle of offering the same high standard for all, regardless of geography, and the variation between fundholders might indicate there is a multi-tiered service rather than a two-tiered service (that is, fundholders and non-fundholders).

Abuse of fundholding budgets Responsibility for hospital treatment costing over £5000 was removed from GP fundholders, and some fundholders might use this to their advantage. Bevan *et al.* (1989) point out that some GPs might delay treating a patient until the problem becomes so serious that it has to be treated as an emergency in hospital, where the cost will be borne by the health areas rather than the GP fundholder.

Cream-skimming Le Grand (1993) argues that in order to cut costs further GP fundholders might 'cream-skim' the healthier (cheaper) patients and discard the more expensive ones from their patient list. However qualitative evidence from Jones *et al.* (1993) suggests that 'cream-skimming' might be limited. On the other hand a survey of one GP fundholding practice showed that the most expensive 5 per cent of patients consumed 68 per cent of practice expenditure – by 'losing' this top 5 per cent huge 'savings' could be made (Glennerster *et al.*, 1993). With the cost of single hospital treatments of £5000 or more being borne by the health areas the incentive to 'lose' high-cost patients might be reduced.

Drug expenditure Spending on drugs might well decrease when GPs' pay for drugs from their own budgets. If expensive drug treatment is effective a reduction in spending on such drugs could well be detrimental to patients. However if the trend is towards dispensing equally effective but cheaper drugs it could be beneficial, allowing more money for other treatments. Given Illich's (1976) point that doctors provide drugs that could well have damaging side effects (iatrogenesis: doctor-induced sickness), then fundholders might attempt to reduce the quantity of drugs they supply. However if it is cheaper to provide drugs than hospital treatment, then patients might well find themselves with a prescription rather than hospital care or even surgery. According to Glennerster *et al.* (1993), their combined sample of GP fundholders and non-fundholders showed a 15 per cent increase in spending on drugs in 1991–2 compared with the previous year; however the fundholders' average increase was only 12 per cent, suggesting that fundholders are doing more to limit their expenditure on drugs.

Health in the market place: the Patient's Charter

The Patient's Charter was announced in 1991 and gave patients in the NHS ten 'charter rights'. Seven of these rights had existed before the charter was announced. The seven existing rights were:

1. Access to health care on the basis of clinical need.
2. To be registered with a GP.
3. To receive emergency medical treatment at any time.
4. To be referred to a consultant and have access to a second opinion.
5. Informed consent to treatment.
6. Access to medical records.
7. Voluntary participation in medical training or research.

The three new rights as of April 1992 were:

1. The right to detailed information about local health services.
2. Admission date for treatment within two years of being placed on a waiting list.
3. Complaints to be investigated and receive prompt reply.

Exercise 10.10 Applying the Patient's Charter

 Conduct a small-scale survey to investigate whether people have heard of the Patient's Charter and what rights they believe they have been given. You might also try to find out whether they realised they had certain rights before the charter came into being. One of the main criticisms of the charter is that few people are aware of their rights. To what extent does your survey support this view?

What is the critique of the Patient's Charter?

Critics have commented that the rights and targets are relatively unambitious. The NHS in Scotland had previously set a waiting list target of 18 months as opposed to the Patient's Charter target of two years. In 1992–3 the target was set at 18 months in line with the NHS Scotland target. Since April 1992 DHAs and GP fundholders have had to provide detailed information about their services in an accessible way through leaflets, helplines or public meetings. The Patient's Charter appeals to a sense of consumerism, implying that consumers have the right to choose and receive quality care. But to what extent do people have the knowledge to make sure their rights are upheld? How easy is it for people, particularly those who are sick, poor, elderly or uneducated, to organise campaigns to support their rights?

Health in the market place: the rise in private health care provision

Although every person in Britain is entitled to free NHS care, the proportion of the population who pay for private medical care has been growing. Private health care includes one-off payments to a private doctor or private hospital. It also includes paying for private medical insurance so that when they are ill the insurance company pays for all or part of their treatment. Users of private health care are often provided with private medical insurance by their company as a fringe benefit (a 'perk' of the job). Three main associations dominate the medical insurance market: BUPA (British United Provident Association), PPP (Private Patients Plan) and the WPA (Western Provident Association). However the market share of these three companies decreased from 91 per cent in 1985 to 79 per cent in 1993 (Laing and Buisson, 1994), suggesting an increase in the number of companies offering private medical insurance.

Demand for private care has certainly been increasing: indeed private health insurers served a total of 3.3 million subscribers in 1993, a twelvefold increase since 1955 (Compendium of Health Statistics, 1994). In 1979 4.3 per cent of the population were contributing to private health care schemes. By 1994 the proportion of the population with private medical insurance had risen to 11.3 per cent and it is estimated that by 1996 13.6 per cent of the British population will be in a private medical scheme. Only 1.1 per cent of the population had private medical insurance in 1955 (Laing and Buisson, 1994). Private health care provision therefore warrants more sociological analysis, particularly when examining access to health services and the quality of care provided by the health services.

Exercise 10.11   Which social groups use private health care?

 1. Which social groups do you believe might use private medicine? Explain your answer.

 2. Do you think the reasons for using private medicine might vary between social groups? Explain your answer.

Gender and use of private health care

Morbidity figures suggest that women use the health services more than men. However it has been pointed out that if we discount consultations about reproductive matters by women aged 15–44 and consultations by elderly women (as elderly women outnumber elderly men they might well report more ill-health), then there is no significant difference between health care use and gender (Macfarlane, 1990).

Two national surveys of private hospitals in 1981 (Williams *et al.*, 1985) and 1989 (Nicholl *et al.*, 1989) showed that women were greater users of private health care than men, even when private abortions were removed from the figures. This may well be questioned as it is not consistent with Macfarlane's (1990) findings. According to the General Household Survey (1987) 8 per cent of sampled males were private policy holders compared with 3 per cent of sampled females. However for *company* organised schemes the figures were more equitable: 9 per cent for males and 8 per cent for females. The relatively recent increase in the number of women employed in the service sector (for example insurance, banking, retail) might account for the number of women in company schemes.

If women are making more use of private health care, sociologists might well ask why. Wiles (1993) attempted to answer this question using data collected by the Wessex regional health authority. The data came from 1070 postal questionnaires (of which 649 were returned) sent to male and female patients in eight private hospitals and pay-bed patients in three NHS hospitals; 10 per cent of the sample were interviewed after discharge from their respective hospitals. Given that both men and women were sampled it is interesting that Wiles uses 'women' in the title of her article ('Women and private medicine') and not 'gender'. Readers may ask why this is the case and what effect treating only women as problematic has on the knowledge produced within the field of sociology of health and illness.

The main reasons people gave for going private were 'to avoid NHS waiting lists', 'to make use of private health insurance' and to enjoy 'better surroundings in private hospitals'; less often cited reasons were being able to 'choose a date for admittance', to have 'a private room' and to have 'better care' (ibid.) Wiles points out that there were no detectable gender differences in the *reasons* for going private; however the *advantages* of the decision to go private were different (ibid.):

Advantages for men of going private:

- Minimal disruption to working or leisure time.
- Better care.
- Shorter waiting lists.

Advantages for women of going private:

- Fits in with 'caring role', for example of elderly relatives or children.
- Health needs met in ways not met within NHS, for example more attention, being taken seriously.
- Allows retention of some dignity and modesty.
- Allows control over their health care, for example more able to negotiate with a consultant.

Exercise 10.12 Gender and use of private medicine

 1. Conduct a small-scale survey of men and women to investigate the use of private medicine. You may wish to find out about the following: Which sex tends to use private medicine more? What reasons do they give for using private medicine? (take care about asking sensitive questions here) Would they use private medicine for all medical problems? Were they satisfied with the private service? Would they use the private service again? In addition, try to apply a suitable measure of social class.

2. From what you have found, is there a relationship between use of private medicine, gender and social class? (Hint: were most of the men and women drawn from any particular social classes?)

Ethnicity and use of private health care

Although the rise in private medical care in the UK is relatively recent, sociologists have shown some interest in the issue of ethnicity and private medicine. Thorogood (1992) examined the issue of private health care from the perspective of black (Afro-Caribbean) women in Britain. Based on in-depth interviews with 32 women living in Hackney, East London, Thorogood used two age groups (16–30 years and 40–60 years) from two locations (a GP's waiting room and word-of-mouth recommendations in the local area). The research shows that 'culture' is not a static entity enabling sociologists to refer to people simply as part of a 'Caribbean culture'. Thorogood cites Giddens (1979) and Gilroy (1987) to show how culture is constantly changing and responding both to past experiences (for example health care in the Caribbean) and present perceptions (for example health care in Britain today). Twenty one of the 32 women interviewed believed private health care was better than the NHS. Fifteen of the women (six young and nine older) had had private treatment and fourteen of the remaining women said they would do so if necessary. Thus private health featured as a prominent choice among the sample.

The women who had had private treatment did not belong to a main insurance scheme such as BUPA, but many were willing (although some were reluctant) to pay for a private consultation with a general practitioner. The main reasons cited were: 'a chance of a second opinion', 'a good going over' and 'more time during the consultation' (Thorogood, 1992).

A more theoretical point about resorting to a fee-paying rather than a free service is the issue of empowerment. Control over health care, particularly in the doctor–patient relationship, appears to be of sufficient concern to lead people to pay for treatment that is available on the NHS free of charge (although it is not always accessible). By directly purchasing a GP consultation many women believed they had more control (that is, became more empowered) than in an NHS consultation. One Afro-Caribbean women in the study commented 'if he's [the GP] horrible he won't get any patient, any private patients, and he won't be able to make any money on the side' (ibid.).

Strong (1979) claims that as women, and particularly as black women, black female patients are often rendered powerless. The sense of powerlessness might stem from a charitable relationship between doctor and patient because the service is provided free 'even for recent immigrants'. Equally it might stem from structural causes: the possible institutional racism that might have caused many ethnic minorities to occupy the worst housing conditions, the poorest standard of social and educational services and the lowest-paid work. This powerlessness could well encourage some people to regain some equality by purchasing health care: the black women in Thorogood's sample were believed to resort to private health care as a means of empowering themselves during the GP consultation.

Exercise 10.13   Evaluating ethnicity and use of private health care

The next paragraph attempts to extend the number of issues any study of empowerment, ethnicity and use of private health care might examine. Read the following and try to add any extra issues or questions you think should be studied in order to provide a detailed examination of ethnicity and private health care.

The concern for empowerment might also apply to other areas, such as social class, status as perceived by the doctor (for example accent, location, profession, educational background), gender, age and disability. Rather than producing a checklist of issues that have already been outlined, why not ask: what is sociologically important about empowerment? What is it that people want from a consultation that will make them feel empowered: politeness, more time, clearer explanations, more prescriptions, more respect for their symptoms? What makes people feel they have little control over consultations with their doctor? Why might people feel the need for empowerment? How might people empower themselves without purchasing health care?

[e] [i]   1. Now rank the preceding questions in order of importance. Explain why you chose the top three answers on your list.

[e]   2. Write down any additional questions you might ask about the relationship between ethnicity and private medicine.

Social class and use of private health care

Since the early 1980s an increasing number of people have been covered by private medical insurance. In 1993, 60 per cent of private medical subscriptions were paid by large business organisations as a fringe benefit for their employees (Laing and Buisson, 1994).

Much like any other commercial good, private medical insurance is distributed unevenly. The General Household Survey (1987) investigated the occupation of those who had private medical insurance and obtained the following figures:

- Professional: 27%
- Employers and managers: 23%
- Intermediate (non-manual): 9%
- Skilled manual: 3%
- Semi-skilled: 2%
- Unskilled: 1%

There clearly is a relationship between social or occupational class and private medical insurance. It is possible to investigate this further, for example are people contributing to an individual scheme or a discounted group scheme, or are they members of company schemes funded by employers? The General Household Survey (1987) shows the percentage of manual workers having individual schemes as opposed to company schemes.

Exercise 10.14   Social class and private health care schemes (per cent)

	Professional	Intermediate	Manual
Individual scheme	21	29	27
Group scheme	28	19	13
Company scheme (employer pays full premium)	25	28	31
Other	36	34	29
Number in sample	177	300	157

(*Source*: Adapted from the General Household Survey, London: HMSO, 1987.)

 1. How might you explain the pattern of private health care cover shown in the table?

 2. What additional variables would you want to see in the table in order to gain a more accurate view of which social groups tend to have private health insurance? (Hint: gender.)

There may be a connection between social class and type of private health insurance. The reasons for having the insurance, and the type of insurance, may well vary both between occupational classes and *within* an occupational class.

Age and the use of private health care

According to the General Household Survey (1987) three main groups of people tend not to have private medical cover: manual workers, the unemployed and old people:

Percentage covered by private medical insurance, 1987

	0–15	16–44	45–64	65–74	75 +
Males	9	10	13	5	3
Females	8	9	10	5	3

(*Source*: Adapted from General Household Survey, London: HMSO, 1987, Table 4.8.)

As can be seen, working people aged 16–44 are most likely to have private medical insurance, particularly males. There may be various reasons for this. The largest increase in private medical insurance, which occurred in the 1980s, coincided with NHS reforms, which encouraged the role of private medical treatment in Britain. Retired people might not have had private medical insurance as part of their fringe benefit package when they were employed. For many elderly people their limited pension will restrict their ability to afford private medical treatment and insurance: their premiums increase with age at the very time their disposable income falls, possibly forcing them to terminate an existing policy.

The state of some people's health may well restrict their eligibility for private medical insurance. It is usually a requirement when applying for insurance that any preexisting medical conditions are declared. People suffering from chronic sickness (which may involve a great deal of expensive care rather than curative treatment) might well be refused cover while others might be deterred from applying. People with limiting long-standing illness tend to be more common in groups such as manual workers, the unemployed and the old. Hence the elderly may well be restricted in their ability to take out private cover, as well as perhaps finding the cost of private cover prohibitive.

ITEM E

Privatisation by Stealth?

'The government introduced the "internal market" to stifle the protests at the continued underfunding of the NHS. . . . The market has forced the pace of closure of NHS beds . . . beds have closed because of underfunding and political decisions not to spend on health care. . . . Faced with decreased NHS capacity and long waiting lists in the public sector, other purchasers such as GP Fundholders have felt they have no choice but to transfer business into the empty, waiting private sector. . . . The private sector has increased its throughput, taking business from the NHS, but it still has plenty of spare capacity.

Patient charging

Trusts and health authorities are increasingly looking at introducing charges for some treatments and services. Patient charges now make up four per cent of NHS income. But in dental care and eye tests, charging is now the rule.

Patient charges make up one third of the £1.2 billion spent on NHS dental care. Each course of treatment requires the adult to pay up to 80 per cent of the costs up to a ceiling of £275. Pregnant and nursing mothers and people on income support are exempt; the elderly are not, unless on income support. The changes in the dental contract have left many parts of the country with a limited supply of NHS dentists. Some dentists will only take on children as NHS patients if their parents agree to go private. The only monitoring of the impact of dental charges is national and local surveys, which point to a growing polarisation of dental disease (standards are worst for disadvantaged groups in society) and a reversal of the trends in improved dental health which have taken place since the 1950s. Dental charges have two effects: they act as a deterrent to seeking help and care at an early stage, but

they also mean that dentists are less likely to set up practice where they are unable to make a good income from private patients.

So, what NHS treatments will be charged for next? One suggestion is that people could start to pay for "predictable" operations and life events such as childbirth. The fact is that in the end all health care has an element of predictability: one in three of us will get cancer; one in 12 women will get breast cancer and most of us will suffer coronary heart disease. Moreover, predictable treatments are only a very small part of what the NHS does. Only seven per cent of the NHS budget is spent on elective surgery, such as hernias and varicose veins, at the cost of about £100 per head of population. The rest of what the NHS does is concerned with emergency work, care of people with devastating diseases, and long-term illness.

The average private health

insurance plan covers people mainly for elective work only, but will cost about £400 to £1000 per year. The cost of the NHS per person is £1035; the difference is that private health insurance covers only seven per cent of the care available on the NHS ...

Patient charges and private health care insurance (the two go hand-in-hand) are hugely inflationary. UK spending on health care is lower than countries with insurance schemes, because the NHS has not had to spend money on administering patient charges; because there are no "middle men" taking a cut in the negotiations between hospitals and insurers; and finally, because the US-style fee-for-service system actually promotes unnecessary intervention. Most importantly however, patient charges create inequities in access and treatments ...

The NHS and Community Care Act has all but destroyed the principle of comprehensive care in the NHS from the cradle to the grave, by opening the door to patient charges. We get the NHS on the cheap; £1035 a year per person for coverage from the cradle to the grave. This is a low price for a fully comprehensive policy with no small print. Private health insurance costs as much and covers less than ten per cent of what the NHS provides.'

(Source: Allyson Pollock, 'Privatisation by stealth?', Health Visitor, vol. 68, no. 3, March 1995.)

ITEM E *Exercise 10.15 Evaluation of private health care*

Read Item E, which evaluates the introduction of private health care and patient charges for health care.

[i] 1. Why does Item E suggest GP fundholders are turning to private health care?

[i] 2. What health care services does private health care tend not to cater for?

[i] 3. What criticisms does Item E make of the introduction of charges for services such as dental care?

[i][e] 4. Copy the table below and in it provide a short critique of private health care using information in Item E.

Critique of Private health care	
For:	Against:

Private health care has grown quite rapidly since the 1980s, and more private health care establishments are able to secure contracts with the NHS and GP fundholders to treat patients. As the future expansion of private health care looks to continue, one main sociological issue that needs to be examined is the potential increase in unequal access to private health care by different social groups: there is a possibility that there will be a decline in free NHS services as private hospitals expand their health care provision; for example fertility treatment might become increasingly harder to obtain within the NHS and thus the fertility service might become more of a private domain.

Evaluating the effectiveness of health care

A number of issues might be relevant to an assessment of the effectiveness of the NHS:

- The NHS and its reforms might be improving standards of health but there is a problem with measuring the quality of services.
- The behavioural model of health: it is the causes of illness (unhealthy behaviour) rather than the symptoms that should be tackled.
- The social model of health: it is the causes of illness (poverty) rather than the symptoms that should be tackled.
- Iatrogenesis: Western medicine (for example the NHS) might be seriously damaging patients' health.
- Orthodox Western medicine is too limited: the contribution of complementary medicine needs to be assessed.

Measuring the quality of services

Morbidity figures

One measure of an effective health service is to examine the incidence of death (mortality rates) and illness (morbidity rates). The problem with morbidity figures is that they depend upon people reporting illness to health officials (rather as crimes need to be reported to the police to be recorded). Not all illness is recorded, therefore the illness figures may simply be the 'tip of the illness iceberg' (see Figure 3.1, p. 47).

The more access people have to health services (for example more local surgeries and more doctors on call) the more likely it is that illness will be recorded. An example of this is shown by a case study of tuberculosis clinics in Puerto Rico (Hunter and Arbona, 1984). The highest TB rates were recorded nearest the clinics, and where there were no clinics there was very little recorded TB. It is possible that the areas without TB clinics had very few cases of TB. However, it is more likely that the existence of clinics in some areas meant that more cases were reported there.

Rather as an increase in police officers means more crime can be detected, the greater the provision of health services the greater the likelihood of an increase in recorded sickness!

Quantitative approaches to measuring the quality of a health service

How should health services be measured? Doll (1973) and Maxwell (1984) offer the following criteria:

Measurements of health care in the NHS

Doll (1973)	Maxwell (1984)
• Medical outcomes	• Access
• Economic efficiency	• Relevance to need
• Social acceptability	• Effectiveness
(ie. patient satisfaction)	• Equity
	• Efficiency
	• Social acceptability
	(ie. patient satisfaction)

Generally, medical performance may be measured in a number of ways, though mainly through quantitative analysis (that is, statistics). One quantitative method used is the number of operations performed over a period of time. A criticism of this method is the problem of comparing the large number of relatively quick and simple operations carried out in one hospital/department with the much smaller number in a hospital or department that specialises in time-consuming and complicated brain surgery or ear, nose and throat operations. Measurements can also be made of hospital waiting times, the number of cancelled operations and the time taken to perform particular operations.

Although medical measurements may be useful, do they actually tell patients and health officials anything valid about the quality of care patients are receiving? In what ways are the figures produced so that consistency (or reliability) is maintained between hospitals and over time? If the rules change in the way a waiting list is compiled, how valid are the figures? At an estimated cost of around £550 000 to produce the medical data, in what ways do the health service and patients benefit from knowing these figures? Given that a survey of 47 GP fundholders' found that their reasons for choosing to send patients to a particular hospital tended to be mainly based on proximity and convenience (Mahon *et al.*, 1993) it seems reasonable to ask how *useful* is the health data. Even if it is useful, just how valid is it as a measure of health care?

Qualitative approaches to measuring the quality of a health service

Rather than attempting to quantify health data (such as the number of operations performed, percentage of patients on a waiting list over a year) some researchers claim that a more qualitative approach using open-ended questionnaires and interviews provides a better measure of patients' (or even health staff's) views about the quality of care received or provided. Indeed qualitative views of health care may be compared with official health data in order to analyse whether the two match, for example a health area's declared hospital waiting time may be contrasted with the time patients claim they have been waiting for surgery.

ITEM F

Jones *et al.* (1993) adopted a qualitative approach in their study of health services for older people. In a study funded largely by the King's Fund Institute (and therefore not government funded) representative samples of elderly people in the general population were drawn from a target population in three district health authorities in South Wales. Very high response rates were achieved: 94 per cent in one of the samples. The respondents were either interviewed or sent postal questionnaires to assess their experiences of the health services before the health reforms had been introduced, and later further samples were chosen to assess the impact of the new health reforms.

Views of the elderly about their GPs, using interviews

There were 1500 respondents in the 'before the reforms' sample in 1990, and 1500 in the 'after the reforms' sample in 1992. These showed:

- Little evidence of the elderly being removed from GP patient lists.
- Many did not receive the compulsory leaflet about the GP practice.
- Many claimed they had not received blood pressure checks.
- An increase in consultations with the doctor.
- An increase in being able to speak to their doctor on the phone.

Views of the elderly about their hospital experiences, using postal questionnaires

There were 960 respondents in the 'before the reforms' sample in 1990, and 1025 in the 'after the reforms' sample in 1992. These found:

- Half of all patients had been categorised as urgent or emergency admissions.
- Over 33 per cent of non-emergency medical needs were treated within a month.
- Few patients in either year reported difficulties in communicating with health professionals.
- Satisfaction was expressed in both years with patient privacy.
- A decrease in the number who felt they had a choice of hospital.
- An increase in offers of a private room within NHS hospitals.
- A slight increase in the number complaining of unclean toilet facilities.
- 34 people before the reforms and 43 after the reforms had waited more than a year to be admitted to hospital.

(Source: Adapted from D. Jones, C. Lester and R. West, 'Monitoring Changes in Health Services for Older People', in R. Robinson and J. Le Grand, eds, Evaluating the Health Reforms, King's Fund Institute, 1993.)

Exercise 10.16   Measuring the quality of a health service: the qualitative approach

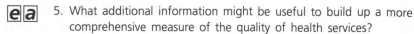

1. Briefly outline the methodology of the study described in Item F.

2. Why is it important to have a high response rate in a survey?

3. State one positive and one main negative finding of the research?

4. Can generalisations be made about the experience of all health service patients from this study?

5. What additional information might be useful to build up a more comprehensive measure of the quality of health services?

The behavioural model of health

The behavioural model of health and illness has often been labelled the individualist model, in that people are 'blamed' for their own symptoms. This perspective has political implications: past health ministers have often turned to the behaviourial model as an explanation of patterns of ill-health. A former Conservative health minister, Edwina Currie, claimed the ill-health of poorer northerners was due to their unhealthy diet and could be best improved by 'impressing upon people the need to look after themselves better'.

A report by the Medical Services Study Group (Connelly and Crown, 1994) investigated 250 cases of individuals who had died before the age of 50. The report claimed that in 98 of the cases the individuals were responsible for their own deaths through their unhealthy behaviour such as smoking, overeating, drinking or failing to comply with treatment.

Research that supports the view that behaviour has a major impact on health was conducted by Belloc and Breslow (1972). The research measured the effects on health of adhering to seven rules:

- Don't smoke cigarettes.
- Sleep for seven hours.
- Eat breakfast.
- Keep weight down.
- Drink alcohol moderately.
- Exercise daily.
- Don't snack between meals.

Longevity increased with the number of rules followed. Life expectancy at age 45 was 11 years longer for those who followed at least six of the rules in comparison with those following less than four (ibid.) However individual behaviour may well be related to structural/material factors such as poverty, unemployment, poor housing and poor working conditions.

Although people may choose to smoke or drink alcohol in excess, there are patterns that suggest working-class people smoke and drink more. This might mean that they are less concerned about their health, but it could equally be that the conditions they experience shape their decisions: coping with life might mean adopting unhealthy lifestyles.

Exercise 10.17 When can an illness be labelled an illness?

Choose the degree to which you would classify the following as an illness by drawing a circle around the appropriate value of your choice (1–4)

	Very ill			Not ill
Migraine symptoms (severe headache, nausea, impaired vision)	1	2	3	4
Anorexia nervosa (severe eating disorder)	1	2	3	4
Hangover (severe headache, nausea)	1	2	3	4
Leukaemia (cancer of the blood)	1	2	3	4
Cirrhosis of the liver (caused by consistent alcohol abuse)	1	2	3	4
Smoker's cough	1	2	3	4
Lung cancer (patient is a heavy smoker)	1	2	3	4
Severe lack of energy	1	2	3	4
Venereal disease due to a holiday romance	1	2	3	4

 1. What influenced your decision to determine whether symptoms were a genuine sickness or not? (Hint: did you consider the seriousness of the complaint, for example how unpleasant the symptoms were and the chances of it being fatal? Did your decision have anything to do with the decisions people might have taken about their lifestyle, for example they drank too much beer hence they suffered a hangover? Are the hangover symptoms similar to those of a migraine?)

 2. If the issue of responsibility influences whether symptoms are considered a genuine sickness (for example hangover is self-induced by drinking alcohol in excess), what implications might this view have in a situation where health service funds are limited. (Hint: treating smokers who develop lung cancer or a football player incurring a sporting injury.)

The government's published health targets outlined in 'Health of the Nation' (DoH, 1992) have emphasised the adoption of healthier lifestyles, and health promotion is now a feature of some outposts' (former regional health authority) policies.

Tannerhill (1987) defines health promotion as involving three overlapping activities: health education, prevention and protection. Whereas health education and prevention were already undertaken by the NHS, the third activity – protection – may allow health organisations to lobby for policy changes that extend beyond simple curative concepts into broader policies, for example on alleviating poverty and unemployment.

Critics argue that the behavioural model diverts attention away from the real cause of ill-health: poverty and exploitation created by the capitalist system. The reason some poor people may adopt unhealthy lifestyles is their structural situation, for example poor people might smoke more cigarettes to relieve the stress caused by their economic position in society and the alienating nature of their work. Furthermore people's 'choices' are shaped by powerful corporate interests in society, such as the tobacco companies' ability to encourage consumers to smoke. Allegedly, early tobacco promotions claimed smoking was good for your lungs. The Marxist critique tends to view people as 'following subtle orders' whereas action theorists are keen to point out that people do make genuine choices: what is important is discovering what it means to be a smoker or heavy drinker and how people make sense of their given situation to make the choices they then exercise.

Link Exercise 10.4   Evaluating the behavioural model of health

Turn to the section 'What is the relationship between income and health?' in Chapter 5 (page 106).

[i] 1. Write one paragraph on how low income can have a damaging effect on health. (Hint: Blackburn's (1991) work examines lack of resources, lack of control, developing coping strategies.)

[a] 2. In no more than two or three sentences suggest how low income might lead to unhealthy behaviour (for example poor diet).

[e] 3. How might you use the information on low income to criticise the behavioural model of illness? (Hint: is illness simply due to inappropriate lifestyle decisions?)

The social model of health

Far from the NHS having made a dramatic improvement in health, the social model argues that improvements in standards of living have had the largest impact on mass health care. McKeown (1976) spent two decades comparing medical records with death records. McKeown claimed that the decline in the death rate in England and Wales in the nineteenth century was not mainly due to improvements in health care: the most common infectious diseases (tuberculosis, scarlet fever, measles) had all virtually disappeared by the time immunisation began. Rather he considered that improvements in the supply of clean water and the disposal of sewage as well as a greater awareness of hygiene had reduced the incidence of diseases transmitted through food and water, for example cholera and typhoid. In addition to the factors that reduced *exposure* to illness, McKeown stressed a main factor in improved health was the increasing ability of people to *resist* disease because they were fitter and stronger and therefore less vulnerable to infections.

Why were people fitter and stronger? McKeown does give some credit to health care provision, but he puts particular emphasis on:

- Better diet.
- Greater awareness of personal hygiene.
- Less overcrowding.
- Better sanitation.

How might the social model of health be applied to social policy today?

The Black Report (Townsend and Davidson, 1980) concluded that inequalities in health had not been effectively reduced by the NHS and therefore more attention needed to be paid to tackling poverty. In the report, low social class had been shown to have a major association with illness: on average those in Class V tended to have a 250 per cent greater chance of suffering from every disease bar breast cancer (which was relatively evenly spread throughout the social classes). The report also argued that better health promotion and primary health care (health centres, family doctors, health visitors) could add to improved health.

Phillimore and Beattie (1994) used a measure of material deprivation in northern England and compared it with measures such as low-birth-weight babies, infant mortality and long-term illness or disability. They found persistent and wide disparities in health between different social groups. These inequalities were evident using both the simple measure of social class (applying the registrar-general's scheme) and a more sophisticated deprivation score based on:

- Employment status, that is unemployed or employed.
- Housing status, that is rented or owned.
- Income and wealth, that is car ownership.
- Household overcrowding (more than one person per room).

Phillimore and Beattie's research supported the findings of the Black Report (Townsend and Davidson, 1980) by finding persistent health inequalities in the north. Their findings also cast doubt on the artefact explanation, which argues that through upward social mobility more people are entering the middle classes, therefore differences in health between those in Class V and those in 'higher' social classes are of negligible importance because fewer and fewer people are affected. In addition, in their opinion the widespread inequalities have been made more persistent by structural changes such as large-scale redundancies in traditional manufacturing and mining areas.

Phillimore and Beattie support the social model of health by arguing that social policy should aim to tackle poverty, unemployment and poor living conditions. The large-scale redundancies that have affected certain areas in particular have caused increasing levels of unemployment, poverty, poor living conditions and overcrowding.

Link Exercise 10.5   Evaluating the social model of health

Turn to Chapter 2 and use Items F, G and I (pages 24–5) to answer the following:

$\boxed{i}$ 1. According to McKeown what were the crucial social policies that decreased the incidence of infectious diseases?

$\boxed{i}\boxed{a}$ 2. What does McKeown's conclusion suggest about the value of a largely curative-based health service such as the NHS?

$\boxed{e}$ 3. What criticisms might be aimed at the social model's conclusions about the value of the health service? (Hint: will improvements to living standards reduce all illnesses?)

Iatrogenesis

Illich (1976) claims that Western style medical treatment is not only ineffective but causes damage to patients. It does this through:

- The undesirable side effects of drugs.
- Technical errors in surgery.
- Removing self-responsibility for health care.
- Claiming to cure illness through medicine rather than by altering human behaviour (more exercise, better diets) or reducing poverty.

Clinical iatrogenesis is illness caused by the side effects of drugs and sometimes surgery. Addiction to depressant drugs or adverse reactions to vaccinations are but two examples of the negative biological effects of medical treatment.

Link Exercise 10.6   Iatrogenesis and the Opren controversy

Turn to Chapter 2, Item D (page 15). Read the case of the anti-arthritis drug, Opren.

$\boxed{i}$ 1. What was one potential side effect of Opren?

$\boxed{a}$ 2. In no more than one paragraph describe how the Opren case illustrates the role of pharmaceutical intervention in the medical industry. (Hint: was Opren safe for all patients?)

Social iatrogenesis refers to the way the medical 'industry' attempts to medicalise human conditions such as sadness which has become a medical problem called depression that can be treated by drugs.

According to proponents of the theory the NHS, having been de-signed by the medical profession, is a curative rather than a pre-ventative system. It is based on developing treatments (new drugs and new technology) that are then produced and sold by private companies for profit. The NHS can therefore be seen as providing a huge market to multinational companies that deal in medical treat-ments. If more money were to be diverted into improving living stan-dards then perhaps less illness would occur, but such measures would do nothing to promote the interests of medical industries such as pharmaceuticals. The medical profession is in the business of pro-moting its own interests by discovering more and more illness to enable it to continue in employment. Profit-making pharmaceutical companies and doctors are in the business of medicalising the human condition (that is, claiming that much of human behaviour is a medical problem, and therefore requires treatment by the medical profession); examples might include treating childbirth as a medical problem to be dealt with by doctors, providing drugs to alter moods, or surgery to alter physical appearance. The NHS is, in its design, a service that might be seen as promoting medical businesses rather than dealing with the underlying causes of ill-health, such as poverty and poor housing.

The notion of iatrogenesis may be useful in analysing the nature of the NHS when considering the ways the health service might actually cause people harm rather than treat them successfully. More research might be needed to show the extent to which some treat-ments can damage patients' health. However there are some illnesses where medical treatments are very effective, so the notion of clinical iatrogenesis may be more applicable to some cases than others. The medicalisation of the human condition, social iatrogenesis, is also worth examining as a critique of the health service. We must be critical of the way certain problems (for example being worried) require a medical response (for example drugs). It might be that people need to rest or attempt to change the stressful conditions in which they live, and then they will not have to resort to medical treatment (cultural iatrogenesis: the inability to cope with problems in life such as grief and pain without resorting to medical treatment). It is also worth examining the way the medical profession resists medicalising certain problems such as repetitive strain injury (RSI), which was discussed earlier in this book. It might be the case that some people want their condition to be medicalised, and therefore the medicalisation of human conditions might not in itself be a criticism of the health service.

Link Exercise 10.7 Medicalisation and the case of RSI

Turn to Chapter 4 and examine 'Convincing others: doctors' in the section 'Being believed' (page 56). Read the account of the RSI sufferer who failed to convince her doctor that the painful symptoms of RSI were a legitimate illness.

 In no more than two or three sentences explain why people such as RSI sufferers may wish to have their condition medicalised.

The role of complementary medicine

Complementary or alternative medicine is the term often given to non-medical treatment. Examples include the following:

- Acupuncture: an ancient Chinese treatment whereby needles are inserted in specific parts of the body. Life is sustained by vital energy force 'Chi' which flows around the body. Acupuncture can restore the bodily flow so that the two elements of Chi (ying and yang) are restored. It is claimed that this treatment is effective for arthritis and chronic head pain.
- Herbal Remedies: certain herbs may be effective in treating illness as they may provoke natural protective bodily responses, for example witch hazel appears to create a tough antiseptic coating over broken skin.
- Homeopathy: this treatment rests on the principle that 'like is cured by like'. Patients are given very dilute doses of a remedy that has been shaken vigorously in preparation. Shaking is supposed to increase the potency of the medicine even though only minute doses are provided. The body then builds immunity to the problem.
- Reflexology: reflexologists believe that different areas of the feet correspond to the different organs of the body. Using a massage technique of applied pressure to the feet the whole body can be treated. This is used to treat migraines, sinus problems, digestive problems as well as tension and stress.
- Osteopathy: the devout American minister, Taylor Still, pioneered this therapy in which the vertebrae are taken to be the centre of bodily disharmony. Taken up by Littlejohn, who had a knowledge of physiology, the therapy was developed further and given a 'scientific' basis. Often used to treat back pains, sciatica and spinal problems by careful manipulation of the body.
- Hypnotherapy: involves creating a trance-like state. Hypnotherapy has been used since (as far back as) 1000 BC. Under hypnosis the patient can be made more receptive to suggestions (for example, to quit smoking) and might retain the advice after the hypnosis has ended.
- Chiropractic: Maladjustment and misalignment of the spine can cause strain on the vertebrae and some joints, causing great pain. Careful manipulation by hand is the standard therapy. Conditions such as sciatica, lumbago and back pain are usually the main problems treated.

Registration urged for unorthodox medicine

'Patients are increasingly likely to turn to non-conventional remedies under the National Health Service, representatives of the orthodox medical profession admitted yesterday.

A report by the British Medical Association acknowledged that many doctors and patients are keen to pursue complementary therapies like osteopathy, homoeopathy, acupuncture, and herbalism.

At the same time, it called for registration and regulation of complementary practitioners to protect the public from quacks.

The report, Complementary Medicine – *New Approaches to Good Practice*, covers the most common techniques of what the BMA calls non-conventional medicine.

The glasnost was summed up at a news conference at the Scottish headquarters when GP committee chairman Dr John Garner was joined by Dr Robert Leckridge, an Edinburgh GP and registered homeopathist.

Dr Garner said the report was not an endorsement of complementary medicine but a pragmatic recognition that patients were exercising choice.

"We want to be sure that the public can make a choice from practitioners who are qualified, have a certain level of training, and follow a code of practice and a disciplinary code," he said.

Other issues covered in the report include the need for patients' GPs to be kept informed if they are undergoing complementary therapy, awareness of the complementary practitioner's limits of confidence, and liability insurance.

Estimates of the number of medically qualified doctors who, like Dr Leckridge, also practise unorthodox techniques, vary from 2 per cent to 15 per cent.

However, a survey of medical students indicated that 69 per cent of them wanted to find out more about complementary techniques.

"Whether or not doctors wish to practise different techniques themselves, it is important they have some way of learning about them in order to advise their patients about what is on offer," said Dr Garner.

The doctors predicted that demand from patients would lead to complementary techniques becoming increasingly available under the NHS, thanks to the introduction of the purchaser–provider split; homoeopathy is already written into the 1949 NHS Act and Greater Glasgow Health Board runs one of the country's most popular courses at its Homoeopathic Hospital.

Up to 160 different non-conventional techniques have been recorded and Dr Leckridge, a member of the faculty of homoeopathy, admitted that there were "many quacks out there waiting to con the public."

"Our fear is that people may be put at risk of emotional or financial abuse from non-medically qualified practitioners, who all operate in the private sphere – they can hook people in and keep them going in order to get their money.

"Another risk is disintegration of care, with people going from one practitioner to another with no communication between them or with the GP.

"I would not have confidence in someone who cleans windows during the week and works as a non-medically qualified practitioner at the weekend." The report recommends statutory registration for those techniques with most potential for risk – either where diagnosis and treatment go hand-in-hand or where invasive or potentially harmful techniques are involved – the statutory scheme recently entered into by osteopaths is recommended as a model.

For others, it says a voluntary registration scheme would be sufficient if it laid down education and training standards and was kept up to date.'

(Source: The Herald, June 1993.)

Exercise 10.18 Monitoring complementary medicine

[i] 1. What evidence does Item G include to suggest that complementary medicine is taken seriously by both patients and doctors?

[i] 2. According to Item G, are complementary techniques likely to become available on the NHS? What evidence suggests that complementary medicine is already available on the NHS?

[i] 3. What problems might both GPs and patients face when deciding to use complementary medicine, according to Item G?

[i][a] 4. Why do you think that complementary medicine should be monitored?

[e] 5. Should all treatments, including those on the NHS (for example drugs and surgery), be monitored? Explain your answer.

[i][a] 6. Turn to the section 'Measuring the effectiveness of therapies' in Chapter 9 (page 248) and identify three problems of trying to monitor a therapy.

Some official medical/health centres use the services of alternative therapists, and hence the term for traditional alternative therapies is complementary medicine as these treatments may add to the existing biomedical service (for example drugs and surgery). There is very little research into the effectiveness of complementary medicine, which makes it difficult to assess. It does, however, appear that there is a demand for complementary medicine. In 1986 a survey of 274 GPs in the Oxford region found that:

- 31 per cent had a working knowledge of at least one non-conventional medicine.
- 41 per cent attended lectures and classes on complementary medicine.
- 16 per cent practised one or more forms of non-conventional medicine, for example manipulation, acupuncture, homeopathy (*Source: Quoted in Health News Briefing, 1989.*)

A further survey of 200 GPs in the south-west found that 38 per cent received training in non-conventional medicine and a further 15 per cent wished to receive training; 72 per cent wished to refer certain patients to a complementary healer rather than treat them personally.

It appears that the NHS is taking a more active interest in complementary medicine. The Marylebone Health Clinic is an NHS holistic centre situated in a crypt in St Marylebone parish church. It was opened in 1987 by the Prince of Wales and includes a member of the clergy, a counsellor, a traditional doctor, a health visitor, a social worker and mind, body and spirit healers. Preventative medicine is a particular focus. While 80 per cent of traditional GP consultations result in a drug prescription, only 34 per cent of consultations at the holistic clinic result in a prescription for drugs. According to Health News Briefing (1989), at that time there were six NHS homeopathic hospitals in Britain. Doctors at the Glasgow Homeopathic Hospital are trained for six months as postgraduates in the Faculty of Homeopathy. The hospital is reported to treat around 2000 patients per year. Thus complementary medicine is becoming more accepted within the official health care system.

ITEM H

Your health in her hands

'Arthritis, back pain, depression? Patients in Devon are being referred by their GPs to a faith healer.

Carole Dommett, 37, took daily tar and oil baths, had ultraviolet treatment, swallowed endless tablets, bought myriad creams and wrapped paste bandages around her entire body for several hours at a time five days a week, in a desperate attempt to fight off the psoriasis that had been plaguing her for four years. Then last year she went to see a healer. "I was a bit skeptical at first. But the first time I saw Gill White she traced my psoriasis back to when my brother had died five years before, at the age of 32. She could sense how I was feeling inside. She talked to me and put her arms around me and I cried uncontrollably. The psoriasis improved within a couple of weeks."

... GP Dr Michael Dixon is currently researching the possible benefits of healing. ... According to Dr Dixon's research of the first 50 patients (patients referred to the healer, Gill White, by the GP practice) more than half said that their main symptom was much better, very much better or had disappeared. "These are good results, particularly when you consider that these patients have tried everything else."

There are more tangible benefits, too. Of those patients whose healing had ended a year prior to analysis, the consultation rate showed a significant reduction from an average of more than 12 consultations a year before the healing to just over 7 during it, and eight in the following year. Thirty-six per cent of the patients either stopped or reduced their medication, which represented an annual saving of £1500 on the practice's drugs bill.'

(Source: Independent, 13 September 1995.)

ITEM H   *Exercise 10.19 Complementary medicine*

[i] 1. Outline the evidence in Item H that suggests that faith healing is effective.

[i] 2. What other benefits might there be in patients consulting a faith healer, according to Item H?

[e] 3. Does the use of faith healing mean that Western medicine is ineffective? (Hint: can faith healing treat all illness – would you use it to treat a broken leg, a cold, a heart attack?)

Alternative therapy in context

Postmodernism argues that a single grand theory (for example Marxism or functionalism) cannot be applied to all social life. For many years sociologists described the Western health service as biomedical (illness has a biological cause and requires medical treatment such as drugs or surgery). However with more of the conventional medical establishment appearing to use complementary medicine sociology must view the health care 'system' in a more sophisticated manner, perhaps viewing the NHS as a fragmentary system: some GPs might use complementary medicine, others might not. On the other hand it might be argued that the way the NHS is drawing in complementary medicine is simply a way of controlling its spread. Complementary medicine might well be shaped into a form that is deemed acceptable to the official medical establishment. It is interesting to investigate which types of complementary medicine are 'accepted' and employed by the NHS and which remain outside the official sphere of health care.

Exercise 10.20   The role of complementary medicine

[a] 1. How does complementary medicine differ from the medical model's approach to health care? (Hint: does complementary/alternative medicine attempt to treat single biological causes; does it treat the body like a machine?)

[a] 2. What evidence is there that complementary health care is becoming more accepted within the NHS?

[e] 3. In no more than one paragraph outline what problems there might be in gaining access to complementary medicine? (Hint: affordability, patients' or GPs' lack of knowledge of alternative treatments.)

What is the role of informal care?

What is meant by informal care?

Formal care is provided by paid carers on an organised basis through a variety of welfare and health agencies. Informal care is provided on an unpaid basis and is usually motivated by love, obligation on duty. Most informal care tends to occur within the family and marital/partnered relationships (Sharkey, 1995). Informal care commonly entails a range of social costs (for example the problem of maintaining relationships because of the time spent caring for others) as well as financial costs, including extra heating, special diets, equipment and the opportunity cost of forgoing paid work and a career. Often the care is very open-ended because the carer is 'on call' 24 hours a day. Around 1.4 million people devote more than twenty hours per week to caring (General Household Survey, 1985). The role of informal care is likely to increase in importance as the proportion of over-75s increases from 1.3 per cent of the population to 7.5 per cent by 2001. To believe *all* elderly people need care is to stereotype; however there are significant needs among this group, and particularly among a proportion of the 'old elderly' (the over 75s). The elderly are not, of course, the only group to require care. But who provides informal care?

Who are the informal carers?

One problem with establishing the extent of informal care is finding accurate figures. It may be difficult to make generalisations from surveys, particularly if key variables such as age, disability, gender, ethnicity and social class are excluded from the study. The General Household Survey is a large-scale, nationally representative survey of over 17 000 adults in over 10 000 households in Britain. It includes questions about unpaid caring, and the response rate is over 81 per cent. The survey excludes informal care provided to people living in residential settings. The main findings (General Household Survey, 1985) show that:

- One adult in seven is a carer.
- 15 per cent of adult women are carers.
- 12 per cent of adult men are carers.
- There are about six million carers in Britain.

One problem with the General Household Survey is that it omits details about emotional support, reassurance or the need for a constant presence (Graham, 1995), and thus it might not capture the real extent of the informal care that is taking place.

Exercise 10.21   Measuring informal care

The way in which informal care was defined and measured in the General Household Survey (1992) involved asking the following screening question: 'Some people have extra family responsibilities because they look after someone who is sick, handicapped or elderly. . . . Is there anyone living with you who is sick, handicapped or elderly whom you look after or give special help to?'

 1. What would your answer be to the screening question?

 2. What ethical questions might you, a sociology student, encounter when asking this question? (Hint: should you ask this question?)

 3. What problems might you have in obtaining a genuine answer?

What is the influence of social policy on informal care?

Informal care has increasingly been the focus of government social policy. The 1981 white paper, 'Growing Older' suggested that community care should not only take place *in* the community but also be provided *by* the community. It was anticipated that this care would be motivated by: 'personal ties of kinship, friendship and neighbourhood ... Care in the community must increasingly mean care by the community' (DHSS, 1981).

A later government white paper, 'Caring for People' (DoH, 1989a) reinforced the emphasis on informal care by pointing out that: (1) most care is provided by family, friends and neighbours, and (2) helping carers to maintain their valuable contribution is a sound investment. However the subsequent National Health Service and Community Care Act 1990, which outlined significant changes to the state health service, did not indicate how informal carers were to be supported. Informal care is likely to increase with future New Right welfare policies: the New Right stresses the role of the individual, particularly within the family, in being self-reliant as well as each family functioning as a self-reliant unit. Therefore future policies might well increase the role of informal care rather than paid formal state care. However many people are not part of a family unit, or do not have a productive relationship with their family: these people therefore have far fewer resources to draw upon.

What social divisions exist in the provision of informal care?

Does the issue of gender apply to informal care?

The General Household Survey (1985) found that 15 per cent of women and 12 per cent of men identified themselves as informal carers. However the extent of informal care may well be underestimated unless the definition of 'informal care' is broadened.

Some feminists argue that informal care is merely an extension of the idea that a woman should be a housewife servicing the needs of her family. It is interesting that the majority of paid caring workers are female: around 90 per cent of nurses are women. Women's traditional domestic role therefore extends into the world of paid employment, reinforcing the patriarchal (male-dominated) notion of woman as carer. Indeed caring has been culturally identified as 'natural' for women (Finch and Groves, 1983).

Women appear to provide more hours of care per week than men. This pattern is most marked for married women. What type of care is provided? Graham (1995) distinguishes two types of care: care provided for someone in the same house (co-resident care) and care for someone living in another household (non-resident care). Using the General Household Survey 1990/1, Graham found that while men and women are equally likely to provide co-resident care, a larger proportion of women provide non-resident care. This difference is most marked between the ages of 45 and 54, when a person is likely to have elderly relatives who might need care.

For whom do men and women care? The General Household Survey (1990/1) shows that:

- 20 per cent of care undertaken by married men and women is for a disabled child.
- 55 per cent of care undertaken by married men and women is for their spouse.
- More married men care for a parent-in-law than for a parent.

It appears that marital status is a major factor in caring as 60 per cent of those caring for elderly parents are single men and women. Married women are far more likely than men to provide non-resident care. Indeed more women than men take the responsibility as main or sole carer, making most of the decisions about care and planning the care. However marital status has much to do with sole caring because virtually all men and women caring for their spouse are the main/sole carers.

The majority of male carers either care for their wives/partners or, if single, for an elderly parent. Men spend fewer hours caring than females, but many men do claim to be carers (12 per cent men, 15 per cent women, General Household Survey, 1985). Ungerson's (1987) study of gender and informal care found that men are more likely to be motivated by love and women by duty. However, for elderly relatives Levin *et al.* (1993) found love to be the main motivating factor for both men and women when they had lived with the elderly relative for a long time. Men have often been viewed as playing little part in informal care and as such would appear to receive even less support than women (who themselves appear to receive very limited support).

To treat everyone as part of one homogeneous (identical) group is somewhat unsophisticated and is likely to obscure differences between social groups. To treat men and women as two large groups would be to repeat the problem. Divisions of ethnicity, age, social class, occupation, marital status and kinship all exist within the broader categories of men and women. The influence of these factors (and others) needs to be borne in mind.

Exercise 10.22   Gender and caring

 Conduct a small-scale research project on gender and caring. Try to find out what proportion of adult males and females would consider caring for (a) wife/husband/partner, (b) mother/father/guardian, (c) a grandparent, (d) sick brother/sister, (e) sick cousin. In addition, find out under what circumstances the respondents would care for another person (for example if the person was ill, infirm or disabled). What do the respondents believe would restrict their opportunity to offer care to another person? From reading the material on gender and caring, what else might you want to find out about?

Does the issue of ethnicity apply to informal care?

Informal care is not a widely documented area: ethnicity and informal care has largely been treated as unproblematic. Whereas the white population in Britain is ageing, ethnic minorities tend to have a younger population; this is due to the pattern of immigration into Britain, largely between the 1950s and the 1970s, in which mainly younger migrants moved to Britain. Thus at present the issue of ageing appears to be less significant for ethnic minorities than for the white British. However Graham (1993a) points out that the relationship between caring, gender and ethnicity is an issue: some black women (and men?) might have a limited family network, perhaps due to migration, which restricts social support between kin. On the other hand this restricted family network might well reduce the likelihood of having to care for an elderly relative in Britain; although the problem could arise of having to care for elderly relatives in the country of origin.

A study by Bhalla and Blakemore (1981) of 400 European, Afro-Caribbean and Asian elders in Birmingham found that 95 per cent of Asian elders, compared with 59 per cent of Afro-Caribbean and 11 per cent European (white?), said that when they were discharged from hospital they were looked after by relatives. One quarter of the Asian respondents had no close relatives in Britain, so who was doing the caring? The study suggests that ethnicity is a variable to be considered when examining informal care.

Gunaratnam (1993) examined the issue of ethnicity and caring, particularly by Asian carers. There might well be large variations in the experience of Asian carers, depending on variables such as individual differences, age, social class, social networks, language, country of origin, religion and customs. Gunaratnam attempts to dispel the myth that all Asians live within extended family networks that enable them to rely on one another for informal support. Although a high proportion might well live in extended families, there are large variations. Gunaratnam interviewed 33 Asian carers from a variety of backgrounds, mainly in London, Birmingham, Bradford and Derbyshire, and found that large variations in informal care exist for

Asians in urban Britain. Cases exist of care by spouses, friends and relatives, both in the home and non-resident.

Gunartanam (ibid.) also found that Asian take-up of health services was very low. However Bhalla and Blakemore (1981) claim that low take-up is largely due to inadequate knowledge of the services and inappropriate publicity. Gunartnam found that 10 out of 33 carers were illiterate in both English and their own language, so even translated information was a problem. Perhaps information other than in written form should be considered? Health and social care workers have become more sensitive to the needs of ethnic minorities and a significant number of publications are being produced in different languages.

Exercise 10.23   Evaluating ethnicity and caring

Read the following critique of ethnicity and informal care. Some of the key words are missing. Use the words below to fill in the gaps.

There is still . . . . . . sociological material on ethnicity and health. When considering available research, the following issues might be considered. Which . . . . . . groups are left out of the study? For what purpose or use is the information? Can . . . . . . be made from the information? Does the information take account of variables such as . . . . . ., age, ..., religion, ..., country of origin, ... and disability? These issues are not the only ones to consider, but may provide a more sensitive and thorough examination of ethnicity as a type of social division.

Key words: social class, limited, generalisations, gender, region, marital status, ethnic.

Does the issue of social class apply to informal care?

Social class is an important variable to consider when examining informal care. Middle-class people may well have more resources and so be able to purchase health care for their relatives or spouses. Middle-class people may have the resources to offer more or better-quality informal care. They may well have more flexible working hours that enable them to assist in the caring of a relative or spouse. However, as with ethnicity, social class and informal care has largely been ignored as a sociological issue, which is curious given the extent to which social class features in other areas of sociology and even within the sociology of health and illness (for example Townsend and Davidson, 1982).

Arber (1989) argues that social class, or rather occupation, is a key variable in both the age of and reason for retirement. Male un-skilled manual workers are more likely than their professional counterparts to retire before the official retirement age due to disability. Indeed some research shows that the early retirement of women is sometimes associated with the ill-health of their spouse, who needs looking after.

Informal networks seem to play a role in 'lay referral', that is, seeking advice from each other rather than from health professionals. McKinley (1973) studied mothers in Aberdeen from unskilled and semi-skilled working-class backgrounds and found that those with closer informal networks experienced a greater degree of 'lay referral'. Those who made most use of antenatal clinics tended to mix more with friends than kin, relying less on lay referral systems. Thus type of kinship network may play a role in informal health-seeking behaviour. Whether sociologists can claim that there are generalisable patterns between social classes is problematic, though useful to explore.

Thus social class appears to be an important consideration when examining informal care and lay referral. The information provided here about informal care and social class gives only a brief outline of the issues.

Link Exercise 10.8   Evaluating social class and informal care

 Turn to Exercise 10.23 (page 299). How might you apply the answers you gave in the exercise to a critique of social class and informal care? (Hint: what issues have not been examined? What relationships have not been explored? For example the relationship between social class and ethnicity)

Does the issue of age apply to informal care?

Age is an important consideration and is one that must be considered alongside other variables, such as social class, gender and ethnicity. Many carers are themselves of retirement age as later in life many people find themselves caring for parents and/or partners. Caring during older age might have important implications for the health of the carer. Atkin claims that 'Older carers are more likely to be in poor health than younger carers and therefore experience greater difficulty with physical care tasks' (Atkin, 1992, quoted in Sharkey, 1995). In response to the demands of caring a charity called Crossroads (named after a TV soap with a disabled actor who became involved with the charity) provides care to carers: the charity sends qualified staff to provide 'respite care' that allows full-time carers to take a short break from their caring role.

A quantitative and qualitative study by Finch and Mason (1993) used a family obligations survey of 978 adults to examine the issue of who should offer kin support for the elderly. Respondents were given case examples and asked who should do the caring:

Case 1: An elderly woman living on her own needing help to get out of bed who has relatives living nearby. Who should be the first to offer help?

Response: daughter, 67.8%; children, 10.4%.

Case 2: Caring for an elderly and confused man who lives alone and needs assistance several times a week.

Response: son, 39%; daughter, 30.6%, children, 9.2%.

Exercise 10.24 Kin and informal care

Examine the text above.

1. Who conducted the research on kin support and how it was conducted?

2. From the response in Case 1, what can you conclude about who was perceived to be the main carer for an elderly female relative?

3. From the response in Case 2, what can you conclude about who it was thought should mainly care for a elderly male relative?

4. What can you conclude overall from the survey about the type of kin (relative) the respondents see as the main person to care for an elderly relative? (Hint: does it depend on the sex of the person needing the care?)

While the respondents in Finch and Mason's survey thought that no specific child (such as the eldest child) should take on more responsibility than another child, there were significant gender differences. Whereas both sons and daughters were expected to provide assistance to parents, in the case of providing money a large proportion of the respondents specified that the son should help. In the role of care provision the crucial variable was the gender of the person needing care: daughters for elderly women and sons for elderly men.

In summary, informal care should be a part of any consideration of health care. Issues such as class, gender, age and ethnicity are important social divisions that may be key variables affecting the extent of care provided. In addition Williams (1993) considers that, for a more thorough examination of informal care, the following areas need to be treated as problematic:

- The *process* of care: the day-to-day experiences of those involved in care (for example the interaction that takes place between care giver and receiver).
- The *context* of care: the variety of historical and cultural aspects of care giving and receiving (for example how ethnicity may affect perceived obligations to provide/receive care).
- The *struggles* of care: the problems and difficulties that care giving and receiving give rise to (for example fear, shame, financial worry, isolation, stigma, uncertainty, balancing other perceived obligations).
- The *rights* of care givers, and in particular of recipients (for example the right to sexual pleasure, the right to be parents, the right to choose the process and type of care received, the right to privacy, the right to deny care).

Turn to Chapter 9 and read the section on community care and the mentally ill (page 229).

[i] 1. In the government reports mentioned, who is assumed to be doing most of the informal care?

[e] 2. What problems can you identify when examining informal care of the mentally ill? (Hint: expertise in caring for the mentally ill?)

Structured exam questions

Question

1. Complete the exercise below to help you understand how to write a response to the following essay question: Assess the view that the power of the medical profession is the main but not the only factor in the continuation of health inequalities. (*25 marks*) (A Level AEB Sociology, June 1991)

(a) Complete the gaps in the following adaptation of a student answer using the key words provided. Read the commentary on skills accompanying each paragraph (in brackets).

Key words: health care, rejected, unhealthy, 'sick roles', material, mobility, power, Black, deprivation, less, lifestyle, Cultural.

Student answer

Parsons (1975) suggested the medical profession allows individuals to take on . . . . . . A sick role is a social role that allows individuals to neglect their usual roles in society, such as their paid working role. Therefore Parsons is suggesting that the medical profession holds . . . . . . over the way in which some people are allowed to adopt the sick role.

Comment *Knowledge and understanding: limited knowledge is shown by the reference to Parsons and the notion of the sick role. The sick role is then related to the question by referring to the medical profession. Interpretation and application: the candidate immediately deals with the issue of the medical profession to ensure the essay question is being addressed. However, perhaps a more explicit connection between the medical profession and health care inequalities needs to be made along with the issue of continuing inequality, which suggests that inequality in the past and present needs to be examined. Evaluation: no evaluation is offered. Perhaps* *a criticism of the power that doctors hold over their official role in legitimating illness could be made.*

The . . . . . . Report (Townsend and Davidson, 1980) suggests that inequalities in health do exist between social classes and that there are alternative reasons to the medical profession being the main cause of these inequalities. The report claims that working-class children are at four times greater risk of accidental death than middle-class children. The report also pointed out that 67 out of 78 causes of mortality are prevalent in the working class.

Comment   *Knowledge and understanding: knowledge is presented that outlines research into alternative reasons why there is social class health inequality. Interpretation and application: the issue of health inequalities is addressed with a relatively accurate interpretation of the Black Report, which is cited in an appropriate context to support the view that inequalities exist. The issue of the continuation of health inequalities is not addressed. Evaluation: alternative explanations are dealt with, which suggests that some evaluation is taking place.*

It might be that some social classes are more healthy than others due to social . . . . . . People who are healthy may remain in their jobs and can continue earning money to maintain or even increase their social class position. Those who are . . . . . . may slide down the social scale. Thus health differences between the social classes may be due to social mobility. In a caste system, as opposed to a social class system, members who become seriously ill still remain in the caste they were born into. Thus there is a distribution of ill-health that remains in each caste. When exploring illness in a system that allows social mobility between the social classes it might be useful to examine the social class origin of the sick person.

Comment   *Knowledge and understanding: although no studies are cited the candidate does offer a brief outline of the social mobility explanation of social class inequality. Interpretation and application: a brief interpretation is provided of the social mobility explanation (also known as the social selection model). Evaluation: the final sentence suggests a possible strength of the social mobility explanation but no criticism, for example serious lack of widespread evidence.*

An alternative explanation is offered by Townsend and Davidson (1982) and Phillimore and Beattie (1994), who suggest that material . . . . . . is also an important factor influencing inequalities in health. Material deprivation is the term given to the lack of material factors such as low incomes and poor housing. Townsend and Phillimore found that those political wards suffering from material deprivation also suffered higher rates of ill-health. Even when looking at manual workers who have the same jobs and the same size family they found that those who lived in more deprived areas were more prone to ill-health than those who lived in less deprived areas. Perhaps deprived areas were least well served by . . . . . . services, which may have contributed to further health inequalities.

Comment   *Knowledge and understanding: an actual study is cited to support an alternative explanation of why health inequalities exist between the social classes. Very little knowledge appears to be presented on the main focus of the essay – the medical profession. Interpretation and application: appropriate use of Townsend and Phillimore to support an 'alternative explanation. An implication of the explanation is that medical services are unequally distributed, thus the candidate is dealing more explicitly with the essay question. Evaluation: a simple juxtaposition is made – one idea or explanation set against another – which hints at evaluation. There is no explicit criticism of the material explanation, for example what about the role of choice and unhealthy lifestyles?*

The Black Report has also suggested that doctors, on average, tend to spend . . . . . . time with working-class patients than middle-class patients. Doctors seem to spend no more than four minutes with the working-class patient and almost ten minutes with the middle-class patient. This itself can be seen as an influence on inequalities caused by the medical profession.

Comment   *Knowledge and understanding: knowledge is presented about the medical profession. Although the Black Report does not tend to deal with doctor – patient dialogue the candidate does make some attempt to refer the reader to a study. It is important for candidates not to refer to a main piece of research as the provider of all studies. The Black Report does not contain every study on health. Interpretation and application: the candidate has addressed the essay question again by examining the role of doctors and inequalities in health. You could update this research with the help of this chapter and Chapter 5 on social class. Again candidates must be careful not to attribute every piece of research on health inequality to the Black Report. Evaluation: no evaluation is offered apart from a simple juxtaposition – that is, that doctors may cause inequality not the material circumstances in which people live. What difference does it make to health inequalities if doctors spend more time with middle-class patients? Is there recent evidence of this? What about issues of gender and ethnic inequalities?*

Rather than examining material factors it might be important to focus on cultural factors that contribute to health inequalities. . . . . . . factors refer to lifestyles adopted by different social groups. Higher rates of smoking, obesity and heart disease have been found in the working-class population. Smoking and drinking may be associated with a 'working-class culture'. The cultural factors may explain some social class health differences. However it might also be that the low incomes and poorer housing associated with the working-class position influence the sort of lifestyle the working-class adopt. Higher levels of stress caused by being in poorer conditions could explain why more working-class people smoke. Thus . . . . . . factors affect lifestyle and cultural factors.

Comment *Knowledge and understanding: key points are provided rather than any sociological data or evidence. Interpretation and application: examples are provided to support the cultural and behavioural explanation, although no sociological research is cited. Evaluation: There is no explicit evaluation apart from, once again, a simple juxtaposition of explanations.*

In conclusion the medical profession does have the power to reduce inequalities in health, but other factors might have greater power. It has been suggested in the Black Report that to reduce inequalities the state could tackle the problem of poverty first and foremost. Only then can the majority of inequalities be eradicated. However this suggestion was . . . . . . by the government and thus inequalities continue.

Comment *Knowledge and understanding: the Black Report is mentioned again and little addition is made to the knowledge presented in the rest of the essay. Interpretation and application: the candidate addresses the essay question again, which is useful as it shows a reasonable interpretation of the question. Evaluation: a hint is provided that social policy needs to be addressed as the Conservative government rejected the Black Report's recommendations. Perhaps the issue of gender and race inequalities could have been mentioned.*

The scores for the candidate were:

- Knowledge: 6/9
- Evaluation and Interpretation: 5/9
- Application: 4/9
- Total mark: 15/27

(b) How could you improve the essay answer?

- Use Chapters 6 and 7 to help you write a paragraph on gender health inequalities that are possibly caused by the medical profession, for example the side effects of contraceptives given to women.
- Use Chapter 7 to help you write a paragraph on ethnic health inequalities that are possibly caused by the medical profession, for example different access to health care for different ethnic groups.
- Use Chapter 10 to help you complete a paragraph on inequalities caused by the 1990 health reforms, for example GP fundholding. Might the patients of GP fundholders receive better-quality health care?
- Use Chapter 10 to help you complete a paragraph on the increase in private health care provision and the distribution of private health care between groups such as social classes. For example might the take-up of private health insurance mean there is better health provision for those who can afford the premiums?

Questions

2. Complete the exercise below to help you write a response to the following essay question: Evaluate the impact of recent government changes to the National Health Service on access to health care. (*25 marks*)

Given the amount of material in Chapter 10 you need to organise the essay into distinct sections. Below is a list of issues you could use to organise a series of paragraphs. Each issue has been expressed in an introductory sentence that you might use to start a paragraph. One criticism has been provided for each introductory sentence. Match the evaluation point with the correct introductory sentence.

Introductory sentences:

(a) The key legislation that changed the NHS in the 1990s was the NHS and Community Care Act. This Act introduced a number of key changes.

(b) The NHS now consists of purchasers of health care and providers of health care.

(c) There is a greater role for private health care under the NHS and Community Care Act.

(d) The creation of GP fundholders allows fundholding pratice to choose which hospital to send their patients rather than having to send them to the local hospital.

(e) The expansion of community care in the 1990s might benefit those who wish to be cared for in smaller community-based programmes.

(f) Tudor-Hart (1971) claimed that under the NHS there is an inverse care law, which describes the situation where those in the poorest areas have least access to quality services. The changes to the NHS might reduce this inequality by allowing GP fundholders to send patients to hospitals offering a quality service.

(g) The Patient's Charter might provide patients with better knowledge of their rights within the NHS and about access to health care.

Key criticisms to be matched with the introductory sentences:

- As health care organisations have to manage their finances they need more administrative staff. This may divert funds away from much needed health care facilities and staff.
- The Patient's Charter only introduced three new rights to the existing seven and these rights might not be widely known.
- Because not all GPs are fundholders there might be inequality of access to health care for those unable to register with a fundholdering GP.
- The expanding role of private health care may only benefit those who can afford to pay for private health insurance.
- The recent legislation may have simply been a measure to reduce spending rather than to improve quality and access to health care.
- The quality of care taking place in the community has been seriously questioned.
- GP fundholders might send patients to hospitals with the cheapest service, not the best-quality service.

3. Write essays on the following exam questions:

(a) 'Health care is more effectively provided by the private sector than by the public sector.' Evaluate the sociological arguments for and against this point of view (25 marks) (AEB November 1994).

(b) Assess the role of the NHS in reducing inequalities in health (25 marks) (specimen exam question).

Summary

This chapter has examined the formal health care structure and informal health care within families. The discussion on formal care mainly examined the development of state involvement in health care during the 1800s and 1900s and the creation of the NHS in 1948. The NHS developed into a largely a curative (sickness treating) rather than preventative health care system (preventing illness from developing through health education, improved living standards and screening).

Recent changes to the NHS have led to a competitive market for health care whereby authorities such as 'regional outposts' and 'health areas' (former regional and district health authorities) purchase medical care from the GPs and hospitals, which provide the medical care. There are repeated claims that by creating a health care market patients will receive a more responsive service that costs less because each business (GP and hospital) will ensure that it limits wastage of its own resources. However inequality and lack of access to these services may be a possible consequence of the government reforms under the 1990 NHS and Community Care Act.

Complementary medicine was also examined as an alternative to the official Western curative model embodied in the NHS, which is based on the medical model (treating the body as a machine to be repaired by drugs and/or surgery).

Informal care, particularly within the family, was contrasted with the formal health care system. Issues relating to ethnicity, social class, gender and age were examined to find out the nature of informal care within these broad social groupings. Informal care is a sociologically neglected area that might become more important because of New Right policies to promote community care programmes that rely upon informal (and particularly, family) care.

11 Perspectives on health care

By the end of this chapter you should be able to:

- outline perspectives on health care;
- evaluate perspectives on health care;
- apply perspectives such as those of the New Right and postmodernism.

Introduction

This chapter begins with an examination of the 'traditional' socio-logical perspectives. The functionalist perspective examines Parsons' (1975) notion of the 'sick role' as well as the view that medical care is useful for society in that it treats people so they are fit to return to their normal social roles, for example to go back to work. The Marxist perspective contrasts with that of the functionalists in that it asks the question: who really benefits from the health care system? Issues such as social control by doctors are examined along with the notion that medical care is just part of capitalism: a means for the bourgeoisie to make money out of persuading people they need to buy medical care (for example drugs and treatment by doctors). The feminist perspective draws attention away from social class and examines a different form of inequality: gender differences. Feminists have examined the way male doctors have created and dominated the NHS and as such continue to impose their values on females. Because of this female patients are controlled by men and the health care women receive may not suit women's needs, for example in the area of child-birth.

The interactionist perspective does not examine the health care system within society but rather focuses on the way the interaction between doctor and patient can affect health care, for example the problem of labelling an illness and the treatment of people suffering from diseases such as AIDS. Postmodernism, which shifts attention away from the concerns of the traditional perspectives, is then explored: the focus is on how notions of the 'body' affect the way illness is perceived, how no theory ('metatheory') is adequate to explain all illness, and how health care may be shifting away from doctor-centred care to patients diagnosing and treating themselves, for example through the use of do-it-yourself kits such as pregnancy testing kits. Finally, the New Right perspective is outlined: this assumes that people should take responsibility for their own health and health care within a free market. The New Right perspective is applied to examine the current state of health care, for example community care, internal markets in health and the growth of private medical care.

When examining the perspectives that follow, think about the usefulness of the different theories in explaining issues of health and health care. It might be that a particular perspective is useful for understanding some issues but not others. This chapter outlines six main perspectives on health care:

- The functionalist perspective.
- The Marxist perspective.
- The feminist perspective.
- The interactionist perspective.
- The postmodernist perspective.
- The New Right perspective.

The structuralist perspective: functionalism

In brief, functionalists tend to assume that the structure of society shapes human behaviour through socialisation. Society requires rules and regulations to create social order. A modern society often develops a large bureaucracy and institutions to cope with the demands of a large population. A division of labour (separate tasks for people, rather than each individual being self-sufficient) is created, with the result that tasks such as education and health care are often performed by specialised, paid people. Thus society is composed of different parts all performing complementary functions; this enables society as a whole to function in an orderly manner.

Parsons (1975) claimed that formal health care performs an important function in modern society by ensuring that ill people are made fit to return to paid work. According to Parsons, when people are ill society tends to release them from normal 'duties' such as going to work. Parsons thought that if too many people claim to be ill it could be dysfunctional for society: not enough work would be completed and a subculture of malingerers, refusing to return to work could develop. For this reason Parsons argued that a 'sick-role' is of crucial importance to society. People can only be legitimately labelled 'sick' if they conform to the elements of the sick role. To acquire the sick role people must:

- Not expect to take care of themselves.
- Want to get better.
- Seek medical advice.
- Comply with the advice given by health professionals.

Ensuring that people seek advice and comply with medical instructions, means that patients will get better quickly and return to work. Formal health care is therefore functional for both individuals and society.

Exercise 11.1 Parsons and the sick role

 Using the preceding information on Parsons' notion of the sick role, complete the following table. Firstly, identify how the sick role should function, according to Parsons. Secondly, for each stage of the sick role there are some issues that Parsons does not treat as a problem: match the stages of the sick role with the issues Parsons fails to treat as problematic. The answers are provided for you below the table.

Parsons' sick role

Stages of the sick role		Areas not treated as problematic
Stage 1:	Individual is sick	
Stage 2:		
Stage 3:	Seek medical advice	
Stage 4:		Medical treatment may cause more harm than good (clinical Iatrogenesis)

Answers to be added to the table:

- Comply with the advice given by health professionals.
- Interpreting symptoms as a 'sickness' may not be straightforward.
- Seeking medical advice may not always be appropriate (for example the role of alternative medicine).
- May not expect to take care of themselves/want to get better.
- Wanting to get better may be quite unrealistic (for example a terminal illness).

Functionalism and the medical profession

The members of the medical profession appear to enjoy high status and high material rewards. Few other organisations have such access to our bodies and/or minds and the authority to treat them in such an invasive way.

According to functionalists, such high status, income and power is justified. In modern industrial societies there is a complex division of labour and the role occupied by doctors is particularly important. They possess specialist knowledge acquired during a long period of training and tested before they are admitted to the profession. Their high reward is not just in recognition of the 'sacrifice' they make by undergoing this training; it is also a recognition of their functional importance to society: their responsibility is to control illness in society – they control access to the sick role and the treatment of the sick.

There may be a danger of doctors abusing their power. Functionalists suggest that a distinctive feature of the doctor's role is that it is not carried out for personal gain ('self-orientation'); rather the interests of the patient and the wider community are paramount ('collectivity orientation').

High standards of conduct are ensured by the profession's ethical codes and disciplinary procedures: the General Medical Council was set up in 1858 to maintain a register of qualified practitioners and to discipline, and possibly 'strike off', those guilty of professional misconduct (for example in 1996 a GP was struck off for using patients as 'guinea-pigs in trials of potentially dangerous drugs'; the doctor was paid by drug companies to conduct the trials and did not obtain the consent of all the patients involved – *Independent*, 23 March 1996).

Criticisms of the functionalist perspective

First, Parsons (1975) assumed that the health care system was the most effective way of creating a fit and healthy society. However according to McKeown (1976) it is improved sanitation, sewage disposal, housing and general welfare that has made the most significant contribution to the nation's health. This alternative model of health is known as the 'social model'.

Second, Illich (1976) claimed that Western style medical treatment is not only ineffective, it also causes damage to patients. This happens through the undesirable side effects of treatments, technical errors during surgery, the removal of self-responsibility for health care, and the claim that medical intervention (rather than reducing poverty or changing people's behaviour) will improve health. The adverse effect of medical treatment is known as iatrogenesis. The medical profession is in the business of promoting its own interests by discovering more and more illness to enable it to continue in employment. Profit-making pharmaceutical companies and doctors are in the business of medicalising the human condition (that is by claiming that much human behaviour is a medical problem requiring treatment by the medical profession). Examples might include treating childbirth as a medical problem to be dealt with by doctors, providing drugs to alter moods, or surgery to alter physical appearance. Whilst functionalists such as Parsons assume that people attempt to define themselves as ill to escape their social roles, Illich claims that the medical industry actively seeks to impose labels of illness on people.

Third, there may be health-seeking routes other than visiting the doctor. Punamaki and Aschan (1994) asked fifty respondents to complete semistructured diaries over a two-week period (details included their daily activities, use of medical services and individual ways of maintaining health). The respondents used a host of alternative health-seeking routes (for example exercise, seeking 'lay' care), which they believed would benefit them more than any official medical intervention.

Link Exercise 11.1   Health-seeking behaviour

Turn to Chapter 3, Exercise 3.6 (page 41).

1. Identify the three most common ways that the respondents in Punamaki and Aschan's (1994) study chose to maintain their health.

2. If these methods were effective how might you use the results to criticise Parsons' concept of the sick role?

In addition, if respondents visit the doctor it is not always the case that they will follow the medical advice they are given. Parsons (1975) considers that patients should comply with medical advice if they are to get better, whereas Illich (1976) stresses that medical advice could have an adverse effect (for example through the side effects of drugs, or failed surgery), and thus non-compliance could be seen as a healthy feature of behaviour. Doctors may view non-compliance as a form of deviance whereas patients may make their own judgments about the advice, distinguishing between what is, from their own perspective, useful advice and what is not.

Finally, a Weberian approach to the study of professions suggests that the power, status and material rewards enjoyed by doctors may not simply be explained by their contribution to the well-being of society as a whole. Rather it may be the result of an occupational group using a range of strategies to improve their position in the job market, largely for their own benefit. The early attempts to exclude women from medicine show how male doctors attempted to limit access to the profession. The lengthy period of medical training may be interpreted as another means of restricting entry to the medical profession. An historical analysis of the development of the medical profession is useful here in showing how doctors have increased their control over health care (for example the registration of qualified doctors after 1858) and tried to maintain this control (for example by insisting, when the NHS was set up, that private medicine should continue).

Link Exercise 11.2   Doctors and labelling illnesses

Examine the section in Chapter 4 on 'Being believed' (page 56).

1. How might you use the example of repetitive strain injury (RSI) to show how doctors could restrict the official 'illness' label although patients regard their symptoms as legitimate?

2. How might you apply a similar issue to the case of mental illness? (Hint: are there disputes about the way in which mental illness is defined?)

3. Using the case of mental illness or RSI, show why Parsons should not have taken for granted the way doctors apply illness labels.

The structuralist perspective: Marxism

Marxists, like functionalists, focus on the structure and influence of the social system rather than on individual behaviour and meaning. However, whereas functionalists focus on stability within society Marxists examine the fundamental nature of conflict within capitalist societies resulting from the inequality produced by the economic system. For Marxists the economic system shapes the rest of society. Therefore within a capitalist society, based on the ownership of private property and the need to create profit, there are two main social classes. Those that own the means of production (the means to produce goods and services, for example factories) are known as the bourgeoisie; they strive to create surplus value (not quite the same as profit, but similar) from the proletariat or workers. Surplus value is the difference between what the worker receives in wages and the total value of what the worker has produced, for example when a worker earning £5 per hour produces goods worth £20, this results in a £15 surplus, which the bourgeois employer uses for his/her own benefit.

The bourgeoisie are believed to influence the rules of society, for example political rules and judicial laws, so that the social and political system continue to allow those who own the economic system, rather than the proletariat, to benefit from it. The proletariat may understand their unequal position (class consciousness) and attempt to enter a class struggle to overthrow the economic system. However many members of the proletariat may be persuaded to believe the system is a fair one (false consciousness). Although many Marxists adopt a similar set of founding principles there are a disagreements within this broad school of thought, particularly with respect to the health system.

The NHS as a means of reproducing the labour force

As discussed above, Marxists claim there are essentially two social classes: the bourgeoisie, or capitalists, who own the means of production and attempt maximise profits by reducing the wages (that is, reduce costs) paid to the proletariat (the workers), who survive on wages for their labour rather than profits from their investments. The view taken by traditional Marxists is that the National Health Service is a way of ensuring workers are sufficiently healthy to continue making profits for their capitalist employers.

The NHS as a working-class victory

A second view taken by some Marxists is that the class conflict between workers and capitalists has resulted in a working-class victory that has secured a free health service for the use of workers. The proletariat have thus diverted the flow of resources to the capitalists by returning some to the workers in the form of a social wage: 'social wage' is the term used to describe state resources that accrue to people other than through their salaries, for example through free health services or free education (Gough, 1979). However critics of the idea that there is health care equality between the social classes, such as Le Grand (1971, 1993), argue that the poorer members of society have not benefited from the free health services as much as the middle-classes. Le Grand refers to the inequality as an 'inverse care law', where the lower social classes receive worse health care provision. Tudor-Hart (1971) suggests that the 1990 NHS reforms are perpetuating unequal health care provision among the social classes.

Link Exercise 11.3 Social class health inequality

Using the answers from Exercise 5.6 (page 83):

1. Write a short paragraph to show that health inequalities exist between the social classes.

2. Write one concluding sentence to show that gender should also be considered when examining social class variations.

Medicine and social control

Some Marxists shift the emphasis away from those who gain financial benefit from the free health care system and focus attention on alternative reasons for a free health care system. Althusser (1969) claims that the capitalist state attempts to exercise social control over its citizens through 'ideological state apparatus' (state institutions) such as the education system and religion. The health service may also be viewed as part of the ideological state apparatus by exercising control over those who are defined as ill, as well as how many can be defined as ill (recent changes in the medical test for disability were introduced to regulate the number claiming invalidity benefit) and what symptoms can be defined as an illness. Doctors working for the Department of Social Security have been advised that patients with ME/chronic fatigue syndrome sometimes exaggerate the effects of their condition.

A dominant theme of ideological control over health (control over the way people *understand* health issues) is that illness is an individual issue in that it is caused by a biological problem (for example gene, a virus) as opposed to structural inequality (for example poverty). If poverty causes ill-health, then the response should not be to increase health care but eradicate inequality. To deal with inequality means changing the economic system from a capitalist system to one in which the proletariat organises the way goods are produced to the benefit of all, instead of just a few. Politically then, the (ideological) notion that illness is an individual biological problem is one that diverts attention away from the social system. For Doyal (Doyal and Pennell, 1979), basing health care systems on curative medicine (drugs and surgery, for example the NHS) rather than preventative medicine (for example addressing issues such as poverty) disguises that fact that illness is socially produced.

Navarro (1979) argues that doctors are merely agents of the state; they act in the interests of the bourgeoisie by promoting the view that illness is an individual problem, a biological not a social issue. The more recent emphasis on health promotion within the NHS (prompted by the government's targets – for example reducing obesity – in the 'Health of the Nation' white paper) shows how the state draws attention away from the social system and towards problems of individual lifestyle. Navarro claims that when the state allowed doctors to exercise a strong influence on the design of the NHS it allowed a dominant group of people to promote a view that illness was a biological problem requiring curative treatment rather than preventative measures.

McKinley (1984) considers that doctors have very little autonomy (freedom). Their professional freedom has systematically been eroded by the state until doctors themselves are merely workers within a vast medical industry that produces marketable health care products (for example drugs) in an effort to generate more surplus value for the bourgeoisie. McKinley tends to focus on the notion of medicine as a commodity whereas Navarro sees medicine more as form of social control.

Exercise 11.2   Brief summary of the Marxist perspective on health

 Using the information on the Marxist perspective, fill in the gaps using the key words provided below.

Marxists believe that the health care system may benefit the . . . . . . because the . . . . . . are treated, enabling them to return to work. Navarro argues that doctors are . . . . . . of the state. Doyal claims that, by adopting the curative approach to illness (that is, drugs and . . . . . .) rather than a . . . . . . approach, the medical profession reinforces the view that illness is an . . . . . . problem and not a social problem, for example caused by . . . . . . McKinley claims that doctors might not be agents of the state, but simply . . . . . . within a large medical . . . . . .

Key words: workers, preventative, individual, bourgeoisie, agents, industry, surgery, poverty.

Exercise 11.3 An evaluation of the Marxist perspective

 Match the first half of each evaluation point with the appropriate ending, then sort each point into strengths and weaknesses of the Marxist perspective.

First half of each evaluation point:

(a) The Marxist perspective encourages us to question the extent to which, and in what ways, doctors are serving the interests of the powerful in society, . . .

(b) Marxists switch attention to social causes of ill-health . . .

(c) In the climate of greater emphasis on health promotion within the NHS (for example of a more healthy lifestyle – more exercise, better choice of diet) sociologists should benefit from asking . . .

(d) Examining health as a product, (for example McKinley, 1984) encourages sociologists to look at the way health has become more 'commodified' . . .

(e) Medicine may be viewed as the ally of capitalism by restricting the number of sick leave certificates and ensuring people return to work. However research suggests that doctors are neither simply a capitalist ally . . .

(f) The debate on health and social control is similar to that on education and social control. State policy may well reflect the interests of capitalists, but the individuals within the sector . . .

(g) Marxists have been criticised on the ground that they ignore the doctor–patient interaction: patients might not simply accept the dominant ideology; they might not believe . . .

(h) Marxists have tended not to conduct empirical tests (find evidence) to support the claim that the concept of dominant ideology . . .

(i) Marxists tend to examine interaction within the health service to show how doctors exert professional . . .

(j) There are health inequalities in socialist societies, so changing the economic system from capitalism to . . .

Second half of each evaluation point:

● unlike the functionalists who suggest doctors serve society as a whole.

● socialism might not improve the quality of health and health care. Socialist societies, like capitalist systems, might benefit from encouraging health to be seen as an individual rather than a social problem, especially if there are insufficient funds to improve people's standard of living.

● why we should examine lifestyle and not the social causes of ill health.

● (that is, more a matter of purchasing care) than an issue of improving the social environment, as McKeown (1976) suggested.

● (for example poverty) rather than individual concerns (for example a virus).

● may not simply be viewed as 'puppets' who are on the side of the capitalist state.

● that their symptoms are biologically induced but might well think the cause lies in social factors such as work and poverty. Indeed doctors themselves may also view illness as having social roots.

- (the prevalence of the medical model of ill-health) exists.
- dominance. On the other hand interactionists, who do examine doctor–patient interaction, often fail to examine the role of dominant ideology and the way it benefits powerful groups in society.
- nor the worker's friend. This issue was raised by Bellaby (1990), who showed how doctors use the medical terminology for 'morning sickness' (hyperemesis) to give some pregnant patients the opportunity to receive sick pay while having time off work.

The feminist perspective

Although there may be as many types of feminism as there are feminists, there are certain views that many feminist theories share. Feminists tend to assume that society is male-dominated or patriarchal and thus that men are in control of the key institutions that shape society and individuals, for example men dominate politics, the judiciary and the health service. Why is it important to consider patriarchy? Whilst feminists might use the term in different ways, male domination is an important consideration in health care. In the past men have excluded women from becoming doctors and have attempted to take control of aspects of women's lives such as childbirth, where previously women health workers tended to dominate (Oakley, 1993). Graham (1984) claims that men still make up the majority of consultants and doctors. Men impose their own values on female behaviour, which means more women are viewed as abnormal and are labelled physically or mentally ill. Symptoms reported by females to male doctors may not be treated as serious conditions, but simply dismissed as 'women's problems'.

Marxist feminists examine women's position within the capitalist system, often viewing women as a 'reserve army of labour' to be used in the economy to increase the labour supply and therefore reduce wage levels. Women not in paid employment may well be full-time housewives, providing free care to their families and keeping them fit for the labour market. Any increase in emphasis on informal care is likely to impact on the traditional female role. Informal care may well be seen as a strategy for cutting the cost of formal care provision (NHS) by passing the workload onto unpaid women.

Radical feminists tend to view men, rather than the economic system, as the primary exploiters of women. No matter what type of society (capitalist or socialist) in which men and women live, men tend to dominate, shaping society to meet their needs rather than the needs of both males and females. Thus any health care system in a capitalist or socialist society may still have a stratum of men who control the nature of medical care. There is a case for a cross-cultural dimension in sociological research to enable comparisons to be made between health care systems in socialist and capitalist societies. In this way sociologists, including radical feminists, could use empirical evidence to test their claim that men dominate irrespective of the type of economic system.

An evaluation of the feminist perspective

The strength of the feminist perspective is that it provides an alternative focus on health inequality from the Marxist exploration of class-based inequality: feminists point out that men dominate in key positions (for example consultants), which might indicate a form of patriarchal control in which men make the key decisions over the health care of women. Oakley's (1993) research, which explores the way men have controlled the management of childbirth in hospital, is particularly relevant here. The radical feminist perspective provides a contrast with that of the Marxists, who assume that health care in a capitalist system benefits the bourgeoisie; radical feminists argue that in any economic system the issue of power differences between men and women is of vital importance, and one to which many Marxists, such as Navarro (1979), have paid insufficient attention.

One major problem with the feminist perspective is that it ignores those males in society who do not hold power over medical care. The control that male doctors and consultants exercise over the provision of medical care might not only harm women (for example through the side effects of recommended contraceptives such as the pill), but might also fail to meet men's health needs (for example the lack of publicity about screening for prostate and testicular cancer). In this way *both* men and women might experience problems with the health care system regardless of the gender of the key health decision makers.

A feminist perspective on postnatal depression

'Postnatal depression (PND) is a condition experienced only by women yet it is mainly treated by a medical profession which is dominated by men. Within the medical model PND is generally perceived as an illness to be dealt with by prescribed treatment ranging from hospitalisation to drug therapy or counselling. This would suggest that PND is indicative of individual pathology; rarely are social or environmental variables taken into consideration ... it is time that PND is reexamined from a feminist perspective, beyond medical parameters ...

A feminist perspective

Feminism seeks to identify women's role in a patriarchal society and addresses issues that concern subordination and oppression of women in everyday life. It challenges the socialisation and stereotyping of women within a society run by men for men's benefit. I suggest that a feminist interpretation of PND would entail:

- a shift in traditional medical thinking as to the nature of motherhood and mothering
- a need to view motherhood in a more realistic and positive sense
- a need to question assumptions that surround not only motherhood but also womanhood.

Women and motherhood

There are many assumptions about motherhood but one of the most damaging is that as women are biologically equipped to bear children they have instinctive knowledge of how to mother. The myth of maternal instinct can create feelings of great inadequacy in mothers who do not feel overwhelming joy and love for the new child and who find child care tiring and irksome. Women are not generally encouraged to voice disappointment over childbirth; many will internalise their feelings; difficulties in coping, when picked up by GP or health visitor, will usually be perceived in medical terms as postnatal depression.

Postnatal depression

... Many of the symptoms diagnosed as PND are indicative of a clinical depression: that is lowness in mood, tearfulness, difficulties in sleeping and eating, mood swings, no interest in sex, general apathy. The major difference with these symptoms displayed postnatally is that they are normally focused on the baby.

Very few women ... will feel alert postnatally. Sex can be unwelcome due to soreness, stitches or just tiredness. Mood swings can be accounted for by the relief when the baby feeds and sleeps without a problem and the almost irrational despair when it does not ... after the birth ... once the initial relief of a safe delivery has worn off, exhaustion and discomfort are apt to take over. When these feelings are combined with the round-the-clock caring for a new baby, it is perhaps inevitable that a mother would appear to be depressed. Feeling depressed is feeling exhausted, bereft of the skills needed to comfort a crying baby ... any man subjected to major surgery and then told to start a new job immediately for which he has had no training and in similarly rigorous conditions would probably also act negatively.

Postnatal care remains in the hands of the medical profession, therefore the general understanding of anxiety in mothers is conceptualised as individual pathology and diagnosed as an illness. To be so labelled can create further distress for many women. Yet it is not so much the identification and definition of PND that creates the problems as the prescribed treatments.

Treatment of PND

The majority of text books which discuss PND are written by the medical profession and tend to stress medical issues.... The unspoken assumptions throughout these texts is that motherhood is intrinsically satisfying and enjoyed by all women and that any other feelings are abnormal. The two most frequently prescribed treatments for PND are anti-depressants/tranquillisers or counselling. The disadvantage of taking medication are now well documented: taking any type of medication can become a career, tranquillisers are notoriously addictive, anti-depressants induce a false coping strategy. No medication solves the cause of any problem and only serves to reinforce poor self-esteem and self blame. . . . It can then become habitual for some women to fall into a sick role with "nervous trouble" rather than learn appropriate coping strategies. . . . It is suggested here that health professionals promote a more positive and realistic concept of motherhood; an aim which can only be achieved through altering existing structures and belief systems held by most members of the medical staff relating to the conditions of womanhood.

(Source: Christine A. Jebali, 'A feminist perspective on postnatal depression', Health Visitor, vol. 66, no. 2, 1993.)

ITEM A   *Exercise 11.4   The feminist perspective on health*

  In no more than one or two paragraphs, outline how you might use the article about PND (Item A) to support the view that men in control of health care might not make decisions that benefit women. Your account should include issues such as medicalisation of the human condition (that is, when rational responses to child care, such as fatigue and inability to cope, are seen as a medical problem), male assumptions about women who do not feel positive about their new baby, and medical treatment and possible clinical iatrogenesis (for example the side effects of antidepressants).

The interactionist perspective

Symbolic interactionism (SI) has provided a micro-sociological perspective that stresses the extent to which individuals shape society; this contrasts with the macro or structuralist perspectives (functionalist and Marxist), which emphasise the extent to which society shapes the behaviour of individuals.

Symbolic interactionism has exerted a major influence by asking different questions from those traditionally asked by functionalists and Marxists. For example interactionists are interested in the way individuals attach meaning to their own and others' behaviour, for example the way doctors impose their views of illness on patients and the way patients attempt to have their views appreciated by the doctor (Hak, 1994). The issue of non-compliance – that is, of patients rejecting the advice of health officials – has become an increasingly popular area for small-scale interactionist research. One problem of such small-scale research is its inability to generalise from its findings that similar interaction is widespread.

Dialogue recorded in small-scale observations between doctor and patient makes it possible to appreciate the way interaction proceeds so that either the doctor or the patient is able to impose their belief about the problem at hand. Bloor (1976) illustrates the way doctors use closed questions to demand very specific responses and therefore to limit their patients' contribution; in this way doctors are imposing interactional dominance in the professional setting.

The issue of labelling, developed by interactionists, has been applied to the study of health and illness. The labelling process is similar to that examined in the sociology of education and deviance:

- People hold perceptions of themselves and others.
- People use these perceptions to understand the characteristics of a person or a group, for example they are criminal, or lazy or have a low pain threshold.
- These labels might well affect the individual, who might live up to the label (a self-fulfilling prophesy) or reject it.
- The label might alter the way people respond to the individual.

How can the issue of labelling be applied? The case of AIDS and HIV

Attitudes among health officials could well shape the quality of care that HIV patients receive. Miller (1989) argued that suicide among diagnosed HIV positive homosexual men could well be related to the manner in which the diagnosis is delivered and the support they receive. Dougal *et al.* (1985) studied homophobia among 128 health carers (physicians and nurses) and discovered that 10 per cent felt that those infected with the virus had 'got what they deserved'. Prejudice against homosexuals seems to be fuelled by the perception that gays are responsible for contracting AIDS. Gillespie (1993) studied a variety of health carers and found that patients with AIDS were rated as more irresponsible, dangerous, unfortunate and hostile than patients with lung cancer. The study clearly shows that health officials might hold values that stereotype or label patients: these officials might well act on these assumptions, leading to inequality of care for those who are labelled.

Link Exercise 11.4 Interactionism and the process of becoming ill

 A further contribution of interactionists has been to raise critical awareness of official statistics. This suspicion of official statistics was explored in Chapter 3 which examined the way people's values and behaviour determine the morbidity figures. Use Stages 3 and 4 (beginning on pages 37 and 40 respectively) to help you write one paragraph showing how the official morbidity figures depend on a number of key decisions made by sufferers (for example deciding how to interpret illness symptoms, choosing whether to visit a doctor).

Criticisms of the interactionist perspective

Structuration

The social structure should be considered in addition to the investigation of the way individuals view the world. According to Giddens

(1991), for too long sociology has been divided between those who support the view that our behaviour is shaped by the environment (structuralists) and those who attempt to understand the choices people make in order to explain their behaviour (agency). The following Diagram shows that both structure and agency are important. Consideration of both these factors is called 'structuration' according to Giddens:

Giddens argues that to understand human behaviour we must examine *both* social structure and the way individuals see the world, that is, both the way society shapes human behaviour through, say, socialisation and the way individuals have choices over their own behaviour. We are all capable of making some choices, for example whether to visit a doctor. However social circumstances such as the cost of the bus fare or the inability to take time off work might prevent us from going to a doctor. Thus both structure and agency need to be examined.

According to Giddens sociological problems are 'structurated': both individual action and the structure of society may contribute to the situation. Structuration appears similar to Karl Marx's notion of dialectics. For Marx, dialectics describe the way people are locked into a process between the changing social structure and their own understanding of the world in which they live. As people change their views (for example people choose no longer to tolerate rape within marriage – this is an example of agency or individual choice) then laws may subsequently alter to suit changes in the way people think (these laws can be considered part of the structure of society). Adjustments to laws may then change other people's views of domestic sexual relationships, that is, agency and social structure are constantly influencing each other. Giddens' notion of 'structuration' shows that interactionism fails to consider the role of the social structure.

People might well make choices about their behaviour, for example whether to visit a doctor, but their choices are constrained by the provision of resources in society, which in turn is determined by the social system in which people live.

Determinism

Determinism means that behaviour is inevitable and predictable; for example, to label people mentally ill may make them feel worse about themselves and possibly alter their behaviour in light of the way they believe they are being viewed. The issue of labelling has often been presented as a cause of behaviour, as if the label actually causes the behaviour to occur. People have the ability to make choices and therefore to defy a label, seeking to ensure the label does not become reality. Interactionism tends to assume that when an individual has been labelled sick or mentally ill, that person will live up to the label. Labelling can therefore be viewed as rather deterministic: that is, assuming that all people will follow the same pattern of behaviour (after being labelled).

Quality of interactionist research

Much argument has taken place about the value of interactionist research. The small-scale nature of the studies means that the samples are small, making it difficult to claim that the results are representative of larger groups of people; that is, the ability to generalise is limited. Lack of objectivity is also levelled against interactionist research. Because observation and interviews are the key methods of gaining interactionist data, some critics suggest that the interviewer might phase the questions in such a way as to gain the desired response, and that the people being observed or interviewed might well change their behaviour to suit what they believe the researcher is looking for, or obscure their normal behaviour. Such problems relate to the issue of validity: does the research produce truthful data? Such research is very difficult to repeat so the question of reliability is raised (replicating or repeating the study to get the same results).

Link Exercise 11.5 Applying the interactionist perspective on health

Examine the extract preceding Exercise 3.7 on doctor–patient interaction (page 43), which shows a doctor attempting to gain control over the dialogue with the patient. This type of small-scale qualitative research into interaction between social actors is an example of an interactionist study. In no more than one paragraph explain why research of doctor–patient dialogue might be worth conducting.

The postmodernist perspective

Why has postmodernism become a concern?

Why is the term postmodernism used? In the same way that early sociologists (the 'founding fathers' of sociology: Durkheim, Marx and Weber) attempted to describe and explain the rapid social changes that stemmed from industrialisation and urbanisation during the industrial revolution, postmodernism appears to have sprung from a rapidly changing society fuelled by advances in technology – particularly computers – and global mass media. Whereas the changes brought about by the industrial revolution were seen to produce a 'modern' society, the recent social, economic and political changes have been viewed by some as producing a 'postmodern' society.

In addition to economic, social and political changes in society, postmodernism is characterised by a distrust of science as the 'truth'. The 'age of reason' (enlightenment) allowed people to disbelieve that God had created the universe, but people have also become less trusting of science to provide the truth and more accepting of their own understanding of the world, according to Baudrillard (1988).

Exercise 11.5 The postmodernist perspective on health

 In no more than 100 words describe any changes in society that might be regarded as postmodern. (Hint: changes in beliefs, in technology, in the economy.)

Postmodern issues

Having explained in a very simple way why the term postmodernism has come to be used today, this section breaks the postmodernist study of health and illness into a series of issues, namely metatheories, discourse, legitimation and resistance, fragmentation, surveillance, and the Body.

Metatheories

Postmodernists are skeptical about the way theories such as Marxism provide one single theory (metatheory) to explain the structure of society and human behaviour. In a rapidly changing, fragmented world no single theory can be viewed as the 'truth'. Why is the world fragmented? Perhaps the answer to this question lies with the number of different groups of people in society, all with their own understanding and experiences of the world. There are men and women, different ethnic groups, social classes, different age groups, all living in different locations. These different groups might share experiences or they might have had very different experiences. No single theory, postmodernists claim, can explain such a wide variation of experiences, and too many theories attempt to place people into a limited number of categories rather than recognising they might have had very different experiences. For example many sociologists have explained social class differences in illness and mortality patterns, yet within the working class lie a number of different groups: men and women, age groups, ethnic groups and locations, occupations and educational experiences. Thus postmodern theories attempt to recognise the fragmented experiences of people.

Postmodernists apply their notion that no single theory/metatheory can account for all experiences to the biomedical theory of illness.

The biomedical view of illness claims that 'illness' is caused by identifiable factors such as a virus or bacteria. Postmodernists do not not accept this as the only legitimate view. Theories might be useful in some circumstances yet insufficient in others. Complementary medicine (for example homeopathy, acupuncture) can therefore exist alongside biomedical knowledge. Postmodernists do not try to state which theory is best (biomedical or complementary) but are more interested in the way that in the 'battle' between dominant biomedical explanations and complementary medicines each attempts to gain status and power over the other. In other words all theories are simply ideas that compete to become recognised as the truth. In a fragmented world there are likely to be a number of competing ideas, some of which may be regarded as more legitimate than others.

Exercise 11.6 Applying metatheories

 Why might Marxist, functionalist and feminist perspectives be described by postmodernists as metatheories?

Discourse

Power is of crucial concern to postmodernists. Power is not necessarily tied to economic control (capitalism) as the Marxists believe, it is more subtle: power must also be considered to lie in language: writers such as Foucault (1963) claim that the way words and phrases are used can affect the way people think. (Language that affects thinking is known as 'discourse'.) Likewise knowledge about the body confers power: those that have this knowledge must ensure that others believe it to be superior. The possessors of this knowledge can then exercise control over others, that is, doctors can claim to have superior knowledge of the body and dismiss their patients' views.

The power of discourse can be illustrated by re-examining a study we looked at earlier, that by Bellaby (1990), who observed the way people in a pottery took time off for illness. Medical discourse (for example a doctor's way of understanding the body and phrasing explanations about the body) tends to carry status for many people. In Bellaby's study doctors occasionally 'medicalised' problems to allow some women to have paid time off work. Morning sickness during pregnancy became 'hyperemesis' and the stress brought about by looking after people at home was called an 'anxiety state'. These examples may be viewed as positive (to workers). However medical discourse has also medicalised human conditions such as being overweight (obesity), being sad (depression) and being worried (anxiety). We might ask what effect the medicalisation of these conditions has on individuals who view themselves as obese, anxious or depressed. In addition Oakley (1993) claims that the medical profession has medicalised childbirth, making it a medical problem rather than a natural process. Women now are encouraged to give birth to their children in hospital rather than at home, as the medical profession is opposed to births taking place outside the traditional hospital environment. We might ask whose interests are being served by this.

Sociology is a discourse that shapes the way people view society: sociology, like any other discipline, simply provides ways of thinking about society rather than producing any truths about human social behaviour. In this sense, postmodernism presents a different set of issues that may affect the way people view society (if they can understand the issues and jargon!). But postmodernism is just a discourse (a kind of language) and provides no truth, because for postmodernists there is no truth, just fabricated knowledge that may or may not gain status.

Link Exercise 11.6 Applying discourse to mental illness

Turn to Chapter 9 on mental illness and examine the section on 'The problems of defining mental illness' (pages 223–4):

 1. In what way might the term mental illness shape the way people think about psychological disorders? (Hint: examine the word 'mental' first then the word 'illness')

 2. How can you apply the notion that discourse is an important consideration when examining health issues such as that of mental illness? (Hint: is illness simply an illness, or does the language we use to describe the illness affect the way we understand the condition?)

Legitimation and resistance

Postmodern writers do not place trust in the notion that scientific knowledge is the truth, all knowledge is simply created by people or 'fabricated' (made up), with some people managing to impose their views as more legitimate than others. The dialogue below illustrates the way a doctor's view is imposed as unquestioningly correct despite the patient's view also being offered (Fox, 1993, p. 54):

Doctor: (to nurse) 'Fix her up with contraceptives, the sheath.'
Patient: 'I thought I'd use an IUD.'
Doctor: 'No, I don't want you on IUD or mini-pill, use the sheath and foam.'

This extract shows how doctors see themselves as possessing legitimate knowledge and when they meet resistance they attempt to assert an unquestioning monopoly over the truth. Doctors are generally considered to support the biomedical view of illness: that illness is caused by bacteria, viruses and disease. The view that all illness is caused by abnormalities within the body (biomedicine) is socially created knowledge that has successfully gained status in many Western health care systems. However such biomedical views are being challenged:

> My doctor initially had only a very limited knowledge of Repetitive Strain Injury, and now we've learned together over the years. For instance my treatment at the beginning was totally wrong so I went back to my doctor and said 'It's not the right treatment'; . . . now she knows not to try that [treatment] with other sufferers (sufferer and support group organiser for RSI) (Arksey, 1994, p. 455).

The extract shows how people can resist the doctor's claim to possess the truth about human conditions such as RSI. Doctors themselves might recognise that medical knowledge is useful for some but not all problems.

Patients opting for complementary medicine further illustrate the way dominant medical knowledge can be resisted and challenged. Yates *et al.* (1993) examined 152 patients with terminal cancer who had opted for non-medical therapies. To have terminal cancer and opt for non-medical therapies is a very a major form of resistance to the medical model of illness. Faith in the medical profession had declined according to Yates *et al.* and patients were choosing to understand their bodily condition in ways that lay outside medical explanations.

Link Exercise 11.7 Patient resistance and social class

Whereas doctors may tend to claim their medical understanding of the body is the truth or legitimate knowledge, patients may resist doctors' attempts to impose their diagnoses. Postmodernists have examined this resistance to the medical approach to illness. Exercise 3.8 (page 44) examines dialogue between doctors and patients of different social backgrounds. Whereas 'resistance' is treated as an overall issue by some postmodernists it might be that some social groups are more able than others to resist the doctor-imposed diagnosis.

[i] 1. Examine the table in Exercise 3.8 and identify which social class expresses most doubt or disagreement with the doctor.

[i] 2. Does the table suggest that we should not treat 'resistance' as a general issue but examine whether some social groups might resist more than others? Answer in no more than two sentences.

[a] 3. Apart from social class, what other social groups might be examined when exploring the degree of resistance between doctor and patient?

Fragmentation

The rolling back of state services means that people are becoming exposed to a greater variety of services controlled by a greater range of people. Ideas are spread easily across the global media (satellite

TV, international radio, international magazines, computer networks and E mail), all of which expose many of us to a larger world. People can be informed of a greater range of health views through the media. People's experiences of health services may well be more varied as they choose from a greater variety of treatments, including conventional medicine and complementary medicine such as acupuncture, herbal medicine and homeopathy. Consumer society contributes to the fragmentation of health views and health care. If people are generally more used to 'shopping around' and choosing from a range of opportunities, then they might also feel inclined to shop around for the most convincing explanation of their illnesses.

Surveillance

Foucault (1963) discusses the way those in power exercise more subtle means of social control than simply through the traditional agencies of control (the police, judiciary and army). Technology can be increasingly used to maintain surveillance over people's behaviour (for example via a video camera). For Foucault, surveillance in the postmodern world is not necessarily exercised by others but by individuals themselves through self-surveillance.

Glassner (1989) uses the popular discourse in the USA of self-health promotion through exercise and dieting to 'enable' or 'force' individuals to monitor their own body and regulate it so that it 'fits' the dominant view of acceptable body size and shape. Self-help groups are an example of the way people are persuaded to regulate their own lives rather than leaving it to the state to take responsibility.

Williams (1989) examines the way a self-help group, the National Ankylosing Spondylitis Society, was set up to support those with a type of chronic arthritis that principally affects the spine. Williams explored how individualistic notions of self-help took the form of a moralistic view of having to cope with illness without complaint: people must do something about their condition rather than simply complain.

Self-care is promoted in popular ideology as part of the NHS and Community Care Act 1990, in which a greater role for self-help groups in providing health care in the community is encouraged. In other words people are to regulate themselves individually rather than through a collectivist notion of state regulation.

Self-surveillance might well be a health strategy of the future. An increasing number of self-diagnosis kits are available for sale: first pregnancy testing kits and now cholesterol testing kits are sold in chemists. People in the future might well be encouraged to purchase such kits rather than visit a doctor. If the tasks carried out by computers continue to expand, then society might experience widespread self-diagnosis, made possible by new technology, rather than doctors' diagnosis. Software might well be created whereby people can input their perceived symptoms and receive a computer-generated diagnosis.

Exercise 11.7 Opportunities for self-care

 Match the following social factors that might limit the opportunities for self-care with the types of self-care that people might be encouraged to practise.

Social factors restricting self-care:

- Shortage of income.
- Lack of medical knowledge.
- Little opportunity for taking sick leave.
- Lack of knowledge about range of alternative healers.
- Cultural influences on diet, for example eating particular foods that can cause heart disease.

Types of self-care:

- Buying a pregnancy testing kit.
- Knowing the symptoms of an illness.
- Being able to rest and recuperate.
- Visiting an acupuncturist.
- Altering nutritional intake.

The body

More attention is being paid to the notion of the body. According to Foucault the body has been conceptualised as a mere physical entity in which any deviation from its 'normal' state is caused by invading bacteria, viruses or other organic causes, that is, the biomedical view of the body.

More recent notions of the body have examined the cultural meanings placed upon it, for example desirable body size, weight and shape. Kirk and Tinning (1994) questioned a sample of Australian adolescent students to examine their perceptions of the body and the way such perceptions affect self-identity (for example self-worth). Consumer societies treat the body as a commodity to be displayed in advertisements, films and media programmes, and products are promoted to change body size through dieting and shape through exercise. The study showed that the students were able to respond critically to these images and ideologies but their effects were still quite powerful.

One postmodern view of the body, proposed by Deleuze and Guattari (1984), sees the body not just as a physical entity with bones, skin and organs but as a culturally defined entity about which people hold all sorts of views, for example ideal body shape and size (though Deleuze and Guattari view the body as a little more complicated than this). Powerful ideas or discourse can shape the way people view their bodies. In fact the body can be viewed as 'one without organs' (Body without Organs, or BwO, Fox, 1993). This notion is merely trying to convey the point that the human body is not just a collection of organs, as the biomedical explanation would have us believe, but something people view through 'cultural glasses': it has a desirable shape, attractive features (for example in relation to the amount of body hair on men and women, desirable height). In other words our view of the body is more than just a collection of organs (kidneys, liver, brain and heart). Indeed illnesses are not simply deviations from the body's normal functioning; being ill can have a number of meanings that extend beyond a simple biomedical view.

Sontag (1993) shows how tuberculosis in the past and AIDS more recently are not just viewed as illnesses; people attach meanings to them, causing them to become 'dirty' and 'unclean' afflictions that 'invade' the body. People who suffer from such stigmatised illnesses may well change the way they view their bodies and their self-identity. In this way the body is not just a collection of organs surrounded by skin and supported by bones; the body exists in the abstract – the concept of a body without organs implies that notions of the body are affected by ideas or discourses that alter the way people view the body.

Link Exercise 11.8 Chronic illness and notions of the 'body'

a Examine the section 'Changes in self-identity' in Chapter 4 (page 63). In no more than one short paragraph show how notions of the 'body' affected the self-identity of those who experienced radical surgery. (Hint: do you believe that notions of how the body *should* appear affected the self-identity of the radial surgery sufferers?)

Exercise 11.8 An evaluation of the postmodernist perspective

i a The following paragraphs provide an evaluation of the postmodern perspective on health. Using the key words provided below, complete the gaps in the text:

Key words: metatheory, differences, discourse, age, acupuncture, poor housing, fragmented, morbidity, health care, Feminists, theory, distribution.

The strength of the postmodernist perspective is that it has attempted to deal not just with patterns of mortality and . . . . . . but a different set of issues such as the power of . . . . . . (language and its influence on thought), which can be applied to mental illness and conditions such as AIDS. Living in a Western society where consumerism is a key feature of everyday life for many people, ... might be seen to be part of a consumer culture in which many 'fragments' of society offer care and treatment. The medical model is therefore not the only influence on the way we understand illness: there are alternative ways of being treated for illness (for example complementary medicine such as . . . . . .). Thus the . . . . . . market for health (where health care is provided by a variety of organisations, not just by traditional medicine) is an issue that should be examined alongside the traditional focus on the medical model of health and health care.

The postmodernists claim that one single . . . . . . cannot explain all of human behaviour in society. An all-embracing social theory is called a . . . . . . This criticism is often made against the Marxists but equally of the functionalist and . . . . . . It is worth pointing out that postmodernism might provide a meta-theory for examining health by focusing on a set of issues (fragmentation, the body, surveillance). However it might also be that postmodernists are merely providing a set of issues to examine in addition to the more traditional sociological concern with patterns of mortality and morbidity.

A further evaluation point focuses on the lack of attention the postmodernist perspective pays to social . . . . . . in society. Postmodernism appears to individualise issues (for example notions of the body) and focuses on the power of discourse rather than the impact on people of structural constraints such as poverty, ..., poor diet, pollution, unhealthy working conditions, inequality in the domestic divisions of labour and in paid work, unequal treatment by the health service, and further issues such as racism, ageism and disability. The world of postmodernists appears to be 'genderless' (except for its focus on notions of the male and female body) and certainly ethnicity appears to be ignored. For example in a recent book by Fox (1993) there is no mention of ethnicity, only four brief references to gender, and no reference at all to social class. It might be that in a postmodern world the importance of class divisions has declined. However many recent statistics still show an unequal . . . . . . of illness between the social classes (DoH, 1995). Traditionally examined social divisions such as ethnicity, social class and gender as well as more recently examined issues of . . . . . . , disability and sexuality cannot be assumed to have vanished in a rapidly changing postmodern world.

The New Right perspective

The New Right (also known as neo-conservative and anticollectivist) philosophy became dominant in the Western world in the 1980s with the election of Ronald Reagan and later George Bush as presidents of the USA and Margaret Thatcher as the prime minister of Britain. The main beliefs of the New Right are:

- The market system can most efficiently supply the goods and services in demand (so for example, make the health service into a market of purchasers and providers, and expand private health care).
- Individual responsibility should be encouraged (so, for example, promote community care, and encourage people to have private health insurance).

Marsland (Marsland and Lait, 1981), a proponent of the New Right, claims that state provision creates a nation of dependants who are unable to exercise individual responsibility for their own welfare. Marsland advocates a reduction in state health provision, greater reliance on voluntary organisations and the encouragement of self-reliance.

The recent health reforms appear to promote the view that people should be more self-reliant. The government white paper 'Working for Patients' (DoH, 1992b) stressed that private provision for health care was to be encouraged. A subsequent increase in the uptake of private health insurance suggests that individuals have responded to the notion that they should accept personal responsibility for their health. In 1979 less than 5 per cent of the population was covered by some form of private health insurance; by 1994 this figure had risen to over 11 per cent of the population. Thus people may well be responding to New Right notions of individual self-reliance. However, people may instead be responding to the problems they are facing with access to state health services, for example long waiting lists and a decline in the provision of services, such as the reported lack of fertility treatment by some health authorities.

Link Exercise 11.9   Inequality and Private Health Insurance

1. Turn to the section in Chapter 10 on 'Social class and use of private health care' (page 277) identify any evidence of possible social class inequality in private health insurance.

2. In no more than two or three sentences explain why individuals might not be equal in the extent to which they can be self-reliant. (Hint: can all social classes equally afford private health insurance?)

Not only does the New Right promote individual self-reliance, it also applies individualism to the health care system itself, for example the 1990 NHS and Community Care Act set in place the purchaser – provider relationship within health care. GPs and hospitals have to compete against one another for patients. Their main income depends either on the number of patients on their list or the number of patients being treated (for example for surgery). Competition has been introduced into the health system because health care providers (GPs and trust hospitals) have to ensure they attract enough patients to stay in business. They have to compete with private hospitals, who are able to enter contracts with GP fundholders (GP surgeries that can spend a proportion of their budget on any health provider, not just their local hospital) to treat their patients (for a fee). Thus health care has become a system in which health care establishments compete with each other to maintain their position in the market. The New Right believes that the introduction of competition to the NHS will make it more efficient (that is, reduce costs) because health managers will seek to minimise costs by using the cheapest drugs and most effective health care treatment (although researching the most effective methods of health treatment itself involves high costs).

The recent promotion of care in the community through the 1990 NHS and Community Care Act is another example of how New Right thinking may have changed the nature of the health care system. Individuals should take care of themselves and individual family units should take care of their own relatives. Informal care is particularly promoted in the 1990 NHS and Community Care Act: families, not just state institutions and care homes, are viewed as source of care for the elderly and mentally ill. It might be that people would prefer to be treated by their family, but not all people have families, or at least families that are willing to care for them. In addition not all families have the resources (for example skills and finances) to look after a family member who needs care.

Link Exercise 11.10 Community care

 Turn to the section 'What are some of the criticisms of community care' in Chapter 9 (page 232). State two reasons why community care might be an inadequate form of health care for the mentally ill.

Health promotion within the NHS is a feature that supports New Right thinking. The notion that people should be responsible for their own lifestyle is one that suits an individualistic style of thinking. By turning attention away from structural causes of illness (for example poverty and poor housing) towards issues that 'appear' to be due to individual choice and lifestyle (for example diet, exercise, smoking) then individuals, rather than the overall structure of society, can be held responsible for their ill-health. However it might be that decisions about smoking and diet are rooted in structural causes, that is, people smoke because of their stressful living and working (or not working) conditions. A focus on the promotion of healthy lifestyles switches the 'blame' for illness away from the structure of society and towards the individual.

Link Exercise 11.11 Structural causes of ill-health

Turn to the section in Chapter 5 on 'Employment and health: are employees aware of the health risks of employment?' (page 97).

i 1. Write one paragraph on the way in which working conditions might affect health.

a 2. At the end of your paragraph write one or two sentences to show that working conditions may not be a matter of individual choice but more a result of people's position position in society. (Hint: being poor and unable to get work in more healthy surroundings.)

e 3. In two sentences suggest how the information on working conditions can be used to criticise the New Right's position on health promotion.

Exercise 11.9 An evaluation of the New Right perspective

i a The following paragraphs provide an evaluation of the New Right perspective on health and health care. Use the key words provided to complete the gaps:

Key words: responsibility, two-tier, powerful, GP fundholder, self-reliant, benefits, competition, working class, private.

The New Right might have made the health care system strive to treat more patients more efficiently by introducing . . . . . . within the health care system. By promoting individual . . . . . . for health the New Right might be making people more aware of their health and ways of improving their health. For some people there might be real benefits of using a . . . . . . who is able to enter into contracts with the 'most suitable' health care provider available. Thus New Right thinking might have suggested ideas to policy makers that have brought some . . . . . . to health care provision.

One criticism of the New Right notion of self-reliance is that not everybody is capable of being . . . . . .: those with more resources are likely to have more choices over their health care provision. The idea of a . . . . . . service is relevant here: those who can afford specialist private treatment might exercise their choice and receive quick treatment; for many others, although private care may be available, the necessary finance might not be.

Marxists claim that by increasing self-reliance and providing fewer state services the state is effectively cutting the 'social wage' (resources that flow to the workers through free state provision); thus the New Right has effectively managed to divert resources away from the . . . . . .

The recent changes to health care might reflect New Right thinking on individual rather than state welfare and health provision. However, whether the ideas of the New Right are dominant throughout society is questionable. It might be that the influence of the New Right has mainly been on . . . . . . members of society, for example the government and its advisors. Less powerful people might not have responded to the individualised notions promoted by New Right thinking. Though the rapid rise in . . . . . . health provision might suggest that people are taking more personal responsibility for health care, they might be doing this reluctantly or because companies have provided the health insurance as a fringe benefit ('perk' of the job).

Structured exam questions

1. To help you apply the issues and practise skills you have learned in Chapter 11, attempt the exercise below, which is based on the following specimen examination question: Evaluate the contribution of the New Right to our understanding of the recent health reforms. (*25 marks*)

Question

(a) Read the following introductory sentences and then research appropriate information to add to each paragraph (part b of the exercise asks you to associate the correct evaluation points with the appropriate introductory sentence(s) featured in part a). Complete the gaps using the key words provided.

Key words: contracts, NHS and Community Care Act, individualism, providers, responsibility, demand, fundholders.

Student answer

(1) The New Right believes that the market system is the most efficient way to supply and distribute health services. In 1990, after the . . . . . . was passed, the health care system was divided into purchasers (for example health authorities) and . . . . . . (for example trust hospitals). Private health care providers have been allowed to compete in the NHS system.

(2) The implication of a market in health care is that the health services that offer the best-quality care for the most cost-efficient price will be in . . . . . . and thus will not only become financially viable but may also have the funds to expand. Those hospitals that do not offer quality care may not receive sufficient . . . . . . to remain in business; therefore, like other business, the hospital will close unless it improves. As such the health reforms might have created a health care system in which services that offer the most effective medical care will expand.

(3) The New Right also believes in . . . . . . as opposed to collectivism: that individuals and not necessarily the welfare state should be responsible for their health care. Thus private health care has been encouraged particularly through allowing GP . . . . . . to use the private hospitals to care for their patients.

(4) To further the notion that individuals should be responsible for their own health care, the community care policy was promoted under the 1990 NHS and Community Care Act. This promotes the idea of families in particular taking . . . . . . for the health of their family members.

(b) Match the following criticisms to the appropriate paragraphs in part a. You may find that more than one criticism can be applied to a paragraph in part one.

- Unlike the Marxists, members of the New Right ignore structural causes of ill-health and promote the notion that decisions individuals make about their lifestyle (for example lack of exercise and poor diet) are the cause of much ill-health.

- However, not everybody is capable of being self-reliant: some people are more able than others to afford exercise, better food and better housing.

- The New Right fails to examine inequalities in health care (for example in connection with social class, ethnicity and gender); by focusing on individual causes of ill-health (for example lack of exercise, poor diet, smoking) the New Right ignores the structural causes of unhealthy lifestyles.

- Not everybody can afford private health insurance, thus for most state health care is the only available form of health care.

- Marxists argue that by promoting private health care the resources secured by the working class in the form of free health care are being eroded through the gradual decline of the NHS. Thus the New Right is transferring resources back to the bourgeoisie.

- Individual lifestyle decisions may be rooted in structural or material factors. For example the decision to smoke cigarettes appears to be an individual choice. However smoking can be caused by the stress of living in poor conditions on a low income and, particularly for women, through being poor and looking after young children. Thus individual decisions might not really be a simple matter of 'free' choice.

Question

2. Write essays on the following specimen exam questions:

(a) Evaluate the contribution of the postmodernist perspective to the area of health and illness (*25 marks*).

(b) Should sociologists search for a single theory to explain all social phenomena? Discuss your answer with reference to the sociology of health and illness (*25 marks*).

Summary

This chapter has explored the main sociological perspectives on health. Each perspective can contribute to different areas of health and health care. Functionalism, Marxism and feminism view health and health care in broad terms, for example who benefits from the health care system? Society as a whole, the bourgeoisie, men? The interactionist perspective explores a more micro or small-scale perspective by focusing on the interaction between social actors such as doctors and patients. Perhaps interactionism and a broader, more structural perspective could be regarded as complementary: as studies of doctor–patient interaction could be combined with, say, Marxism, so questions of power within society could be addressed and the structure of society explored. Feminism (and a consideration of ethnicity, perhaps) could also be applied to provide a broader view of health and health care. The perspectives do not have to be seen as mutually exclusive: they can be used in conjunction with one another.

The postmodernist perspective attempts to address a different set of issues that may be of value in examining some issues in health care (metatheories, discourse, legitimation and resistance, fragmentation, surveillance, the body). However in isolation postmodernism may shift attention away from inequality in society. The New Right may be regarded as having influenced many of the changes in health care since 1990: community care, the internal market in health care (for example trust hospitals and GP fundholders) and the growth of private health care. Evaluation of the New Right perspective shows that competing perspectives, for example Marxism, can be applied to offer an alternative account of the health care system.

References

Abbott, P. and C. Wallace (1990) *An Introduction to Sociology: feminist perspectives* (London and New York: Routledge).

Abel-Smith, B. (1960) *A History of the Nursing Profession* (London: Heinemann).

Abraham, J. (1994) 'Bias in Science and Medical Knowledge', *Sociology*, vol. 28, no. 3 (August).

Acheson, E. (1990) 'Edwin Chadwick and the world we live in', *Lancet*, no. 336.

Ahmad, W. (ed) (1992) *The Politics of Race and Health* (Race Relations Research Unit University of Bradford).

Ahmad, W. *et al.* (1992) 'An exploration of White, Asian and Afro-Caribbean people's concepts of health and illness causation', *New Community*, vol. 18, no. 2 (January).

Althusser, L. (1969) *For Marx* (London: Allen Lane).

Amin, K. with C. Oppenheim (1992) *Poverty in Black and White: deprivation and ethnic minorities* (London: CPAG with the Runneymede Trust).

Anderson, I., P. Kemp and D. Quilgers (1993) *Single Homeless People* (London: HMSO).

Andrews, A. and N. Jewsen (1993) 'Ethnicity and Infant Deaths', *Sociology of Health and Illness*, vol. 15, no. 2.

Arber, S. (1989) 'Class and the elderly', *Sociology Review*, vol. ??

Arber, S. (1995) 'Gender differences in Informal caring', *Health and Social Care in the Community*, vol. 3.

Arber, S. and J. Ginn (1991) *Gender and Later Life* (London: Sage).

Aries, P. (1973) *Centuries of Childhood* (Harmondsworth: Penguin).

Arksey, H. (1994) 'Expert and lay participation in the construction of medical knowledge', *Sociology of Health and Illness*, vol. 16, no. 4.

Association of Community Health Councils in England and Wales (1989) 'The state of non-conventional medicine – the consumer's view', *Health News Briefing*.

Baker, A. and S. Duncan (1986) 'Prevalence of child sexual abuse in Great Britain', *Child Abuse and Neglect*, vol. 9.

Balarajan, R. and Raleigh, V. (1990) *Perinatal Health and Ethnic Minorities*, (Institute of Public Health, University of Survey).

Barker, J. (1984) 'Black and Asian Old People in Britain' (London: Age Concern).

Barton, N. (1989) 'Repetitive Strain Disorder', *British Medical Journal*, no. 299, pp. 405–6.

Bateson, G., D. Jackson, D. Haley and J. Weakland (1956) 'Toward and theory of schizophrenia', *Behavioural Sciences*, vol. 1, pp. 251–64.

Baudrillard, J. (1988) *Selected Writings* (Cambridge Polity Press).

Becker, H. (1963) *Outsiders: studies in the Sociology of Deviance* (New York: Free Press).

Bellaby, P. (1990) 'What is genuine sickness? The relation between the work-discipline and the sick role in a pottery factory', *Sociology of Health and Illness*, vol. 12, no. 1.

Bendelow, G. (1993) 'Pain perceptions, emotions and gender', *Sociology of Health and Illness*, vol. 15 no. 3.

Bergin, A. (1971) 'The Evaluation of Therapeutic Outcomes', in A. E. Bergin and S. L. Garfield (eds), *Handbook of Psychotheraphy and Behaviour Change: An Empirical Analysis* (New York: Wiley).

Bernard, J. (1982) 'The Wife's Marriage', in M. Evans (ed.) *The Women Question* (London: Fontana).

Bevan, G., W. Holland and N. Mays (1989) 'Working for which patients and at what cost?', *Lancet*, i.

Beveridge, W. H. (1942) *Social Insurance and Allied Services. Report by Sir William Beveridge, Command Paper 6404* (London: HMSO).

Bhalla, A. and K. Blakemore (1981) *Elders of the Ethnic Minority Groups* (Birmingham: All Faiths for One Race).

Blackburn, C. (1991) *Poverty and Health* (Milton Keynes: Open University Press).

Blakemore, K. and M. Boneham (1993) *Age, Race and Ethnicity in Britain* (Milton Keynes: Open University Press).

Blaxter, M. (1983) 'The cause of disease: women talking', *Social Science and Medicine*, vol. 17.

Blaxter, M. (1990a) *Health and Lifestyles* (London: Tavistock).

Blaxter, M. (1990b) 'Evidence on inequality in Health from a National Survey', *Lancet*, ii.

Bleuler, E. (1911) *Dementia Praecox or the group of schizophrenias* (New York: International University Press).

Bloor, M. (1976) 'Professional autonomy and client exclusion: a study in ENT clinics', in M. Wadsworth and D. Robinson (eds), *Studies in Everyday Medical Life* (London: Martin Robertson).

Bond, J., P. Coleman and S. Peace (1993) *Ageing in Society* (London: Sage).

Booth, C. (1989) *Labour and Life of the People*, vol. 1 (London: Williams and Norgate).

Boulton, M., D. Tuckett, A. Olesen and A. Williams (1986) 'Social class and the general practice consultation', *Sociology of Health and Illness*, vol. 8, no. 4.

Bowler, I. (1993) 'They're not the same as us: midwives stereotypes of South Asian descent maternity patients', *Sociology of Health and Illness*, vol. 15, no. 2.

Brent Census SASPAC (London Borogh of Brent, 1991).

Brown, C. (1984) *Black and White Britain: The Third PSI Survey* (London: Heinemann).

Brown, G., M. Brolchan and T. Harris (1975) 'Social class and psychiatric disturbance among women in an urban population', *Sociology*, vol. 9.

Brown, K. (1992) *Introduction to Sociology* (Cambridge: Polity Press).

Bury, M. (1982) 'Chronic Illness as Biographical Disruption', *Sociology of Health & Illness*, vol. 4. pp. 167–82.

Bury, M. (1991) 'The sociology of chronic illness: a review of research and prospects', *Sociology of Health and Illness*, vol. 13, no. 4.

Calnan, M. (1987) *Health and Illness: the Lay Perspective* (London: Tavistock).

Calnan, M. and S. Williams (1992) 'Images of scientific medicine', *Sociology of Health and Illness*, vol. 14, no. 2.

Cartwright, A. and M. O'Brien (1976) 'Social Class variations in Health Care', in M. Stacey, *The Sociology of Health and Healing* (London: Unwin Hyman).

Castledine, G. (1994) 'Elder abuse by Nurses is on the increase', *British Journal of Nursing*, vol. 3, no. 13.

Centre for Disease Control (1992) 'TB among homeless shelter residents', *Journal of the American Medical Association*, no. 267.

Charmaz, K. (1983) 'Loss of self: fundamental form of suffering in the chronically ill', *Sociology of Health and Illness*, vol. 5.

Chevannes, M. (1991) 'Access to health care for black people', *Health Visitor*, vol. 64, no. 1.

Clarke, A. (1919) *Working Life of Women in the Seventeenth Century*, (London: Routledge & Kegan Paul; reprinted 1982).

Clausen, J. and M. Kohn (1959) 'Relation of schizophrenia to the social structure of a small city', in G. Davison and J. Neal, *Abnormal Psychology*.

Coleman, P., J. Bond and S. Peace (1993) *Ageing in the Twentieth Century* (London: Sage).

Collet, D. (1992) *Annual Practice Report* (Oxford: Luther Street Centre).

Connelly, J. and J. Crown (eds) (1994) *Homelessness and ill health* (London: Royal College of Physicians).

Cooley, C. (1902) *Human nature and social order* (New York: Shocken).

Cox, B. (1987) *Health and Lifestyle Survey: Preliminary Report* (London: Health Promotion Research Trust).

Creighton, S. S. (1990) Child Abuse in 1989. Research Briefing No. 11 (London: NSPCC).

Crichton, M. (1988) *Travels* (London: Pan Books).

Crombie, D. (1984) 'Social class and health status: inequality or difference', *Journal of the Royal College of GPs*, Occasional Paper 25.

Culley, L. and Dyson S. (1993) 'Race, Inequality and Health', *Sociology Review*, September.

Cumming, E. and W. Henry (1961) *Growing Old: The process of disengagement* (New York: Basic Books).

Currer, C. (1983) *The Mental Health of Pathan Mothers in Bradford: A Case Study of Migrant Asian Women* (Coventry: University of Warwick).

Dahrendorf, R. (1987) 'The erosion of citizenship and its consequences for us all', *New Statesman*, 12 June.

Deane, P. (1989) *The State and the Economic System* (Oxford: Oxford University Press).

Denker, R. (1990) 'Results of treatment of psychoneurosis by the general practitioner : A follow up of 500 cases', in R. Gross, *Key Studies in Psychology* (Sevenoaks: Hodder & Stoughton).

Deleuze, G. and Guattari, F. (1984) *Anti-Oedipus: Capitalism and Schizophrenia* (London: Athlone).

Deutsch, A. (1949) *The Mentally Ill in America* (New York: Columbia University Press).

d'Houtard, A. and M. Field (1984) 'The Image of Health: variations in perceptions of social class in a French population', *Sociology of Health and Illness*, vol. 6.

DHSS (1981) 'Growing Older', (London: HMSO).

Dobraszczyc, U. (1989) *Sickness, Health and Medicine* (London: Longman).

DoH (1989a) 'Caring For People' (London: HMSO).

DoH (1989b) 'Working For Patients' (London: HMSO).

DoH (1991a) 'Implementing Community Care' (London: HMSO).

DoH (1991b) 'Purchase of Service' (London: HMSO).

DoH (1992a) 'The Health Of The Nation' (London: HMSO).

DoH (1992b) 'Working for Patients' (London: HMSO).

DoH (1995) 'Variations in Health' (London: HMSO).

Doll, R. (1974) 'To measure NHS progress', *Fabian Occasional Paper*, no. 8, Summerville Hastings Memorial Lecture (London: Fabian Society).

Donnellan, C. (ed.) (1994a) *Disabilities and Equality* (Cambridge: Independence Publishers).

Donnellan, C. (ed.) (1994b) *Alternative Medicine* (Cambridge: Independence Publishers).

Donnellan, C. (ed.) (1995) *Mental Health* (Cambridge: Independence Publishers).

Donovan, P. (1984) 'Ethnicity and Health: a research review', *Social Science and Medicine*, vol. 19, no. 7, pp. 663–70.

Dougal, C., C. Kalman and T. Kalman (1985) 'Homophobia among physicians and nurses', *Hospital Community Psychiatry*, vol. 36, no. 12, pp. 108–11.

Douglas, M. (1966) *Purity and Danger* (London: Routledge & Kegan Paul).

Doyal, L. (1985) 'Women and the National Health Service: the careers and the careless', in E. Lewin and V. Oleson (eds), *Women, Health and Healing*, (London: Tavistock).

Doyal, L. and I. Pennell (1979) *The Political Economy of Health* (London: Pluto Press).

Drake, R. and L. Sederer (1986) 'The adverse effects of intensive treatment of chronic schizophrenia', *Comprehensive Psychiatry*, vol. 27, pp. 313–26.

Durkheim, E. (1970) *Suicide: A Study in Sociology* (London: Routledge & Kegan Paul).

Emerson, J. (1972) 'Behaviour in private places: sustaining definitions of reality in gynecological examinations', in Dreitzel, *Recent Sociology*.

Etkind, S., J. Ford, E. Nardell and J. Boutotte (1991) 'Treating Hard to Treat TB Patients in Massachusetts', *Seminars in Respiratory Infections*, no. 6.

Ewan, C., E. Lowy and J. Reid (1991) 'Falling out of culture: The effects of repetition strain injury of sufferers' roles and identities', *Sociology of Health and Illness*, vol. 13, no. 2.

Fennell, G., C. Phillipson and H. Evers (1988) *The Sociology of Old Age*. (Milton Keynes: Open University Press).

Ferriman, A. (1995) 'Looking Younger on Prescription', *Independent on Sunday*, 25 August, 1995.

Finch, J. (1986) *Research and Policy: The Uses of Qualitative Methods in Social and Educational Research* (Lewes: Falmer Press).

Finch, J. and D. Groves (eds) (1983) *A Labour of Love: Work and Caring*, (London: Routledge & Kegan Paul).

Finch, J. and J. Mason (1993) 'Filial obligations and kin support for elderly people', in *Community Care: a reader* (London: and Milton Keyness: Macmillan and Open University Press).

Findlay, I. *et al.* (1991) 'Coronary Angiography in Glasgow', *British Heart Journal*, no. 66.

Foucault, M. (1976) *The Birth of the Clinic: An Archaeology of Medical Perception* (London: Routledge).

Foucault, M. (1973) *The Order of Things: An archaeology of the Human Sciences* (New York: Vintage/Random House).

Fox, N. (1993) *Postmodernism, Sociology and Health* (Milton Keynes: Open University Press).

Fromm-Reichmann, F. (1952) 'Some aspects of psychoanalytic therapy with schizophrenics', in G. Davison and J. Neale (eds), *Abnormal Psychology* (Chichester: John Wiley and Sons).

General Household Survey (various years) (London: HMSO).

Gerhardt, N. (1989) *Ideas about Illness: An intellectual and political history of medical sociology* (London: MacMillan).

Giddens, A. (1979) *Central Probems in Social Theory* (London: MacMillan).

Giddens, A. (1991) *Modernity and Self-Identity: Self and Society in the Late Modern Age* (Cambridge: Polity Press).

Gillespie, F. (1993a) 'HIV/AIDS: a study of doctors, nurses and counsellors/therapists attitudes towards HIV and AIDS issues, policies and practices in a psychiatric setting', *International Journal of Psychology and Medicine*, vol. 4, no. 2.

Gillespie, F. (1993b) 'Health carers' attitudes to HIV infection and AIDS', *British Journal of Nursing*, vol. 2, no. 10.

Gilroy, P. (1987) *Ain't no Blacks in the Union Jack* (London: Hutchinson).

Glassner B. (1989) 'Fitness and the postmodern self', *Journal of Health and Social Behaviour*, vol. 30.

Glennerster, H., M. Matsaganis and P. Owens (1993) 'GP Fundholding: Wild card or winning Hand', in R. Robinson *et al.* (eds), *Evaluating the Health Reforms* (London: Kings Fund Institute).

Goffman, E. (1968) *Asylums – essays on the social situation of mental patients and other inmates* (Harmondsworth: Penguin).

Goldblatt, P. (ed.) (1990) *Mortality and alternative social classifications*, in *Longitudinal Study 1971–1981: Mortality and social organisation* (OPCS LS series, no. 6.

Goldthorpe, J., C. Llewellyn and Paynes, C. (1980) *Social Mobility and Class Structure in Modern Britain*, 2nd edn (Oxford: Clarendon).

Gough, I. (1979) *The Political Economy of the Welfare State* (London: Macmillan).

Graham, H. (1984) *Women Health and the Family* (Brighton: Wheatsheaf).

Graham, H. (1985) *Health and Welfare* (Edinburgh: Nelson).

Graham, H. (1986) *Caring for the family* (London: Health Education Council).

Graham, H. (1993a) 'Feminist perspectives on caring', in J. Bornat *et al.* (eds), *Comunity Care: a reader* (London and Milton Keynes: Macmillan and Open University Press).

Graham, H. (1993b) 'Women's smoking: government targets and social trends', *Health Visitor*, vol. 66, No. 3.

Graham, H. (1995) 'Diversity, inequality and official data: some problems of method and measurement in Britain', *Health and Social Care in the Community*, vol. 3.

Griffiths, R. (1988) *Community Care: Agenda for Action* (London: HMSO).

Gunaratnam, Y. (1993) 'Breaking the silence: Asian carers in Britain' in J. Bornat *et al.* (eds) *Comunity Care: a reader* (London and Milton Keynes: Macmillan and Open University Press).

Hak, T. (1994) 'The interactional forms of professional dominance', *Sociology of Health and Illness*, vol. 16, no. 4,

Harrison, A. (ed.) (1994) *Health Care UK 1993/94* (London: King's Fund Institute.

Harrison, P. (1995) 'Schizophrenia: a misunderstood disease', *Psychology Review*, vol. 2, no. 2.

Hart, N. (1985) *The Sociology of Health and Medicine* (Ormskirk: Causeway Press).

Havinghurst, R., B. Naugarten and S. Tobin (1968) 'Disengagement and patterns of ageing', in B. L. Neugarten (ed.) *Middle Age and Ageing* (Chicago: University of Chicago).

Havinghurst, R., B. Naugarten and S. Tobin (1968) 'Disengagement and patterns of ageing', in B. L. Neugarten (ed.) *Middle Age and Ageing* (Chicago: University of Chicago).

Health and Safety Commission (1994) *Health and Safety Statistics, Statistical Supplements to the 1993/94 Annual Report* (London: HSE Books).

Health News Briefing (1989) *The State of Non-conventional Medicine: The Consumers' Views* (London: Association of Community Health Councils in England and Wales).

Heather, N. (1976) *Radical Perspectives in Psychology* (London: Methuen).

Helman, C. (1984) 'Feed a cold, starve a fever', in N. Black *et al.* (eds), *Health and Disease: a reader* (Milton Keynes: Open University Press).

Hollingshead, A. and F. Redlich (1958) *Social Class and Mental Illness: a community study* (New York: Wiley).

Hopkins, E. (1979) *A Social History of the English Working Classes* (Leeds: Edward Arnold).

Hunt, L. (1996) 'GP attacked for removing a 6-a-day smoker from list', *Independent* (London), 26 February 1996.

Hunt, P. (1978) 'Cash transactions and household tasks', *Sociological Review*, vol. 26, no. 23.

Hunter, J. and S. Arbona (1984) 'Disease rate as an artifact of the health care system. Tuberculosis in Puerto Rico', *Social Science and Medicine*, vol. 19, no. 9.

Huskisson, E. (1992) *Repetitive Strain Injury: the keyboard disease* (London: Charterhouse Health Series).

Illich, I. (1976) *Limits to Medicine: Medical Nemesis* (Harmondsworth: Penguin).

Illsley, R. (1986) 'Occupational Class, Selection and the Production of Inequalities in Health', *Quarterly Journal of Social Affairs*, vol. 2, no. 2.

Iverson, L. (1979) 'The chemistry of the brain', *Scientific American*, no. 241.

James, W. (1892) *Psychology: The Briefer Course* (New York: Holt, Rinehart & Winston).

Jebali C. (1993) 'A feminist perspective on postnatal depression', *Health Visitor*, vol. 66, no. 2.

Jenkins, R. (1971) *The Production of Knowledge in the IRR* (London: Institute of Race Relations).

Jones, D., C. Lester and R. West (1993) 'Monitoring Changes in Health

Services for Older People', in R. Robinson and J. Le Grand (eds), *Evaluating the Health Reforms* (London: King's Fund Institute).

Jones, L. (1994) *The Social Context of Health and Health Work* (London: Macmillan).

Judge, K. and M. Benzeval (1993) 'Health Inequalities: new concerns about the health of single mothers', *British Medical Journal*, vol. 3, no. 6.

Kelly, M. (1992) 'Self, identity and radical surgery', *Sociology of Health and Illness*, vol. 14, no. 3.

Kenward, H. and D. Hevey (1992) 'The Physical Effects of Abuse and Neglect', in W. Stainton Rogers, D. Hevey, J. Roche and E. Ash (eds) (1992) *Child Abuse and Neglect* (Milton Keynes: Open University Press).

Kimble, G., N. Garmezy and E. Zigler (1980) *Principles of General Psychology* (New York: Wiley).

Kingston, P. and C. Phillipson (1994) 'Elder abuse and neglect', *British Journal of Nursing*, vol. 3, no. 22.

Kirk, D. and R. Tinning (1994) 'Embodied self-identity, healthy lifestyles and school physical education', *Sociology of Health and Illness*, vol. 16, no. 5.

Kohn, M. (1973) 'Social class and schizophrenia: a critical review', in G. Davision and J. Neale, *Abnormal Psychology* (Chichester: John Wiley).

Kossof, J. (1995) 'Second Class Males', *Time Out*, 1–8 February.

Laing and Buisson (1994) *Private Medical Insurance Update* (London: Laing and Buisson).

Laing, R. D. and A. Esterson (1970) *Sanity, Madness, and the Family* (Penguin: Harmondsworth).

Laqueur, W. (1990) *Making Sex, Body and Gender from the Greeks to Freud* (Cambridge, Mass: Harvard University Press).

Last, J. (1963) 'The illness iceberg', *Lancet*, 6 July.

Lawrence, S. and K. Bendixen (1992) 'His and Hers: Male and Female Anatomy in Anatomy Texts for US Medical Students', *Social Science and Medicine*, vol. 35, no. 7.

Lee-Treweek, A. (1994) 'Bedroom abuse: the hidden work in a nursing home', *Generations Review*, vol. 4, no. 1, pp. 2–4.

Leff, J. (1992) 'Over the edge: stress and schizophrenia', *New Scientist*, March.

Le Grand, J. (1982) *The Strategy of Equality* (London: Allen & Unwin).

Le Grand, J. (1993) 'Market-orientated health care reforms: impact on equity and efficiency', in R. Robinson and J. Le Grand (eds), *Evaluating the Health Reforms* (London: King's Fund Institute).

Lemert, E. (1962) 'Paranoia and the dynamics of exclusion', *Sociometry*, vol. 25.

Levin, E., I. Sinclair and P. Gorbach (1993) 'The Supporters of Confused Elderly Persons at Home', in J. Bornat *et al.* (eds), *Community Care: a reader* (London and Milton Keynes: Macmillan and Open University Press).

Levitt, R. and A. Wall (1994) *The Reorganised National Health Service* (London: Chapman & Hall).

Lewis, G. (1976) 'A view of sickness in New Guinea', in J. B. Louden (ed.), *Social Anthropology and Medicine* (London: Academic Press).

Lindsay, W. (1982) 'The effects of labelling: blind and non-blind ratings of social skills in schizophrenic and non-schizophrenic control subjects', *American Journal of Psychiatry*, no. 139, pp. 216–19.

Lissauer, T. (1994), in J. Connelly and J. Crown (eds), *Homelessness and Ill Health* (London: Royal College of Physicians).

Littlewood, R. and M. Lipsedge (1982) *Ethnic Minorities and Psychiatry* (Harmondsworth: Penguin).

Lloyd, P. (1992) 'Introduction to Psychology – an integrated approach', in R. Gross, *Psychology: The Science of Mind and Behaviour* (London: Hodder & Stoughton).

Macfarlane, A. (1990) 'Official statistics and women's health and illness', in H. Roberts (ed.), *Women's Health Counts* (London: Routledge & Kegan Paul).

Macran, S., L. Clarke., A. Sloggett and A. Bethune (1994) 'Women's socio-economic status and self-assessed health: identifying some disadvantaged groups', *Sociology of Health & Illness*, vol. 16, no. 2.

MacVicar, J. (1990) 'The Asian Mother and Child', in B. McAvoy and L. Donaldson (eds), *Health Care for Asians* (Oxford University Press).

Mahon, A., D. Wilkin and C. Whitehouse (1993) 'Choice of Hospital for Elective Surgey Referrals: GPs' and Patients' Views', in R. Robinson and J. Le Grand (eds), *Evaluating the Health Reforms* (London: King's Fund Institute).

Marmot, M., G. Davey-Smith, S. Stansfield, C. Patel, F. North and J. Head (1991) 'Health Inequalities among British Civil Servants: the Whitehall Study II', *Lancet*, 337.

Manchester Health Needs Survey (1993) (Manchester Public Health Resource Centre).

Manchester Public Health Resource Centre (1992) *The Manchester Health Needs Survey: Topic Report no. 1, Smoking Version 1.1* (Manchester City Council).

Marsland, D. and Anderson, D. (1981) *Breaking the Spell of the Welfare State* (London: Social Affairs Unit).

Martin, E. (1989) *The Woman in the Body: a cultural analysis of reproduction* (Milton Keynes: Open University Press).

Maxwell, R. (1984) 'Quality assessment in health care', British Medical Journal, vol. 288, pp. 1470–2.

McKeown, T. (1976) *The Role of Medicine: Dream, Mirage or Nemesis* (London: Nuffield Provincial Hospitals Trust).

McKeown, T. (1979) *The Role of Medicine: Dream, Mirage or Nemesis* (Oxford: Basil Blackwell).

McKinlay, J. (1984) *Issues in the Political Economy of Health Care* (London: Tavistock).

Mead, G. (1934) *Mind, Self and Society* (Chicago: University of Chicago Press).

Medical Services Group (1978) 'Medical Services Group of the Royal College of Physicians of London Deaths under 50', *British Medical Journal*, vol. 2, pp. 1061–2.

Mednick, S., Machon, R., Huttunen, M. and Bennett, D. (1988) 'Fetal viral infection and adult schizophrenia', *Archives of General Psychiatry*, vol. 45, pp. 189–92.

Miller, D. (1989) *Living with AIDS and HIV* (London: Macmillan).

Ministry of Agriculture, Fisheries and Food, (1989) *Household Food Consumption and Expenditure*, Annual Report of National Food Survey Committee (London: HMSO).

Morris, J., D. Cook and A. Shaper (1994) 'Loss of employment and mortality', *British Medical Journal*, vol. 308, 1135–9.

Mullen, K. (1992) 'A question of balance: health behaviour and work context among male Glaswegians', *Sociology of Health and Illness*, vol. 14, no. 1.

Murray, C. (1984) *Losing Ground* (New York: Basic Books).

National Children Homes (1991) 'Poverty and Nutrition Survey', in J. Connelly and J. Crown (eds), (1994) *Homelessness and Ill Health* (London: Royal College of Physicians).

Navarro, V. (1979) *Medicine Under Capitalism* (London: Croom Helm).

Neal, D. (n. d.) 'The Sociology of Health and Illness', unpublished manuscript.

Nicholl, J., N. Beeby and B. Williams (1989) 'Comparison of the activity of short stay independent hospitals in England and Wales 1981, 1986 and 1989', *British Medical Journal*, no. 298.

Oakley, A. (1993) *Women, Medicine and Health* (Edinburgh: Edinburgh University Press).

Oliver, M. (1992) 'Changing the Social Relations of Research Produciton?', *Disability, Handicap & Society*, vol. 7, no. 2.

OPCS (1978) *Trends in Mortality* (London: HMSO).

OPCS (1991) Census (London: HMSO).

OPCS (1992) *Mortality Statistics: General Review of the Registrar General on Deaths in England and Wales* (London: HMSO).

OPCS (1995) *Population Trends*, no. 82 (London: HMSO).

Osborne, A. and A. Morris (1979) 'The rationale for a composite index of social class and its evaluation', *British Journal of Sociology*, vol. 30, no. 1.

Pahl, J. (1983) 'The allocation of money and the structuring of inequality within marriage', *Sociological Review*, vol. 31, pp. 237–62.

Parsons, T. (1975) 'The sick role and the role of the physician reconsidered', *Health and Society*, vol. 53, no. 3.

Peeke, A. (1993) *Waiting times for GP Fundholder procedures* (Oxford: Performance Monitoring Department, Oxford Regional Health Authority).

Phillimore, P. and A. Beattie (1994) *Health and Inequality: The Northern Region* (Newcastle: Dept. of Social Policy, University of Newcastle).

Phillimore, P., A. Beattie and P. Townsend (1994) 'Widening inequality of health in northern England', *British Medical Journal*, no. 308, p. 1126.

Pill, R. and N. Scott (1982) 'Concepts of illness causation and responsibility: some preliminary data from a sample of Working class Mothers', *Social Science and Medicine*, vol. 16, no. 1.

Pollock A. (1995) 'Privatisation by stealth?', *Health Visitor*, vol. 68, no. 3.

Pui-Ling Li (1992) 'Health Needs of the Chinese Population', in W. Ahmed (ed.), *The Politics of Race and Health* (Race Relations Research Unit, University of Bradford).

Punamaki, R. and H. Aschan (1994) 'Self-care and mastery among primary health care patients', *Social Science and Medicine*, vol. 39, no. 5.

Raftery, J., D. Jones and M. Rosato (1990) 'The mortality of first and second generation Irish immigrants in the UK', *Social Science and Medicine*, vol. 31, pp. 577–84.

Ranade, W. (1994) *A Future for the NHS?* (London and New York: Longman).

Roberts, H. (1993) 'Women, Health and Health Care', *Sociology Review*, April.

Rosenhan, D. (1973) 'On being sane in insane places', *Science*, no. 179, pp. 250–8.

Rosenhan, D. and M. Seligman (1989) *Abnormal Psychology* (New York: W. W. Norton).

Rowntree Report (1995) *Inquiry into Income and Wealth: A Summary of Evidence* (York: Joseph Rowntree Foundation).

Sacks, O. (1985) *The Man Who Thought His Wife Was A Hat* (London: Picador).

Sarbin, T. and J. Mancuso (1980) *Schizophrenia: Medical Diagnosis or Moral Verdict?* (New York: Pergamon).

Sayce, L. (1993) 'Preventing breakdown in women's mental health', *Health Visitor*, vol. 66, no. 2.

Scheff, T. (1966) *Being Mentally Ill: a sociological theory* (Chicago: Aldine).

Schneider, K. (1959) 'Primary and Secondary Symptoms in Schizophrenia', in S. R. Hirsch and M. Shephard (eds) (1974) *Themes and Variations in European Psychiatry* (New York: John Wright).

Sharkey, P. (1995) *Introducing Community Care* (London: Collins Educational).

Shilling, C. (1993) *The Body and Social Theory* (London: Sage).

Skrimshire, A. (1978) *Area Disadvantage, Social Disadvantage and Health Service* (Oxford: Oxford University Press).

Slater, E. and M. Roth (1977) *Clinical Psychiatry*, 3rd edn (London, Ballière Tindall & Cassell).

Social Trends (various issues) (London: HMSO).

Sontag, S. (1983) *Illness as Metaphor* (Harmondsworth: Penguin).

Sontag, S. (1990) *AIDS and its Metaphors* (Harmondsworth: Penguin).

Stacey, M. (1988) *The Sociology of Health and Healing* (London: Unwin Hyman).

Stainton Rogers, R. (1993) 'The Social Construction of Child-Rearing', in A. Beattie, M. Gott, L. Jones and M. Sidell (eds), *Health and Wellbeing: a reader* (London: Macmillan).

Starr, I. (1991) in R. Webb and D. Tossell, *Social Issues for Carers* (London: Edward Arnold).

Stevens, R. (ed.) (1993) *Health Inequalities and Manchester in the 1990s* (Manchester Health for All Working Party).

Strong, P. (1979) *The Ceremonial Order of the Clinic* (London: Routledge).

Szasz, T. (1961) *The Myth of Mental Illness* (London: Paladin).

Tannerhill, A. (1987) 'Regional health promotion planning and monitering', *Health Education Journal*, vol. 46, no. 3, pp. 125–7.

Taylor, S. (1986) *Health and Illness* (London: Longman).

Taylor, S. (1992) 'Measuring Child Abuse', *Sociology Review*, February, p. 24.

Taylor, S. (1994) 'Beyond the medical model' *Sociology Review*, September.

Thompson, P. (1993) 'The labour process: changing theory, changing practice', *Sociology Review*, vol. 3, no. 2.

Thorogood, N. (1992) 'Private medicine: "you pay your money and you gets your treatment"', *Sociology of Health and Illness*, vol. 14, no. 1.

Townsend, P. (1981) 'The structured dependency of the elderly: creation of social policy in the twentieth century', *Ageing and Society*, vol. 1, pp. 5–28.

Townsend P. and N. Davidson (eds) (1982) *The Black Report on Inequalities in Health* (Harmondsworth: Penguin).

Townsend, P., N. Davidson and M. Whitehead (1987) *Inequalities in Health: The Black Report and the The Health Divide* (Harmondsworth: Penguin).

Trowler, P. (1989) *Investigating Health, Welfare and Poverty* (London: Collins Educational).

Tuckett, D. (ed.) (1976) *An Introduction to Medical Sociology* (London: Tavistock).

Tudor Hart, J. (1971) 'The Inverse Care Law', *Lancet*, 1.

Turner, B. (1984) *The Body and Society: Explorations in Social Theory* (Oxford: Basil Blackwell).

Ungerson, C. (1987) *Policy is Personal* (London: Tavistock).

Ungerson, C. (1993) 'Caring and citizenship: a complex relationship', in J. Bornat *et al.* (eds), *Community Care: a reader* (London and Milton Keynes: Macmillan and Open University Press).

van der Gaag, N. (1995) 'Ageing with Attitude', *New Internationalist*, no. 264.

Victor, C. (1989) in J. Connelly, P. Roderick and C. Cohen, 'Use of hospital services by homeless families in an inner London district', *British Medical Journal*, vol. 299.

Victor, C. (1992) 'Health status of the temporarily homeless population and residents of the North West Thames Region', *British Medical Journal*, no. 305.

Wadsworth, M. (1995) 'Serious illness in childhood and its association with later-life achievement', in J. Westergaard, *Social Science Teacher*, vol. 24, no. 2.

Wadsworth, M., W. Butterfield and R. Blaney (1971) *Health and Sickness: the choice of treatment* (London: Tavistock).

Wagstaff, A., Doorslaer, E. and Rutten, F. (eds) (1991) *Equity in the Finance and Delivery of Health Care* (Milton Keynes: Open University Press).

Watterson, A. (1994) 'Threats to health and safety in the work place in Britain', *British Medical Journal*, vol. 308, pp. 1115–2116.

Webster, C. (1988) 'The crisis of the hospitals during the industrial revolution', in M. Stacey, *The Sociology of Health and Healing* (London: Unwin Hyman).

Westergaard, J. (1996) 'Class today: fashion at odds with facts', *Social Science Teacher*, vol. 25, no. 2.

Whitehead, M. (1994) 'Equity issues in the NHS: who cares about equity issues in the NHS?', *British Medical Journal*, vol. 308, pp. 1284–7.

Whitehead, M. (1992) 'The Health Divide', in *Inequalities in Health*, (Harmondsworth: Penguin).

Whitehead, M. (1993) 'Is it fair? Evaluating the equity implications of the NHS Reforms', in R. Robinson and J. Le Grand (eds), *Evaluating the NHS Reforms* (London: King's Fund Institute).

Wiles, R. (1993) 'Women and private medicine', *Sociology of Health and Illness*, vol. 15, no. 1.

Wilkinson, G. (1986) *Class and Health* (London: Tavistock).

Williams, B., J. Nicholl, K. Thomas and J. Knowlden (1985) *A study of the relationship between the private sector of health care and the NHS in England and Wales* (Dept of Community Medicine, University of Sheffield).

Williams, F. (1993a) 'Anthology: Care', in J. Bornat *et al.* (eds), *Community Care: a reader* (London and Milton Keynes: Macmillan and Open University Press).

Williams, F. (1993b) 'Women and community', in J. Bornat *et al.* (eds), *Community*

Care: a reader (London and Milton Keynes: Macmillan and Open University Press).

Williams, G. (1984) 'The genesis of chronic illness: narrative reconstructions', *Sociology of Health and Illness*, vol. 6.

Williams, G. (1989) 'Hope for the humblest? The role of self-help in chronic illness: the case of ankylosing spondylitis', *Sociology of Health and Illness*, vol. 11, no. 2.

Williams, R. (1983) 'Concepts of health: an analysis of lay logic', *Sociology*, vol. 17.

Williams, R. (1992) 'The health of the Irish in Britain', in W. Ahmad (ed.), *The Politics of Race and Health* (Race Relations Research Unit, University of Bradford).

Willis, P. (1990) *Common Culture* (Milton Keynes: Open University Press).

Yates, P. *et al.* (1993) 'Patients with terminal cancer who use alternative therapies: their beliefs and practices', *Sociology of Health Illness*, vol. 15, no. 2.

Zborowski, M. (1952) 'Cultural components in response to pain', *Journal of Social Issues*, no. 8.

Zola, I. (1966) 'Culture and Symptoms: an analysis of patients presenting complaints', *American Sociological Review*, vol. 31.

Zubin. J. and B. Spring (1977) 'Vulnerability: a new view of schizophrenia', *Journal of Abnormal Psychology*, vol. 86, pp. 103–26.

Author Index

Subject Index

abnormality 218
see also mental illness
acupuncture 290
age
access to treatment for mental
illness and 246
chronic sickness and 191
definitions of health and 6
ethnicity and 162
extraneous variable and 85
ill health and 188
informal care and 300
social construction of 188
use of private health care
and 274
visits to doctor and 193
ageing
abuse of elderly 205–7
'burden of dependency' and 198
dependency 198
ethnicity and 200
gender and 201–2
ill health and 201–3
population 261
prejudice 198, 199, 200
theories of 203–5
ageing population 189, 190, 261
agency 323
Asian carers 298
AIDS 62, 73, 132, 322, 331
alcohol 93
alternative medicine *see*
complementary medicine
anxiety state 56
artefact explanation
ethnicity and 178
social class and 88
arthritis 293

barber-surgeons 12
bed and breakfast (B&B)
accommodation 121, 173
behavioural model of health 284
being believed 56–9
'being sane in insane places' 225
see also mental illness
Beveridge Report 108, 255
Black Report 80–1, 83, 84, 96,
112
Black women 17, 148
Body without Organs 330

Body, the
feminism and 27
medical model and 26–7
phenomenological perspective of
the 27–8
postmodernism and the 330
power relations 61
social constructionists and 27
the sociology of, explanation
of 26
bourgeoisie 13, 14
Bovine Spongiform Encephalopathy
(BSE) 87, 96
British Geriatrics Society 206
British Heart Foundation 37–8
British Medical Association 111
British United Provident
Association (BUPA) 273, 276

cancer 195
breast 38, 115, 139, 149
cervical 116, 139, 149
lung 92
mortality and social class 81
mortality rates 81
prostate 149
screening 149
testicular 149, 319
throat 169
'Caring for People' White
Paper 296
certainty 68
child abuse 195–7
childbirth 17, 19, 139, 148
childhood 193–5
Chinese Health Resources
Centre 170
chiropractic 290
chronic illness 53, 54, 58, 84, 191,
254
clinical iceberg 47
Community Care 229–33
explanation of 230
evaluation of 232–3
outline of 229
stigmatization and 233
complementary medicine
evaluation of 293, 294
extent of 292
monitoring of 292
postmodernism and 328

mortification of self 228, 239
myalgic encephalomyelitis (ME)
        63, 69, 137, 138, 139, 315

narrative reconstructions 54, 55
National Association of Health
        Authorities 243
National Health Service 10, 14, 255
    administration costs 259
    aim of 109
    and Community Care Act 229,
        263, 296, 329, 333
    changes in 19, 110
    definitions of health and 7
    dentists 113
    development of 23
    equity and 268
    explanations of rising costs 258–61
    GP fundholders 269–72
    hospital waiting lists 271
    measuring quality of 281–3
    organisation in 1948 256
    Patient's Charter 272–3
    problem of rising cost of 257
    purchasing and providing within
        the 266
    reforms in 1980s 261–5, 278
    screening 149
    use of technology 259
    see also health care
neonatal mortality 179
'New Gaze' 14
New Right
    evaluation of 334–5
    health service 262
    outline of 332–4
    social class, ill health and 91, 109
NHS and Community Care
        Act 229, 263, 296, 329, 333
nurses 19, 147
    Nurses Act 1943 19

old age *see* ageing
'One Flew Over the Cuckoo's
        Nest' 228, 247
    see also mental illness
Opren 15
osteopathy 290
outposts 264
overcrowding 287

pain 39–40
Parkside Survey 121
Patient's Charter
    critique 273
    outline 272
    see also NHS
patient-centred model of
        illness 21–2

evaluation of 22–3
    explanation of 21–2
perinatal mortality 179, 180
peripheral workers 103
physicians 12
pill, the 17
population of Brent 161
Poor Law, the 253, 254
post-Fordism 102, 103
postmodernism
    ageing and 204
    discourse and 224, 326
    evaluation of 331–2
    fabrication and 204
    fragmentation and 328
    importance of 324–31
    legitimation and resistance
        327–8
    metatheories and 12, 75, 178,
        294, 325–6
    self-identity 61
    surveillance and 329
    the body and 330–1
postnatal depression 320
postnatal mortality 179
poststructuralist 223
poverty
    ageing and 201
    Birmingham Local Poverty
        Survey 172
    coping with illness and 59–60
    gender and 144
    Islington Local Poverty
        Survey 172
    medical treatment and 241
    social process of becoming ill
        and 36
    unemployment 144
preventative medicine 260, 316
private health care
    age and 278–9
    ethnicity and 276–7
    evaluation of 279–80
    gender and 274–5
    growth of 273–4
    New Right and 333
    social class and 277–8
Private Patients Plan 273
privatisation 279–80
proletariat 14
prostate 141
prostitution 123
providers *see* purchasers, NHS
Public Health Act, the 254
purchaser–provider relationship
    critique of 267–8
    diagram 266
    outline 266
    see also NHS

'quacks' 12, 13
qualitative measure of health
    care 282–3
quantitative measure of health
    care 282

race 158
Race Relations Act 159
racial discrimination 175, 177, 178
radical surgery 53
redundancy 288
reflexology 290
Regional Health Authorities 7,
    116, 264, 265
Registrar General's Scale 77
Repetition/Repetitive Strain Injury
    (RSI) 3, 21, 45, 47, 55, 56,
    60, 68, 101, 143, 289, 290
residential homes 207
resistance 326–8
respiratory tuberculosis 24, 25
retirement 299
rheumatism 194
role negotiation 67–8
Rowntree Report 106

sanitation 254, 287
schizophrenia 217
    causes 234–40
    ethnicity and 166, 243
    explanation of 234
    homelessness and 123
    neurological theory 237
    problems of diagnosis 234
screening 149
self-care 41
self-fulfilling prophecy 65
self-help groups 63, 99
self-identity
    AIDS and 62
    changes and 63
    discourse and 62
    explanation of 60–1
    intimate relationships and 66
    models of 65–66
    self-help groups and 63
    the body and 330
    total institutions and 239
    types of 64
self-presentation 64
sick leave 56
sick notes 3, 42, 57
sick role 58, 67, 150, 151
    Parsons and 58–9
sick pay 102
sickle cell anaemia 160, 176
sickness 8
side effects 17, 148, 319
single-parent households 144

smoking
    ethnicity and 168
    GP patients and 111
    gender and 107, 140, 141
        145–6
    social class and 92, 93, 96
    structural causes 334
social class
    access to treatment and 241
    classlessness and 75
    extraneous variables and 85–7,
        104, 117
    GP consultations 113–15
    gradients 81–2
    health and 75, 79–81
    health and explanations of
        88–115
    homelessness 118–24
    informal care and 299
    locality and 115–18
    measurement of 76–7, 79
    measurement problems 77–8
    membership 76
    mobility and 90
    morbidity (illness) and 83–5
    mortality and 81–3
    postmodernism and 75
    schizophrenia and 237–8
    stratification and 75
    use of private health care
        277–8
social constructionists 12–14
social mobility 175
social model
    disability and the 211
    evaluation of 25
    evaluation of NHS and 286–7
    explanation of 23–5
social process of becoming ill
    culture and 38
    doctor–patient negotiation
        42–5
    family and 38
    gender and 39–40
    health-seeking behaviour
        .and 40–2
    interpretation of symptoms
        and 37
    labelling and 42
    mass media and 38
    types of symptoms and 36
    vulnerability to illness and 36
social selection explanation 89
social wage 315
Standardised Mortality Ratio
    (SMR) 81, 83, 86, 88, 116
statutory sick pay 59
stereotypes 177, 243
stigmatization 233, 247